Hobbes to Hume

Contents of *A History of Western Philosophy,* SECOND EDITION

W. T. JONES

California Institute of Technology

Hobbes
to Hume

A History of Western Philosophy
SECOND EDITION

Harcourt Brace Jovanovich, Inc.

NEW YORK   CHICAGO   SAN FRANCISCO   ATLANTA

ISBN: 0-15-538314-0

Library of Congress Catalog Card Number: 69-14397

Printed in the United States of America

LIST OF COPYRIGHTS AND ACKNOWLEDGMENTS

The author records his thanks for the use of the selections reprinted in this book by permission of the following publishers and copyright holders:

GEORGE BELL AND SONS, LTD., for excerpts from *Ethics* by Spinoza, translated by R. H. M. Elwes.

THE BOBBS-MERRILL COMPANY, INC., for excerpts from *Dialogues Concerning Natural Religion* by David Hume, edited by Norman Kemp Smith. Copyright 1947 by Thomas Nelson & Sons, Ltd. Reprinted by permission of the Liberal Arts Press Division of The Bobbs-Merrill Company, Inc.

CAMBRIDGE UNIVERSITY PRESS for excerpts from *The Passions of the Soul, Meditations on First Philosophy*, and *The Principles of Philosophy* by René Descartes, translated by E. S. Haldane and G. R. T. Ross, in *The Philosophical Works of Descartes*, Vols. I and II; and from *The Sidereal Messenger* by Galileo, translated by E. S. Carlos, in *Cambridge Readings in the Literature of Science*.

E. P. DUTTON & CO., INC., for excerpts from *Two Treatises of Civil Government* by John Locke (Everyman's Library).

FORTRESS PRESS for excerpts from *The Works of Martin Luther*, Vol. I, translated by W. A. Lambert; Vol. II, translated by W. A. Lambert and C. M. Jacobs; and Vol. III, translated by C. M. Jacobs. And for excerpts from *Secular Authority: To What Extent It Should Be Obeyed* by Martin Luther, translated by J. J. Schindel, in *The Works of Martin Luther*, Vol. III.

HOUGHTON MIFFLIN COMPANY for excerpts from *Masters of Political Thought: Plato to Machiavelli* by M. B. Foster.

HUMANITIES PRESS, INC., NEW YORK, for excerpts from *The Metaphysical Foundations of Modern Physical Science* by E. A. Burtt.

THE NEW AMERICAN LIBRARY, INC., for an excerpt from *The Inferno* by Dante, translated by John Ciardi. Copyright 1954 by John Ciardi. Reprinted by arrangement with The New American Library, Inc., New York.

NORTHWESTERN UNIVERSITY PRESS for excerpts from *Dialogues Concerning Two New Sciences* by Galileo, translated by H. Crew and A. De Salvio. Published in 1950 by Northwestern University Press, Evanston, Ill.

GISELA M. A. RICHTER for excerpts from *The Literary Works of Leonardo Da Vinci*, edited by J. P. and I. A. Richter.

Preface

The changes incorporated into this revision of A *History of Western Philosophy* reflect what I have learned, in the seventeen years since the book was first published, about the history of philosophy, the nature of the philosophical enterprise itself, and the role that philosophy plays in the general culture. They also reflect a good deal of thought about what characteristics make a textbook useful.

The most noticeable innovation is the division of the book into four separate volumes: *I. The Classical Mind; II. The Medieval Mind; III. Hobbes to Hume;* and *IV. Kant to Wittgenstein and Sartre.* This division has provided space for expansion of the text, especially in the fourth volume. It also conforms to the way in which courses in the history of philosophy are now organized and enables the reader to choose the periods on which he wishes to concentrate.

In my revision I have been able to condense and at the same time clarify the exposition materially. In addition, I have greatly simplified the elaborate system of subheadings used in the first edition, for I believe that today's generation of students no longer needs such a complex set of guideposts. The condensation of material and the elimination of superfluous heads have allowed me to expand the discussions of a number of thinkers and to add discussions of many others who were omitted from the earlier edition. For instance, in Volume I, I have added a short section on axiomatic geometry and a longer section on Greek Scepticism, with extracts from the writings of Sextus Empiricus. In Volume II, I have added a discussion of Gnosticism and have balanced this with a section on physical theory in the late Middle Ages, illustrated by quotations from John Buridan. It is Volume IV, however, that contains the most extensive additions. The sections on Hegel, Marx, and Nietzsche have been completely rewritten and greatly expanded; there are entirely new chapters on Kierkegaard, Wittgenstein, Husserl, and Sartre.

There are also a great many changes—some of them major—in my interpretation and evaluation of individual thinkers and their theories. For instance, I have softened my criticisms of Greek Atomism and of Augustine, and in the sections on St. Paul and on the author of the Fourth Gospel I have taken account of recent scholarship. There is, indeed, hardly a page that has not undergone extensive revision. This edition is a thoroughgoing and rigorous updating of the first version.

Despite all these alterations, my point of view remains basically the same. In revising, as in originally writing, this history, I have been guided by four principles—concentration, selectivity, contextualism, and the use of original sources.

An historian of philosophy can either say something, however brief, about everyone who philosophized, or he can limit himself to giving a reasonably consecutive account of a number of representative thinkers, omitting discussion of many second- and third-flight philosophers. I have chosen the latter approach, for two reasons. First, many works based on the first approach are already available, and I see no good reason for adding to their number. Second, such works are likely to be unintelligible to the beginning student. I still recall my own bewilderment as an undergraduate in seeking to understand a complicated theory that some expositor had "boiled down" to a summary. The principle of concentration rests on the thesis that it is better to understand a few theories than to be superficially acquainted with a great many.

But concentration implies selectivity, and I can hardly hope that even those who accept the principle of concentration will approve all my selections. There will probably be no difference of opinion about the great figures of the remote past. Everyone will surely agree that Plato and Aristotle are the masters of their age. And perhaps there will be general agreement that Augustine and Thomas occupy similar positions in the Middle Ages—that Augustine demands more attention than, say, Boethius, and Thomas more attention than Duns Scotus. But how is one to choose among philosophers of more recent times? Here one must try to anticipate the judgment of time. To some extent, I have simply avoided the issue by dealing with more philosophers in the modern period. The result is that, whereas the first two volumes cover more than two millenia, the last two focus on hardly more than four hundred years.

Even so, I have been forced to be selective by my determination that here, as in the earlier periods, I would not mention a philosopher unless I could deal with his views in some detail. Thus I have repressed a natural desire at least to mention Fichte and Schelling, in order to provide extended analyses of Hegel and Schopenhauer. All these thinkers represent reactions to Kantianism, and although they differ among themselves in many ways, it is better, I believe, to select and concentrate on a few than to attempt to give a complete enumeration.

Also underlying the writing of this history is the generally recognized but seldom adopted principle that philosophers are men, not disembodied spirits. Some histories of philosophy treat theories as if they were isolated from everything except other philosophical theories. But all the great philosophers have actually been concerned with what may be called "local" problems. To be understood, their theories must be seen as expressions—doubtless at a highly conceptualized level—of the same currents of thought and feeling that were moving the poets and the statesmen, the theologians and the playwrights, and the ordinary men, of the age. Otherwise, how could their philosophies ever have been accepted? These philosophers furnished satisfactory answers only because they were alert to the problems that were exercising their contemporaries and because they were harassed by the same doubts. The cultural milieu in which a given philosophy emerges can be ignored only at the risk of making the philosophy seem a detached (and so meaningless and inconsequential) affair.

In carrying out this principle I have begun my account of Greek philosophy by describing the state of affairs in Athens at the end of the Peloponnesian War, and I have drawn on the plays of Euripides and Aristophanes to illustrate the mood of the times. This, I believe, is a necessary setting for Plato, because his central thesis—the theory of forms—was an attempt to answer the scepticism and cynicism of his age. Plato's insistence on the existence of "absolute" standards for conduct and for knowledge is understandable only as a reflection of the social, economic, and political chaos and the moral and religious collapse that occurred at the end of the fifth century.

Similarly, my discussion of medieval philosophy is prefaced with an account of the dissolving Roman Empire, and I have tried to indicate the rich and diversified cultural background within which Christian philosophy developed. In discussing the theories of Augustine and Thomas I have kept in mind that, whereas Augustine expressed the eschatological fervor of a new sect fighting for its life, Thomas embodied the serenity of an imperial and universal religion whose piety had been softened by a new sense of responsibility for "that which is Caesar's."

Finally, in discussing the development of early modern philosophy I have tried to show the many factors—exploration and discovery, the rise of money power, Humanism, the Reformation, and above all the new scientific method—that combined to overthrow the medieval synthesis and to create new problems that philosophy even today is struggling to resolve. In a word, I have conceived the history of philosophy to be a part of the general history of culture and hence to be intelligible only in its cultural context.

The fourth principle is my conviction that in philosophy—or in any discipline, for that matter—nothing takes the place of a direct, patient, and painstaking study of a great and subtle mind. For this reason there is much to be said for the use of a source book. But a source book alone has serious limitations, because its selections are apt to be discontinuous and difficult to follow. The advantage of a text is that it can explicate obscure passages and draw comparisons. Even so, explication and interpretation are not substitutes for the documents themselves. Therefore, each of the volumes in this series stands halfway between textbook and source book and tries to combine the advantages of both: I have set out a philosopher's thought in his own words by a careful selection of key passages and have bound these together with my own comment and criticism. The quoted passages constitute about one third of the contents.

To undertake to give an account of the history of philosophy in its cultural context is a formidable and perhaps presumptuous task for a single expositor. In this undertaking I have received help from a wide variety of sources. In addition to those who have read and commented on the first edition, whose names I shall not repeat here, I wish to thank many friends and colleagues who have called my attention to points that needed correction: Stanley M. Daugert, Stewart C. Easton, Robert L. Ferm, John H. Gleason, Douglas Greenlee, Raymond Lindquist, Edwin L. Marvin, James A. McGilvray, Philip Merlan, John E. Smith, Robert T. Voelkel, Culver G. Warner, Rev. S. Y. Watson, S.J., and R. M. Yost, Jr. I am much indebted to Robert J. Fogelin, from whom I learned a great deal during the years we taught a joint course on nineteenth-century philosophy, and to Clark Glymour, who has sent me extensive notes, especially on the history of science. My greatest appreciation is due to Cynthia A. Schuster, who read the revised version of Volumes I, II, and III and commented in immense—and immensely helpful—detail, and to Stephen A. Erickson, on whom I have constantly leaned for advice about matters small as well as great and whose detailed comments both on the first edition and on successive drafts of the revision have been invaluable. These readers have saved me from many errors of fact and interpretation; for errors that remain I must be responsible, and I shall be grateful if any that come to notice are pointed out to me.

I am obliged to the many publishers and copyright holders (listed on pages iv–v) through whose cooperation the quotations used in these volumes appear. Since I have followed the style of the various writers and translators I have quoted, there is some variation in spelling, capitalization, and punctuation in the reprinted passages. Full bibliographical notes, keyed to the text by letters rather than numbers, appear at the end of each volume.

For the secretarial work on the manuscript I am chiefly indebted to Helen Armstrong, Dorothy Overaker, Catherine Tramz, and Judith Strombotne, who divided the typing. I am also grateful to Paul Cabbell, who checked all references in the first three volumes and made many helpful suggestions, to Joan McGilvray, who performed a similar function for the last volume, and to my good friend Margaret L. Mulhauser, who generously allowed me to impose on her the onerous task of proofreading.

W. T. Jones

Contents

6

7

8

9

10

Introduction

Just as Greek philosophy, with its emphasis on independence, autonomy, and self-realization, seemed irrelevant to the survivors of the collapse of classical culture and the wreck of the Roman Empire, so medieval philosophy, with its emphasis on an infinitely good God and its assumption of man's finitude and sin, could not satisfy the Renaissance man who emerged in the fifteenth and sixteenth centuries. Shaped by capitalism and the new money power, by the idea of sovereignty and the ideals of Humanism, by the discovery of America and the Protestant reformation, this new man was an individualist increasingly concerned with this world and its values. (Chapters 1 and 2.)

Perhaps the most momentous element in the great change from medieval to modern times was the development of the scientific method. Indeed, if it can be said that classical philosophy was overthrown by the Christians' discovery of God, then it can be said that medieval philosophy was overthrown by the scientists' discovery of nature. This discovery was not a mere revival of classical naturalism and secularism; it was the discovery of a world of facts that seemed indifferent to man and his affairs. But how in this neutral and predictable world of facts could a place be found for man, with his capacity to choose freely among goods, a capacity that the new-style man of the Renaissance deeply valued? (Chapter 3.)

This soon became a central question for the philosophers of the early modern period. Hobbes, the first of these thinkers, wholeheartedly adopted what seemed to him the new scientific world view. Only matter in motion exists; men's thoughts and desires are but the by-products of motions occurring in their cortices and caused by events in the physical environment. It follows that there are no metaphysically based standards by which to determine the objective truth of thoughts or the true value of desires. Accordingly, Hobbes concluded that men need a sovereign who by arbitrary decree establishes, and by overwhelming force maintains, what is "true" and what is "good." (Chapter 4.)

It is not surprising that most philosophers drew back from so radical a position. Descartes replaced the materialistic monism of Hobbes with a metaphysical dualism. There are two kinds of substance, Descartes held—material substance, for which the laws discovered by the new physics hold true, and mental (or spiritual) substance, for which the old insights about man as a teleological being with an immortal soul are still applicable. But this Cartesian compromise broke down on the mind-body problem. Man, it would appear, is a material substance, for the movements of his body are a part of the physical universe and as such are completely predictable; but he is also a spiritual substance and can freely choose to follow (or neglect, as the case may be) God's commands. How can two such radically different substances interact, as they seem to do whenever a man wills to move his arm or his leg? (Chapter 5.)

Both Spinoza (Chapter 6) and Leibniz (Chapter 7) retained the Cartesian concept of substance as the cornerstone of their theories; they sought to reconcile physics with theology by denying that interaction occurs and by downgrading sense perception (which seems to present us with evidence of interaction) to the level of "confused" thought.

Locke adopted a very different strategy for dealing with the problems with which all these philosophers were wrestling. Instead of dismissing perception as unreliable and holding that pure reason can work out a correct metaphysical solution, he held that the concepts of reason must meet the test of what he called "the historical plain method"—that is, they must be verified in sense experience. (Chapter 8.)

Though Locke handled this new empirical criterion of meaning rather gingerly, Berkeley used it effectively against the concept of material substance. According to Berkeley, there is nothing in experience named by the term "matter" that is not already named by such terms as "light," "heavy," "solid," "fluid," and "red." At one blow, half the Cartesian system disappeared. (Chapter 9.)

In Hume's hands the empirical criterion of meaning became an even more formidable weapon; judged by this standard, "self," "cause," and "external world"—even "God"—become merely empty noises. Thus Hume exploded, one after the other, all the basic concepts in terms of which Western men had organized and interpreted their experience for more than two millennia. (Chapter 10.)

These conclusions were revolutionary, but though the men of the Age of Reason were aware that they had broken with the past, they did not realize how truly radical this break was. They were convinced of their own achievements and optimistic about the future, certain that they lived in the best of all possible worlds. From the perspective of almost two centuries, however, their self-appraisal seems exaggerated. Classical philosophy had been summed up in the syntheses of Plato and Aristotle, and medieval philosophy in the synthesis of St. Thomas—metaphysical schemes that gave unity and cohesion to the culture and to the intellectual life of these periods. In contrast, the early modern period was characterized, not by a set of enduring answers, but by a set of stubborn, persistent questions.

And new philosophy calls all in doubt,
The element of fire is quite put out;
The sun is lost and the earth, and no man's wit
Can well direct him where to look for it.

JOHN DONNE

O brave new world,
That has such people in 't.

SHAKESPEARE

Renaissance

The Place of Value in a World of Fact

For the men of the Middle Ages the world was created by a supremely good power for the discipline of man, with a view to his salvation. Since medieval men believed that God had created everything for this purpose, they held that the way to explain anything was to show how it promotes this end. The result was that medieval science was teleological in form. And since, of course, the underlying purpose was that of the one supreme and totally good God, the medieval sciences all pointed beyond themselves to religion. The universe was a vast sacerdotal system: It had no meaning or value in itself; its importance lay in the role it played—partly symbol, partly stage-set—in the drama of man's salvation. Everything meant something beyond itself in this religious drama.

Nothing was simply what it was. A tree was not merely a tree; a bird was not merely a bird; a footprint in the sand was not merely a footprint—they were all signs, just as the particular footprint Robinson Crusoe saw was a sign to him that he was not alone on the island. And what was true of the rest of the created universe was true of man. He was not merely man; he was a child of God. And his supreme task was to get back into that right relation with God that his first parent had lost.

Beginning in the Renaissance, beliefs gradually changed. The one supremely important vertical relationship of man to God, which absorbed all the attention of men of the Middle Ages, was eventually replaced by a network of horizontal relations connecting every individual to his social and physical milieu. For modern men, the good life no longer consists in achieving a right relation with God, but in effecting an efficient relation with one's fellow men.

In this respect the modern view is similar to the classical, but there are also important differences. For the classical mind, the universe, if not sacerdotal, was at least teleological. If the classical mind did not conceive of everything as worshiping God, it at least conceived of all things as subserving some purpose and aiming at some good. Hence, for the classical mind, as for the medieval, purpose was the primary mode of explanation. In contrast—and as a result of the success of the new physics, which was rigorously nonteleological in orientation—the modern mind became hostile to the use of purpose as an explanatory principle.

The modern mind also came, eventually, to differ from both the medieval mind and the classical mind in its attitude toward values. It never occurred to the medieval mind that values might not be objectively real. Although it certainly occurred to the Greek Sophists that values are merely the ways individuals feel about things, Plato's and Aristotle's reaffirmation of objectivity was for the most part accepted. The fact that men of the classical period and the Middle Ages agreed that values are objectively real is connected, of course, with the teleological conception of the universe that they shared. If the purpose anything subserves gives it value, and if purposes are objective, values will be objective. Anything will be good (really good, apart from some individual's feeling about it) insofar as it consciously or unconsciously realizes its purpose; anything will be bad insofar as it fails to accomplish its purpose. The same consideration also yields a hierarchy of goods, for values can be compared in terms of the relative height and significance of the purposes they subserve.

It follows that, in abandoning the teleological conception of the universe, the modern mind abandoned this easy way of establishing the objectivity of value. Moreover, modern men did not merely abandon the teleological conception of the universe; gradually they substituted for it a conception of the universe that seemed incompatible with the objectivity of values. This is, of course, the conception of the universe as a vast set of facts—facts that are indifferent to men's values, facts that no one planned with any end in view but that just happen to stand in the sorts of spatiotemporal relations that can be ascertained by the techniques of modern science.

The role that scientific instruments came to play in the accession of factual knowledge had an important bearing on this development. Where would astronomy be without the telescope? biology without the microscope? But these instruments, which have led to the discovery of innumerable astronomical and biological facts, throw no light at all on values. When a scientist dissects a corpse in a laboratory, he finds no evidence of the courage or magnanimity the living man displayed. Nor do microscopes or telescopes reveal God or freedom or immortality. As long as men believe that these instruments give them the whole truth about the universe, it is difficult for them also to believe that God, freedom, and immortality, courage, justice, and piety are objective realities. It is difficult, that is, for them not to assume that what the instruments reveal—the facts in their spatiotemporal relations—is reality, and that what the instruments do not reveal—the souls, the forms, and the values that classical and medieval minds conceived to be constituent elements in the universe—is merely subjective feeling.

Most of the early modern philosophers sought to save themselves from this drastic conclusion by drawing a sharp distinction between minds (souls, spirits) and all the rest of nature. These philosophers considered everything in nature except minds to have just the characteristics and the properties that the new physics reported: Everything was material, was unthinking, was in motion, was completely determined in its behavior. Minds, on the other hand, knew eternal truths, including the truths of physics; minds were free to choose between goods and evils and so were responsible for their bad choices; minds were capable of contemplating and so getting themselves into a right relation with God, who was also supposed to exist outside the material universe. He was supposed to have created the universe and then left it strictly alone to behave in accordance with the laws of motion that the physicists were discovering.

This dualistic metaphysics had an initial plausibility: It divided the universe into two realms, matter and mind, allotting one to the science of physics and the other to the sciences of theology and ethics; and it argued that if each science remained within its own domain, there could be no quarrel between them. Unfortunately, from the outset this dualistic solution was in serious trouble; eventually, it was in effect wholly exploded by Hume's formidable critique. The new beginning that became necessary was launched by Kant. Kant himself and post-Kantian developments are treated in the last volume of this series. This volume, which is devoted to philosophical theory from Hobbes to Hume, will review the series of increasingly involved attempts to save the basically dualistic formula.

Before these attempts are examined, some of the major changes in the culture that affected the overall course of philosophical development must be reviewed. For convenience, the discussion of this complex of changes will be organized under three familiar rubrics—"Renaissance," "Reformation," and "Rise of Science"—which will be taken up in turn in this and the following two chapters. But it is important not to be misled by names, or by chapter divisions. The Renaissance, for instance, was not a homogeneous "something" that can be sharply and unambiguously distinguished from another homogeneous something, the Reformation. Nor—though people do, on occasion, call these the "causes" of modern culture—should we allow ourselves to think that what was occurring was even remotely analogous to what occurs on a billiard table when one ball is set in motion by successive impacts from other balls. If an analogy is wanted, it is better to think of a vast network of interweaving strands crisscrossing in all sorts of directions in something like a web. This complex pattern of interweaving strands is not the cause of something else, modern culture; it *is* that culture as it emerges from a different pattern, the Middle Ages.

This chapter, then, will examine some of the strands that compose the section of the web called (for convenience) the Renaissance. We shall begin with a strand that may be labeled "Exploration and Discovery."

Exploration and Discovery

One of the marks of the beginning of modern times was a new spirit of adventure and curiosity, reflected in, among other things, the many voyages of exploration during the fifteenth century. Of course, there was nothing absolutely new about an interest in travel. The Crusaders, for instance, had certainly been travelers; a great many of them had been adventurers motivated by all sorts of this-worldly ambitions. And two hundred years before the high tide of exploration, Dante's Ulysses could experience a sentiment that people think of as peculiarly modern:

> "Shipmates," I said, "who through a hundred thousand
>   perils have reached the West, do not deny
>   to the brief remaining watch our senses stand
>
> experience of the world beyond the sun.
>   Greeks! You were not born to live like brutes,
>   but to press on toward manhood and recognition!"[a]

It is suggestive, however, that Dante resorted to the use of a figure drawn from classical mythology as a symbol of this spirit of adventure. Had he written at the end of the fifteenth century instead of at the beginning of the fourteenth, he would have found it difficult to choose among the many contemporaries who eminently exemplified this spirit. For, though there were medieval explorer-adventurers, the fifteenth century was characterized by a rapid acceleration of discovery. In 1415, the Portuguese captured Ceuta, thus gaining a foothold in Africa. Before the middle of the century, adventuring farther southward into the Atlantic, they reached the mouth of the Senegal. By 1484 they reached the mouth of the Congo, and the next year Diaz rounded the Cape of Good Hope.

Not only was there a marked increase in exploration in the fifteenth century, but the motives for exploration seem to have gradually changed. Prince Henry, the energizing force behind the Portuguese activity, had been moved by a characteristically medieval ambition: By landing on the African coast he hoped to attack from the rear the Mohammedan infidel, who was securely lodged on the Mediterranean coast of Africa. This grandiose scheme naturally came to nought, but it was soon found that the black men who lived in Africa could be sold in Europe at a handsome profit. For a long while Christian piety continued to express itself in an interest in the salvation of souls and the spread of the Kingdom of God by the conversion of the Negro, but as time went on, economic motives came to dominate.[1] This was especially true after men realized that beyond the southern tip of Africa lay the fabulous Indies.

COLUMBUS

Meanwhile, Columbus had conceived of the possibility of an even more direct route to the Indies. Since it had long been accepted that the earth is round, he argued that by sailing due west one ought to be able to reach the east coast of Asia. Columbus' bold scheme was not welcomed in the citadels of naval power. Venice and Genoa refused to back him; since they were the termini of the long eastern (overland) route, the possibility of a new trade route that would by-pass them was a threat to their preeminence. Portugal was uninterested, for it was concentrating on completing the route around Africa. The advantage of backing a winner therefore fell to one of the newer states that had yet to stake a claim for itself in the world. That it happened to be Spain was an accident that had important consequences in the shift in the balance of power during the coming centuries.

---

1 This mixture of motives is plainly visible in Columbus' letter announcing his first voyage. The natives, he wrote, were "willing to exchange valuable things for trifles. . . . But I forbade giving them a very trifling thing . . . because it was plainly unjust; and I gave them many beautiful and pleasing things, which I had brought with me, for no return whatsoever, in order to win their affection, and that they might become Christians and inclined to love our King and Queen . . . for what I believe our most serene King especially desires is their conversion to the holy faith of Christ; for which, indeed, so far as I could understand, they are very ready and prone. . . . Therefore let King and Queen and Princes, and their most fortunate realms, and all other Christian provinces, return thanks to our Lord and Savior Jesus Christ . . . that so many souls of so many people heretofore lost are to be saved; and let us be glad not only for the exaltation of our faith, but also for the increase in temporal prosperity, in which not only Spain but all Christendom is about to share"—text and translation printed under title *Columbus' Letter to Raphael Sanchez* (Boston Public Library, 1891).

News of Columbus' success stimulated the Portuguese to greater efforts to open up *their* route to Asia (for this, of course, is what everyone supposed Columbus had reached), and in 1498, after a voyage of ten and a half months from Lisbon, da Gama reached India via the Cape of Good Hope. Soon, despite the antagonism of the Mohammedans, who objected to the appearance of rivals, the Portuguese had established trading headquarters. It was obvious that this all-sea route had great advantages over the old route across the Mediterranean and overland from Egypt or Syria to the Indian Ocean. Transport by sea was not only less expensive, but it avoided the delays entailed by numerous transshipments.

With the impetus of Columbus' and da Gama's successes, exploration continued at an increasing rate. In 1496 the English king, disappointed at having missed Columbus' great prize, licensed John Cabot of Bristol to explore westward in the northern latitudes and "to set up our . . . banners and ensigns in any town, city, castle, island or mainland whatsoever, newly found by them; [to] conquer, occupy and possess [them] as our vassals and governors."[b] But it was Spain, eager to determine the nature and extent of its new possessions, that led the field. Pinzón discovered the coast of South America in 1499, and by 1506, the year in which Columbus died, seven thousand miles of the coast had been sighted. It was becoming increasingly evident that Columbus had discovered not a new route to Asia but a new continent. In 1518 the Spaniards sailed into the Gulf of Mexico, and a few years later Cortés invaded and conquered the country. Shortly thereafter a huge treasure began to pour out of Mexico toward Spain. By 1525 the Spaniards had crossed the Isthmus of Panama, and in 1532 they invaded Peru, opening the great wealth of that country to European expropriation.

ECONOMIC EFFECTS OF THE DISCOVERY OF AMERICA

At the end of a single century of exploration, Europe found itself facing west instead of east. Increasingly, commercial preeminence passed from Mediterranean powers, like Genoa and Venice, and from the inland cities, like Nuremberg and Augsburg, to the Atlantic powers. Indeed, the political and military history of the sixteenth century can in large measure be read as the repeated attempts of the Spanish Crown to secure hegemony over Europe. Nor were Spain's ambitions exclusively political and economic. This nation was also engaged in a great struggle to suppress the Protestant heresy. Those who resisted Spain, like the English seamen who captured the Spanish king's treasure ships on the high seas, could congratulate themselves on their service to their country and to the cause of Protestantism — not to mention the profits from their piracy. But it was not only Drake and the other English captains who grew wealthy at Spain's expense. Directly or indirectly, the whole economy of Europe was stimulated by the inflow of bullion, and the development of a new kind of economy was enormously accelerated.

SOCIAL AND POLITICAL EFFECTS

Nor was it only on the European economy that the age of discovery, especially the discovery of America, had an impact; the extension of physical horizons expanded mental and social horizons. The early explorers may have thought they had nothing to learn from naked savages; but contact with other cultures, however primitive, gave them a stronger sense—if only by contrast—of the solidarity of Europe, and later, in the eighteenth century, it provided the basis for criticism of European culture, which seemed decadent in comparison to the simple life of the savages.

Quite early, America came to be thought of as a refuge for those who, for religious or political reasons, could no longer remain in their homelands. The earliest of these settlements was made by Frenchmen in 1555, in Brazil. Its short history is an ironical comment on the foibles of human nature. Though these settlers were reformers who had left France because they held the dominance of the Catholic faith inimical to their Protestantism, they would tolerate no theological differences among themselves, and the new settlement was quickly dissolved. At the beginning of the next century, however, British colonization on a large scale began, and the foundations of a new England were laid by men seeking the freedom to worship as they pleased—though, like the French in Brazil, they were unwilling to extend tolerance to other dissenters.

For whatever reasons the colonists ventured across the Atlantic, they found an immense and fertile land of virgin forests and mighty rivers and great extremes of temperature. The very words "New World" suggest the almost limitless opportunities that awaited enterprising individuals. In the frontier settlements that men were hacking out of the wilderness, the social distinctions that had loomed so large in Europe tended to fade. Instead, a new set of values, grouped around the qualities that facilitated successful living in this very different world, began to appear. Just as in the decaying Roman imperium, values of a transcendental kind had emerged because there was no longer any opportunity for, or any utility in, the civic virtues that Plato and Aristotle had admired, so in the new societies of the Western world practical skills, ingenuity, and initiative took precedence over outmoded medieval otherworldliness.

It would be absurd, of course, to attribute the overthrow of medievalism exclusively to the spirit of adventure or to one of the great consequences of that spirit, the discovery of America. The New World was a powerful solvent of the old culture and its values only because many other reagents were operating at the same time in the Old World.

Rise of the Money Power

The medieval economic system, like the feudal political structure, consisted largely of self-contained units. Since individual estates tended to be self-supporting, there was little need for money, especially in the country areas. It is true, of course, that in order to finance their wars kings borrowed from (and often failed to repay) medieval bankers. It is also true that considerable money was needed for the trade with the Orient, especially since the flow of European goods eastward was insufficient to pay for the Eastern silks and spices in such great demand in the West. But in the early Middle Ages payment was largely rendered in services or in kind: Instead of paying rent in money, the feudal retainer paid his lord in produce or in so many days' work on the lord's land; instead of being obligated to pay taxes to a central government, the local lord was obligated to his overlord for service on the field of battle; and so on up the line.

THE CHANGE TO MODERN ECONOMY

The change from medieval to modern economy consisted primarily in a radical increase in the use of money. That is to say, the early modern period was not so much marked by a dramatic increase in the volume of commerce or by a change in the instruments of production (the latter, of course, did not occur until the late eighteenth century, with the so-called Industrial Revolution) as by a change in the method of financing commercial transactions.

The discovery of the uses to which capital could be put caused a gradual redistribution of power. A new class emerged, imbued with a new spirit and without the traditions and prejudices of the old feudal nobility. Those who owned money acquired prestige and power, which they used to remake political institutions so as to facilitate their transactions. In this way, the feudal organization of Europe, which was incompatible with the new economy, was replaced by a new political structure favorable to trade and commerce. The medieval organization of economy on a municipal and local-unit basis gave way to a large-scale economic structure. Because trade came to be regarded by the Crown as a principal source of strength, it was favored and encouraged by monarchs everywhere. Thus, an alliance of the new money power with the old royal power produced the national territorial state, the instrument of capitalistic advance.

A sign of the profound alterations that were occurring in men's values was the change in attitude toward moneylending. In the Middle Ages the money-lender was looked down upon because it seemed that he alone profited from his transactions. Also, moneylending was associated in the public mind with the Jews, who were hated as the slayers of Christ. A third reason for the contempt heaped on moneylenders in the Middle Ages was the dominance of the ideas of chivalry. As long as writers and thinkers were drawn from the noble class or held views that had been colored by the values of this class, "trade" was considered to be demeaning, and tradesmen inferior.

Long before the end of the Middle Ages, however, the Church found it necessary, or at least expedient, to modify its position on usury.[2] It decided that though the lender might not charge interest during the time of the loan, he might levy a fine as a penalty for late payment. These concessions, of course, made it easy to conform to the letter of the Church's injunctions while profiting from moneylending. One had only, by mutual agreement with the borrower, to predate the time for the loan's repayment, so as to be assured of the "fine" for late payment. Or again, one could write a higher figure into the note than was actually lent and so receive a premium on repayment. As the opportunities for profit by putting money to work became more and more obvious, the temptation to avoid the injunctions against usury became too strong to resist, and gradually a distinction came to be drawn between interest and usury. Interest, it was held, was a "fair" return on one's investment, whereas the term "usury" came to be applied only to exorbitant rates.

These changes in usage show that a fundamental shift in the *attitude* toward money was occurring. The Church's hostility toward usury had simply reflected the conditions of life in an economically static society. In such a society a man had no use for money unless he wanted to buy something. Since most of his wants were satisfied by barter or by the services of his tenants and retainers, his store of money lay idle in his strongbox until he required it. Since it was useless all this time, there was no reason why he should not lend it without charge to a neighbor, just as, if you have an injured hand and cannot use your fountain pen, you might as well let someone else use it.

But when it was found that money could be useful in ways other than in the purchase of an occasional luxury from a passing peddler, this theory broke down. As soon as the notion of investment became widespread, the theological objections to usury could not survive; and as soon as the advantages of investment came to be recognized, the old chivalric prejudice against trade began to vanish. By the middle of the sixteenth century the Protestant reformers could insist that what a man did for a living was less important than how he did it. In any occupation, however humble it might be in an aristocratic social scale, a man might, with God's grace, find his "calling." How was a man to know that he had found his calling? One of the marks was worldly "success and lawful gain," which showed God's favor. Profit-making, indeed, became one of man's duties to God, and the parable of the talents was interpreted as meaning that we should cultivate all our talents, including our talent for trade.[3] "If God show you a way," declared one Protestant divine, "in which you may lawfully get

---

2 But the medieval view was a long time dying out. R. Ehrenberg, in *Capitalism and Finance in the Age of the Renaissance* (Cape, London, 1928), pp. 42–43 and 242, notes that even in the fifteenth century merchants sometimes obtained legal opinions on what was permitted and what forbidden under canon law (as a modern businessman might employ counsel on income tax matters), and as late as 1530 jurists at the university of Paris made a study of whether the business practices at Antwerp were in accord with canon law.

3 See p. 32.

more than in another way, if you refuse this and choose the less gainful way, you cross one of the ends of your calling, and you refuse to be God's steward."[c]

How was the discovery made that money can breed money? Perhaps the question had better be put the other way around—why did this, to modern men, elementary truth have to be laboriously discovered and put into practice? The answer to this question lies in the fact that manufacturing was in the hands of guilds whose primary concern was for the well-being of the master craftsmen who collectively formed the guild. Difficulties in the way of transport and the lack of money—not to mention the whole spirit of the age—discouraged any attempt to expand on a large scale beyond local areas. Hence the attention of the guilds was focused on dividing a known, local market, and individual initiative and enterprise were frowned on. Since both supply and demand were inelastic, the expansion by any individual of his share of the market would have entailed corresponding losses for the other members of his guild.

This does not mean that there was no interregional trade. On the contrary, it was extensive; but here again medieval practice ran counter to large-scale employment of capital in the modern sense. Trade was on a municipal, rather than a national, scale (for as yet there were no "nations" in the sense in which we understand the term); and the various municipalities engaged in exclusive practices. Partly, this was a result of suspicion of "foreigners"; when they were allowed to trade, it was only with all sorts of restrictions, which once again limited initiative. Partly, it was a result of the belief that the city would profit most when it secured complete control of a given trade. In the Middle Ages this was relatively easy to do since the overland trade routes tended to converge on a few points (Aleppo and Alexandria, for instance, were the termini of the routes from the Indies), and in the days when ships seldom ventured out of sight of land, it was possible for a city that commanded a portion of the Mediterranean coast to exclude all its rivals. Thus, like the manufacturing system of the guilds, established trade practices were in terms of an inelastic economy.

How were these restrictions broken down? The answer involves many inter-weaving strands in the web of cultural change. One of these was the discovery of the compass and other navigational aids, which enabled seamen to strike out across the sea and so ended the trade monopolies of certain cities. Much later, the new sailing routes shifted the weight of trade to the high seas, which, more than the Mediterranean, were open to all competitors. Success there went to the most energetic.

Another strand in the web was the development, at Antwerp, of a new trading policy. Instead of trying to maintain a monopoly for its own merchants, Antwerp welcomed any kind of trade whatever: Foreigners were hospitably received instead of being excluded; the various toll stations along the Scheldt River, leading from the sea to the city, were bought up so that merchants would have a duty-free port. These novel measures to encourage trade, which were in essence merely a development of the local, temporary fairs that were widespread in the Middle Ages, made Antwerp a kind of "permanent fair."

Such fairs as those held in the thirteenth century in Champagne had been neutral points at which merchants could come together to exchange goods, and over the years an international "law merchant," as it was called, had gradually developed, quite distinct from the codes that governed the inhabitants of each local community. Further, at these fairs a merchant could buy (and sell) on credit, instead of paying on the spot for each of his purchases. Then, at the end of the fair, when his various debits and credits had been totaled up, he would make one definitive settlement. Similarly, "bills of exchange" were developed. If A at Bruges owed B at Troyes a sum of money, and if C at Troyes owed D at Bruges a sum of money, arrangements were made for A to pay D and for C to pay B. This made the payments internal transactions at Troyes and Bruges respectively, thus avoiding the dangers and delays involved in the transfer of gold or silver coin between Troyes and Bruges.

Such innovations as these laid the basis for the appearance of a new kind of economy. Antwerp, with its regular facilities for credit and its hospitality to trade from all quarters, proved that these practices could be used to great advantage. The opportunities for investment drew money from all over Europe, and the hectic search for wealth produced speculation on a large scale. The whole quality of life—the pattern of daily behavior and the system of values that motivated this behavior—was radically different from that of the typical medieval town.

INCREASE IN VOLUME OF MONEY

So far discussion has centered on the appearance of techniques for the expansion of credit. But while this was going on the volume of money rapidly increased. About the middle of the fifteenth century a new method for separating silver from copper was discovered, and many deposits that had formerly been useless because the two metals were mixed in the same ore became workable. As a result, between 1450 and 1530 there was perhaps a fivefold increase in the output of silver, and before the latter date the treasures of Spanish America had begun to flow into Europe. This huge increase in the quantity of money had, of course, a markedly inflationary effect. The larger the volume of money available, the lower its unit value, as with any other kind of goods. Since money was worth less because there was more of it, prices rose and business was greatly stimulated. At the very moment, therefore, when men were discovering profitable uses for capital, there occurred an immense increase in the amount of capital available. As silver and gold flowed into Western Europe, men no longer stowed their capital in strongboxes. They began, as they said, to make it "turn over," and as it turned over it multiplied manyfold.[4]

4 Between 1511 and 1527 the Fuggers increased their capital from 196,760 gulden to 2,021,202 gulden. "At this time, they were making about 55 percent annually on their investments"— M. M. Knight, H. E. Barnes, F. Flügel, *Economic History of Europe* (Houghton Mifflin, Boston, 1928), p. 322.

The capitalist[5] who put up the money to finance a voyage to the Indies expected three-fourths of the profits, whereas the adventurer who conducted the voyage received one-fourth. Since the profits of a successful voyage were large, the penniless adventurer soon became a capitalist himself, investing money in his own subsequent voyages or helping to finance others.[6] In this way, new fortunes were rapidly created—in itself a startling development in a society in which power had hitherto rested in land and in arms.

DECLINE OF THE GUILD

The new capitalism was not content merely to exploit trade. It soon infiltrated manufacturing, where it destroyed the guild system. Formerly the trader bought the finished product; he now purchased raw or semifinished material and employed workmen to manufacture it for him. Production thus came more and more into the hands of individuals who had connections in other trading centers and whose concern was to exploit these distant markets, and manufacturing became, from the point of view of the new owners, merely one phase of a long process. The ultimate aim of this process was profit for the individual owner, who was now a capitalist rather than a craftsman. The guild as a corporate body gradually disappeared, and the sense of a corporate responsibility for the quality of the goods and for the well-being of all members was replaced by each owner's determination to fend for himself.

This sense of enterprise is one of the hallmarks of the modern spirit. Here we see it at work in the traders and capitalists just as we saw it operate increasingly in the explorers who discovered a new world and laid the foundations for empire. It would be ridiculous, of course, to say that no one in the early Middle Ages showed initiative, that everyone was otherworldly. Nevertheless, the number of enterprising men increased as the Middle Ages drew to a close—indeed, what is meant by the closing of the Middle Ages is in part simply the increased frequency with which such men appeared. Here again it is not so much a matter of radical novelty as the acceleration of already discernible trends.

It would be possible to mention many merchants whose careers exemplified this new spirit—the Fuggers, for instance, or the Medici. But for purposes of illustration it will suffice to cite but one. Jacques Coeur (1395–1456), the son of a small merchant, became by his industry, enterprise, and competence the

---

5 It has been much debated whether "capitalism" was or was not an invention of the new era. This is largely a matter of definition. If capitalism is defined as the ownership of money, there have always been capitalists—at least since the invention of money. What distinguishes the capitalist of early modern times from the capitalists of other eras is what he did with his capital and how he felt about what he did.

6 These practices began as early as the twelfth century. Somewhat later, permanent associations appeared in which a number of investors owned "shares." This may be described as the beginning of the joint-stock company.

wealthiest Frenchman of his time and one of the most powerful men of the kingdom. He "sold every sort of merchandise," a contemporary marveled, "that the brain of man could think of or imagine." He was "the first in his day," another noted,

> . . . [to cause] to be constructed and equipped ships which transported to Africa, throughout the Levant, and even to Alexandria in Egypt, cloths, woolens, and other articles fabricated within the realm. On the return voyage these ships brought back different varieties of silks and all sorts of spices, and perfumes which were marketed in the provinces reached by the water of the Rhone, or in Catalonia and in neighboring lands, *a practice which was then entirely new in France,* for theretofore this commerce had long been carried on through the medium of other nations.[d]

At the apex of his career, Coeur owned lead, copper, and silver mines, a silk factory at Florence, and a paper mill at Bourges; he operated a passenger service for pilgrims to the Holy Land, maintained business houses in all the principal cities in France, and had, in all, three hundred representatives scattered through Europe and the East. He built himself a splendid palace in Bourges, was a patron of the arts, a friend of popes and kings. He lent Charles VII huge sums to maintain his army and to consolidate the kingdom by driving the English out of France, and in the ensuing campaigns he took an active part. He represents admirably that rising man of middle-class stock who, not so much earlier, would have been the prisoner of his status unless he entered the Church, but who could now achieve a position of power by an alliance with the Crown against the old feudal aristocracy—that man who knew how to make use of the new money power and who had the energy in the fluid circumstances of a changing world to make the most of every opportunity. It is appropriate that, playing on his name, Coeur should have chosen as his motto, when his sovereign ennobled him, "To the Valiant Heart [*coeur*] Nothing Is Impossible."

The New Political Ideal

One of the major results of the economic changes just discussed was the emergence of a new political entity, the nation-state. But the nation-state and the realignment of political forces that accompanied it also helped make possible these economic changes. Here again, events are reciprocally causes and effects of each other, thus validating the analogy of interweaving strands. Let us now focus attention on the political strands in this network of events.

Two of the most important of these are the closely connected ideas of nationalism and of sovereignty. A third involves not so much a change in content as a change in attitude toward the phenomena of politics. This new attitude has been variously called "naturalism" (to contrast it with the ethical and religious perspective from which the Middle Ages had studied politics), "positivism" (to emphasize its empirical and secular point of view), and "realism" (to bring out its rejection of the idealistic tendencies of traditional political theory). This terminology will become clearer as we proceed. Meanwhile, let us examine these three strands in turn, attempting to see the ways in which they interact among themselves and with the other strands that, collectively, we call the Renaissance.

NATIONALISM

How did the local loyalties of feudal society come to be broken down so that the nation-state could come into being? In the Middle Ages a man thought of himself as owing allegiance to a particular noble; he was the Earl of Norfolk's man or the Duke of Burgundy's man. How did he come to conceive of himself as a citizen of England and a subject of the English king? It is reasonable to suppose (though there is no direct evidence to substantiate this view) that the Crusades were instrumental in the dissolution of medieval localism. Just as when Americans go abroad local differences fade out and Californians and Texans come to have a fellow feeling as Americans, so men from different English villages turning up in Palestine to fight the Saracens doubtless found themselves uniting as Englishmen in the face of the greater differences that marked them off from French or German villagers.

It seems likely, too, that the development of the vernacular languages as literary forms played a part in the emergence of the nation-state. The fact that Dante wrote in Italian and Chaucer in English, rather than in the cosmopolitan Latin, indicates the existence, as yet rudimentary no doubt, of a national feeling, and the use of national languages to communicate ideas reinforced this feeling. Later on, in the fifteenth century, the invention of printing powerfully encouraged this trend. The existence of the press allowed the possibility of addressing a larger audience, who knew no Latin; hence the profit motive led the printers to exploit the vernacular languages and to assist in their development.

While such causes as these were operating, as it were, in the background, and while economic changes were undermining the old nobility and bringing a new class into prominence, there appeared on the thrones of France and England men of the shrewd, self-reliant type that we have already encountered in trade and banking. Such a man was Louis XI of France. When he succeeded to the throne in 1461, France was still largely a feudal kingdom. Louis, therefore, set himself to subdue his great vassals. Some, like the Count of Armagnac, ruler of great territories in the southwest, he mastered by force of arms. Others, like the Albrets, who lived beyond their means despite huge feudal revenues, he won over with large pensions.

During this period the Crown was also gradually strengthening its position in the fiscal and military realms. Even as late as the early part of the fifteenth century, the king, lacking the right to levy taxes on his own initiative, had to rely on his private fortune and special grants for revenue. Gradually, however, the right to levy regular taxes was acquired by the Crown. In the same way, the Crown began to affirm its exclusive right to raise and maintain troops. In place of the ramshackle assemblage of unreliable men-at-arms, supported by and loyal to the great vassals, there was now the beginning of a national army, well disciplined, trained to fight together, and paid by the Crown.

Even the Church failed to withstand the drive of Louis' ambitions. Though he was superstitious, and even devout in his way, Louis did not scruple to play fast and loose with the Church's interest in his kingdom when it served his advantage. Like any other capitalist, he understood the value of money; he held that every man had his price, and he was usually able to discover what it was. He found ambitious men of the middle class, paid them well, and was indifferent to their morals or their avarice as long as they served him effectively; but he was ruthless when confronted with treason or incompetence. He was shrewd, cold-blooded, and pitiless, untroubled by conventional moral patterns, and completely cynical when it came to his fundamental passion, which was a desire for power.

Just as Louis XI was a radically different kind of man from his saintly ancestor, Louis IX, so Henry VII of England was not remotely like his Plantagenet predecessors. While maintaining the peace of England by playing off the continental powers against each other, Henry managed to make favorable commercial agreements with them. He secured special trading privileges for his subjects in Flanders and succeeded in breaking into the monopolies the Germans had long enjoyed in the Baltic trade and the Venetians and the Florentines in the Mediterranean. Henry was a careful man of business who knew how to profit from the increasing prosperity of his kingdom and so could dispense with those frequent appeals to Parliament for grants that had weakened his predecessors' positions. When he died in 1509, the nobility had been pretty well brought under control; only the Church remained largely independent of royal authority. The problem of asserting the supremacy of the secular sovereign against this formidable opponent was solved by his heir, Henry VIII.

In England, as well as in the other states, there was a long history of opposition to papal financial policy and to the practice, which had been increasing over the years, of extracting all sorts of fees and percentages for the support of the Roman Curia. As early as 1279, the Statute of Mortmain sought to prevent the pious from bequeathing land to the Church. In 1351 the Statute of Provisors forbade appointment to English benefices by the pope; two years later the Statute of Praemunire forbade appeal from English courts to the Roman Curia. Thus Henry VIII was not the first English king to move in the direction of a national church; but no king before him had moved so far or so effectively, for no earlier king, even had he wished to do so, would have had the necessary power.

Henry's quarrel with the Church came to a head over the question of his divorce from Catherine of Aragon. Only a sickly daughter had survived all the years of their marriage. Henry had a strong dynastic sense and he knew well from the history of the preceding century what happened in a state when the succession failed or was in doubt. Hence he was not moved simply by his desire to marry Anne Boleyn, who had refused to become his mistress. He wanted, both for the sake of his family's future and for the good of the state, a male heir. When he failed to obtain papal consent to a divorce, Henry took matters into his own hands. By a series of skillful moves he secured the submission of the English clergy, and in 1534 Parliament passed the Act of Supremacy that made the king head of the English Church.[7]

Henry's next step was to dissolve the monasteries. This served a double purpose: It brought him great personal wealth and the support of a group of powerful men, his upper-class subjects, to whom he granted the monastic lands and who, as a result, gained a strong motive for backing their king against the papacy. Had the monasteries not been dissolved, it is doubtful that the separation of the English Church from Rome would have been permanent.

Thus, first in France and then in England, a succession of aggressive monarchs—themselves in many ways representative of the new-model man who participated in trade and in banking—created nation-states in which a single, central power made itself felt in every department of life and throughout a whole territory, which, only a short time earlier, had been a hodgepodge of virtually independent units.

All these changes in political circumstances were naturally reflected in political philosophy. Because the centralizing tendency was a new phenomenon, it required explanation and justification. But the concept of sovereignty, which was to provide the needed rationale, developed only slowly and by stages.

DANTE AND THE INDEPENDENCE OF THE TEMPORAL POWER

The first step in the emergence of the concept of sovereignty was the denial of the claim, made by Aquinas and other writers in the popes' behalf, that the temporal power was simply an agency through which God's vicar and Peter's successor chose to rule. Dante's *De Monarchia* is representative of this first shift from the orthodox medieval position. Dante was not only a poet; he was a thoughtful observer of the political scene. Since he believed that the primary causes of the troubles of his own day were the papacy's temporal ambition and its persistent interference in secular affairs, he held it essential to find a theoretical justification for confining the papacy to its spiritual sphere. This task was complicated by the fact that in other respects Dante was a thoroughgoing

---

7 Henry was no Protestant reformer. In 1521 he had written an attack on the Lutheran heresy that had earned him from the pope the splendid title "Defender of the Faith" (a title retained to this day as a part of the royal style). Henry had no taste for heresy. What he attacked was not the Church's theology but its temporal power, and that only insofar as it conflicted with his own. The Reformation in a religious sense came to England only gradually, toward the end of Henry's reign and under Edward VI and Elizabeth.

Thomist. He had therefore to find a way of avoiding Thomas' conclusions about ecclesiastical supremacy while accepting Thomas' basic premises.

Dante argued as follows: The ultimate purpose of political association is "the calm and tranquillity of peace," for it is only when men live in peace that each can "freely and easily" perform those various activities in which, according to Thomas (and Aristotle), human happiness consists. If, then, peace is the purpose of political association, how is it to be achieved? The answer to this question seemed obvious to Dante. To live in peace, the members of any society—whether it be a family, a village, or a city—require "one to rule and regulate them."

> Let the first [argument] be drawn from the authority of the philosopher [Aristotle] in his *Politics*. For there his venerable authority asserts that when more things than one are ordained for a single purpose, needs must one of them guide or rule, and the others be guided or ruled. And to this not only the glorious name of the author, but inductive argument also forces assent.
>
> For if we consider an individual man, we shall see that this is true of him; since whereas all his faculties are ordained for felicity, the intellectual faculty is the guide and ruler of all the others, else he cannot attain to felicity. If we consider the family, the goal of which is to prepare its members to live well, there must needs be one to guide and rule whom they call the pater-familias, or his representative. . . . And if we consider a city, the end of which is to live well and suitably, there must be a single rule. . . . For if it be otherwise . . . the very city itself ceases to be what it was. If finally we consider a kingdom, . . . there must be one king to rule and govern, else . . . the kingdom itself lapses into ruin.[e]

But kings can fall out just as easily as villagers; hence, if villagers require a head man, so do kings. And the "head man" of kings is the emperor. It is thus "plain that the Empire is necessary to the welfare of the world." Since his argument was designed to appeal to the Thomists, Dante assumed that Thomas was correct about man's end and merely urged (1) that peace is the means to this end and (2) that a universal secular sovereign is the indispensable condition of peace.

But Dante still had to rebut the claims of the papal jurists, who relied on the Donation of Constantine and other legal documents that purported to commit secular authority to the bishops of Rome. He was not in a position as sixteenth-century antipapists were to be [8] to argue that the documents were forgeries. Instead, he pointed out that they lacked the authority of Scripture. "The traditions of the Church are after the Church. It follows that the Church has not its authority from traditions, but rather the traditions from the Church." Hence, in the final analysis, the papal claims must appeal, not to documents

8 See p. 37.

or traditions, but to Scripture. And a careful reading of Scripture justifies these claims nowhere.

It follows that, since

> . . . political authority does not depend on the vicar of God, it depends on God. . . . Providence, then, has set two ends before man to be contemplated by him; the blessedness, to wit, of this life, which consists in the exercise of his proper power . . . , and the blessedness of eternal life. . . .
>
> Now to these two as to diverse ends it behoves him to come by diverse means. For to the first we attain by the teachings of philosophy. To the second by spiritual teachings which transcend human reason. . . . Wherefore man has need of a twofold directive power according to his twofold end, to wit, the supreme pontiff, to lead the human race, in accordance with things revealed, to eternal life; and the emperor, to direct the human race to temporal felicity in accordance with the teachings of philosophy. . . .
>
> Thus, then, it is plain that the authority of the temporal monarch descends upon him without any mean from the fountain of universal authority. Which fountain, one in the citadel of its simplicity, flows into manifold channels out of the abundance of its excellence.[f]

Dante's reasoning in this passage is still thoroughly medieval: His argument works backward from divine ends to means. Nor is his conclusion as "modern" as some have held it to be. It is a mistake, for instance, to hail Dante as the first *inter*nationalist when he had hardly the faintest conception of nationality. He was reaffirming the old ideal of a universal Christendom, rather than anticipating the modern notion of a union of secular and sovereign states. Nevertheless, Dante at least adumbrated the breakup of the medieval position. In his political theory there is a new emphasis on this-worldly problems; the peace he held to be the end of political association was not the peace that passeth understanding but the security that makes ordinary living possible.

Dante did no more than free the secular power from ecclesiastical dominion. He left the two powers equal under God, each sovereign in its own sphere. But how were the two spheres to be distinguished? Dante said only that the secular power was concerned with "those things which are measured by time," but this, certainly, is not very helpful. Since, in the world of politics, things temporal and things spiritual interpenetrate, a solution based on the distinction between time and eternity collapses as soon as it gets down to particulars.

MARSIGLIO AND THE SUPREMACY OF THE TEMPORAL POWER

Dante's younger contemporary, Marsiglio of Padua,[9] saw that it was not enough for the secular power to be independent; it must be supreme. Marsiglio

---

9 Marsiglio (about 1274–about 1343) appears to have studied medicine and to have been, briefly, rector of the university of Paris. In 1326 he went to the court of Louis of Bavaria to escape the pope's authority and became an adviser to the emperor and an inspirer of imperial policy.

adopted the so-called double-truth doctrine of Occam and the Averroists. According to this doctrine, reason and revelation are completely separate spheres. Since they are independent, there is no possibility of conflict between philosophy and theology. Philosophers may therefore develop an entirely rational —and secular—theory of politics without regard to the teachings of the Church, which are based exclusively on revelation. This is obviously a most convenient thesis for a thinker who wanted to maintain the autonomy of the secular power; it enabled Marsiglio to take the drastic step that Dante's more orthodox mind resisted.

Marsiglio's argument begins with the familiar Greek thesis that the state is an organism whose well-being consists in the healthy functioning of its various organs. Marsiglio thought that Aristotle's account of the various social groups— the farmers, artisans, middle class, and so on—was satisfactory, but that it required supplementation in one important respect. Because Aristotle knew nothing about the Christian clergy, he naturally did not discuss its function. The primary problem of the political theorist was therefore to bring Aristotle up to date by ascertaining the proper function of this group. This inquiry was the more pressing since the clergy had gotten out of hand and laid claim to functions that properly reside in other groups.

What, then, is the proper role of the clergy in the state? In accordance with the double-truth doctrine, Marsiglio maintained that there are two answers to this question—the answer yielded by revelation and the answer yielded by reason. According to theology, and thus from the point of view of revelation, the function of the clergy is to teach us how to attain eternal salvation. However, because this is such an elevated affair, philosophy cannot take account of it.

> What eternal life is, the whole company of philosophers have not been able to show; nor is it among the things which are manifest in themselves; therefore, the philosophers have not concerned themselves with teaching the things which pertain to that sort of life. But concerning living and living well, in the mundane sense of the good life, . . . renowned philosophers have given an almost complete demonstration. They have reached the conclusion that for fulfilling that life a civil community is necessary.[g]

According to philosophy, and thus from the point of view of reason, the clergy have no special status; they are to be considered on exactly the same basis as blacksmiths, doctors, or soldiers: What do they contribute to the "sufficiency" of the state?

Under the guise of exalting revelation, Marsiglio removed it from consideration, and with it went any need for allowing the claims of the clergy to a special status in the state. Thus, in place of Dante's dualism of spheres, Marsiglio proposed a dualism of points of view. For Dante, even the secular arm had to allow the validity of the spiritual arm's claims in its own realm. For Marsiglio, from the secular point of view there was no spiritual realm at all.

The double-truth doctrine also enabled Marsiglio to distinguish between divine and human law in such a way as to give a completely secular account of the latter.

> Divine law is a command of God directly, without human deliberation, about voluntary acts . . . to be done or avoided in this world but for the sake of attaining the best end . . . in the world to come. . . .
>
> Human law is a command of the whole body of citizens, or of its prevailing part, arising directly from the deliberation of those empowered to make law, about [things] to be done or avoided in this world, for the sake of attaining the best end . . . in this world. I mean a command the transgression of which is enforced in this world by a penalty or punishment enforced on the transgressor.[h]

This definition contrasts sharply with that given by Thomas. Thomas held that human law is simply the application of God's universal decrees to particular, local situations. He also held that the principal characteristic of law everywhere is rationality; ultimately, law is the expression of the divine intellect. But Marsiglio defined law in terms of will, that is, command. Divine law is the command of God; human law is the command of the people or of their agents. Further, what cannot be enforced is, properly speaking, an "entreaty," not a command; hence, without power, there is no law. "A law is useless if it is not obeyed." But not every command backed by power is law, nor is every commander a legal authority. To be law, according to Marsiglio, a command must issue from the proper authority ("the whole body of citizens or its prevailing part"), and it must be directed toward the common good. Thus, though he rejected a religious sanction for law and other human institutions, Marsiglio retained a moral sanction.

This is a long way from Dante and a still longer way from Thomas. Dante might object to the canon lawyers and insist that Holy Scripture is a higher authority than canon law. But Marsiglio was far more drastic. By his definition, canon law is not law at all; it does not issue from the whole people, nor has it the power to enforce its commands. In Marsiglio's view, the whole system of ecclesiastical courts, exemptions, and prerogatives by means of which the Church had gradually made itself a state within a state had no more legal standing than the house rules of a private club. In fact, though he was thinking chiefly of the Church and its claims, his arguments applied equally well against any other group (for example, the feudal barons) who might conceivably claim independent jurisdiction. There exists in a state, Marsiglio believed, but one jurisdiction—that exercised in the name of the whole people. What distinguishes the state from every other community is the presence in it of a plenary power,[10] which issues commands having the character of laws and which has the strength

10 Of course, Marsiglio held this power to be subject to the moral restrictions noted above.

to enforce its rules on all groups in the state, including the clergy. This, in fact, may be said to be Marsiglio's definition of a state; it is a society in which such a power exists.

Marsiglio's notion of plenary power is a considerable advance toward the conception of sovereignty, but Marsiglio's classical studies seem to have had a greater influence on his thinking than his close association with imperial policy. When he talked about a supreme secular power, he was not thinking of the medieval ideal of a universal empire and still less of the nation-state that was to emerge in the next century. He was thinking primarily of smaller entities, more on the order of the Greek city-state, in which the body of citizens, taken collectively, constituted the state's power. Thus Marsiglio was not looking forward into the future but back into a remote past.

Moreover, even at the city-state level there are problems that Marsiglio barely touched: How is plenary power to express itself? It can hardly do so save through some agent—council, king, parliament. But what is the relation of this agent to those on whose behalf the agent acts? Again, what is the relation between power and right? What happens if the possessor of power legislates against the common good? Since Thomas defined law in terms of right reason, his answer was unambiguous: Immoral legislation, even when amply backed by force, is not law. But since Marsiglio defined law in terms of will, it would seem to follow that any decision the ruler can enforce has the status of law.

BODIN AND THE CONCEPT OF SOVEREIGNTY

The first effort to answer these questions in a systematic way was made by Jean Bodin.[11] In order to understand his answers it is necessary to realize that, although the French Crown had swept away the great feudalities by the end of the sixteenth century, it had not succeeded in reducing the laws, customs, and traditions of the various provinces to uniformity; its power was still limited by many local and ecclesiastical privileges.

Bodin gave numerous examples of the ways in which ancient prerogatives prevented the development of a uniform administrative policy. For instance:

> Notwithstanding the ordinance of Louis XII, the chapter of the church at Rouen claims to have the right of granting pardon in honour of its patron, St. Romain. Before the feast of that saint the chapter forbids the judges to execute any condemned persons, as I myself saw when I served on the commission for the reform of Normandy. Now, on one such occasion the courts had a condemned prisoner executed despite the wishes of the chapter.[i]

11 Bodin (1530–96) was educated as a lawyer and wrote on legal theory, on the methods of historical study, and on economics, as well as on politics. He held an important magistracy in Laon and served in the States General of 1576. In attempting to compromise between the Catholics and French Protestants, he lost the king's favor and was accused of heresy in 1590.

The chapter was furious at this neglect of its ancient right, and since it chanced to "have for its head one of the princes of the blood," it was able to make great trouble for the unfortunate magistrates who were attempting to enforce the King's justice in Rouen.

Meanwhile, the Lutheran heresy had spread to France, and the country had become bitterly divided on the religious issue. Just at this point the throne was occupied by a succession of weak princes, who were incapable of handling the situation, and the country was plunged into civil war.

It was against the background of these events that Bodin developed his political theory. It was natural for him to insist that the times required a single authority in the state, powerful enough to bring all the divisive elements into order. This authority, which Bodin called "sovereignty," occupied the central position in his thought. In insisting on the primacy of sovereignty, Bodin of course reflected the whole trend of political development in western Europe; but whereas politicians such as Louis XI and Henry VIII had long acted like sovereigns, and whereas thinkers such as Marsiglio had adumbrated the idea, no one before Bodin, as he proudly recognized, had stated the concept of sovereignty formally.

> A state is a lawful government of many families and of what is common to them, together with a supreme sovereignty. . . . We [say that it] is a *lawful* government, in order to distinguish it from a gang of robbers or of pirates. . . . However much such a gang may seem to form a society, and its members to live in amity among themselves, we ought not to call it a "society" or "state," . . . because it lacks the principal mark of a peaceful society, namely, a lawful government according to the laws of nature.[j]

Thus, even more explicitly than Marsiglio, Bodin incorporated in his conception of the state both the notion of power and the notion of neutral right. In emphasizing right he was a continuator of the classical and medieval traditions, according to which the primary function of political theory is the evaluation of political institutions in terms of a set of absolute norms. But as a man of his own times, sensitive to the new developments in politics, he saw that power is also an essential political element. From this point of view, the primary function of the political theorist is descriptive, not normative. In its empirical orientation this view anticipated the ethically neutral methodology of modern physical science. Just as the latter produces information about the behavior of the physical universe that technologists can put to use, either for human weal or for human woe, so the political theorist provides information that princes can apply, either in their own interests or in those of their subjects.

When Bodin was thinking in terms of *right,* that is, when he was trying to "justify" the existence of an independent secular power, his reasoning was far more modern than was Marsiglio's. Whereas Marsiglio had rested his case for the independence of the secular arm on a tenuous distinction between reason and revelation, Bodin pointed out that the old decentralized state that had served well enough in the Middle Ages was no longer practical in the changed conditions of the sixteenth century. The best way to achieve an "assured state," that is, a condition of peace and security, was to concentrate power in the hands of one man.

Bodin was, however, more concerned with description than with justification; what chiefly interested him was the techniques for acquiring and maintaining power. His account of how a prudent prince should deal with religious dissent will illustrate his approach.

It is obvious that factions or parties (religious or otherwise) are dangerous and pernicious in any kind of state. It is best, therefore, to take counsel to prevent their formation; or if this be impossible, to prevent any dangerous developments by employing any medicines which will cure them. . . . When I say "faction" I do not mean every little handful or society of subjects whatever. I mean a good-sized group banded together against some other group in the state. For if the numbers be small, the sovereign can usually bring them to reason by putting their differences in the hands of impartial and dispassionate judges for settlement. But if the groups be large and violent, or if they be not appeased by justice and judgment, the sovereign must not delay until they grow still stronger. He must act promptly, employing force to extinguish the faction utterly, a thing which he can accomplish at that stage by punishing a few of the ring leaders. . . .

Among the many causes for internal faction is religion. Changes in the religion of a state, as we have seen in the German empire, Sweden, England, and other countries, are always accompanied by extreme violence and bloodshed. Therefore the maxims just asserted should be followed with respect to religion. In the first place, then, if a state be so fortunate as to have a religion universally followed by all the inhabitants, the greatest care should be taken to prevent its being questioned or brought into dispute. . . .

But what if there exist several religions in the state? This is unfortunate, but not necessarily fatal. For we have many examples from history of wise kings who ruled successfully and peacefully over subjects divided into many distinct sects. Theodosius the Great, for instance, found many of the Arian sect in the Roman Empire. . . . Although he was opposed to their beliefs, he did not wish to force them to accept his or to punish them for being Arians. On the contrary, he rescinded previous edicts against them, permitted them to live in liberty of their conscience, to worship according to their own rites, and to bring up their children in their faith. Nevertheless, he succeeded in considerably reducing the number of Arians in Europe. . . .

I will not here try to determine which religion is the best and truest (though there can be but one truth, one divine law, issuing from the mouth of God). But if a prince be well assured of his possession of the true religion and if he wish, therefore, to draw his subjects to it, he should not, in my opinion, use force. For the more one tries to force men's wills, the more unwilling and stubborn they become. . . .

Except, therefore, where a dissenting sect becomes seditious, a good prince will not try to destroy it. For those who have been forbidden their own religion and who are disgusted with all other kinds become atheists and, after having lost their fear of God, they know no restraint, and commit all manner of crimes and impieties, which it is impossible to correct by any human laws or other devices. The prudent prince, therefore, will remember that just as the worst tyranny is less miserable than anarchy . . . , so the worst superstition is far less detestable than no religion at all. . . . For in the reverent fear which religion awakes, there lies a mighty power for controlling a tumultuous people. . . . Indeed, even atheists themselves agree that nothing is more useful in maintaining a state than is religion and that it is the chief support on which the power of kings and princes rests.[k]

When Bodin's attention was focused on such questions as the problems of efficient administration, moral considerations dropped out of the picture. His account of the source of law is a case in point. He held that since customs are difficult to determine with precision, and since they vary from one region to another, efficient administration requires a single, explicitly defined code of laws. This, in turn, requires a single legal authority, a final court of appeal to resolve conflicts in the interpretation of the laws. In other words, efficient administration demands that the source of law be the sovereign's will, backed by force.

Despite this emphasis on the sovereign's power as the source of law, Bodin never altogether forgot the medieval thesis that God is the ultimate source of law. Like Thomas, he distinguished between force and law, or, in his own terminology, between "the way of fact" and "the way of justice." Taken by itself, the assertion that the sovereign is the source of law seems to imply the "positivistic" (or "realistic")[12] corollary that whatever is decreed by the person (or persons) in authority is *ipso facto* law. But Bodin added that the sovereign ought "to obey the laws of nature—that is, he ought to govern his subjects in accordance with natural justice."[1] This amounts to saying that the king is not the source of law at all; he merely enunciates God's law and enforces it. And power is legitimate—morally justified—only when it is in the hands of a good king, that is, when it is employed in accordance with natural law.

Clearly, Bodin was no more successful than Marsiglio in reconciling the medieval view that law is a reflection of the divine intellect and will with the view that law is whatever the sovereign promulgates. Reconciling the concept of right with the concept of power was to remain a central problem of political theory for the next two or three hundred years—as long as men took seriously the concept of an absolute moral criterion in terms of which all actual legislation should be evaluated.

NATURALISM

Reference to the concept of power brings us to naturalism, the last of the three strands in Renaissance politics to be examined here. "Naturalism" is a

12 See p. 14.

term that people use in a number of different ways. For present purposes, it may be defined as the disposition to ignore moral considerations and to concentrate on ascertaining the facts about power and the means of attaining it. The political naturalist is uninterested in criteria for evaluating political institutions, because he suspects that moral criteria (such as those employed by Plato or Thomas) are no more than private preferences. If the naturalist is also an egoist, he may evaluate political institutions by the extent to which they promote his own personal ends—the maintenance of the status quo, if he is already in power, or its overthrow, if he wishes to secure power.

There is, of course, nothing novel about naturalism; it is at least as old as Thrasymachus. But the point is that after lying buried for centuries beneath the prevailing religious orientation of the Middle Ages, it began to emerge again during the fifteenth century as a part of that complex of changes called the Renaissance. It was in Italy that a purely naturalistic political theory—as distinct from the mixed, or dilute, theories of Bodin and Marsiglio—was first explicitly formulated. Indeed, the conditions of life there were particularly favorable to the development of political naturalism.

In the first place, since feudalism never gripped Italy as firmly as it did northern Europe, less effort was required for Italians to break away from the medieval system of values. In addition, during the whole of the Middle Ages municipal life was vigorous in Italy; the Italian cities knew how to maintain their independence, and great trading centers like Venice and Genoa soon learned how to put the piety of the north to use in promoting their own commercial life. What is more, during the period when the medieval kings in France and England were emerging as monarchs of new nation-states, the Italian cities continued to maintain their independence. There was, in fact, no medieval Italian king to initiate the movement toward unity. There was only a German emperor, faraway, preoccupied, and weak, by no means an object on which nascent emotions of Italian nationalism might fix.

Thus the political life of Italy was organized into small-scale units, each a center of vigorous this-worldly activities and a focus of intense local self-interest. Anyone who was sufficiently bold, vigorous, and unscrupulous might win a state for himself. Ambitious *condottieri* like Jacopo Sforza and shrewd bankers like Cosimo de' Medici found it easy to establish dynasties, though in the ruthless competition of the age it required even more of the same qualities, together with an almost complete absence of nerves, to hold on to one's newly acquired state for any appreciable length of time.

It is not surprising, therefore, that the new man we have already encountered in France and England appeared in Italy in even greater numbers. And it is obvious that this new man, with his new values, would conceive of politics in a far less moralistic way than did Bodin, for instance, with his emphasis on natural law.

For one thing, this new man's point of view was intensely dynamic. It was not merely that he was ambitious—there was nothing new about ambition; but now, no longer confined to a static society, no longer hemmed in by moral sanctions, an ambitious man was free to choose among almost limitless possibilities, regardless of his birth or background. In this fluid milieu, the old virtues proved to be vices. Piety and charity, for instance, were positively dangerous to cultivate in the new society. A man who felt bound by contracts and promises would obviously be severely limited in this life (whether he might receive a recompense in heaven had become an irrelevant consideration); moral and religious scruples were a handicap. In place of such old values, power became the focus of attention. Power was desirable because it enabled one to hold on to what one already had, and to acquire more of what one wanted. Power was desirable because it could buy those this-worldly goods in which the new man delighted—clothes, women, palaces, classical manuscripts, adulation. Above all, power was good because it brought with it the sense of being unrestricted.

Ambition and power are, of course, two aspects of the same phenomenon— the secularization of value. Indeed, the infinity of ambition's range is reflected in the fact—soon recognized during the Renaissance—that power has no maximum. The religious motive of the Middle Ages had a maximum in the sense that when one "saw God," one could want nothing more; this was the final good. But no matter how much power one possesses, one wants and needs more. And whereas "seeing God" was not only a maximum but also a common value (in the sense that it could be shared without loss), power is obviously an exclusive value. Since one's own power is relative to others' lack of it, the pursuit of power for oneself implies the denial of power to others. Thus the competitive character of the new society was also reflected in the competitive character of its new good.

Machiavelli

Less significant than the fact that power politics was a characteristic product of the Renaissance in Italy is the fact that this kind of politics was analyzed with great penetration by an Italian contemporary of the first *realpolitikers*. What Bodin did for the idea of sovereignty, one of the great ideas operative in the France of his day, Machiavelli[13] did for the idea of power politics, one of the great ideas operative in the Italy of his day. Each of these writers, because of the peculiar circumstances in which he happened to be placed, was able to recognize and to isolate for study one of the leading elements in the new political ideal of the West.

13 Niccolo Machiavelli (1469–1527), a citizen of Florence, served the Florentine government of his day in a variety of capacities at home and abroad until 1512, when the Republic was overthrown and the Medici (the family that had ruled Florence during most of the preceding century) were restored to power.

CONCEPTION OF HUMAN NATURE

The essence of Machiavelli's conception of politics lies in his conviction that most men are stupid and irrational, quite incapable of governing themselves intelligently. "Those who have been present at any deliberative assemblies of men will have observed how erroneous their opinions often are; and in fact, unless they are directed by superior men, they are apt to be contrary to all reason."[m]

Most men are moved by passion rather than by reason, and one of the greatest of the passions that move them is ambition. It is

> . . . so powerful in the hearts of men that it never leaves them, no matter to what height they may rise. The reason of this is that nature has created men so that they desire everything, but are unable to attain it; desire being thus always greater than the faculty of acquiring, discontent with what they have and dissatisfaction with themselves result from it.
>
> . . . .
>
> As human desires are insatiable (because their nature is to have and to do everything whilst fortune limits their possessions and capacity of enjoyment), this gives rise to a constant discontent in the human mind and a weariness of the things they possess.[n]

For the rest, Machiavelli held that men are moved by fear and envy, by desire for novelty, by love of wealth, by hatred of any kind of restriction on their activities, and by a desire for security. Since it is obvious that such a concatenation of drives can lead only to strife and competition, whether between individuals or states, it follows that the only feasible government is a strong monarchy.

It has not always been thus, Machiavelli believed. Human nature has deteriorated from the nobility that made the ancient Roman Republic possible. Here, of course, Machiavelli betrayed that nostalgia for the classical past with which Italians of his generation were imbued and which, in other individuals, led to the revival of learning that will be examined in the concluding section of this chapter. Machiavelli naturally asked himself what had caused this decline from ancient virtue, and he decided that the corrupting influence of the Christian religion was chiefly responsible. Its exaltation of meekness, humility, and otherworldliness had gradually undermined the ancient civic virtues.

> Reflecting now as to whence it came that in ancient times the people were more devoted to liberty than in the present, I believe that it resulted from this, that men were stronger in those days, which I believe to be attributable to the difference of education, founded upon the difference of their religion and ours. For, as our religion teaches us the truth and the true way of life, it causes us to attach less value to the honours and possessions of this world; whilst the Pagans, esteeming those things as the highest good, were more energetic and ferocious in their actions. . . . Besides this, the

Pagan religion deified only men who had achieved great glory, such as commanders of armies and chiefs of republics, whilst ours glorifies more the humble and contemplative men than the men of action. Our religion, moreover, places the supreme happiness in humility, lowliness, and a contempt for worldly objects, whilst the other, on the contrary, places the supreme good in grandeur of soul, strength of body, and all such other qualities as render men formidable; and if our religion claims of us fortitude of soul it is more to enable us to suffer than to achieve great deeds.

These principles seem to me to have made men feeble, and caused them to become an easy prey to evil-minded men, who can control them more securely, seeing that the great body of men, for the sake of gaining Paradise, are more disposed to endure injuries than to avenge them.º

CONCEPTION OF SOVEREIGNTY

Machiavelli's admiration for the pagan past did not make him unrealistic about the present. Although ideally "governments of the people are better than of princes," the student of politics must deal with things and with men as they are, not as they might be.

It is vain to look for anything good from those countries which we see nowadays so corrupt, as is the case above all others with Italy. France and Spain also have their share of corruption, and if we do not see so many disorders and troubles in those countries as is the case daily in Italy, it is not so much owing to the goodness of their people, in which they are greatly deficient, as to the fact that they have each a king who keeps them united, not only by his virtue, but also by the institutions of those kingdoms, which are as yet preserved pure. . . .

The only way to establish any kind of order . . . is to establish some superior power which, with a royal hand, and with full and absolute powers, may put a curb upon the excessive ambition and corruption of the powerful.ᴾ

Machiavelli realized that since the prince is a man, he is subject to the same irrational passions that infect the mass of mankind.[14] Men are so selfish and so shortsighted that a strong power is required to keep them from destroying themselves; unfortunately, the man who holds this power is likely to be as selfish, if not as shortsighted, as his subjects. Hence, since "a prince's private interests are generally in opposition to those of his subjects," most princes are tyrants. Fortunate indeed is a people ruled by a virtuous prince. Of course, when Machiavelli talked about a "virtuous" prince, he did not mean one who exemplifies the standard Christian virtues of charity and forbearance. He meant a ruler who is shrewd enough to serve his own interests well without so crossing those of his subjects as to make them rebellious.

14 This realistic insight contrasts with the cheerful facility with which Bodin and the medieval theorists wrote about what a "good king" will do for his people.

In general, by "virtue" Machiavelli meant any behavior that promotes the acquisition and maintenance of power; by "vice" he meant behavior that decreases or destroys power. These definitions may sound paradoxical, but they follow from Machiavelli's assumptions about human nature. After all, according to a respectable Greek usage, the "virtue" of anything is simply that thing's way of functioning efficiently and realizing itself. Plato's list of virtues differed from Machiavelli's because, having a different view of human nature, Plato reached different conclusions about how men function efficiently.

Plato would have allowed, of course, that many men, perhaps most men, take power as their end—after all, he was acquainted with Thrasymachus and Callicles. But he distinguished between what men actually do and what they ought to do; beyond the facts, he believed, there exists a set of norms by which the facts are to be assessed. The function of political theory, according to Plato, is to ascertain these norms.

Machiavelli rejected this conception of political theory. For him there were only two questions. First, what do men aim at? This aim, whatever it is, is their good. Second, what acts on their part will produce this good? These acts, whatever they are, are their virtues. This is the point of view of the political naturalist.

These are both purely factual questions. Machiavelli's answer to the first was that every man aims at maintaining and expanding his own power. His answer to the second is the heart of his political theory, for in his view political theory is nothing but the exposition of the political virtues, that is, the best techniques for securing and maintaining power. Machiavelli's conception of these techniques was determined by his belief that human beings are stupid and venal; the intelligent prince, that is, plays upon those passions by which, according to Machiavelli, all men are moved.

The two principal instruments at the disposal of the prince are force and propaganda. As regards force, the chief rule is to employ it ruthlessly.

> Whoever becomes the ruler a free city and does not destroy it, can expect to be destroyed by it, for it can always find a motive for rebellion in the name of liberty and of its ancient usages, which are forgotten neither by lapse of time nor by benefits received. . . .
>
> It is to be noted, that in taking a state the conqueror must arrange to commit all his cruelties at once, so as not to have to recur to them every day, and so as to be able, by not making fresh changes, to reassure people and win them over by benefiting them. Whoever acts otherwise, either through timidity or bad counsels, is always obliged to stand with knife in hand, and can never depend on his subjects, because they, owing to continually fresh injuries, are unable to depend upon him. For injuries should be done all together, so that being less tasted, they will give less offence. Benefits should be granted little by little, so that they may be better enjoyed. And above all, a prince must live with his subjects in such a way that no accident of good or evil fortune can deflect him from his course; for necessity arising

in adverse times, you are not in time with severity, and the good that you do does not profit, as it is judged to be forced upon you, and you will derive no benefit whatever from it.[q]

Doubtless, these policies will make the prince hated; but if one has to choose, it is much better to be feared than to be loved.

> From this arises the question whether it is better to be loved more than feared, or feared more than loved. The reply is, that one ought to be both feared and loved, but as it is difficult for the two to go together, it is much safer to be feared than loved, if one of the two has to be wanting. For it may be said of men in general that they are ungrateful, voluble, dissemblers, anxious to avoid danger, and covetous of gain; as long as you benefit them, they are entirely yours; they offer you their blood, their goods, their life, and their children, as I have before said, when the necessity is remote; but when it approaches, they revolt. And the prince who has relied solely on their words, without making other preparations, is ruined. . . . And men have less scruple in offending one who makes himself loved than one who makes himself feared; for love is held by a chain of obligation which, men being selfish, is broken whenever it serves their purpose; but fear is maintained by a dread of punishment which never fails. . . .
>
> How laudable it is for a prince to keep good faith and live with integrity, and not with astuteness, everyone knows. Still the experience of our times shows these princes to have done great things who have had little regard for good faith, and have been able by astuteness to confuse men's brains, and who have ultimately overcome those who have made loyalty their foundation. . . .
>
> A prudent ruler ought not to keep faith when by so doing it would be against his interest, and when the reasons which made him bind himself no longer exist. If men were all good, this precept would not be a good one; but as they are bad, and would not observe their faith with you, so you are not bound to keep faith with them. Nor have legitimate grounds ever failed a prince who wished to show colourable excuse for the nonfulfilment of his promise. Of this one could furnish an infinite number of modern examples, and show how many times peace has been broken, and how many promises rendered worthless, by the faithlessness of princes, and those that have been best able to imitate the fox have succeeded best. But it is necessary to be able to disguise this character well, and to be a great feigner and dissembler; and men are so simple and so ready to obey present necessities, that one who deceives will always find those who allow themselves to be deceived.
>
> I will only mention one modern instance. Alexander VI[15] did nothing else but deceive men, he thought of nothing else, and found the occasion for it; no man was ever more able to give assurances, or affirmed things with stronger oaths, and no man observed them less; however, he always succeeded in his deceptions, as he well knew this aspect of things.[r]

15 [See pp. 48–49—AUTHOR.]

So much for force, the first instrument of princes. Although it is indispensable, it is expensive. Therefore the wise prince will use propaganda to win the people over to his side: He will persuade them that he is devoted to their interests, though in point of fact he makes no real concessions to them. Of course, it is important not to depend on propaganda alone. Propaganda must always be backed by force; the prince must be ready to deal firmly with those who are not easily duped.

Of all the propaganda techniques at a prince's disposal, one of the most valuable is religion.

> Whoever reads Roman history attentively will see in how great a degree religion served in the command of the armies, in uniting the people and keeping them well conducted, and in covering the wicked with shame. . . . In truth, there never was any remarkable lawgiver amongst any people who did not resort to divine authority, as otherwise his laws would not have been accepted by the people; for there are many good laws, the importance of which is known to the sagacious lawgiver, but the reasons for which are not sufficiently evident to enable him to persuade others to submit to them; and therefore do wise men, for the purpose of removing this difficulty, resort to divine authority. Thus did Lycurgus and Solon, and many others who aimed at the same thing. . . .
>
> And therefore everything that tends to favour religion (even though it were believed to be false) should be received and availed of to strengthen it; and this should be done the more, the wiser the rulers are, and the better they understand the natural course of things. Such was, in fact, the practice observed by sagacious men; which has given rise to the belief in the miracles that are celebrated in religions, however false they may be. For the sagacious rulers have given these miracles increased importance, no matter whence or how they originated; and their authority afterwards gave them credence with the people. Rome had many such miracles; and one of the most remarkable was that which occurred when the Roman soldiers sacked the city of Veii; some of them entered the temple of Juno, and, placing themselves in front of her statue, said to her, "Will you come to Rome?" Some imagined that they observed the statue make a sign of assent, and others pretended to have heard her reply, "Yes." Now these men, being very religious, as reported by Titus Livius, and having entered the temple quietly, they were filled with devotion and reverence, and might really have believed that they had heard a reply to their question, such as perhaps they could have presupposed. But this opinion and belief was favoured and magnified by Camillus and the other Roman chiefs. . . .
>
> It does not seem to me from my purpose to adduce here some examples to show how the Romans employed religion for the purpose of reorganizing their city, and to further their enterprises. . . .
>
> The system of auguries was . . . the cause of the prosperity of the Roman republic. . . . Amongst other auspices the armies were always accompanied by a certain class of soothsayers, termed Pollari (guardians of the sacred fowls), and every time before giving battle to the enemy, they required these

Pollari to ascertain the auspices; and if the fowls ate freely, then it was deemed a favourable augury, and the soldiers fought confidently, but if the fowls refused to eat, then they abstained from battle. Nevertheless, when they saw a good reason why certain things should be done, they did them anyhow, whether the auspices were favourable or not; but then they turned and interpreted the auguries so artfully, and in such manner, that seemingly no disrespect was shown to their religious belief. . . . Nor had this system of consulting the auspices any other object than to inspire the soldiers on the eve of battle with that confidence which is the surest guaranty of victory.[s]

CONTRAST WITH BODIN

It is interesting to contrast this passage with Bodin's discussion of religion. Unlike Machiavelli, Bodin lived through the wars of religion; he knew even better than Machiavelli the potential political power of the religious passion. But he was also a deeply religious man. For him, religion was not only power; it was also the thrust of the soul toward God. The question for him, therefore, was how to hold on to the truths of religion while utilizing it as a political instrument. This gave Bodin's view an ambivalence and a tension that were lacking in Machiavelli's completely secular conception of religion. For Machiavelli, religion was just one more evidence of man's irrationality, just one of many forces with which the ruler had to reckon. In itself, Machiavelli held it to be as neutral as, say, gravity—another force with which men must reckon. Misused, it is "bad"; but the intelligent man can put it to use in getting what he wants, just as he can use gravity in shaking down the apple that is out of reach at the top of the tree. The "goodness" of gravity depends on whether it can be made to promote a man's ambitions. And, according to Machiavelli, the same is true of religion and all the other social, economic, and physical forces that make up life.

The state, in his view, is not a divine institution, and it has no supernatural end. It is as much a neutral object of study as any other natural phenomenon, though, of course, it is more complicated than most. To understand it, we do not make a teleological inquiry into purposes, divine or human; rather, we describe the interactions of the various forces that constitute it. The goal of this descriptive science is the power that such knowledge yields. The way to be happy is to manipulate these forces so as to achieve one's own private ends. This requires foresight, skill, and, above all, cold-blooded calculation of self-interest. "Before deciding upon any course, . . . men should well consider the objections and the dangers which it presents; and if its perils exceed its advantages, they should avoid it, even though it had been in accordance with their previous determination."[t]

Of course, not even the most intelligent and enlightened of egoists can expect always to control the forces that play upon him. In part, the success or failure of men depends not so much on themselves as on their manner of suiting their conduct to the times. "It is an incontrovertible truth, proved by all history, that men may second Fortune, but cannot oppose her; they may develop her designs, but cannot defeat them."[u] This anthropomorphic language should not lead one to suppose that Machiavelli was covertly reintroducing a kind of divine or supernatural causality, even in the person of chance. As a matter of fact, exactly the opposite was his intention. In emphasizing that there is a basic element of irrationality in the universe, that some things "just happen," Machiavelli meant to deny that the universe is the wholly rational structure that theologians like Thomas had argued it must be because it was created by an omnipotent God. Since Machiavelli lived before the dawn of modern science, with its concept of a rational but secular system, he could deny divine causality only by affirming chance. Saying that the world is not wholly rational was, from Machiavelli's point of view, simply a way of saying that it is wholly natural, and that life is an adventure that, to be enjoyed, must be lived at maximum pitch and savored to the full in all its tension and variety, in all its strangeness and excitement, in all its novelty and passion.

Humanism and the Revival of Learning

The men of the Middle Ages were, of course, immensely learned—learned in the Church fathers, in the commentators, in Aristotle. But the learning that was revived in the Renaissance was the secular learning of the ancients, the poems, dramas, essays, that had been lost for centuries.

This interest in pagan literature did not arise suddenly in the fifteenth century. Dante, who was the most medieval of men in his system of values, chose no Christian saint but the author of the *Aeneid* as his guide through hell and purgatory. But what was occasional in the thirteenth century had become a dominant passion by the end of the fifteenth, and this new passion had brought with it a new educational and social ideal and a new conception of human nature.

What produced this change? It will not do to say that as soon as the long-lost classical texts were rediscovered, their beauty shone forth for all to appreciate. For the texts had been available previously to anyone who cared to look for them. There must have been a change in taste that led men to seek out manuscripts that had long lain neglected in monastic libraries.[16] Of course, the new taste for the classics grew as men became more widely acquainted with them.

16 Several generations of scholars rang the changes on Petrarch's personification of these manuscripts as gentle prisoners awaiting release from barbarous jailers. Poggio, for instance, who discovered the *Institutions* of Quintilian at the Abbey of St. Gall, said that Quintilian "seemed to be stretching out his hands calling upon the Romans," beseeching them to free him from the foul dungeon to which he had been consigned by the ignorant monks.

At the outset, the movement characterized by this taste was too diffuse to have a sense of identity. But as it gradually spread, it acquired self-consciousness; those who shared the new taste found for themselves the name by which they are called to this day. They described themselves as "humanists" because they were students of what they called "litterae humaniores"; since they studied this literature as a model for the new values they were introducing into life, it is fair to take the term "Humanism" as a token of the shift in the focus of values to man and his affairs.

PETRARCH

Petrarch (1304–74) was one of the fashioners of the Humanistic point of view. He was indeed representative of the first stage of Humanism, when the movement had not yet become pagan and secular, when it had not yet cut itself off from the Middle Ages. Petrarch's family were Italians who moved to Avignon[17] when he was a boy. He never forgot, however, that he was Italian, and he felt very strongly the decline of Italy from its past greatness. The papal court's subservience to the French king seemed to him a symbol of that decline. On his first visit to Rome, in 1336, he was much impressed by the contrast between the meanness of the modern city and the grandeur, even in ruin, of the surviving monuments of ancient Rome. Petrarch's desire to revive pagan learning was therefore not unconnected with nostalgia for the great past.[18]

Petrarch was also representative of the Renaissance in his enjoyment of nature. It was symptomatic of the new spirit that was emerging that he climbed a mountain not merely to get to the other side but also to look at the view. Nature had not interested the typical medieval mind, which saw in it only a series of symbols—God's instructions to erring humanity. This new attitude toward nature, the attitude that made it possible for men simply to enjoy a view, soon came to show itself in every department of human activity—in a new art that sought to render real-life people in real landscapes; in a curiosity about the facts that eventually resulted in the development of science in the modern sense;[19] in the discovery that the state, as well as man himself, is a natural organism whose life history can be made a neutral object of study like the rest of nature.

Petrarch's ascent of Mont Ventoux, then, was one of the first recorded signs of a reviving naturalism. But it marked only a beginning: The letter in which he described his expedition is a blend of old and new attitudes and shows that in his eyes the ascent was to a large extent an allegory of a spiritual struggle like that of St. Augustine.

17 This was the period of the "Babylonish captivity" of the papacy (see p. 45).
18 Compare Machiavelli's contrast between "ancient virtue" and "modern degeneracy," pp. 27–28.
19 See Chapter 3.

Today I ascended the highest mountain in this region, which, not without cause, they call the Windy Peak. Nothing but the desire to see its conspicuous height was the reason for this undertaking. For many years I have been intending to make this expedition. . . . So I was at last seized by the impulse to accomplish what I had always wanted to do. It happened while I was reading Roman history again in Livy that I hit upon the passage where Philip, the king of Macedon—the Philip who waged war against the Roman people— "ascends Mount Haemus in Thessaly, since he believed the rumor that you can see two seas from its top: the Adriatic and the Black Sea." Whether he was right or wrong I cannot make out because the mountain is far from our region, and the disagreement among authors renders the matter uncertain. I do not intend to consult all of them: the cosmographer Pomponius Mela does not hesitate to report the fact as true; Livy supposes the rumor to be false. I would not leave it long in doubt if that mountain were as easy to explore as the one here.

. . . .

At first I stood there almost benumbed, overwhelmed by a gale such as I had never felt before and by the unusually open and wide view. I looked around me: clouds were gathering below my feet, and Athos and Olympus grew less incredible, since I saw on a mountain of lesser fame what I had heard and read about them. From there I turned my eyes in the direction of Italy, for which my mind is so fervently yearning. . . .

One could see most distinctly the mountains of the province of Lyons to the right and, to the left, the sea near Marseilles as well as the waves that break against Aigues Mortes, although it takes several days to travel to this city. The Rhone River was directly under our eyes.

I admired every detail, now relishing earthly enjoyment, now lifting up my mind to higher spheres after the example of my body, and I thought it fit to look into the volume of Augustine's *Confessions* which I [keep] always in my hands. . . . It is a little book of smallest size but full of infinite sweetness. I opened it with the intention of reading whatever might occur to me first. . . . Where I fixed my eyes first, it was written: "And men go to admire the high mountains, the vast floods of the sea, the huge streams of the rivers, the circumference of the ocean, and the revolutions of the stars—and desert themselves." I was stunned, I confess. I bade my brother, who wanted to hear more, not to molest me, and closed the book, angry with myself that I still admired earthly things. Long since I ought to have learned, even from pagan philosophers, that "nothing is admirable besides the mind; compared to its greatness nothing is great." . . .

How often, do you think, did I turn back and look up to the summit of the mountain today while I was walking down? It seemed to me hardly higher than a cubit compared to the height of human contemplation, were the latter not plunged into the filth of earthly sordidness. This too occurred to me at every step: "If you do not regret undergoing so much sweat and hard labor to lift the body a bit nearer to heaven, ought any cross or jail or torture to frighten the mind that is trying to come nearer to God and set its feet upon the swollen summit of insolence and upon the fate of mortal men?" [v]

Some characteristic motifs of the Renaissance are apparent in this passage. One is reliance on pagan literary sources. The reference to Livy was not just a display of erudition, though Petrarch liked to display his immense learning. It was surely also a survival of the medieval desire to cite authorities. The Renaissance was quite unmodern and unscientific in this respect. It did not abandon the appeal to authority; it simply relied on different authorities. Yet appeal to an authority that itself relied on rational, rather than on supernatural, grounds introduced a new tone, and eventually infused a more critical spirit, into the work of Renaissance writers.

Petrarch could be quite critical about some things. He scorned the Scholastic technique of comment and exegesis. "There are people who do not dare to write anything of their own. Eager to write, they become interpreters of the works of others. Like those who have no notion of architecture, they make it their profession to whitewash walls."ʷ Though they regard themselves as learned, they merely compile uncritically all sorts of rubbish and unverified gossip, such as

> . . . how many hairs there are in the lion's mane; how many feathers in the hawk's tail; with how many arms the cuttlefish clasps a shipwrecked man; . . . how the hunter fools the tiger with a mirror; . . . how whales turn over on their backs and thus deceive the sailors. . . .
>
> All this is for the greater part wrong, as has become manifest in many similar cases when animals were brought into our part of the world. The facts have certainly not been investigated by those who are quoted as authorities for them; they have been all the more promptly believed or boldly invented, since the animals live so far from us. And even if they were true, they would not contribute anything whatsoever to the blessed life. What is the use—I beseech you—of knowing the nature of quadrupeds, fowls, fishes, and serpents and not knowing or even neglecting man's nature, the purpose for which we are born, and whence and whereto we travel?ˣ

DEVELOPMENT OF TEXTUAL CRITICISM

In place of a Scholastic education consisting merely in the accumulation of an encyclopedic mass of information, Petrarch advocated study of the classics, which he believed to produce "a good and well-trained mind." At the outset, he and the other Renaissance writers were primarily interested in the classics from a literary standpoint. Their ideal was to achieve a style modeled on the best Latin writers—not to copy them slavishly, but to achieve, as Petrarch said, a "family resemblance."

More important than this interest in style was the technique of textual criticism that emerged from it. When several manuscripts of the same poem or essay came to light, they were collated and compared; great ingenuity was exercised in interpreting copyists' mistakes and in determining an accurate version of the original work.

The seeds of this scholarly methodology planted by Petrarch and other early students bore vigorous fruit in the next century. Lorenzo Valla (1406–56), for instance, examined the so-called Donation of Constantine in this spirit and showed that the text did not mention events that would almost certainly have received notice had it been written, as purported, in the early fourth century; on the contrary, the text contained terms and references to institutions of a much later origin. Valla's analysis left no doubt that this document, on which the Church rested its claim to temporal authority, was a forgery.

Less dramatic but in the long run more significant was the textual criticism of the Vulgate, as the Latin version of the Bible was called. This translation, made by St. Jerome, was regarded by the Church as a product of revelation—divine, immutable, and absolutely definitive. But the Renaissance search for manuscripts turned up numerous versions of the Old and New Testaments. By collating these, many of which had not been accessible to Jerome, Renaissance scholars showed that the saintly writer had in places misunderstood and mistranslated.

It should not be supposed that this scholarly research was motivated by irreligion. Lorenzo Valla was by no means a sceptic; Petrarch's admiration for pagan learning did not mean that he was a pagan. Like Augustine, Petrarch held that learning should have a "sober use." One should seek in it "nothing but to become good." Without this ultimate, and religious, purpose, learning "inflates, it tears down. . . . It is a glittering shackle, a toilsome pursuit, and a resounding burden for the soul." There are only two things absolutely indispensable for happiness, and neither of them is learning. They are, Petrarch held, "Faith and Immortality." [y] For the most part, then, the scholars of the early Renaissance were pious men who thought they were rehabilitating and purifying Christian doctrine.

But though their intention was devout, these scholars were undermining, at least by implication, the Church's claim to be the exclusive vessel of Christian truth. For the logical corollary of their method was an affirmation of the supremacy of reason over the authority of revelation. This may not be obvious at first sight. But the growth of an historical sense was bound to undermine the doctrine of revelation. It is significant, indeed, that the notion of *document* first came into prominence during this period. Documents are natural objects, capable of objective investigation; documents have a temporal locus, and a knowledge of the historical context in which a document was written is obviously highly relevant to an understanding of the document. Of course, during the early Renaissance, no one held that the truth was any less revealed; men simply came to hold that since God always spoke through individuals living in a particular historical milieu, it was important, for understanding His message, to understand this milieu. Thus the right of the Church to the last word on revelation came to be questioned. When this line of reasoning is extended, the real expert proves to be not a divinely inspired institution but a competent scholar; and scholarship, being a matter of training and education, is open to all. Hence, the conclusion is inescapable that the ultimate authority on God's message is the reason of individual men. When men finally reached this conclusion, the Middle Ages were over.

What is surprising, therefore, is not that the Church came to oppose this critical activity but that it actually dallied so long with the Renaissance, encouraging its scholarship and cultivating its scholars. Nothing, as a matter of fact, shows so well the depth and pervasiveness of the Renaissance spirit as the long and active patronage on the part of the Church. Indeed, it was not until the Reformation brought the Church face to face with destruction that it reacted against the new learning.

A NEW CONCEPTION OF VALUE

So far the linguistic and scholarly aspects of the revival of learning have been considered. But though the Renaissance's original interest in the classics was focused on literary form, it proved impossible to emulate an author's style without absorbing something of his point of view with respect to the world, and gradually the old classical conception of man as an autonomous, independent, rational being began to revive. The long-forgotten appreciation of the value and dignity of human personality, of pride and self-respect, now reemerged.

Pico della Mirandola's[20] *Oration on the Dignity of Man* is a good example of this new spirit:

> At last it seems to me I have come to understand why man is the most fortunate of creatures and consequently worthy of all admiration and what precisely is that rank which is his lot in the universal chain of Being—a rank to be envied not only by brutes but even by the stars and by minds beyond this world. . . .
>
> God the Father, the supreme Architect, had already built this cosmic home we behold, the most sacred temple of His godhead, by the laws of His mysterious wisdom. The region above the heavens He had adorned with Intelligences, the heavenly spheres He had quickened with eternal souls, and the excrementary and filthy parts of the lower world He had filled with a multitude of animals of every kind. But, when the work was finished, the Craftsman kept wishing that there were someone to ponder the plan of so great a work, to love its beauty, and to wonder at its vastness. Therefore, when everything was done (as Moses and Timaeus bear witness), He finally took thought concerning the creation of man. . . .
>
> Assigning him a place in the middle of the world, [He] addressed him thus: "Neither a fixed abode nor a form that is thine alone nor any function peculiar to thyself have We given thee, Adam, to the end that according to thy longing and according to thy judgment thou mayest have and possess what abode, what form, and what functions thou thyself shalt desire. The

---

20 Pico, who was born in 1462, almost one hundred years after Petrarch's death, was one of the leading members of Lorenzo de' Medici's Florentine Academy.

nature of all other beings is limited and constrained within the bounds of laws prescribed by Us. Thou, constrained by no limits, in accordance with thine own free will, in whose hand We have placed thee, shalt ordain for thyself the limits of thy nature. We have set thee at the world's center that thou mayest from thence more easily observe whatever is in the world. We have made thee neither of heaven nor of earth, neither mortal nor immortal, so that with freedom of choice and with honor, as though the maker and molder of thyself, thou mayest fashion thyself in whatever shape thou shalt prefer. . . ."

O supreme generosity of God the Father, O highest and most marvelous felicity of man! To him it is granted to have whatever he chooses, to be whatever he wills. Beasts as soon as they are born (so says Lucilius) bring with them from their mother's womb all they will ever possess. Spiritual beings, either from the beginning or soon thereafter, become what they are to be for ever and ever. On man when he came into life the Father conferred the seeds of all kinds and the germs of every way of life. Whatever seeds each man cultivates will grow to maturity and bear in him their own fruit. If they be vegetative, he will be like a plant. If sensitive, he will become brutish. If rational, he will grow into a heavenly being. If intellectual, he will be an angel and the son of God. And if, happy in the lot of no created thing, he withdraws into the center of his own unity, his spirit, made one with God, in the solitary darkness of God, who is set above all things, shall surpass them all. Who would not admire this our chameleon? . . .

But why do we emphasize this? To the end that . . . we may not, by abusing the most indulgent generosity of the Father, make for ourselves that freedom of choice He has given into something harmful instead of salutary. Let a certain holy ambition invade our souls, so that, not content with the mediocre, we shall pant after the highest and (since we may if we wish) toil with all our strength to obtain it.

. . . Let us also, therefore, be emulating the Cherubic way of life on earth, by taming the impulses of our passions with moral science, by dispelling the darkness of reason with dialectic, and by, so to speak, washing away the filth of ignorance and vice, cleanse our soul, so that her passions may not rave at random or her reason through heedlessness ever be deranged.

Then let us fill our well-prepared and purified soul with the light of natural philosophy, so that we may at last perfect her in the knowledge of things divine.[z]

THE HUMANISTIC IDEAL

Thus the revival of learning was far more than a mere achievement in scholarship. Acquaintance with, and interest in, the classics as literature broadened into an ideal of self-culture, with emphasis on human, rather than supernatural, values.

Earlier Humanists like Petrarch had thought of this ideal of humane culture as merely supplementing the moral ideal of the Church. But as the movement developed, the new ideal gradually replaced the old Christian conception. This concentration of interest on man and his possibilities for self-culture, which Pico and other Humanists described, was naturally reflected in educational practice.

What kind of instruction in what subjects would realize these possibilities and produce a cultivated man of the world? One of the earliest and most influential of the Renaissance schools was that of Vittorino da Feltre (1397–1446), established in 1425 at the request of Gian Francesco Gonzaga, Marquis of Mantua. Vittorino wished to produce a well-rounded individual. He aimed at a culture that would not only satisfy the needs of the religious and contemplative life but also prepare his pupils for the duties of citizenship. In accordance with the Humanistic program, the Latin classics were the basis of the curriculum: The children read history and Stoic ethics as well as poetry and drama, and they learned to compose in both Latin and Greek. Vittorino made a place in the curriculum for the arts (music and singing) and the sciences (geometry, astronomy, and natural history); he also insisted, in accordance with his classical models, that his pupils develop their bodies as well as their minds. Training was provided in riding and swimming and in the military arts, and all sorts of outdoor activities were encouraged. Finally, good manners, along with manliness and morals, were stressed.

As Vittorino's fame spread, children were sent to his school from the various princely courts of Italy and even from Germany. Nor were his pupils confined to the aristocracy; at his own cost, Vittorino established scholarships with which he maintained as many as seventy children from poor families. The Renaissance ideal was not exclusive; though "good" birth and an adequate income were desirable, they were not indispensable. The important thing was the talents one had and the use one made of them. The ideal was, in fact, not so much that of a nobleman as that of a gentleman. It was democratic in its range, while remaining aristocratic in its conception of quality. Thus, just at the moment when changing economic and social conditions were dissolving the old stratifications of feudal society and permitting the rise of a new class, the Renaissance Humanists formulated an ideal appropriate for it. The new economic and social man was not fitted temperamentally to model himself on the old feudal ideal, but the new ideal of a cultivated gentleman was exactly in accord with the urban, secular, and individualistic spirit of the new age.

Typical of the illustrious alumni of Vittorino's school was Federigo di Montefeltro. Federigo (1422–82), a Renaissance prince and a successful *condottiere*, maintained a magnificent establishment at Urbino from the income paid him by grateful popes and kings. He built

> . . . the most beautiful [palace] in all Italy . . . and furnished it with . . . silver vases, hangings of richest cloth-of-gold and silk, and other similar things,—but for ornament he added countless antique statues in marble and bronze, pictures most choice, and musical instruments of every sort, nor would he admit anything there that was not very rare and excellent. Then at very great cost he collected a goodly number of most excellent and rare books

in Greek, Latin and Hebrew, all of which he adorned with gold and with silver, esteeming this to be the chiefest excellence of his great palace.[a]

Duke Federigo employed thirty or forty "scrittori" in various places to copy manuscripts for his library, which possessed the complete works of Thomas and other leading Scholastics, of Dante and Boccaccio, of Sophocles, Pindar, and Menander. There were also catalogues of the libraries of the Vatican, of San Marco at Florence, and even of Oxford. And this was the library, not of a scholar, but of a soldier.[b]

CASTIGLIONE'S *BOOK OF THE COURTIER*

After Federigo's death, his son continued to maintain a court that attracted accomplished men and women. Among these was Baldesar Castiglione (1478–1529), whose *Book of the Courtier* sums up the outlook of Renaissance Humanism—its concept of the ideal at which men ought to aim. To Castiglione it was obvious that "the principal and true profession of the courtier ought to be that of arms." He should therefore be "bold and strong, and loyal to whomsoever he serves," and courageous in small things as well as in great ones. He should be "very bold [and] stern . . . where the enemy are to be seen, [but] in every other place, gentle, modest, reserved, above all things avoiding ostentation and that impudent self-praise by which men ever excite hatred and disgust in all who hear them."[c]

The French, Castiglione held, were quite mistaken in thinking that "letters are injurious to arms" and in "holding all men of letters most base." On the contrary, literature is "the true and principal ornament of the mind," as all the greatest heroes of antiquity—Alcibiades, Alexander, Scipio Africanus, Pompey, Brutus, Hannibal—well knew. It is necessary, therefore, that the courtier be

> . . . more than passably accomplished in letters, at least in those studies that are called the humanities, and conversant not only with the Latin language but with the Greek, for the sake of the many different things that have been admirably written therein. Let him be well versed in the poets, and not less in the orators and historians, and also proficient in writing verse and prose, especially in this vulgar tongue of ours; for besides the enjoyment he will find in it, he will by this means never lack agreeable entertainment with ladies, who are usually fond of such things.[d]

Similarly, he should "be also a musician" and "play upon divers instruments," and he should "know how to draw and have acquaintance with the very art of painting."[e]

So far, it will be noted, we have considered only Castiglione's discussion of the cultivation of personal values and talents. In fact, he had little to say regarding the courtier's political life, probably because of the structure of Italian society in his day. According to Castiglione, the courtier's political life consists in loyalty to the prince to whom he is bound as servant or companion. Since most princes are "corrupted by evil customs and by ignorance and mistaken self-esteem," the chief function of the courtier is to try, by example and advice, "to lead his prince along the thorny path of virtue, decking it as with shady leafage and strewing it with lovely flowers to relieve the tedium of the weary journey to one whose strength is slight."[f]

Emphasis on the courtier's duties as schoolmaster to his prince suggests that the perfect courtier must be well advanced in years. What then? Can he not love? Obviously, to be unable to love would be a deficiency in the ideal of a well-rounded, integrated personality. But Castiglione held this criticism to be based on a superficial conception of the nature of love. Actually, "old men can love more happily than young": The latter are misled by their appetites and seek to satisfy this highest of all drives by means of "unchaste desires with the women whom they love." This mistaken pursuit of physical beauty ends either in "satiety and tedium" or in unsatisfied longing for something better—in either case, in unhappiness.

How much more beautiful than any woman is "this great fabric of the world, which was made by God for the health and preservation of every created thing. The round firmament, . . . the earth in the centre, surrounded by the elements and sustained by its own weight; the sun, which in its revolving illumines the whole. . . . They have [so much] beauty and grace that human wit cannot imagine anything more beautiful."[g]

And there is a still higher beauty, one "identical with the highest good, which by its light calls and attracts all things to itself, and not only gives intellect to the intellectual, reason to the rational, sense and desire for life to the sensual, but to plants also and to stones communicates motion and that natural instinct of their quality, as an imprint of itself."[h] It is essential, then, for the proper perfection of a courtier, to "show him how to love beyond the manner of the vulgar crowd"—the well-rounded life is not complete without religion. But the religion Castiglione was thinking of was more Platonic than Christian; it was the religion of the *Symposium* rather than the religion of the Gospels.

This conception of the gentleman—of the value of personal development and self-culture—soon spread from Italy to the rest of Europe.[21] It survived, indeed, down to the nineteenth century, when an industrial and mass-democracy culture began to develop another conception of man, with an emphasis on equal opportunities for all, rather than on the cultivation of the talents of a small elite. The Renaissance conception of man, however, still haunts many minds. It is fair to say that one of the problems of education today is how to revive this ideal of man within the conditions of modern life.

21 The *Book of the Courtier* was first printed in 1528. Within less than forty years, translations had appeared (in this order) in Spanish, French, English, Latin, and German. Opdycke (*Book of the Courtier,* pp. 419–22) lists more than one hundred and forty separate editions published before 1900.

How much the Humanistic conception of man owed to the classical world—to Aristotle, for instance, in his conception of law and rulership, and especially to Plato in the *Republic* and the *Symposium*—is obvious. Yet it was no mere revival of the classical view; as one of Castiglione's characters remarked when the similarity of his concept of the gentleman to the Platonic ideal was pointed out, "I am far from sure . . . that Aristotle and Plato ever danced or made music in their lives, or performed any other acts of chivalry."[1]

As a matter of fact, even when it was trying most self-consciously to be classical, the Renaissance ideal maintained a character of its own. For though classical learning might be revived, the milieu in which that learning had originally developed did not, and could not, revive. Except in Italy, from which leadership in the modern world soon passed, the milieu of the new ideal was neither the Greek city-state nor the universal imperium of Rome. It was that new phenomenon, the national territorial state, sovereign in its own domain and confronted with a plurality of political units as independent as itself. In this milieu the individual person was neither submerged, as in the Roman Empire, nor yet simply a member of an interdependent social group bound together by ties of blood and traditions, as in the Greek *polis*. The new political and social milieu, the rise of money power, and the physical expansion of Europe to America and Asia combined to create an unstable society in which the energetic and ambitious could rise. The new-model man of the Renaissance was therefore more dynamic, more individualistic, and more self-centered than the typical classical man.

These are important cultural differences that prevented the Renaissance ideal from being a mere "renaissance" of the classical ideal. The chief difference, however, lies in the fact that, despite the naturalism that came increasingly to the fore, the new culture remained for several centuries stubbornly Christian. The new world might turn its back on St. Peter and his successors, but it still tried to make peace with the Gospels.

CHAPTER 2

Reformation

Like the term "Renaissance," "Reformation" names not a single, self-contained entity but a section of a complex web of interweaving strands. Indeed, many of the strands that we have already considered as phases of the Renaissance—nationalism and the revival of learning, for instance—also operated, though in different ways, in the Reformation. Let us try, then, to see how events produced the changes in religious thought and practice that were the central phenomena of the Reformation and how these changes in turn reacted on the political and cultural milieu.

The Reformation was the emergence of a conception of man's relation to God that was radically different from that which had dominated the Middle Ages. At the same time, it was a revolt against the papacy and the Church. These movements were connected because, for men of the Middle Ages, the Church and the papacy were the links between man and God.

Let us first consider the revolt against the papacy. The changes in point of view and in political organization that have already been considered were inevitably inimical to all conservative institutions, whether secular or ecclesiastical. Like the feudal lords, the Church found its traditional sources of revenue no longer sufficient in the changing economic scene; like them, it had to secure access to the new money power or perish. And just as the measures by which the barons sought to increase their income caused peasant revolts, so the measures the papacy took to increase its revenues ran headlong into the ambitions of new sovereigns and newly awakened national sentiments.

Ecclesiastical Corruption

The worst of the papal "abuses," as Christendom came to call the practices it detested, began early in the fourteenth century. At the end of the preceding century, as a result of an increase in the power of the French kings and a succession of French popes, the papacy became hardly more than an instrument of French policy. A sign of the strength of French influence was the removal of the papal court to Avignon early in the fourteenth century. This "Babylonish captivity" at Avignon produced, by way of reaction to the preponderance of France in the determination of papal policy, a tendency in the other European states toward the creation of national churches concerned with supporting the policies of the temporal rulers.

But worse was to follow. When, after three quarters of a century, the papacy returned to Rome and an Italian-born cardinal was raised to the throne, the French faction of the College of Cardinals proceeded to elect another, pro-French pope. Christendom was thus confronted with the absurdity of having two popes. This situation, known as "the Great Schism," persisted for almost forty years. In 1409, in an attempt to mend the breach, both the pope and the antipope (who was pope and who antipope depended, of course, on one's point of view) were deposed and a new election was held. But since each of the deposed popes had a large following, the election only resulted in the installation of a third pope.

It would be difficult to overestimate the damage to the prestige of the papacy caused by the Schism. Not only was the spectacle of rival claimants to papal authority a scandal to the pious; the situation also called in question the theory that the choices of the College of Cardinals were divinely inspired, thus undermining the doctrinal basis of papal authority.

PAPAL FISCAL POLICY

Unfortunately for the popes, at the very time when they were losing prestige as a result of the Schism, they were making enemies by their fiscal policy. One of the principal sources of papal revenue and one of the bitterest causes of complaint were the annates. The annates (which amounted to the new incumbent's first year's income) had originally been assigned for some local use, such as the repair of a church building. But the popes had gradually claimed them for their own use, so that eventually the first fruits of every parish and see in Europe went directly to Rome to support the papal court in luxury greater, even, than that of the secular princes.

The collection of the annates and of similar fees was generally farmed out to a banker or to an expert in the art of extracting the last penny from unwilling debtors. Because reluctance to pay made collection difficult, costs were high—in some cases amounting to as much as 50 per cent of the fee. Naturally, this created a vicious circle. Since the popes received a relatively small portion of the fees paid in, they constantly tried to raise the fees. But this resulted in greater opposition to them, in increased costs of collection, and finally, in a search for new sources of revenue.

One such source was the sale of benefices and offices. Accordingly, the right of cathedral chapters and monastic bodies to elect their heads was constantly abrogated. It even became the practice to sell appointments in advance, and clerics often bought the next vacancy, or even the next but-once, in expectation of later recovering their investment by means of the income from endowments with which the faithful had long ago enriched the benefice. As a result of such complications, titles often became suspect and new incumbents had to face expensive lawsuits in order to establish their claims. The Roman pontiff, however, made a threefold profit on each such transaction: First the benefice was sold, then the annates were collected, and finally the court costs were assessed. The papal court was, indeed, so useful a source of revenue that the popes gave it a primary jurisdiction over cases that had formerly been heard in episcopal courts. Here were additional grounds for complaint by the bishops, who once again lost revenue to Rome. Moreover, as a result of the flood of business, the papal court became slow and venal. Cases took years to come to trial, and the trials themselves cost, in bribes, from twenty-five to forty times the regular official fees.

INDULGENCES

Though these practices were offensive, the historically crucial abuse proved to be the selling of indulgences. This practice had a harmless origin in the primitive Church. There, when a backsliding member repented, he confessed his misdeeds before the congregation, which then determined what "satisfaction" (as it was called) he should make—whether he should fast, suffer lashes, or make a contribution to charity. This act of satisfaction, it was held, served a double purpose: It was an outward sign that an inward change had really occurred, as the penitent claimed, and it was in itself an act well pleasing to God. Since the congregation determined the nature of a satisfaction, it had the right, naturally, to remit or reduce it. Thus, if a penitent who had been ordered to fast fell ill, the satisfaction might be changed, or, if the congregation concluded that further evidence of repentance was not needed, it might be canceled altogether.

In the course of centuries, both the practice and the theory underwent change. When confession came to be private, instead of public, determination of the nature of the satisfaction passed from the congregation to the priest. Also, a distinction was drawn between "eternal" and "temporal" punishments. From the former the priest might, if he saw fit, absolve the penitent. After he did so, he imposed a penance to be worked off as a temporal punishment. But what if the penitent died before completing his penance? Or, even more alarming, what if the priest, who was mortal and fallible, underestimated the gravity of the sin and so the severity of the punishment God wished to have exacted? To meet these difficulties a third idea was developed, the notion of a treasury of merit—a kind of bank account at the pope's command, composed of the good deeds of the saints and the supreme goodness of Jesus. A papal indulgence was, as it were, a draft against this inexhaustible fund, drawn to make up the deficit between what the individual sinner had done for himself (or what his confessor had mistakenly required of him) and what God really demanded of him.[1]

This doctrine of the pope's right to draw against a treasury of merit in the interest of individual sinners reflects the medieval man's acute sense of sin and his deep need for the security of salvation. Indeed, terror of damnation was so great that a distinction came to be drawn between "contrition" and "attrition." The former, defined as sorrow arising from one's love of God, was the only frame of mind that the early Church had allowed as a basis for repentance. Beside this high and difficult doctrine there grew up the notion that attrition, defined as sorrow arising from some lower consideration, such as fear of punishment, would also serve—not, it is true, as well as pure contrition, but, withal, adequately. Being inferior, attrition required a greater penance, but this could be taken care of by a larger draft against the treasury of merit.

Thus, by the fifteenth century, a view of indulgences had been developed that could easily lead to serious abuse. As the moral standards of the papacy declined, the substantial market value of indulgences was not overlooked, and the popes went into a large-scale business of selling insurance policies against

---

1 The doctrine of indulgences was underwritten by the great Scholastics of the thirteenth century, who, finding the practice well established, conceived it their duty to find rational arguments to support it. Thus, according to Thomas, "The universal Church cannot err. . . . The universal Church approves and grants indulgences. Therefore indulgences have some value . . . ; for it would be blasphemy to say that the Church does anything in vain" (*Summa Theologica*, Pt. III, Supplement, Ques. xxv, Art. 1). It does not follow, of course, that Thomas would have approved the abuses to which the sale of indulgences later led.

possible inconvenience in the life to come. It was unnecessary for the purchaser to feel truly contrite; payment of a sufficient sum assured him of safety, regardless of the inner state of his soul.[2] Despite the refusal of some rulers to permit the sale of indulgences inside their states, despite repeated assurances from the popes themselves that they would put an end to the practice, needy pontiffs continued to make use of indulgences throughout the fifteenth century and into the sixteenth.[3]

THE WORLDLINESS OF THE POPES

There was, of course, nothing unique about the popes. Men everywhere were becoming more this-worldly; it is not surprising that the Church was affected by so pervasive a change in values and in outlook. But though a secular prince, a merchant, or a banker could devote himself to this-worldly ends without scandal, the Church and its head were supposed to be otherworldly. Of course, the Church had never succeeded in living up to this ideal, but the worldliness of the Renaissance popes was on a much greater scale than that of any of the medieval popes.

Leo X (1513–21), for instance, inherited the extravagant ideas and the excellent taste of his father, Lorenzo the Magnificent. Leo's values were essentially pagan. He had a concern, naturally, for the prosperity and influence of his family, but his primary interest lay in the enjoyment of life. To him this meant experiencing the whole gamut of esthetic satisfactions and shutting out, as far as possible, anything that might interfere with the cultivation of an exquisite and refined sensitivity. "God has given us the papacy," he said to his brother upon his elevation to the throne; "let us enjoy it." And enjoy it he did, without realizing that the structure that made his life possible was collapsing around him.

Far more serious, however, than Leo's hedonism was the corruption of such a pope as Alexander VI (1492–1503). Though much that was reported of him

---

2 In 1517, for instance, the following fees were charged: for an indulgence in a case of sodomy, 12 ducats; for sacrilege, 9 ducats; for murder, 7; for witchcraft, 6; and so on down the line. According to an eyewitness, when Tetzel, the dispenser of these indulgences, approached a town, "all the priests and monks, the town council, the school masters and their scholars, and all the men and women went out to meet him with banners and candles and songs, forming a great procession; then all the bells ringing and all the organs playing, they accompanied him to the principal church. . . . One might think they were receiving God Himself"—quoted in T. M. Lindsay, *A History of the Reformation* (Scribners, New York, 1906), Vol. I, p. 213. A few words from one of Tetzel's sermons show how he played upon mass emotion. "Do you not hear your dead parents crying out, 'Have mercy upon us? We are in sore pain and you can set us free for a mere pittance. We have borne you, we have trained you and educated you, we have left you all our property, and you are so hard-hearted and cruel, that you leave us to roast in the flames when you could so easily release us'"—quoted in McGiffert, *Martin Luther: The Man and His Work*, p. 81.

3 On no less than five separate occasions between 1500 and 1517, indulgences were offered for sale.

by his contemporaries is now rejected as gossip, his career was unusually vicious, even when judged by the standards of the secular princes of the day. His values were quite different from Leo's, and reflect less the esthetic side of the Renaissance than its thrust to power. He was certainly neither the first nor the last pope to use the papacy as an instrument for promoting the personal ambitions of his "nephews" (as the illegitimate sons of the popes had come to be called), but no other pope was as cynical or as unscrupulous as he in accomplishing this end.

From every side, then, the policy of the papacy and the character of the popes were such as to cause hostility. On the one hand, they offended the piety of Europe, which was still deep. It is a mistake to suppose that the Reformation had its origins chiefly in the scepticism and rationalism that were growing during this period. On the contrary, in its essential being, the Reformation was a protest against these novelties, and especially a protest against the fact that the Church had been infected by them. On the other hand, among those who did not criticize papal morals, because they shared them, the papacy was equally opposed. The reasons were various, but the sentiments were uniformly hostile. Ecclesiastics who were not shocked by the papacy's secularization were offended by the loss of revenue that this secularization entailed. Italians saw that the papacy deliberately kept the country in a state of open warfare.[4] And in every one of the new nation-states, the Crown regarded papal claims to universal dominion as an insult to its own claims to supremacy, and it deeply resented papal attempts to interfere in internal policy.

Attempts at Reform

THE CONCILIAR MOVEMENT

All during the fifteenth century, attempts had been made to induce the papacy to reform itself. Of these, the chief was the Conciliar Movement, which originated in the series of councils called to try to settle the Great Schism. Thus the Council of Pisa maintained, first, that "the pope, as pope, is a man; as a man and so as pope he is liable to sin and error," and, second, that a council, which represents the Church Universal, is "superior to the pope in authority, in dignity, and in office. . . . It has the authority to limit the pope's authority. . . . The pope must obey such a council in all things. . . . If he does not, the council has the right to depose him."[a]

At the next council (that of Constance, in 1417) an attempt was made to put this theory into practice.[5] But these good intentions came to nothing. As

---

4 Compare Machiavelli on this point, p. 28.
5 Among the abuses on which this council decreed that the pope must take action were the annates, reservation of benefices, indulgences, and the jurisdiction of the papal court.

soon as the council disbanded, the pope denied its claim to supremacy, and shortly after the middle of the century, a papal decree was issued expressly banning appeals against the pope to any future council. It was unrealistic to hope to persuade the popes to reverse the policy by which they had made themselves absolute sovereigns of the Church and to agree to serve as constitutional monarchs responsible to a kind of ecclesiastical parliament. The Conciliar Movement failed because it assumed the popes to be reasonable and compliant, as they clearly were not—and because it ran counter to the whole absolutist trend of the times.

THE CHRISTIAN HUMANISTS

Another group who undertook to reform the papacy were the Humanists. But here a distinction must be made; not all the Humanists, by any means, were reformers. Some, especially in Italy, were much too worldly and too cynical to think of becoming crusaders for right.[6] Representative of many was the historian Guicciardini:

> No man is more disgusted than I am with the ambition, the avarice, and the profligacy of the priests, not only because each of these vices is hateful in itself, but because each and all of them are most unbecoming in those who declare themselves to be men in special relations with God. . . . Nevertheless, my position at the Court of several Popes[7] forced me to desire their greatness for the sake of my own interest. But, had it [not] been for this, I should have loved Martin Luther as myself, not in order to free myself from the laws which Christianity, as generally understood and explained, lays upon us, but in order to see this swarm of scoundrels put back into their proper place, so that they may be forced to live either without vices or without power.[b]

But other Humanists, especially in Germany, were deeply religious men who sought to adjust their new values to what they took to be the religious values of Christianity. These Christian Humanists, as they are called, naturally applied the techniques they used in reading and editing Cicero to their reading of the Christian classics, above all the Bible. This brought them into direct conflict with Scholasticism and its carefully worked out method of reaching the rational truth. In particular, the Christian Humanists deprecated the Scholastic practice of taking a line of Scripture out of context and using it to "prove" some thesis already adopted on other grounds. The Humanists held that one ought to study a text as a whole, in its historical setting. To understand the Epistle to the Romans, for instance, one must know as much as possible not only about St.

---

6 Giovanni de' Medici (Pope Leo X) was just such a Humanist on the throne of St. Peter.
7 [Guicciardini was in the employ of Leo X and Clement VII—AUTHOR.]

Paul and the kind of man he was but also about his correspondents and the kind of men they were. For, obviously, what one says to an audience and how one says it are affected by who the members of the audience are.

All this implied a new definition of Christianity. The Church had managed to reconcile its view of itself as the interpreter of a once-for-all revelation with its changing historical life only by insisting on the authority of tradition. In and through tradition the timeless and eternal communicated itself to, and took on the form of, the changing and the historical. To put this differently, for the medieval Church, Christianity *was* the tradition, codified and systematized by the method of Scholasticism. Thomas and the other medieval doctors never asked themselves whether a doctrine or a practice had originated in the primitive Church;[8] they were satisfied if it had come, in the course of time, to be generally accepted. Their function was to give it intellectual authority by demonstrating its logical consistency with all other accumulated beliefs and practices.

Hence, to want to go back to sources, to claim that the doctrines of the original, primitive Church were wiser and truer than the gradually accumulated mass of interpretation and comment, was to strike at the root of Catholic Christendom. As soon as scholars began to investigate what the primitive Church had believed and done, there was no doubt that the Church had changed greatly during the centuries. If it had not grown in wisdom and in strength, there was no excuse for the changes; Christianity ought to return to its original state.

Many considerations led the Christian Humanists to this radical conclusion. In the first place, the fundamental presupposition of the method of classical scholarship was that the earlier is truer than the later: The classical scholar wanted to establish Cicero's text to find out what Cicero himself had said, not what some later copyist thought he had said. Again, this conclusion obviously accorded with the belief that the Church had been instituted by a divine founder. Just as Cicero himself knew better than the later copyists what he wanted to say, so Jesus and the inspired apostles knew better than any later Churchmen what the Christian Church should be.

Finally, what their method disclosed about the beliefs of the primitive Church accorded with the Christian Humanists' own religious conceptions. They found in the primitive Church a pure and austere ethics, with all the emphasis on inwardness, none at all on those externalities that had, they thought, perverted the contemporary Church. Like other thinking people of the day, the Christian Humanists were appalled by the abuses to which the papacy seemed wedded. They viewed the doctrine of indulgences as a superstition utilized for an evil end. And the whole institutional system of the Church, of which the sacrament of penance was but one instance, seemed a device to keep men from God. As for the monastic orders, these urbane scholars held that the asceticism that the monks preached was as ignoble as their falling away from their ideals was contemptible. Hence ethical considerations as well as scholarly inclinations led

8 See p. 47, n. 1.

them to urge a return to the original Christianity taught, or so they held, in the Bible and by the earliest fathers.

Erasmus (1466–1536) was representative of this group. Though he was the greatest classical scholar of the time, his central interest was the reform of religion. His scholarship was directed first toward establishing the correct text of the New Testament and then toward rendering it into the national language for the use of the ordinary man. Erasmus held God's word to be so plain and simple, once divested of the encrustations of later commentators, that one needed but to read it to understand, but to understand to be convinced, and but to be convinced to experience that inward change that was salvation.

> Other philosophies, by the very difficulty of their precepts, are removed out of the range of most minds. [But] no age, no sex, no condition of life is excluded from [comprehending the Christian philosophy of life]. The sun itself is not more common and open to all than is the teaching of Christ. For I utterly dissent from those who are unwilling that the sacred Scriptures should be read by the unlearned and translated into their vulgar tongues. . . . I long that the husbandman should sing portions of them to himself as he follows the plough, that the weaver should hum them to the tune of his shuttle, that the traveller should beguile with their story the tedium of the journey.

Thus, Erasmus rather naïvely expected the simple truths at the core of the Christian religion—love, humility, and piety—to work a gentle reformation in the mind and heart of Europe. He could help, he thought, by holding the present bloated regime up to ridicule and by deflating its pretensions with biting irony. His little book, *The Praise of Folly*, pricked all sorts of balloons of egoism, snobbishness, and vanity. Its sharpest needle, however, was reserved for the clergy, ridiculing the ignorance of the Scholastic theologians, satirizing the immorality of the monks, and pouring scorn on the vulgar version of Christianity currently taught by the Church.

But Erasmus' writings were not a source of real danger, for he was unwilling to take the drastic steps necessary to change the status quo. It was not merely cowardice that held him back. It is true that he was timid, but the real keys to his behavior were his conservatism and his belief in gradualism. On the one hand, he thought that the sudden overthrow of an institution so deeply involved in the whole life of the time would do more harm than good. On the other hand, it was his fond belief that enlightenment—the kind of reasonableness classical scholarship inculcated—would gradually effect the reformation that all sought. This was why the work of editing and translating the New Testament seemed to him of supreme importance. For these reasons, when the outbreak finally came, Erasmus sided with Church, papacy, and tradition.

Although Erasmus and the other Christian Humanists were not out out to lead a popular movement, they nevertheless contributed indirectly to the Reformation. Their version of Christianity was, at least implicitly, an attack on the institution of the church. Their satiric attacks on ecclesiastical abuses reached and moved a large audience. Their scholarship displayed the sixteenth-century Church as a monstrous aberration from the intentions of the Founder. Finally, the failure of such basically sympathetic and conservative critics to induce reform was a demonstration to the more vigorous reformers that sweet reasonableness would not suffice.

THE GERMAN MYSTICS

Still a third group of would-be reformers emerged during the fifteenth century: the Christian mystics of Germany and the Low Countries. The Brethren of the Common Life, the Brethren of the Free Spirit, the Friends of God, differed in certain respects that were doubtless important to themselves, but seen from the distance of five centuries they show a marked similarity. Generally speaking, they advocated a return to the simple life of primitive Christianity, abandonment of the worldliness and corruption that had infected the Church, and a moderate asceticism. They were no more interested in the new Humanism than in the old Scholasticism. They were mystics, and like all mystics, they held that the way to God was personal, requiring neither the apparatus of rational theology nor the elaborate organization of the Church.

Had the popes cared to mobilize the zeal of these mystics, the result might have been another great reforming order or a movement like St. Francis' Friars. But without guidance from higher ecclesiastical authorities, the mystics were content to purify their own lives. Though their numbers were considerable, they formed a backwater of sentiment that had no immediate influence on the larger life of the Church. But they were important because, though loyal and Catholic themselves, their feeling for the privacy of religion and the directness of man's relation to God contained the seeds of Protestantism.

MOUNTING PRESSURES FOR REFORM

Thus, by the end of the fifteenth century, and quite apart from the political antagonism papal policy had created, there had developed inside the Church itself a body of opinion inimical to the existing regime. Centered in the Conciliar Movement, in the Christian Humanists, and in the German mystics, it called in question, with varying degrees of consciousness, the whole sacerdotal system of the medieval Church. Starting from different premises, various groups had reached remarkably similar conclusions—that in determining faith and doctrine it was necessary to go back to the Bible; that the Bible contains the clear and unmistakable word of God; that it ought therefore to be made available to laymen; that the Scholastic summas and commentaries were unnecessary, indeed, harmful; that every individual soul stands in a direct relationship with God, or rather, *can* stand in such a relationship if God so wills; that the achievement of this relationship (which is salvation) is not man's doing but God's; that therefore the apparatus of confession, penance, and indulgence, which the Church held to be the sole route by which sinful man might reach God, was not only worthless but detrimental; that this very structure of ceremonies and ritual had enwrapped the Church in worldliness, luxury, and vice; that the Church ought therefore to give up meddling in civil affairs and to return to the poverty and simplicity of former days.

Nevertheless, there was as yet no thought of breaking up the Church. The reformers regarded themselves as members, along with those whom they opposed, of one Holy and Apostolic Church; they believed themselves to be right about the inner nature of this Church, and they wanted to bring those who differed with them around to their views. They did not challenge the preeminence of the pope, even though they questioned his complete supremacy. They did not (except for what might be called the lunatic fringe) question the desirability of having an ecclesiastical institution of some sort. Because they had not thought their objections through to their logical conclusion, they could still call themselves, and feel themselves to be, faithful Catholics. They were not yet rebels; they were reformers.

These religious opinions, when added to the secular objections to the papacy's political and fiscal policies, created a potentially very dangerous situation. But it was not yet explosive. What focused all this discontent and exploded the charge that had been accumulating for two hundred years? It was the personality of Martin Luther, working on the piety of Germany.

Luther

Martin Luther (1483–1546) was the son of peasants, who, though poor, managed to send him to the university of Erfurt, then one of the leading universities of Germany and a center of Humanistic studies. However, being already deeply concerned with theological questions, Luther had little contact with the Humanistic circle at Erfurt, and in 1505, despite his father's desire that he become a lawyer, he suddenly joined the Augustinian Friars. Many explanations of this abrupt decision have been proposed. According to Luther himself, the strict life his parents had required of him as a child[9] sent him into holy orders. Some have thought that he took the sudden deaths of two close friends as a warning to prepare himself to meet his Maker. It is clear that, like Augustine and so many other Christians, Luther was oppressed by a sense of sin and convinced that his primary need was to find God. Initially it must have seemed appropriate

---

9 "They meant well," Luther later wrote of his parents, "but they did not understand the art of adjusting their punishments."

to Luther to seek Him in a monastery, by means of the penances that the monastic rule provided and that, so the Church assured him, would lead to his salvation. But though the very rigorous program of ascetic observances that he set himself won him a reputation for saintliness among his brother monks, it was all in vain. Monastic discipline did not bring the sense of God's forgiveness for which he yearned. "If ever a monk could have got to heaven by monkery," he later said, "I would have."

Failing here, he had recourse to his Bible—despite the objections of his superiors, who warned him, "Brother Martin, let the Bible alone; read the old teachers; they give you the whole marrow of the Bible. Reading the Bible simply breeds unrest." As events proved, these monks were quite correct, and much shrewder than was Erasmus about the likely effect of indiscriminate Bible-reading on the Christian mind. Luther discovered that there was more to the Bible than was given in the Church's services. Looking back much later on this period of his life, he said, "The Bible was [then] unknown. The Prophets were treated as if they were impossible to understand. I was twenty years old before I had even seen a Bible. I had no idea there was anything more to the Epistles and the Evangels than was read in the lessons. Finally I found a Bible in the library at Erfurt which I often read with great amazement."

As Luther now studied St. Paul, and especially that letter to the Romans that St. Augustine had read many centuries earlier in the garden at Milan, it seemed to him that all the commentators and Scholastics were mistaken. What Luther found in Paul was the doctrine of salvation, or justification, by faith alone, rather than by the "works" of penance, almsgiving, or monkish asceticism. He had been oppressed (as Augustine had been) by the appalling gulf that separated depraved man from his God. How could sinful man achieve union with God? Luther himself had tried in every conceivable manner, and he had failed. He now realized that it was the most damnable pride to suppose that man could bring about his own salvation. Is the human predicament, then, hopeless as well as helpless? No, God is not only just; He is merciful: He sent His only begotten Son to save us. As he read St. Paul, Luther saw that, though God is supremely perfect and man utterly depraved, the incarnation, in which God took on human form, demonstrated that the gulf is not impassable. But the mediator, by whose aid we cross the gulf, is Christ, not the Church and its works. What, then, must we do to be saved? Believe in the Lord Jesus and have faith in the mercy of God, as Christ's gospel teaches.

JUSTIFICATION BY FAITH

The implications of this view were inconsistent with fundamental theses of the medieval Church. Indeed, the doctrine of justification by faith undermined the whole sacerdotal system of the Church and, with it, the institutions that administered, licensed, and perpetuated it.

Many have thought Christian faith to be an easy thing. . . . This they do because they have had no experience of it, and have never tasted what great virtue there is in faith. . . . But he who has had even a faint taste of it can never write, speak, meditate or hear enough concerning it. For it is a living fountain springing up into life everlasting. . . .

It is evident that no external thing, whatsoever it be, has any influence whatever in producing Christian [faith]. . . . All manner of works, even contemplation, meditation, and all that the soul can do, avail nothing. One thing and one only is necessary for Christian life, righteousness and liberty. That one thing is the most holy Word of God, the Gospel of Christ. . . . Let us then consider it certain and conclusively established that the soul can do without all things except the Word of God, and that where this is not there is no help for the soul in anything else whatever. . . .

You ask, "What then is this Word of God, and how shall it be used, since there are so many words of God?" I answer, The Apostle explains . . . in Romans i, . . . "The just shall live by his faith." . . . Hence it is clear that, as the soul needs only the Word for its life and righteousness, so it is justified by faith alone and not by any works; for if it could be justified by anything else, it would not need the Word, and therefore it would not need faith. . . .

It is clear then that a Christian man has in his faith all that he needs, and needs no works to justify him.[c]

If the sacraments are unnecessary, it follows that priests are not needed to mediate between the worshiper and his God. The doctrine of justification by faith entails the doctrine of the universal priesthood of believers. If God's grace, insofar as it operates at all, operates directly on each individual, if it is not canalized and filtered through the ceremonies and ritual of the Church, then every man can be his own priest.

This became clear to Luther only gradually; it was not until 1520 that he explicitly formulated it:

Faith . . . unites the soul with Christ as a bride is united with her bridegroom. . . .

Hence we are all priests and kings in Christ, as many as believe on Christ. . . .

It is pure invention that pope, bishops, priests and monks are to be called the "spiritual estate"; princes, lords, artisans and farmers the "temporal estate." That is indeed a fine bit of lying and hypocrisy. . . . All Christians are truly of the "spiritual estate." . . .

Through baptism all of us are consecrated to the priesthood, as St. Peter says in I Peter ii, "Ye are a royal priesthood." . . .

To make it still clearer. If a little group of pious Christian laymen were taken captive and set down in a wilderness, and had among them no priest consecrated by a bishop, and if there in the wilderness they were to agree in choosing one of themselves, married or unmarried, and were to charge him with the office of baptising, saying mass, absolving and preaching, such a man would be as truly a priest as though all bishops and popes had consecrated him. . . . It was in [this] manner . . . that Christians in olden days chose from their number bishops and priests, who were afterwards confirmed by other bishops, without all the show which now obtains. . . .

Therefore a priest in Christendom is nothing else than an office-holder. While he is in office, he has precedence; when deposed, he is a peasant or a townsman like the rest.[d]

LUTHER'S ATTITUDE TOWARD THE BIBLE

Much the same conclusions follow if one considers, not the doctrine of justification itself, but the means by which Luther reached it—through his own reading of the Epistle to the Romans. Let every man read his Bible for himself; he will find therein, Luther was persuaded, the same doctrine. It is unnecessary, therefore, to have the word of God interpreted for us by the Church. "The Holy Ghost is the all-simplest writer and speaker that is in heaven or on earth. Therefore His words can have no more than one simplest sense which we call the scriptural or literal meaning." The authority of the Bible, as interpreted by every individual for himself, is thus substituted for the authority of the Church. "The Bible belongs to all, and so far as is necessary for salvation is clear enough."[10] "It belongs to each and every Christian to know and to judge of doctrine, and belongs in such wise that he is anathema who shall have diminished this right by a single hair."

Thus, the position Luther had reached from reflecting on St. Paul's message and from his own struggle with sin and his own experience of grace was inconsistent not only with papal supremacy but also with institutional Christianity as the medieval Church conceived of it, a holy, apostolic, and exclusive system. But this consideration of the full implications of Luther's Bible-reading has taken us far ahead of Luther himself. It took a long time for him to formulate these conclusions, and he might never have done so but for a series of circumstances—particularly, his opposition to indulgences—that forced him to define his position.

THE INDULGENCE QUESTION

Luther did not object to the sale of indulgences on political or economic grounds, as some German princes did; he objected to it on religious and moral grounds. It seemed to him to "promote a servile righteousness, and to do nothing but teach the people to fear, to flee, to shudder at the punishment of sin, instead of the sin itself." Indulgences were well named, "because to indulge is to permit and indulgence is impurity and permission to sin, and hence to avoid the Cross of Christ." Good works, whether they are ascetic devotions performed in monas-

10 Luther added, characteristically, that we should be content with the simple but all-important truths necessary for faith. The Bible is "dark enough for souls that long and seek to know more."

teries or contributions to the building of a new St. Peter's, avail us nothing. What is necessary for salvation is the grace a merciful God bestows on a truly contrite and trusting soul.

When Tetzel[11] reached the neighborhood of Wittenberg in the course of promoting the sale of indulgences, Luther felt that he had to take a stand against the practice. He drew up a list of ninety-five propositions, covering various aspects of the indulgence question, that he was willing to defend against all comers, but to which he did not yet commit himself except for the purposes of debate. Learned disputations of the kind Luther proposed were common among scholars and as a rule excited no interest among the laity. But to his surprise, his theses were translated into German, published, and circulated in great numbers; suddenly he found himself a public figure and the spokesman for a cause.[12]

The chief points Luther made in these ninety-five theses were (1) that the notion of a "treasury of merit" had never been clearly defined, (2) that priests could commute only penalties they themselves had imposed, not those God had imposed, and (3) that, in any case, the truly contrite Christian has already been forgiven by God and so requires no indulgence.

When the matter was referred to Rome, Leo X was at first disposed to view it as only a foolish monkish dispute. But it soon became clear that the agitation against indulgences would have an adverse effect on papal finances, and it was decided to discipline Luther. Vastly underestimating the strength of the feeling that Luther had aroused in Germany, the authorities in Rome condemned him without a hearing, thus only adding to popular indignation. Luther's sovereign, the Elector of Saxony, protected him, and the emperor Maximilian, who shrewdly perceived that all this hubbub might be put to use, advised the Elector to "take good care of the Wittenberg monk; we may want him some day."

Though the authorities in Rome realized at this point that they were confronted with a delicate situation, there was no agreement about how to handle it. Some, including the Pope, believed that a diplomatic approach should be adopted; others, especially the Dominicans, held that conciliation would be a mistake.[13] While Rome was hesitating, the Dominicans began an attack on

---

11 See p. 48, n. 2.

11 See p. 48, n. 2.

12 Luther seems to have been embarrassed by the stir he caused. "In fourteen days the theses ran through all Germany. . . . I became famous, because at last some one had appeared who dared to take hold of the business. But the glory of it was not agreeable to me . . . ." And, again, "I hoped the pope would protect me, for I had so fortified my theses with proofs from the Bible and papal decretals that I was sure he would condemn Tetzel and bless me. But when I expected a benediction from Rome, there came thunder and lightning instead."
    Catholic historians regard these protestations as disingenuous. Some conceive of Luther as a Machiavellian plotter who seized on the indulgence question as a "favorable opportunity" for securing wide publicity for his "novel and erroneous teachings" (see, for instance, P. F. O'Hare, *The Facts About Luther* [Putset, Cincinnati, 1916]). Others, like H. Grisar, the Jesuit, hold that sudden fame went to Luther's head.

13 This is the position of some modern Catholic commentators (see, for instance, H. Grisar, *Luther* [K. Paul, Trench, Trübner & Co., London, 1913–17], Vol. I, p. 365).

Luther that was skillfully designed to drive him into making statements so flagrantly heretical that there would be no alternative but to condemn him. This they accomplished. In a debate with Dr. John Eck, one of the chief theologians in Germany, Luther was outmaneuvered. Eck took the natural line that since indulgences were authorized by the pope, they could not be questioned without denying papal authority. Did Luther, then, question the supreme authority of the popes? Did he deny that the Council of Constance itself had acknowledged the supremacy of the pope in matters of doctrine? Did he perhaps even question the authority of a council? The Council of Constance had condemned Huss[14] and his views—did Luther deny the justice of this condemnation?

Luther hesitated for a moment, then he replied, quite honestly, that he thought that some of Huss's opinions were correct. "A council cannot make divine right of what is not by its nature such, nor can it make that heresy which is not against divine right." This caused a great sensation, and Eck virtuously retorted, "If you believe this, you are to me a heathen and a publican." The debate had moved a long way from the question of indulgences, and Luther was now in open opposition to the Church. Doubtless this was what his position had always implied, and as soon as he was forced to face the issue squarely, his course of action was decided—his conviction of the rightness of his interpretation of the Bible was so overwhelming that, as he said, he could not do otherwise than to take this stand.

THE CREATION OF A NEW THEOLOGY

Once Luther had taken his stand, the only question was whether the Church would be able to destroy him. That this could have been a question shows how far from medieval norms society had already moved by the beginning of the sixteenth century. In the Middle Ages no secular ruler would have dared, or cared, to protect such flagrant heresy. But times had changed. The German princes who supported Luther did so because they sympathized with his attack on papal abuses, because he had an immense popular following that it would be dangerous to oppose, and because they saw that they could use the religious revolt to free themselves from foreign ecclesiastical control and to extend their power in their own states. Though only a minority of the princes backed Luther, the majority did not oppose the heresy very actively. They were loath to obey the Pope's command to use force against their brother princes lest they should thereby establish a precedent that could someday be used to justify interference in their own domestic affairs.

Despite the help he got from the princes, Luther's revolt succeeded only because he founded a new church and so gave the dissidents a strength they

14 John Huss (1373–1415) was a Bohemian reformer who attacked clerical corruption and the selling of indulgences. He was tried for heresy, condemned, and, in spite of having been given an imperial safe-conduct, burned at the stake.

lacked as individuals. Though it was essential for the preservation of the movement, the new church created a painful dilemma for Luther. For it naturally required a new confession of faith to distinguish its members, and the defense of this faith required a new theology. Thus Luther found himself in the position of the earliest Christians, who had had to choose between individual religion and the requirements of institutionalism.

The new theology soon became as inflexible and as orthodox as the old. Those who opposed it by even a hair's breadth were cast into outer darkness along with the Catholics. The Anabaptists, for instance, who denied the need for infant baptism (on the reasonable ground that "God would not damn a little child for the sake of a drop of water"), were treated without mercy.[15]

What concern did Luther have with the sacrament of baptism when he had rejected the sacrament of penance on the ground that each individual soul is in direct relation with God? It is doubtless possible for theologians—and Luther was an acute one—to draw subtle distinctions here, but he was probably motivated to accept the sacrament of baptism less by considerations of logic and evidence than by the exigencies of institutionalism. In theory, there might be a universal priesthood of believers; but if there was to be a church organization, there had to be a definite mark of membership. Moreover, doctrinal considerations led Luther to the same conclusion. His conviction of man's helplessness without the gift of God's grace made it impossible for him (precisely as it had made it impossible for Augustine) to allow that man is born sinless. As regards the Eucharist, since he did not see how it was possible to get around Jesus' explicit statement, "This is my body," he felt that he had to insist on the Real Presence of Christ's body, "corporeally extended in space," in the visible bread.

Hence Luther insisted on the sacraments of baptism and the Eucharist even though he could not reconcile the importance he attributed to them with his central thesis, justification by faith. If the sacraments were efficacious without faith, how could he claim that faith was all-important as Paul and Augustine had taught him to believe; but if the sacraments depended on a prior act of faith, how could he claim that they were indispensable?

Justification by faith also committed Luther to Augustine's denial of free will. If man was incapable of helping himself, it followed that his destiny was completely in God's hands:

> Since the fall of Adam, . . . free will exists only in name . . . .
> Such teachings [as the official, Thomistic conception of free will] are invented only to insult and overthrow the grace of God, to strengthen sin

15 In 1536, Melanchthon, Luther's coadjutor, sat in judgment on a number of Anabaptists. He prayed over them "in a friendly and Christian fashion" and warned them that they should "have regard to the Scriptures" (that is, accept the Lutheran view of the Scriptures). When they replied that "they would abide by what God had taught them" (which, of course, was precisely Luther's own reply to the Catholics), they were sentenced to death (Beard, *The Reformation of the Sixteenth Century*, pp. 195–98).

and increase the kingdom of the devil. . . . The folly and blindness of the pope and his followers could be tolerated, to be sure, in other matters, but in this chief article of faith it is a pity that they are so senseless, for by it they entirely destroy everything that we have from God through Christ. . . . Who denies Him more than those who ascribe too little to His grace and too much to the free will? . . .

Therefore I wish that the word[s] "free will" had never been invented.[e]

This revives all the difficulties of Augustine's position. If God is to get the credit for one man's salvation, must He not be blamed for another's damnation? If God is a loving father in that He mercifully saves some sinful men, is He not a cruel tyrant in that He allows others to remain helplessly in sin? Why urge men to answer God's call if they cannot do so unless God wills that they answer? How is it possible to reconcile the proposition that "the salvation of all men is the earnest will of God" with the proposition that "God foreknows all things and all things come to pass according to His will"?

No wonder Luther thought that, like free will, "predestination" was a word that ought never to have been invented. "When a man begins to discuss predestination, the temptation is like an inextinguishable fire; the more he discusses, the more he despairs. . . . We ought, therefore, avoid any discussion of predestination. . . . In trying to understand it we forget God, and instead of praising Him, we blaspheme."[f]

Nor were the problems of free will and predestination the only difficulties created by the doctrine of justification by faith. Why are not such good works as truth-telling, promise-keeping, and almsgiving as irrelevant and extraneous to salvation as are the various works of penance? Why should not the former be thrown out along with the latter? This, as a matter of fact, was the drastic conclusion reached by some of the more extreme Protestants. Luther abominated their views, but how could he, logically, avoid them as long as he maintained that faith justifies? Luther's only reply was that, though faith *alone* justifies, faith manifests itself in active works. The true Christian does good works, not in order to acquire merit, but merely from the love of God that He infuses into the believer's heart.

So a Christian . . . undertakes all things that are to be done, and does everything cheerfully and freely; not that he may gather many merits and good works, but because it is a pleasure for him to please God thereby, and he serves God purely for nothing, content that his service pleases God. . . .

And this is what makes it a Christian work to care for the body, that through its health and comfort we may be able to work, to acquire and to lay by funds with which to aid those who are in need, that in this way the strong member may serve the weaker, and we may be sons of God, each caring and working for the other. . . . Lo, this is a truly Christian life, here faith is truly effectual through love; that is, it issues in works of the

> freest service cheerfully and lovingly done, with which a man willingly serves another without hope of reward, and for himself is satisfied with the fulness and wealth of his faith.[g]

Although this formulation had the advantage of providing a basis for the development of an ethics that was in harmony with the new spirit of enterprise and initiative,[16] it hardly satisfies the logical requirement of reconciling good works with justification by faith. It may be a psychological fact that the saved soul delights in good works; but this has no more a moral character than does any other psychological fact, for example, that a hungry man enjoys eating. And why, indeed, should good works please God as Luther claimed they do? If He is indifferent to them before our salvation, why should they seem important to Him afterwards?

But passing over these difficulties, what, according to Luther, are the good works that God requires of us in "this alien land" where we are now sojourning? Luther's answer was that God has established three great institutions by means of which He governs mankind and through which men, in their turn, serve Him. Our specific duties are determined by our calling, that is, by our position in respect to these institutions. They are the priesthood, marriage, and civil government.

As we have already seen, the notion of a special institution of priesthood is not easily reconciled with the notion of a universal priesthood of believers. As regards marriage, it exists specifically for the procreation of children and the perpetuation of the race. Marriage exists for the sake of the family, and the family for the sake of the children, who are to be brought up as loyal and dutiful citizens and as devout and pious Christians.

POLITICAL THEORY

This brings us, finally, to Luther's political theory, which is contained in his account of the institution of civil government. Just as the final end of the institution of marriage is "the preservation and education of posterity," so the final end of the state is "the preservation of the peace." Men are so sinful and vicious that without a sovereign to keep them in order they would "quickly despatch one another out of this world."

> Since few believe and still fewer live a Christian life, . . . God has . . . subjected them to the sword, so that, even though they would do so, they cannot practice their wickedness, and that, if they do, they may not do it without fear nor in peace and prosperity. Even so a wild, savage beast is fastened with chains and bands, so that it cannot bite and tear as is its wont.[h]

16 See pp. 8–11.

This line of reasoning was backed up by a second argument to the effect that, since the salvation of one's soul is the only really important thing in life, even the worst of rulers can do no serious harm to the believing Christian. The temporal power,

> . . . whether it do right or wrong, cannot harm the soul, but only the body and property. . . . To suffer wrong destroys no one's soul, nay, it improves the soul, although it inflicts loss upon the body and property. . . .
>
> Therefore, also, the temporal power is a very small thing in God's sight, and far too slightly regarded by Him, that for its sake, whether it do right or wrong, we should resist, become disobedient and quarrel. [i]

Luther's conclusion—"Men sin . . . if they lie to the government, deceive it, and are disloyal, [or if they disobey what] it has ordered and commanded, whether with their bodies or their possessions"[j]—is poles apart from the medieval ideal of the limited monarchy and fully underwrites even the most extreme claims of the new-type sovereign: "Wicked authority is still always authority in the sight of God."

But while insisting on the subject's absolute duty of obedience to his prince, Luther had to find a way to extricate the Protestant princes from a corresponding duty to obey their overlord, the Catholic emperor. Hence he argued that

> . . . every father is bound to protect wife and child as far as he can against violent death, and there is no difference between a private murderer and the emperor, when the latter goes beyond his office and makes use of unjust force, particularly force notoriously unjust; for by natural law open violence does away with all duty between subject and ruler. The present case [that is, when the emperor is interfering with *Protestant* princes] is of this sort, since the Emperor wishes to compel his subjects to blasphemy and idolatry. . . .
>
> [Nor need] the defender . . . wait until his enemy actually begins the attack. [k]

It is clear, of course, that everything Luther said here would equally justify the peasants' revolt (1525) against *their* lords, which Luther bitterly opposed. But once again, his views were wholly in accord with the new notion of national territorial sovereignty, in contrast to the old notion of universal empire.

Finally, what of the relation between church and state? Here, too, Luther was ambivalent. On the one hand, he insisted that civil authority had no rights in the field of religion. "Worldly government has laws which extend no further than to life and property. . . . Over the soul God can and will let no one rule but Himself. . . . Every man is responsible for his own faith, and he must see to it for himself that he believes rightly. . . . For faith is a free work, to which no one can be forced."[l] These are noble words, and it cannot be doubted that the position is the logical corollary of Luther's central conception of justification by faith. But on the other hand, to enforce institutional conformity, to regularize worship and purge the damnable papists, he needed the help of the secular arm. "It is the business of . . . your Electoral Grace . . . ," he wrote to the Elector of Saxony in 1522, "to keep false preachers out, and to permit, or if necessary, to compel the installation of a proper preacher, seals, letters, custom and law to the contrary notwithstanding."[m] When, however, the shoe was on the other foot, when he was thinking of the possibility of a Catholic regime requiring Protestant conformity, he expressed himself quite differently. "All Christians have the power and the right to judge all doctrines and to separate themselves from false teachers. . . . If we seek to depend upon human councils and counsels, we lose the Scriptures altogether and remain, hair and hide, the devil's prey."[n]

Such inconsistencies as these are not exclusively, or even chiefly, due to the exigencies of politics. They also reflect the difficulty of reconciling the essentially mystical doctrine of justification by faith with the facts of social life. It is not an accident that Protestantism has never produced a theology comparable to the achievements of Scholasticism: The very core of the Protestant insight is the certainty of every individual conscience, a belief that is incompatible with theological system-building. Protestantism rests on the immediate, felt data of conscience, not on the accumulated, sifted, public data of tradition.

ATTITUDE TOWARD REASON

This is strikingly apparent in Luther's equally ambivalent attitude toward reason. When he was attacking what he regarded as the superstition of the Catholic Church, he sounded like a Humanist—or even an eighteenth-century rationalist: "What is contrary to reason is certainly much more contrary to God. For how should not that be against divine truth which is against reason and human truth?" And again, "Reason is the chief of all things, and among all that belongs to this life the best, yea, a something divine." But when he recalled the paradoxes into which reason can lead men, reason seemed to him sterile in comparison with the sweetness and light that pours into the pious heart.

> It is a quality of faith that it wrings the neck of reason. . . . But how? It holds to God's Word: lets it be right and true, no matter how foolish and impossible it sounds. So did Abraham take his reason captive and slay it, in as much as he believed God's word, wherein was promised him that from his unfruitful and as it were dead wife, Sarah, God would give him seed. . . . There is no doubt faith and reason mightily fell out in Abraham's heart about this matter, yet at last did faith get the better, and overcame and strangled reason, that all-cruellest and most fatal enemy of God. So, too, do all other faithful men who enter with Abraham the gloom and hidden darkness of faith: they strangle reason . . . and thereby offer to God the all-acceptablest sacrifice and service that can ever be brought to Him.[o]

Compared with conscience, reason seemed to him as fallible as the Church. He would always reject it if and when it conflicted with individual, private, and subjective feeling. Hence Luther was fundamentally an antirationalist. But the real extent of his antirationalism was hidden from him; the certainty of his own convictions persuaded him that his conscience bespoke *the* rational truth, which others would also see if only they would look. However, consciences may disagree; they may reveal a variety of individual certainties. If our criterion of truth is the certainty of individual conscience, there is no basis for rational choice among these conflicting private certainties: The unity of Christian doctrine has been shattered.

Luther's commitment to the primacy of conscience was an expression of one of the basic motifs of the new world that was dawning—individualism. From this point on, emphasis in literature, in art, in morals, in religion, was to be on what is subjective and private—on the dictates of the individual conscience; on the political liberties of the individual citizen; on the enjoyment, in poetry and painting and music, of the flow of subjective feeling. This has added a new dimension to modern culture. It has also created some of the fundamental problems of modern society—how to balance the need for order, discipline, and obedience against the value of freedom and spontaneity; how to achieve the controls necessary for economic and political survival without destroying civil liberties. The outcome of Protestantism, it would seem, is not only as many priests, but as many truths, as there are believers. Thus the great strength of Protestantism is also its great weakness.

Renaissance and Reformation

It is plain, then, that although the Renaissance and the Reformation agreed in many respects, they differed in many others. They agreed in attacking the medieval synthesis, but they did so on quite different grounds. Even though both were conservative in the sense of wanting to go back to the past, they valued different pasts. For the Renaissance, it was the pagan past of Greece and Rome; for the Reformation, it was the Christian past of the primitive Church. And whereas both the Renaissance and the Reformation were to this extent conservative movements, they were in other and more important respects radically innovative. Neither the Renaissance nor the Reformation could have succeeded in going back to its chosen past; neither really wanted to do so. For each, the idealized past was essentially a springboard from which to develop a new program accommodated to the new times. The Renaissance and Reformation therefore had a vigor that twentieth-century veneration for the past, which is largely antiquarian in outlook, lacks. Both the Renaissance and the Reformation, in a word, were engaged in fashioning a new-model man, a man who was like the Christian and pagan past chiefly in being radically different from the medieval conception of man.

Although the Renaissance and the Reformation were certainly not in entire agreement about the nature of this new-model man, both saw him as an individual, superior to the institutions of which he was a member. Of course, the Reformation was thinking of the Church, and the Renaissance was thinking of feudalism and medieval economic and social practices; but the important thing is that, whereas the Middle Ages had prized institutions, both the Renaissance and the Reformation deprecated the value of institutions as compared with individuals. They did so because they thought it easy for the individual to break away from institutions, easy for him to make a fresh start, easy for him to preserve his independence and determine his own destiny.

Again, although they differed about what it was that made the individual superior and capable of fending for himself—the Renaissance thought it was power; the Reformation thought it was conscience—they were alike in that power and conscience both contained a deep antirationalist strain, a suspicion that the universe was not the rational, systematic order that the Middle Ages had conceived it to be. This feeling was also evidenced by the growth of witchcraft and alchemy—practices that rest on a belief that, even though natural events can be controlled (by magical means), they cannot be rendered intelligible.

Though hints of this strain appeared in Luther, and though it was quite manifest in Machiavelli, several centuries were to pass before the West became fully conscious of all that the new attitude involved and of the choices with which, as a result, the new age was faced. At the outset, as a matter of fact, the new age believed itself to be thoroughly rationalistic; indeed, it would have said that the major difference between itself and the Middle Ages lay in the fact that it was an age of reason whereas the Middle Ages had been an age of faith, or, as the rationalists would have preferred to put it, an age of superstition. The next chapter will deal with the development of modern science, one of the chief evidences that the new age would have adduced to defend its claim to rationalism, but also, as we shall see, one of the chief instruments by which its ambivalence toward reason was gradually to be revealed.

Science and Scientific Method

Like "Renaissance" and "Reformation," the term "science" is an abstraction. Because we cannot think about everything at once, we have to isolate Renaissance from Reformation and science from both. But the development of scientific method was a part of the whole context of events—in some respects an "effect" of the changes that we have been considering, in other respects one of their "causes." For, while economic and social developments were fashioning a man who was intent on this-worldly affairs, the new method was revealing a completely secular universe to this new man and showing him how he could satisfy his new desires.

This new method involves the combination of two different elements, one empirical and one deductive. From a very early stage in the development of this method, as it began to yield reliable results, almost everyone saw that both these elements were necessary. But there was by no means agreement—nor is there yet—on exactly how they contribute to the formation of scientific knowl-edge. Emphasis on the primacy of one or the other led to radically different metaphysical and epistemological theories and to different conceptions of the implications of scientific method for ethics and religion. Since almost all modern philosophers have been involved in these disputes, it is essential to have a clear grasp of these two elements and their interrelationship if one is to understand the history of modern philosophy.

The Empirical Spirit

Before there could be science in the modern sense, it was necessary for men to develop a lively curiosity about the world they lived in and to try to satisfy this curiosity by looking at the world rather than by peering into ancient tomes written by Aristotle or Galen or Augustine or Isidore of Seville. There had to be, in a word, a drastic change in the conception of authority, from that of the written word, especially the inspired word of God, to that of nature and empirical fact. How did this great change come about?

Insofar as it was a matter of questioning old authorities, the development of scientific method was simply a part of the widespread movement of thought reflected in the transformation of political and moral ideals and in the weakening of the Church's hold on society. Insofar as it was specifically an interest in nature, the empirical spirit manifested itself, for instance, in Petrarch's appreciation of the view from Mont Ventoux, and in Chaucer's realistic portraits of his fellow pilgrims and his delight in the sounds, smells, and sights of spring. It was also at work in the growing passion for exploration that sent men in search of new routes to the Indies, as well as in the concern for correct rendering of the human figure and the devotion to problems of perspective shown by the painters of the fifteenth century.

There is also a relation between this empirical spirit and the revival of learning. The Humanists and the empiricists (if they may be so described) were at one in rejecting the authority of the Church, but the empiricists did not share the Humanists' veneration for classical antiquity. In fact, insofar as the Humanists merely substituted one authority (pagan literature) for another (the Bible and the Church fathers), Humanism and empiricism were poles apart. However, since admiration for the classics caused the Humanists to admire whatever their classical authorities admired, the revival of learning brought with it, if only as a by-product, an interest in nature. Here the empirical spirit and Humanism found a meeting ground. It was no accident that the gold backgrounds with which the painters of the Middle Ages enclosed their saints now disappeared, or that the artists of the fifteenth century portrayed their patrons, the Renaissance princes and Humanists, seated before distant perspectives of mountain, vale, and hill.

So far, of course, we have considered merely a new attitude of mind and a new object of attention—nature. There is nothing specifically "scientific" about the *Canterbury Tales* or about Piero della Francesca's portrait of Federigo di Montefeltro. One of the earliest instances of this new interest applied in a way that *was* scientific was the medical schools of northern Italy.

At first, naturally, physicians relied on the Arabian and Greek texts that were becoming available, but gradually the more empirical spirit of these new authorities evoked a response in their readers. Physicians began to study patients and their symptoms in detail and to record diagnoses and treatments with care. Dissections of the human body were increasingly performed. By the fifteenth century, the method and point of view of the anatomists was utterly different from the combination of rationalism and authoritarianism taught by the Scholastics. Though we will not examine this development in detail, let us look briefly at the writings of one of these anatomists.

Leonardo

Leonardo da Vinci (1452–1519) was a universal genius for whom painting was hardly more than a sideline. He busied himself in an enormous variety of occupations—sculpture, architecture, city planning, military engineering, astronomy, botany, geology, mechanics, hydraulics, physical geography. Indeed, his curiosity about the natural world—about man and his environment—was unlimited. Though his project for a treatise on anatomy was never brought to completion, the introduction he wrote for it shows the careful groundwork he had laid.

> The mental matters which have not passed through the sense are vain, and . . . as such discourses spring from poverty of genius, such discourses are always poor. . . .
>
> And you, who say that it would be better to watch an anatomist at work than to see these drawings, you would be right, if it were possible to observe all the things which are demonstrated in such drawings in a single figure, in which you, with all your cleverness, will not see nor obtain knowledge of more than some few veins, to obtain a true and perfect knowledge of which I have dissected more than ten human bodies, destroying all the other members, and removing the very minutest particles of the flesh, by which these veins are surrounded, without causing them to bleed, excepting the insensible bleeding of the capillary veins; and as one single body would not last so long, it was necessary to proceed with several bodies by degrees, until I came to an end and had a perfect knowledge; this I repeated twice, to learn the differences.[a]

The large number of short maxims Leonardo set down show how much he was preoccupied with the problems of scientific knowledge and how clearly he recognized the novelty of the empirical method:

> All our knowledge has its origin in our perceptions.

> But first I shall test by experiment before I proceed further, because my intention is to consult experience first and then with reasoning show why such experience is bound to operate in such a way.
>
> And this is the true rule by which those who analyse the effects of nature must proceed; and although nature begins with the cause and ends with the experience, we must follow the opposite course, namely . . . , begin with the experience and by means of it investigate the cause.

> Experience, the interpreter between formative nature and the human race, teaches us how that nature acts among mortals; and being constrained by necessity cannot act otherwise than as reason, which is its helm, requires it to act.

> Experience never errs; it is only your judgments that err by promising themselves effects such as are not caused by your experiments.

> . . . Men wrongly complain of Experience; with great abuse they accuse her of leading them astray. Let experience alone, and turn your complaints against your ignorance, which causes you to be carried away by vain and foolish desires as to expect from it things that are not in her power. . . .

> . . . But before you found a law on this case test it two or three times and see whether the experiments produce the same effects.

> Mechanics are the Paradise of mathematical science, because here we come to the fruits of mathematics.

> There is no certainty in sciences where one of the mathematical sciences cannot be applied, or which are not in relation with these mathematics.

> Any one who in discussion relies upon authority uses, not his understanding, but rather his memory. . . .

> Those who fall in love with practice without science are like a sailor who enters a ship without a helm or a compass, and who never can be certain whither he is going.[b]

These remarks are immensely suggestive, as one would expect the observations of a genius of Leonardo's order to be; but they are, nevertheless, only hints. Leonardo seems to be saying that there exists in the universe a *rational* structure (which he conceived to be a projection, as it were, of the divine intellect), and that this structure is reflected in the natural world in such a way that it can be got at only by somehow combining a painstaking observation of nature with mathematics. Many earlier thinkers, of course, had held that there is a rational explanation of the universe's behavior. But that it was to be got at, not through a Platonic dialectic, not through syllogistic inference, not through the analysis of concepts, but through the "application" of mathematics to natural occurrences—this notion was indeed a novelty. But how, exactly, was mathematics to be applied to nature, and why should this combination yield a superior type of knowledge? Leonardo did not say. And even his hints, buried in his notebooks, were soon forgotten. When the first tentative answers to this central question began to appear one hundred years later, it was the result of independent reflection.

William Gilbert

In William Gilbert[1] of Colchester, in England, this same empirical spirit was at work, not pouring itself forth with the prodigality of genius in a thousand different directions, but patiently and laboriously devoting itself to the detailed study of one group of natural phenomena. His great study, *On the Loadstone and Magnetic Bodies* (1600), contains the same more or less unconscious presuppositions that underlay Leonardo's more varied activities. There is the assumption, first, that natural knowledge is possible—that is, that there are uniformities in nature that close observation, coupled with "experiment," will reveal. There is the assumption, second, that this natural knowledge can be put to use— specifically, that it could be used effectively in the new power systems that the conditions of life were creating in Gilbert's time. It is no accident that, in an age when colonization of the New World was just beginning, Gilbert should have emphasized the application of his new scientific knowledge of the magnet to the improvement of the compass, the determination of latitude, and other navigational aids. But it was not merely the possible utility of this new knowledge that set Gilbert to work on his experiments. It is clear that if he was moved by the thought of power, he was also moved by the thought of truth—by curiosity about what the facts are.

Gilbert prefaced his account of his experiments with a rapid survey of the state of knowledge (or lack of it) before he began his work. The loadstone, he pointed out, had been described by a great number of ancient writers, but

---

1 Gilbert was born in 1544, the year after Copernicus' death and two years before Luther's; he died in 1603, when Kepler, Galileo, and Bacon were reaching their full maturity. Gilbert was educated at Cambridge and possibly also at Oxford. After three years of study and travel in Italy, he returned home to practice medicine; eventually he became president of the Royal College of Physicians and personal physician to Queen Elizabeth.

. . . by all, the subject is handled in the most careless way, while they repeat only the figments and ravings of others. . . .

Many have . . . wasted oil and labor, because, not being practical in the research of objects in nature, being acquainted only with books, being led astray by certain erroneous physical systems, and having made no magnetical experiments, they constructed certain ratiocinations on a basis of mere opinions, and old-womanishly dreamt the things that were not. . . .

But we do not propose just now to overturn with arguments either these errors and impotent reasonings, or the other many fables about the loadstone, [such as] that a loadstone placed unawares under the head of a sleeping woman drives her out of the bed if she be an adulteress; . . . or that it withdraws bolts and opens locks, as Serapio insanely imagines; . . . or that . . . there are in Indian seas certain sharp-pointed rocks abounding in loadstone, the which draw every nail out of ships that land alongside them; . . . or that . . . when held in the hand it cures pains of the feet and cramps; or that . . . it . . . makes one eloquent. . . . Many others I pass by of purpose . . . who . . . like furbishers send forth ancient things dressed with new names and tricked in an apparel of new words as in prostitutes' finery; . . . who seem to transmit from hand to hand, as it were, erroneous teachings in every science and out of their own store now and again to add somewhat of error.[c]

Nothing could be in greater contrast to this farrago of superstition than Gilbert's own careful experiments, one of the chief of which was designed to show that the earth itself is a great magnet whose poles are nearly coincident with its geographical poles.

Get a circular planed board with diameter of at least six finger-lengths, which is to be fastened to one face of an upright square post and to rest on a wooden base. Divide the periphery of the instrument into four quadrants, and then each quadrant into ninety degrees. In the centre of the instrument drive a brass nail, and in the centre of its head bore a small hole well reamed and smoothed. Adjust to the instrument a circle or ring of brass about two finger-breadths wide, with a transverse plate or flat bar of the same metal fastened across the middle of the ring and serving for horizon. In the middle of this horizon bar bore another hole which shall be exactly opposite to the centre of the instrument, in which a hole was already bored. Next get a steel wire such as is used for compass needles, and at the exact middle of it and at right angles to it pass a very thin iron axis through it so that the middle of the axis and the middle of the needle shall exactly meet; let this inclination (dipping) needle, the ends of the axis having been inserted into the holes, be suspended so that it may move freely and evenly. . . . The needle thus nicely balanced, now rub skilfully at both ends with the opposite poles of a loadstone, but do this with the greatest care lest the wire be in the least bent; for unless you do all this with great skill and dexterity, you will reach no result. . . . The instrument being now complete, set it up perpendicularly with the small versorium on the base, so that when thus erected exactly upright it may tend to the true point of the magnetic direction. Then that one of the needle's ends which in northern latitudes looks to the north dips below the horizon; but in southern latitudes the end of the needle that looks south tends toward the earth's centre in a certain ratio (afterward to be explained) of the latitude of the region in question from the equator on either side. . . .

As in other magnetic movements there is strict agreement and a clearly visible, sensible accordance between the earth and the loadstone in our demonstration, so in this inclination is the accordance of the globe of the earth and the loadstone positive and manifest.[d]

Though Gilbert's theories often outran their experimental basis, he was rightly impressed by his discovery that there was a "wondrous combination, harmony, and concordant interaction of the earth and the loadstone." He was rightly impressed by the fact that this interaction had been "made manifest by our theory." His work helped to bring the earth down to scale, to show that it is a natural object among others, and to demonstrate the pervasiveness and simplicity of natural law (that there is, for instance, a behavior pattern common to things as different in shape, size, and general appearance as the earth and a loadstone). But more important than Gilbert's conclusions was the method by which he reached them. He was scrupulous in describing everything he did in such a way that it would be possible for others to check his findings. He was willing to accept the facts as he found them. His work was one of the first attempts to use experiment, not merely to illustrate conclusions already reached by other means, but to test hypotheses and so to extend knowledge.

Francis Bacon

From the point of view of the historian of philosophy, Bacon is perhaps more interesting than either Leonardo or Gilbert, for he was even more articulate and self-conscious about the new method and its importance than they had been. His work was programmatic, not only in the sense that, like Leonardo, he was too busy and too impatient to finish anything that he began, but in the fuller sense that he deliberately set himself to sketch the outlines of a vast undertaking that he intended other hands to perform. Bacon was one of the earliest deliberate publicists for science. He wished to "sell" it, and his point of view was characteristically modern, pragmatic, and utilitarian. "Knowledge is power" was his recurrent theme, the knowledge in question being, of course, natural knowledge. He was poles apart from the medieval view, both in his conception of man's end and in his conception of the means to achieve it.

LIFE

Bacon was born in 1561, in the full tide of the English Renaissance. Since his father was a great state official and since his uncle by marriage, Lord Burghley, was the most powerful man in the kingdom, Bacon looked forward to a great career. At twelve he was sent to Trinity College, Cambridge, where he discovered the "unfruitfulness" of Aristotle. At sixteen (such was the precocity of the era), he was on the staff of the English ambassador to France. But when his father died two years later, his position suddenly altered. Despite constant importuning of Burghley (who had to think first of his own son and who appears to have disliked his nephew), Bacon's advance in the great world was painfully slow.

He became a member of Parliament, however, in 1584, and finally, on James's accession, he was knighted (Bacon's pride was offended and his pleasure diluted because he had to share this honor with "300 other gentlemen"). Thereafter he rose steadily. In 1607 he was appointed Solicitor-General; in 1613, Attorney-General; in 1617, Lord Keeper and Chancellor. Shortly afterwards he was created Baron Verulam and Viscount St. Albans. But disgrace only too soon followed success. In 1621 he was convicted of taking bribes and was removed from office. He spent his last years (he died in 1626) unsuccessfully trying to regain his place at court.

THE BACONIAN IDEAL

Bacon liked to maintain (and had probably persuaded himself) that his only ambition was in the intellectual sphere and that he asked of Burghley or the Queen but the modest competence that would enable him to carry on his experiments. In a letter to Burghley that he wrote at the age of thirty-one, Bacon declared that his "civil ends" were as moderate as his "contemplative ends" were vast. "I have taken all knowledge to be my province; and if I could purge it of two sorts of rovers, whereof the one with frivolous disputations, confutations, and verbosities, the other with blind experiments and auricular traditions and impostures, hath committed so many spoils, I hope I should bring in industrious observations, grounded conclusions, and profitable inventions and discoveries."

And in *The Interpretation of Nature,* he wrote:

> I set myself to consider in what way mankind might be best served. . . .
> Now among all the benefits that could be conferred upon mankind, I found none so great as the discovery of new arts. . . . But if a man could succeed, not in striking out some particular invention, however useful, but in kindling a light in nature—a light that should . . . illuminate all the border regions that confine upon the circle of our present knowledge . . .—that man (I thought) would be the benefactor indeed of the human race—the propagator

of man's empire over the universe, the champion of liberty, the conqueror and subduer of necessities.[e]

But Bacon was no selfless experimenter interested only in ascertaining the facts. It is not that he was uninterested in "the Truth," as he called it; what interested him about it was chiefly its possibilities for exploitation. What he sought, in his own pregnant phrase, was "that knowledge whose dignity is maintained by works of utility and power."

Bacon was, in fact, a man of the new type that we have already encountered in politics and in business, a man whose dominant motive was power and the good things of this life that power brings in its train. What distinguished Bacon from Caesar Borgia or Louis XI or Machiavelli was his discovery that science is a road to power. But since he could never quite make up his mind whether it was a surer route than the more obvious path through politics, he undertook to follow both roads at once. Today no one would dream of taking more than a tiny segment of knowledge for his province, and even so one would expect to have to devote one's whole life to "research" in this limited area. But Bacon could range over the whole field of natural knowledge in his spare time, while concentrating his major attention on politics and law. This is the best evidence not only of his genius but also of the opportunities that exist at the inception of a new age, when old patterns of thought and action have broken down and everything is fluid.

THE "GREAT INSTAURATION"

The vast scheme (truly "without precedent," as Bacon claimed) by which he proposed to make his fortune was nothing less than a "total reconstruction of the sciences, arts and all human knowledge." Underlying this "great instauration," as Bacon called it, were two basic assumptions: (1) that virtually everything that had so far passed for knowledge was error (otherwise there would be no need for *total* reconstruction), and (2) that the human mind is an adequate instrument for obtaining knowledge (otherwise there would be no possibility of such a reform).

The second basic assumption seems at first sight to contradict the first. For if the mind is the adequate instrument that Bacon supposed it to be, how did it come about that man had fallen into hopeless error? Bacon would have replied that it is necessary to distinguish between the native state of the mind, in which it *is* an adequate instrument, and its present degenerate state, in which it is most inadequate. The mind has gotten itself into bad habits and these must be unlearned, along with the errors that these habits have foisted upon us. When this purging process has been completed, the mind, restored to its original condition, will once more be adequate. In a word, since "the human intellect makes its own difficulties," it can be "restored to its perfect and original condition." Originally, the mind was "like a fair sheet of paper with no writing on it," or (in another metaphor) "like a mirror with a true and even surface fit to reflect the genuine way of things." In the course of time, men's minds have become "strangely possessed and beset so that there is no true and even surface left to reflect the genuine rays of things." We must, therefore, first restore the surface and then "make provision for finding the genuine light of nature and kindling and bringing it to bear."[f]

This notion of a renovation of the human mind that would take it back to its original state parallels the great religious reform that had just been achieved and that was itself a casting off of false accretions and complications in order to return to the original purity of the gospel message. Probably this parallel never suggested itself to Bacon's mind; rather it seems that in many departments of life the notion of *change*, which was so prominent in the thought of the new age, was colored by the thought of *return*. Indeed, in both Luther and Bacon, who differed in so many respects, the myth of Adam's fall can be seen at work. Quite unconsciously Bacon applied the metaphor of the loss of paradise to the analysis of scientific method. Just as man's original, moral will had been corrupted and had become enslaved to sin, so his original power of knowledge had become diseased and had led him into sins against the "Truth," namely, the acceptance of all sorts of errors and mistakes. Both Luther and Bacon passed in silence over the awkward question, "How did the fall come about?" in order to concentrate on the practical question, "How can fallen man be redeemed and restored to his pristine state?"

Thus Bacon's position is a kind of epistemological Protestantism: "Works" are not necessary for salvation. Knowledge, like grace, is not something that we achieve by our efforts; it comes to us from outside. "Truth" will write in its own fair hand upon our intellects as soon as faith has made them ready to receive it.

Whatever may be the *theological* solution of the controversy over faith and works, Bacon's account of the knowledge situation was mistaken. His metaphors about the smooth, even surface and the fair sheet of paper sound plausible, but a mind empty of all preconceptions would be as incapable of getting at the facts as a baby's, for it would be helpless to organize and interpret the experiences before it.

Moreover, even if emptiness were a desirable state of affairs, no mind except a newborn baby's could possibly achieve it. Immediately after birth, habits or routines for organizing experience begin to develop. The problem is not to get rid of them but to keep them flexible. The basic criticism of Bacon is not that he failed to free his mind from all preconceptions, but that, because he naïvely thought that he *had* done so, he was quite uncritical about those he unconsciously retained.[2] This erroneous conception of the mind's relation to truth was all but inevitable, given the circumstances in which Bacon wrote. Because the precon-

2 See pp. 85–87.

ceptions of medieval science were so flagrantly wrong, it was easy to assume that if men could only rid themselves of them, everything would be smooth sailing.

BACON'S CRITICISM OF MEDIEVAL SCIENCE

Accordingly, before we proceed, let us examine Bacon's criticism of medieval science.

> The propositions[3] now in use, having been suggested by a scanty . . . experience and a few particulars of most general occurrence, are made for the most part just large enough to fit and take these in. . . . And if some opposite instance, not observed or not known before, chance to come in the way, the proposition [instead of being abandoned as false] is rescued and preserved by some frivolous distinction.[g]

Moreover, the main tendency of medieval science had been to start from propositions of the highest order of generality[4] and then, assuming their incorrigibility, to deduce propositions of lower generality from them. Bacon saw that a purely deductive science was not a *natural* science. "The syllogism consists of propositions, propositions consist of words, words are symbols of notions. Therefore if the notions themselves (which is the root of the matter) are confused and over-hastily abstracted from the facts, there can be no firmness in the superstructure." What the new science had therefore to aim at was not "propositions established by argumentation [that is, by the methods of deductive logic], . . . but propositions duly and orderly formed from particulars."[h]

In order to understand what Bacon was criticizing and why, we must recall that what passed as scientific explanation in the universities of his day frequently amounted to no more than empty verbiage. For example, it was still possible for the learned to "explain" the ignition of one object by another already on fire in terms of the Aristotelian concepts of form and matter: Contact with the flame, in which the form of fire is actual, brings to actuality the form of fire that remains potential in the second object until it is ignited.

Bacon saw that even when Scholastic science was not as completely trivial as this explanation of ignition, everything depended on the major premise; if it did not correspond to the facts, the conclusion might also fail to do so. Hence the crucial question seemed to him to be obtaining a major premise that corresponds to the facts. Scholastic science went astray because it failed to make certain of this. How, Bacon asked himself, can modern science avoid this mistake?

---

3 [Bacon used the Latin word *axiomata* here, but the English term "axiom" is now a misleading translation—AUTHOR.]

4 "The conclusions of human reason as ordinarily applied in matter of nature I call *Anticipations of Nature* (as a thing rash or premature)"—*Novum Organum*, I, 26.

In the first place, he thought, we must uproot the "false notions" and "prejudices" that plunge us into hasty generalizations and prevent us from seeing the exceptions to them. There are, Bacon thought, four types of these "idols" that now have possession of the mind:

> The Idols of the Tribe have their foundation in human nature itself, and in the tribe or race of men. For it is a false assertion that the sense of man is the measure of things. On the contrary, all perceptions, as well of the sense as of the mind, are according to the measure of the individual and not according to the measure of the universe. And the human understanding is like a false mirror, which, receiving rays irregularly, distorts and discolours the nature of things by mingling its own nature with it.
>
> The Idols of the Cave are the idols of the individual man. For every one (besides the errors common to human nature in general) has a cave or den of his own, which refracts and discolours the light of nature; owing either to his own proper and peculiar nature; or to his education and conversation with others; or to the reading of books, and the authority of those whom he esteems and admires; or to the differences of impressions, accordingly as they take place in a mind preoccupied and predisposed or in a mind indifferent and settled; or the like. So that the spirit of man (according as it is meted out to different individuals) is in fact a thing variable and full of perturbation, and governed as it were by chance. Whence it was well observed by Heraclitus that men look for sciences in their own lesser worlds, and not in the greater or common world.
>
> There are also idols formed by the intercourse and association of men with each other, which I call Idols of the Market-place, on account of the commerce and consort of men there. For it is by discourse that men associate; and words are imposed according to the apprehension of the vulgar. And therefore the ill and unfit choice of words wonderfully obstructs the understanding. Nor do the definitions or explanations wherewith in some things learned men are wont to guard and defend themselves, by any means set the matter right. But words plainly force and overrule the understanding, and throw all into confusion, and lead men away into numberless empty controversies and idle fancies.
>
> Lastly, there are idols which have immigrated into men's minds from the various dogmas of philosophies, and also from wrong laws of demonstration. These I call Idols of the Theatre; because in my judgment all the received systems are but so many stage-plays, representing worlds of their own creation after an unreal and scenic fashion. Nor is it only of the systems now in vogue, or only of the ancient sects and philosophies, that I speak: for many more plays of the same kind may yet be composed and in like artificial manner set forth; seeing that errors the most widely different have nevertheless causes for the most part alike. Neither again do I mean this only of entire systems, but also of many principles and axioms in science, which by tradition, credulity, and negligence have come to be received.
>
> But of these several kinds of idols I must speak more largely and exactly, that the understanding may be duly cautioned.

The human understanding is of its own nature prone to suppose the existence of more order and regularity in the world than it finds. . . . Hence the fiction that all celestial bodies move in perfect circles. . . .

The human understanding when it has once adopted an opinion (either as being the received opinion or as being agreeable to itself) draws all things else to support and agree with it. And though there be a greater number and weight of instances to be found on the other side, yet these it either neglects and despises, or else by some distinction sets aside and rejects; in order that by this great and pernicious predetermination the authority of its former conclusions may remain inviolate. . . . And such is the way of all superstition, whether in astrology, dreams, omens, divine judgments, or the like; wherein men, having a delight in such vanities, mark the events where they are fulfilled, but where they fail, though this happen much oftener, neglect and pass them by. . . . Besides, independently of that delight and vanity which I have described, it is the peculiar and perpetual error of the human intellect to be more moved and excited by affirmatives than by negatives; whereas it ought properly to hold itself indifferently disposed towards both alike. Indeed in the establishment of any true axiom, the negative instance is the more forcible of the two. . . .

The human understanding is no dry light, but receives an infusion from the will and affections . . . . What a man had rather were true he more readily believes. Therefore he rejects difficult things from impatience of research; sober things, because they narrow hope; the deeper things of nature, from superstition; the light of experience, from arrogance and pride . . . ; things not commonly believed, out of deference to the opinion of the vulgar. Numberless in short are the ways, and sometimes imperceptible, in which the affections colour and infect the understanding.

. . . .

The *Idols of the Cave* take their rise in the peculiar constitution, mental or bodily, of each individual; and also in education, habit, and accident. . . .

Men become attached to certain particular sciences and speculations, either because they fancy themselves the authors and inventors thereof, or because they have bestowed the greatest pains upon them and become most habituated to them. But men of this kind, if they betake themselves to philosophy and contemplations of a general character, distort and colour them in obedience to their former fancies; a thing especially to be noticed in Aristotle, who made his natural philosophy a mere bond-servant to his logic, thereby rendering it contentious and well nigh useless. The race of chemists again out of a few experiments of the furnace have built up a fantastic philosophy, framed with reference to a few things; and Gilbert also, after he had employed himself most laboriously in the study and observation of the lodestone, proceeded at once to construct an entire system in accordance with his favourite subject.

. . . .

But the *Idols of the Market-place* are the most troublesome of all: idols which have crept into the understanding through the alliances of words and names. For men believe that their reason governs words; but it is also true that words react on the understanding; and this it is that has rendered philosophy and the sciences sophistical and inactive. Now words, being commonly framed and applied according to the capacity of the vulgar, follow those lines of division which are most obvious to the vulgar understanding. And whenever an understanding of greater acuteness or a more diligent observation would alter those lines to suit the true divisions of nature, words stand in the way and resist the change. . . .

The idols imposed by words on the understanding are of two kinds. They are either names of things which do not exist (for as there are things left unnamed through lack of observation, so likewise are there names which result from fantastic suppositions and to which nothing in reality corresponds), or they are names of things which exist, but yet confused and ill-defined, and hastily and irregularly derived from realities. Of the former kind are Fortune, the Prime Mover, Planetary Orbits, Elements of Fire, and like fictions which owe their origin to false and idle theories. . . .

But the other class, which springs out of a faulty and unskilful abstraction, is intricate and deeply rooted. Let us take for example such a word as *humid;* and see how far the several things which the word is used to signify agree with each other; and we shall find the word *humid* to be nothing else than a mark loosely and confusedly applied to denote a variety of actions which will not bear to be reduced to any constant meaning.

. . . .

But the *Idols of the Theatre* are not innate, nor do they steal into the understanding secretly, but are plainly impressed and received into the mind from the play-books of philosophical systems and the perverted rules of demonstration. . . .

For the Rational School of philosophers snatches from experience a variety of common instances, neither duly ascertained nor diligently examined and weighed, and leaves all the rest to meditation and agitation of wit.

There is also another class of philosophers, who having bestowed much diligent and careful labour on a few experiments, have thence made bold to educe and construct systems; wresting all other facts in a strange fashion to conformity therewith.

And there is yet a third class, consisting of those who out of faith and veneration mix their philosophy and theology and traditions; among whom the vanity of some has gone so far aside as to seek the origin of science among spirits and genii. So that this parent stock of errors—this false philosophy—is of three kinds: the Sophistical, the Empirical, and the Superstitious.

The most conspicuous example of the first class was Aristotle, who corrupted natural philosophy by his logic . . . .

But the empirical school of philosophy gives birth to dogmas more deformed and monstrous than the Sophistical or Rational school. . . . Of this there is a notable instance in the alchemists and their dogmas; though it is hardly to be found elsewhere in these times, except perhaps in the philosophy of Gilbert. . . .

But the corruption of philosophy by superstition and an admixture of theology is far more widely spread, and does the greatest harm . . . .

Of this kind we have among the Greeks a striking example in Pythagoras, though he united with it a coarser and more cumbrous superstition; another in Plato and his school, more dangerous and subtle. It shows itself likewise in parts of other philosophies, in the introduction of abstract forms and final causes and first causes, with the omission in most cases of causes intermediate, and the like. Upon this point the greatest caution should be used. . . .

So much concerning the several classes of Idols, and their equipage: all of which must be renounced and put away with a fixed and solemn determination, and the understanding thoroughly freed and cleansed; the entrance into the kingdom of man, founded on the sciences, being not much other than the entrance into the kingdom of heaven, whereinto none may enter except as a little child.[i]

COMMENT ON BACON'S ACCOUNT OF THE IDOLS

This is excellent as far as it goes, but (as Bacon saw) it is merely the negative stage of resurfacing the mirror of our minds. It must be supplemented by a stage in which the "genuine light of nature" is "kindled and brought to bear" on the mirror.[5] Laying aside metaphor, what is required as the next step is an inductive procedure that utilizes the "evidence of the senses."

> In order to penetrate into the inner and further recesses of nature, it is necessary that [our] notions . . . be derived from things by a more sure and guarded way. . . . We must lead men to the particulars themselves, and their series and order; while men on their side must force themselves for awhile to lay their notions by and begin to familiarise themselves with facts.[j]

In other words, though observation is fundamental, it is not sufficient. "The evidence of the senses," Bacon recognized, must be helped and guarded by a certain process of correction. If it is essential that the scientist "start directly from single sensuous perceptions," it is equally essential that observation "be guided at every step."[k] It is necessary to

> . . . provide helps for the sense—substitutes to supply its failures, rectifications to correct its errors; and this I endeavour to accomplish not so much by instruments as by experiments. For the subtlety of experiments is far greater than that of the sense itself, even when assisted by exquisite instruments; such experiments, I mean, as are skillfully and artificially devised for the express purpose of determining the point in question. To the immediate and proper perception of the sense therefore I do not give much weight; but I contrive that the office of the sense shall be only to judge of the experiment, and that the experiment itself shall judge of the thing.[l]

5 See p. 76.

BACON'S INDUCTIVE METHOD

This is admirably put, but those who recall the modesty of the experimental techniques with which Bacon was acquainted and which he himself employed will not expect his detailed analysis to live up to this prospectus. Bacon's own example of the application of his inductive method was an investigation of the cause of heat.

First, he held, it is necessary to draw up a list of all known cases in which the phenomenon of heat occurs. This he called the "Table of Essence and Presence." Bacon's own list, which he recognized to be incomplete, contained twenty-seven entries. Among them were:

> 1. The rays of the sun, especially in summer and at noon.
> 2. The rays of the sun reflected and condensed, as between mountains, or on walls, and most of all in burning-glasses and mirrors. . . .
> 4. Burning thunderbolts.
> 5. Eruptions of flame from the cavities of mountains.
> 6. All flame. . . .
> 8. Natural warm-baths. . . .
> 11. Certain seasons that are fine and cloudless by the constitution of the air itself, without regard to the time of year. . . .
> 13. All villous substances, as wool, skins of animals, and down of birds, have heat.[m]

Second, one must make a "Table of Deviation, or of Absence in Proximity"— that is, a list of cases that are akin to each of the positive instances but in which the phenomenon of heat does *not* occur. For instance, the moon, the stars, and comets are heavenly bodies like the sun (positive case 1) but do not give off heat as it does. And, as regards flame (positive case 6):

> All flame is in all cases more or less warm; nor is there any Negative to be subjoined. And yet they say that the *ignis fatuus* (as it is called), which sometimes even settles on a wall, has not much heat; perhaps as much as the flame of spirit of wine, which is mild and soft. But still milder must that flame be, which according to certain grave and trustworthy histories has been seen shining about the head and locks of boys and girls, without at all burning the hair, but softly playing round it. It is also most certain that about a horse, when sweating on the road, there is sometimes seen at night, and in clear weather, a sort of luminous appearance without any manifest heat.

Bacon recognized that he did not have sufficient knowledge about most of the positive instances to draw up definite negative instances. At best he could only suggest certain experiments that, if they were performed, might determine whether such-and-such was in fact the negative instance it appeared to be. For instance, positive case 2 is the rays of the sun reflected in (among other things) a magnifying glass. If it turns out that the flame of a candle fails to generate heat under this condition, the candle flame will be a negative instance. Therefore, "let a burning-glass be tried with common flame," and again, "let the experiment be carefully tried, whether by means of the most powerful and best constructed glass the rays of the moon can be so caught and collected as to produce even the least degree of warmth." Over and over again Bacon simply remarked, "On this instance should be made more diligent inquiry."

"Thirdly we must make a presentation to the understanding of instances in which the nature under examination [heat in this case, of course] is found in different degree, more or less. . . . This Table, therefore, I call the Table of Degrees or the Table of Comparison." Bacon listed forty-one instances in this table, among which were:

> 10. When attacked by intermittent fevers, animals are at first seized with cold and shivering, but soon after they become exceedingly hot, which is their condition from the first in burning and pestilential fevers.
>
> 11. Let further inquiry be made into the different degrees of heat in different animals, as in fishes, quadrupeds, serpents, birds; and also according to their species, as in the lion, the kite, the man; for in common opinion fish are the least hot internally, and birds the hottest; especially doves, hawks, and sparrows.
>
> 12. Let further inquiry be made into the different degrees of heat in the different parts and limbs of the same animal. For milk, blood, seed, eggs, are found to be hot only in a moderate degree, and less hot than the outer flesh of the animal when in motion or agitated. But what the degree of heat is in the brain, stomach, heart, &c. has not yet been in like manner inquired. . . .
>
> 15. By the tradition of astronomers some stars are hotter than others. Of planets, Mars is accounted the hottest after the sun; then comes Jupiter, and then Venus. Others, again, are set down as cold; the moon, for instance, and above all Saturn. Of fixed stars, Sirius is said to be the hottest, then Cor Leonis or Regulus, then Canicula, and so on. . . .
>
> 22. I think also that the flame which results from some imperfect metals is very strong and eager. But on these points let further inquiry be made.

The fourth step in Bacon's method he called the "Process of Exclusion." This is needed because, although God and the angels could doubtless grasp the nature of heat directly from the three tables, "this assuredly is more than man can do." The scientist must therefore "set induction to work" on these instances to find some factor (or "nature") always present when heat is present, always absent when heat is absent (for example, something in the sun but not in the moon), and present in greater or lesser degree as the objects in question are more or less hot. He should proceed by way of negation, excluding those factors (or natures) that obviously fail to satisfy these conditions. Since the sun is such an obvious instance of heat, he might be tempted to leap to the conclusion that the cause of heat has something to do with being a heavenly body; but

this cannot be, for the table of positive instances shows that there exist subterrane-
ous fires, "which are the most remote and most completely separate from the
rays of heavenly bodies." Nor can light be the cause of heat, because the moon,
which is light, is not hot. Nor can rarity be the cause of heat, because gold
and other dense metals are capable of being hot; and so on. In all, Bacon listed
fourteen factors excluded in this way, adding that his list was "not perfect but
meant only for an example."

This "Process of Exclusion," Bacon held, is "the foundation of true induction."
But it is immensely time-consuming and, unless the scientist can be sure that
he is dealing with "simple natures,"[6] not necessarily accurate. For instance,
heavenly bodies and rarity have been excluded. But both these notions are "vague
and ill defined." What men call rarity may well be a compound, one element
of which is the very nature the scientist seeks. An even "more powerful aid
for the use of the understanding" is therefore needed, and this will proceed
by way of affirmation, though only tentatively. This Bacon called "the Indulgence
of the Understanding, or the Commencement of Interpretation, or the First
Vintage." It amounts to a preliminary hypothesis, or guess, as to what the causal
factor in question is.

> It is to be observed that the Form of a thing is to be found (as plainly
> appears from what has been said) in each and all the instances, in which
> the thing itself is to be found; otherwise it would not be the Form. It follows
> therefore that there can be no contradictory instance. At the same time
> the Form is found much more conspicuous and evident in some instances
> than in others; namely in those wherein the nature of the Form is less
> restrained and obstructed and kept within bounds by other natures. Instances
> of this kind I call Shining or Striking Instances. Let us now therefore proceed
> to the First Vintage concerning the Form of Heat.
>
> From a survey of the instances, all and each, the nature of which Heat
> is a particular case appears to be Motion. This is displayed most conspic-
> uously in flame, which is always in motion, and in boiling or simmering
> liquids, which also are in perpetual motion. It is also shown in the excitement
> or increase of heat caused by motion, as in bellows and blasts; on which
> see Tab. 3. Inst. 29.; and again in other kinds of motion, on which see Tab.
> 3. Inst. 28. and 31. Again it is shown in the extinction of fire and heat by
> any strong compression, which checks and stops the motion; on which see
> Tab. 3. Inst. 30. and 32. It is shown also by this, that all bodies are destroyed,
> or at any rate notably altered, by all strong and vehement fire and heat;
> whence it is quite clear that heat causes a tumult and confusion and violent
> motion in the internal parts of a body, which perceptibly tends to its
> dissolution.
>
> When I say of Motion that it is as the genus of which heat is a species,
> I would be understood to mean, not that heat generates motion or that motion
> generates heat (though both are true in certain cases), but that Heat itself,

6 For a discussion of this concept, see p. 87.

its essence and quiddity, is Motion and nothing else; limited however by the specific differences which I will presently subjoin.

According to Bacon, the specific differentiae of the motion that is heat are (1) expansive, (2) toward the circumference and upward, (3) lacking in uniformity, and (4) rapid. The final stage in his inductive method is verification: This hypothesis regarding the nature of heat must be checked against all cases in the tables. In every case, "whether the body be elementary or subject to celestial influence; whether it be luminous or opaque; rare or dense; locally expanded or confined within the bounds of its firm dimension; verging to dissolution or remaining in its original state; animal, vegetable, or mineral, water, oil, or air, or any other substance whatever," it turns out that heat is felt when motion of the kind described occurs, that it is not felt when this motion does not occur, and that the degree of heat experienced varies with the amount of motion occurring.

COMMENT ON BACON'S INDUCTIVE METHOD

As one reads through this analysis of the nature of heat, it is difficult to avoid the suspicion that the whole proceeding has been "cooked up"—that the tables were constructed to fit the hypothesis rather than that the hypothesis grew out of the tables. It is hard to believe that any reasonable hypothesis could ever emerge from the jungle of assorted cases of heat presented in the Table of Essence and Presence, and certainly no real-life scientist has used tables like Bacon's, nor has any important scientific law been brought to light by Baconian induction.

What went wrong with an account that began so sensibly? The first thing that was wrong was simply Bacon's assumption, already mentioned, that the mind is like a mirror, needing only to be made even and smooth to present us with a perfect reflection of external reality.[7] With his thinking about method dominated by this analogy, it was inevitable that Bacon would oversimplify the technique of reaching hypotheses, making it appear that an hypothesis leaps to mind fully blown from a mere inspection of enough assorted facts. But this puts the cart before the horse: We cannot collect facts that will be of much use unless we have some sort of hypothesis already formed. It is clear that Bacon entirely neglected to consider the role of hypothesis in directing the search for facts and in determining what experiments are tried.

Further, though Bacon believed that he had put Scholasticism and all its works behind him, he actually retained one of its prime notions—the concept of substance. He took for granted that the universe is composed of individual substances and that various of these substances share certain properties (or "natures," as he sometimes called them). Thus, according to Bacon's view, if a scientist wants to study "man," he looks for the *something* that makes all particular men, men. If this something, whatever it is, is absent, he is not dealing with man; if

7 See p. 76.

it is present, regardless of what *other* properties may be present or absent, he is. What the scientist has to do, then, is to isolate this essential something.

Here are our old friends, universals, on whose existence almost all earlier philosophers had agreed, even while differing widely about their nature. Since all these philosophers had also held that universals are the true objects of scientific knowledge, it is not surprising that Bacon did not ask himself whether there are universals, but merely whether the Scholastics had gone about finding them in the right way. It was clear to him, of course, that the Scholastic way of discovering universals was not correct and that as long as science clung to this method it would stagnate. For Scholastic science proceeded by way of a "scanty experience," first to generalize and define the essential properties of man—to say that he "is a rational being" or that he "has an immortal soul"—and then to deduce the corollaries of these definitions.

Now Bacon, as we have seen, realized the inadequacy of this procedure. What he proposed was a new method for ascertaining natures, or essences[8]—a method that he called "induction" (not a "scanty experience," but a *full* experience of instances). But the point is that he still assumed that there *is* a nature to be discovered and that this nature is a simple, self-contained something, either wholly present or wholly absent[9] in the various particulars of sensation. He merely proposed what he believed to be a better method for getting at the same sort of thing that the Scholastics had failed to get at. He did not see that what the new method was competent to reveal about the world was really something altogether different from natures. What it could discover was *relations* (spatial or temporal) between various occurrences. Thus, when Bacon said that heat "is" a motion of a certain kind, he supposed the verb "is" to be functioning in the same way that it functions in the sentence "Man is a rational animal." That is, he supposed himself to be saying that the "essence" of heat is motion, just as a medieval thinker might have affirmed that the essence of man is rationality. But what Bacon's new method really showed was something quite different, namely, that whenever we have an experience of a certain kind, a

---

8 He also held, rightly, that the nature "man" is too complex for this kind of analysis. He wished to distinguish between such forms and those "simple" forms that he believed to be the constituent elements of the more complex ones: "The forms of substance . . . are so perplexed as they are not to be inquired; no more than it were either possible or to purpose to seek in gross the forms of those sounds which make words, which by composition and transposition of letters are infinite. But on the other side to inquire the forms of those sounds or voices which make simple letters is easily comprehensible; and being known induceth and manifesteth the form of all words, which consist and are compounded of them. In the same manner to inquire the form of a lion, of an oak, of gold; nay, of water, of air, is a vain pursuit; but to inquire the forms of sense, of voluntary motion, of vegetation, of colours, of gravity and levity, of density, of tenuity, of heat, of cold, and all other natures and qualities, which, like an alphabet, are not many, and of which the essences (upheld by matter) of all creatures do consist, to inquire, I say, the true forms of these, is that part of metaphysics which we now define of"—*Advancement of Learning*, in *The Works of Francis Bacon* (Spedding, Ellis, Heath), Vol. II, pp. 38–39.

9 The implications of the Table of Degrees are, of course, quite inconsistent with this doctrine.

motion of a certain kind is occurring—in other words, that two experiences of ours (one the felt, inner sensation called "heat" and the other the observed, outer experience called "motion") are regularly juxtaposed.

Unfortunately, because Bacon never quite realized the radically different conception of reality that the new method implied, he set it to work pursuing natures, or essences, which are not within the compass of this method. It should occasion no surprise, therefore, that it did not capture any. Bacon failed to give a correct formula for procedure under the new method because he failed to understand the implications of the empirical point of view, and he failed to understand these implications because he had not rid himself of the presuppositions of the old, substantival metaphysics.

To put this difficulty somewhat differently, Bacon proposed to use the new method to discover the natures whose reality the old metaphysics had assumed, but the new method actually implied an altogether different conception of reality—it implied that the real constituent entities of the universe are not natures at all, but events. This is an instance of the general truth that the way people believe they know things has a bearing on what they think they can know. For instance, anyone who holds (as did Plato) that knowledge is dialectical will probably conceive that reality is not sensuous and that universals are the most real things of all. On the other hand, anyone who holds that all real knowledge is obtained through perception will probably conclude that reality consists of concrete particulars and that universals are mere names. In other words, theory of knowledge and theory of reality are always correlative. Yet Bacon was attempting to retain the old conception of reality while adopting a very different conception of knowledge.

Stated this way, his mistake may seem elementary. But since nothing is more difficult for us than to be critical of those basic concepts that seem a part of the very fabric of our universe, his was a mistake made by many other thinkers. As we shall see, much of the new philosophy was devoted to an ill-fated attempt to accommodate the concept of substance to the new science.

The final weakness in Bacon's view to be considered stemmed not from his missing the point of empiricism but from his being too exclusively empirical. Let us suppose for the sake of argument that Bacon's method of induction is satisfactory and that by its means we have obtained a series of true propositions about the causes of various phenomena—"heat is so-and-so," "light is such-and-such," "density is such-and-such," and so forth. We now have some knowledge of nature, but do we have a science of nature? According to Bacon's own view, we do not. Science, he held, is more than a simple collection, or assortment, of true propositions; it must be a cohesive body of knowledge. That is, there must be a rationale that connects the propositions to one another, a rationale by which one moves, *at the propositional level*, by logical sequences (all the while, of course, making sure by inductive means that the facts correspond to the propositions in question). But though Bacon described this ideal and vividly painted its utility, he did not fashion an instrument for attaining it.

The Mathematical Spirit

In order to understand the nature of the mathematical element in the new methodology, let us contrast crime detection (a science in which the mathematical element is largely lacking) with physics (in which the mathematical element is manifestly present). In the course of investigating a crime, say, a murder, a detective sooner or later forms an hypothesis about the identity of the criminal—an hypothesis that he will wish to test. He may reason as follows: "If so-and-so is the murderer, as I think he is, he will react to an accusation of guilt in a way in which he would not react if he were innocent—he will turn pale and fall in a faint or make a break and run for it, and so on. Therefore I can test my hypothesis by accusing him and watching his reaction."

With this hypothesis of the detective, contrast the following: "If there are ten stones in this pile and five in that one, there are fifteen stones in both piles." Now, it is possible to miscount—counting is the empirical element here, corresponding to Bacon's observation that fire is hot or to the detective's noting of a footprint or a fingerprint. But if one has counted correctly, the inference to the total number of stones is certain, for it is based on the laws of arithmetic. The detective's inference, on the other hand, is based on an empirical generalization—a generalization about how people behave under conditions of stress. This generalization is fallible. Suppose so-and-so does faint when charged with the murder. Does this prove that he is guilty? Not at all. His fainting may be evidence of fright, not of guilt.

Now suppose that we want to study a freely falling body. If we merely look at it, we can say little more than that it falls "pretty fast." This may be called the level of simple empirical generalization from direct observation, which is about all that Bacon's method by itself could yield. Suppose, however, that we follow Bacon's advice and conduct an experiment; and let our experiment, unlike Bacon's own, take the form of *measuring* what is measurable about the behavior of a freely falling body. And suppose that measurement results in the following tables, quite different from Bacon's tables of qualitative differences:

TABLE I: VELOCITIES

End of 1st second	32 feet per second
End of 2nd second	64 feet per second
End of 3rd second	96 feet per second

TABLE 2: DISTANCES

During 1st second	16 feet
During 2nd second	48 feet
During 3rd second	80 feet

What we do when we measure is to convert a quality (fast, long, hot) into a quantity (32 feet per second, 10 miles, 98°). The practical advantages of making such a conversion are as obvious as they are great. If, for instance, we want to buy a carpet for a room, we stand a better chance of obtaining the right size if we go to the shop with quantitative information obtained by measurement ("The room is thirty feet by eighteen feet") than if we carry only qualitative information ("Well, it is really quite a nice big room").

Less obvious but equally important are the theoretical advantages of converting qualities into quantities. In order to understand these advantages, let us study the interrelations among the quantitative data obtained by measurement and set out in the above tables. What are the relations, in the first table, between the numbers representing successive velocities? Since we are dealing with simple quantitative data, it is easy both to frame an hypothesis and to test it. The velocity at the end of the second second is twice the velocity at the end of the first second (2 × 32 = 64), and the velocity at the end of the third second is three times the velocity at the end of the first second (3 × 32 = 96). This suggests the hypothesis that the velocity at the end of any second n will be n times the velocity at the end of the first second. It follows that the velocity at the end of the fourth second should be 128 feet per second (4 × 32). Obviously, the hypothesis can be tested by measuring the velocity at the end of the fourth second.

The same may be done for the second table. Forty-eight (the distance fallen through in the second second) is three times 16 (the distance fallen through in the first second), and 80 (the distance fallen through in the third second) is five times 16. In other words, the numbers 16, 48, 80, are in the same ratio to one another as the numbers 1, 3, 5. This suggests the general hypothesis that the distance fallen through in successive seconds varies with the series of odd numbers. It follows, if this hypothesis is correct, that the distance fallen through in the fourth second will be a multiple of the next odd number, or 7 × 16 = 112, and this conclusion can easily be checked by further measurements.

Now, by adding together the distances fallen through in successive seconds (given in the second table), *accumulated* distances at the end of each second may be obtained:

TABLE 3: ACCUMULATED DISTANCES

End of 1st second	16
End of 2nd second	64 (16 + 48)
End of 3rd second	144 (16 + 48 + 80)
End of 4th second	256 (16 + 48 + 80 + 112)

Let us see whether the successive numbers are multiples of 16. Sixty-four proves to be four times 16; 144 is nine times 16; 256 is sixteen times 16. So we can say that at the end of the second second, a body will have fallen four times the distance it fell during the first second of its fall; at the end of the third second, nine times; and at the end of the fourth second, sixteen times. But four (the multiple of the original distance for the second second) is the square of two; nine (the multiple of the original distance for the third second) is the square of three; and sixteen (the multiple of the original distance for the fourth second) is the square of four. Hence it seems reasonable to formulate an hypothesis to the effect that the accumulated distances fallen through at the end of successive seconds vary with the square of the time. At the end of the nth second, the accumulated distance will be $16n^2$. This can be tested for any second we choose. Note that to obtain this third formula it has not been necessary to make fresh observations and collect new data—the formula has been derived entirely by manipulation of the numerical data that are contained in Table 2 (page 88).

Contrast the detective's use of hypothesis with this procedure. Here, inference moves against a background quite different from the empirical generalizations that perforce guide inference in crime detection. By converting qualitative data into quantities, we have obtained numbers. We are therefore dealing not with empirical things but with abstractions whose relations are certified by the "laws of combination" (addition, division, multiplication, and so forth) that hold in arithmetic. There is, of course, an empirical phase at the beginning (when we measure the velocities and distances) and at the end (when we check the conclusions we have deduced). But the middle section of our procedure—the section in which we derive our hypothesis and formulate our scheme for testing it—is not empirical at all. It is "pure" mathematics, and it has the certainty of any purely mathematical knowledge. Its *relevance* depends, of course, on the empirical phases at the beginning and the end—the accuracy with which we have observed and measured.

Now, it is precisely this middle section that is neglected in Bacon's account of scientific method. The reasons for this neglect are obvious. Medieval science emphasized almost exclusively what is often called validity, which it understood as correct inference from premises to conclusion in syllogistic reasoning. Rarely were either the premises or the conclusions checked against the facts. Had they been checked, they would have been found to be sadly irrelevant to the actual world, however valid the logical relations among them. Men like Bacon, men who saw the importance of relevance (what has been called the empirical phases at the beginning and the end), naturally reacted against the incompetence of medieval science by exaggerating the importance of the empirical factor that assures that all concepts correspond to the facts and that all relevant facts have been observed.[10] But with the concentration of attention on relevance, logical cohesion suffered; in rejecting the irrelevant rationalism of medieval science, there was a tendency to throw out *all* rationalistic elements.

---

10 Bacon's tables were designed to lend just this assurance.

One should not suppose that Bacon himself fell into this particular trap. On the contrary, he prided himself on having "established forever a true and lawful marriage between the empirical and the rational faculty, the unkind and ill-starred divorce and separation of which has thrown into confusion all the affairs of the human family."[n] But, though Bacon was entirely correct in holding that human knowledge would remain in confusion until the two faculties were lawfully married, he did virtually nothing toward effecting their union. He seemed somehow to expect to utilize syllogism to sire a rational structure for the generalizations provided by induction, for his criticism of medieval science was not an attack on syllogism per se—he did not attack the logic of syllogism, but merely the irrelevance of the premises from which it started. But he did not develop this line of reasoning in detail, and, in any case, his interest in syllogism was actually a blind alley. The rational structure of the new science was to be provided, not by a syllogistic, but by a mathematical, logic.

What is more, had Bacon been more alert to developments on the Continent, he would have seen that a new method of precisely the type required—a method that was empirical *and* rational in character—was emerging. Mathematics was the instrument by which the marriage of fact and deduction was at last effected. We must now turn to a consideration of how this came about, for the consequences of this marriage were so fundamental that three hundred years later we are still far from understanding all its implications.

Copernicus

ANCIENT ASTRONOMY

It is no accident that astronomy was the science to which mathematics was first applied. The wonderful regularity of the movements of the planets has, of course, impressed all peoples; and the important role the heavenly bodies played in most religions, combined with the influence their behavior had on economic life, caused men to study them. From very early times, this study issued in generalizations accurate enough to permit predictions about astronomical events (eclipses, for example), which were deemed to have religious or other significance. Thus the regularity that stimulated man's imagination and aroused his curiosity provided him with a means of satisfying that curiosity.

The ancients, of course, had not only accumulated information about the movements of the planets; they had also constructed theories that would explain the movements observed. Some early thinkers—the Pythagoreans, for instance—maintained that the earth moves, and Aristarchus (third century B.C.) even held that the sun is the center of the whole system. But these conclusions seemed too paradoxical to meet with general acceptance, and opinion gradually settled down into a first premise that accorded with the apparently obvious fact that the planets turn around the earth. The problem, then, was to describe their manner of turning. Aristotle, for instance, held that the planets are contained in translucent, crystalline spheres fitted one inside another and that the movements we observe are compounded of the simple rotating motion of the various spheres. As time went on and further observations were made, revision of the theory became necessary. Ptolemy (second century A.D.) was able to show that the observed data accorded reasonably well with the hypothesis that the planets' paths are epicycles.[11] For instance, suppose that on successive nights we see a planet advancing against the background of fixed stars and that then one night it begins to retrogress. This is just what would happen if the planet moved in an epicycle as it rotated around the earth.

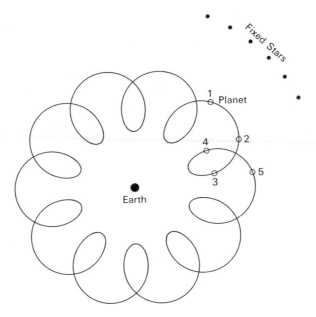

The successive observed positions advance (against the fixed stars) from 1 to 2, advance from 2 to 3, move backwards from 3 to 4, and move forward again from 4 to 5.

From Ptolemy's time down to the fifteenth century, little progress was made in astronomical theory; for the most part, men had neither the interest nor the mathematical competence for this kind of work. But in the general relaxing of tradition and in the new curiosity about the natural world that occurred in

---

11 An epicycle is a circle on a circle. Suppose that, as a horse walks in a circular path around a barn, a would-be rider runs in circles around the horse. The man's path would be an epicycle, that is, the center of his path is a successively advancing point on the perimeter of the horse's path. His actual path is a series of loops.

that century, astronomical speculation revived, and a number of tentative suggestions were made to the effect that perhaps the earth rotates on its axis.[12] It was not until Copernicus,[13] however, that this idea was taken up seriously.

COPERNICUS' CONCEPTION OF THE HELIOCENTRIC HYPOTHESIS

It is not clear whether Copernicus first derived the idea of a heliocentric system from the Pythagoreans and other authors whom he mentioned or whether he regarded them, in the Scholastic fashion, merely as authorities to be cited in support of the view.[14] But surely it was only in an age that was becoming scornful of Aristotle and the Aristotelians that the geocentric view sanctioned by that august authority could be questioned. Thus the Neoplatonic and Pythagorean revival, whether or not it actually suggested the idea to Copernicus, created a climate of opinion in which it was natural to believe that the universe runs in accordance with simple mathematical principles. The grafting of Pythagoreanism onto Christianity resulted in the concept of an omnipotent creator god who was an omniscient mathematician—exactly the kind of view that would lead to the mathematical study of nature. It is one of the more pleasant ironies of history that the driving force behind the development of the new physics and astronomy was a semimystical religion.

Given this notion of a divine mathematician, criticism of the Ptolemaic scheme was inevitable. Even a fallible human mathematician would hardly stoop to designing a planetary system that involved seventy-nine epicycles and in which, even so, motion was not absolutely uniform. However, if the earth turns (as quite a respectable number of ancient writers *had* supposed), some of the movements that, on Ptolemy's geocentric hypothesis, had to be attributed to the planets themselves and that accordingly required seventy-nine epicycles, will be apparent only—a projection, as it were, of the earth's movement.[15]

But how can the motions that we mistakenly read into the planets on the old assumptions of the earth's immobility be distinguished from the motions

---

12 For instance, by Cardinal Nicholas of Cusa (1401–64).

13 Nicolaus Copernicus (1473–1543), a Pole, was educated at the university of Cracow. His uncle was a great political bishop in the Baltic area, which even in those days was in dispute between the Germans and the Poles. In this political struggle Copernicus seems to have played a not unimportant part, though he also found time to make translations from the Greek, to compose a treatise on currency reform, and to work away at the astronomical studies that were his principal interest.

14 For instance, in his letter to Pope Paul III, Copernicus said, "According to Cicero, Nicetas had thought the earth was moved. . . . According to Plutarch, . . . certain others had held the same opinion. When from this, therefore, I had conceived its possibility, I myself also began to meditate upon the mobility of the earth"—quoted in Burtt, *The Metaphysical Foundations of Modern Physical Science*, p. 38.

15 "If . . . any motion is attributed to the earth, there will appear in all the bodies outside the earth a motion of equal velocity, but in the opposite direction, as though these objects were moving past the earth"—quoted in E. Rosen, *Three Copernican Treatises* (Columbia University Press, 1939), p. 26.

the planets really make? This obviously depends on what motion is attributed to the earth. Copernicus assumed (1) that it revolves on its axis, and (2) that it turns in a circular path around the sun between Mars and Venus, carrying the moon with it on an epicycle.[16] He further assumed that all this happens within the sphere of the fixed stars. In other words, as was entirely sensible, he made no more changes from the base hypothesis than seemed absolutely necessary. He then recalculated all the observed and recorded positions of the planets and found that he had a workable scheme.

> I found at length by much and long observation, that if the motions of the other planets were added to the rotation of the earth and calculated as for the revolution of that planet, not only the phenomena of the others followed from this, but also that it so bound together both the order and magnitudes of all the planets and the spheres and the heaven itself, that in no single part could one thing be altered without confusion among the other parts and in all the universe. Hence for this reason . . . I have followed this system.
>
> . . . .
>
> We find, therefore, under this orderly arrangement, a wonderful symmetry in the universe, and a definite relation of harmony in the motion and magnitude of the orbs, of a kind it is not possible to obtain in any other way.°

Copernicus was, however, very hesitant about publishing his theory, perhaps because he was not sure what the Church's reaction would be.[17] He need not have distressed himself. Far from suddenly overthrowing the medieval world view, his book aroused little interest. The Church only became alarmed some sixty years later, when Galileo gave the heliocentric view sensational publicity.

Nevertheless, Copernicus had, as it were, loosened the bonds in which astronomical thought had been imprisoned for two thousand years. Astronomers—even those who, like Tycho Brahe,[18] rejected the heliocentric theory—saw that his criticisms of the Ptolemaic scheme were cogent. Revisionism was now in the air, and though Tycho's own hypothesis was of little value,[19] he invented valuable astronomical instruments and used them to make a large number of careful observations that provided the empirical data without which further progress would have been impossible.

16 He also assumed a third motion, a motion of the earth's axis, which can be left out of account.
17 He did not release it for publication until just before his death, and, as it was, it appeared with a preface (inserted without Copernicus' knowledge) denying that the author claimed the theory to be true.
18 Like so many other men of this age, Tycho (1546–1601) was anything but a specialist. He prepared horoscopes and calendars for the Danish and the Hapsburg courts, studied medicine and chemistry, manufactured glass, ran his own printing press, hobnobbed with royalty, and corresponded extensively with other scientists and with princely dilettantes.
19 Tycho assumed, with Ptolemy, that the earth is at the center of the whole universe; he then argued that the sun, the moon, and the fixed stars turn about it, and that Jupiter, Saturn, Mars, Venus, and Mercury turn about the sun as it turns about the earth—in other words, that their orbits are concentric epicycles on the sun's orbit.

Tycho left his incomplete data to his assistant and protégé, Johann Kepler, with the excellent advice to "lay a solid foundation for his views by actual observation and then by ascending from these to strive to know the causes of things."

Kepler

Kepler (1571–1630) was not a great observer, but he had the kind of generalizing and synthesizing mind that could discover the simple uniformities hidden beneath the rich diversity of concrete facts. Together, he and Tycho represent two of the main elements in scientific method.

The motivating drive behind Kepler's inquiries was a deep religious piety. "I am a Christian," he said on one occasion, "attached to the Confession of Augsburg [that is, he was a Lutheran] by a thorough examination of doctrine, not less than by the instruction of my parents. That is my faith; I have already suffered for it, and I know not the art of dissembling. Religion is for me a serious affair, which I cannot treat with levity."[p] Fortunately for the development of science, Kepler's piety was colored by a Pythagorean mysticism that convinced him that God had created the universe in accordance with certain simple mathematical harmonies. This conviction gave him the fortitude to see the failure of one formula after another without giving up hope that there was a formula to be found. But it was a very great mathematical imagination that suggested the formulas to Kepler, and it was a very high order of mathematical competence that enabled him to test them.

This imagination, urged on by Pythagoreanism, sometimes led him into fantasy,[20] but, all the same, had he approached Tycho's factual data with the empty mind that Bacon recommended, he would never have reached any conclusions at all. In this way, by conceiving hypotheses and trying to verify them, Kepler eventually worked out his so-called three laws, which are very general descriptions, in mathematical terms, of Tycho's data.

THE THREE LAWS

According to the first law (this is the logical order, not the historical order in which Kepler conceived them), the planets describe orbits that are ellipses,

---

20 He held, for example, that the planets actually make music as they swing around the sun. Saturn is a basso profundo, Jupiter a bass, Mars a tenor, the earth a contralto, Venus a soprano, and Mercury (nearest the sun and with the shortest orbit and the highest velocity of all) a falsetto. The earth, for instance, sings the notes *mi, fa, mi*, "so that you may guess from them that in this abode of ours Misery and Famine prevail" (quoted in Rufus et al., *Johann Kepler*, p. 77). It will be noted that the planets sing (or rather, think) in both Latin and English (*fa* is the opening syllable of both "famine" and its Latin equivalent *famus*, and *mi* of both "misery" and *miseria*), but not in German, Russian, or Hindustani.

with the sun in one focus. Kepler had started on the Copernican assumption that the paths are circular, but Tycho's observations showed that Mars does not move in a circle. Hence, since Kepler assumed the basic Copernican hypothesis that the planets turn about the sun, not about the earth, it was necessary for him to try other curves in order to find one that Tycho's observations fit. Eventually Kepler tried an ellipse. He found that, if he took account of the fact that the earth moves around the sun in an elliptical orbit, all the recorded positions of Mars lay along such a curve. And so for all the other planets.

The second law states another regularity that can be formulated from observations of the planets' paths. Until Kepler's day, men had assumed that the planets move at constant speeds (there being no reason why an omniscient and omnipotent force could not move them in what was, obviously, the simplest way). And as long as it was supposed that each planet travels in an epicyclical path, it was possible to hold that the velocity is constant and only seems to slow down as the planet is turning around one of its epicycles. On the supposition, however, that the paths are elliptical, it had to be admitted that the planets speed up and slow down again, like an absent-minded driver on a highway, as they orbit around the sun.

But Kepler did not believe that the planets are absent-minded. It was his deepest conviction that nothing happens without a reason and that these reasons (God being a mathematician) have a mathematical form. Hence he started with the presupposition that the changes in planetary velocity are not arbitrary (like those of the absent-minded driver, which seem to be the product merely of the random play of impulses across his cortex), but conform to some pattern that can be stated mathematically.

Kepler's initial belief was that there must be some direct relation between velocities and times. For instance, if it could have been established that the planets' velocities increase during times t^1 to t^4, then decrease during times t^5 to t^8, then increase again from t^9 to t^{12}, and so on, he would have found the kind of relation he sought. But all the formulas of this type that he tried failed. Finally, instead of a relation between velocities and times, he hit upon one between velocities and areas, and so the belief in regularity was vindicated. The planets are not absent-minded drivers. Their behavior (at least with regard to their speeding up and slowing down) conforms to a pattern, and this pattern can be stated in simple mathematical terms: In any two equal periods of time, equal areas are swept out by a line from the sun to the planet.

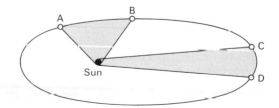

Thus, as a planet travels from A to B along its orbit around the sun (S), a certain region of the ellipse, ABS, is swept out; as it moves from C to D, another region, CDS, is swept out. The second law says that if the times from A to B and from C to D are equal, the regions ABS and CDS are equal. Times are proportional, not to the distances traveled (for the distance AB is much greater than the distance CD), but to the areas swept out.

The first two laws concern individual orbits, but Kepler was convinced that when God created the several planets, He did not leave each a sheerly arbitrary unit of fact, like a series of independent drivers who happen to take the same road from Washington to New York. As a young man, even before he met Tycho, Kepler had worked out an ingenious formula based on the assumption of circular paths. But this was exploded by Galileo's discovery of the satellites of Jupiter.[21] Though painful, the failure of his hypothesis did not cause Kepler to abandon his search for *some* description that would relate the orbits of the various planets, and his delight at finally finding one was unbounded. "What sixteen years ago I urged as a thing to be sought, . . . for which I have devoted the best part of my life—at length I have brought to light, and recognized its truth beyond my most sanguine expectations. It is now eighteen months since I got the first glimpse of light, three months since the dawn, very few days since the unveiled sun, most admirable to gaze upon, burst out upon me."[q]

This new light was the third law: The squares of the periodic times are proportional to the cubes of the mean distances from the sun. That is to say, every planet takes a certain time t to circle the sun. Let the earth's periodic time be Et, Mars's time, Mt, Jupiter's, Jt, and so on. Again, as each planet moves in its elliptical path, its distance from the sun varies. By averaging out these various distances, a mean distance is obtained for each planet. Then the earth's mean distance can be designated as Ed, Mars's as Md, and so on. These distances, of course, are all different; since Mars's path is outside the earth's, its mean distance is greater than the earth's, Jupiter's is still greater, and so on. Then $(Et)^2:(Ed)^3::(Mt)^2:(Md)^3$, and so on for each of the other planets, as the following table shows. Regardless of the enormous differences in actual distance and time for, say, Mercury and Jupiter, the *proportion* is the same.[r]

	Time in Earth Years	Distance in Earth Distance	t^2	d^3
MERCURY	.241	.387	.058	.058
VENUS	.615	.723	.378	.378
EARTH	1.000	1.000	1.000	1.000
MARS	1.881	1.524	3.538	3.538
JUPITER	11.862	5.203	140.70	140.83
SATURN	29.457	9.539	867.70	867.92

21 See pp. 99–100.

SIGNIFICANCE OF THE THREE LAWS

Kepler's three laws were an immense achievement. The two main steps on which they depend—(1) the framing of hypotheses and (2) the mathematization of the data that confirm or disconfirm them—provide useful corrections to the pure empiricism of Bacon's method. They are a great advance over his inductive tables.

But after all, Kepler's laws are merely three independent generalizations. They are not connected by any rationale; thus they cannot be *demonstrated*, that is, derived logically from the same basic principles. It is not unfair, therefore, to describe them, as some writers have done, as "empirical generalizations," on a par (except, of course, as regards generality) with our generalization about the velocity of falling bodies. It was in Galileo's work that the final element involved in scientific method first emerged—the rationale that makes it possible to organize a number of separate empirical truths into a deductive and demonstrative structure.

Galileo

Galileo (1564–1642), the son of a Florentine nobleman, was a little older than Kepler and almost an exact contemporary of Bacon. He died the year Newton was born. Though Galileo's interests ranged over the whole field of knowledge—he attained more than mere competence in music, drawing, and poetry, for instance—his central passion was the study of physical nature. As a child he showed a remarkable ability in constructing mechanical toys. And the story of his discovery of the "law of the pendulum" is often recounted. As a medical student, sitting one day in the cathedral at Pisa, he watched an attendant lighting a lamp suspended from the ceiling. In order to reach the lamp, the attendant had to draw it to one side; after it was released, it naturally swung back and forth in gradually reducing arcs until it once more hung perpendicularly from the ceiling.

All this had happened thousands of times, and it had been observed by thousands of young men, but without issue. It was characteristic of Galileo that he did not merely look; he also *counted*. And what he discovered when he counted (using his pulse beat in lieu of any other timepiece) was a pattern of regularity, a pattern that might never have become known had he not conceived of the idea of translating the qualitative succession into quantities. He found that, though the arcs traversed by the swinging lamp constantly diminished, the time intervals remained constant. Obviously, if one had a way of recording the number of swings the lamp made, one would have a reliable chronometer; thus the idea of the pendulum clock was born. But far more important than this technological application[22] was the attitude of mind that led to the discovery.

In 1589 Galileo was appointed to a professorship at Pisa, but the tactlessness with which he demonstrated the falsity of Aristotelian dogmas about motion, coupled with the painfully honest criticism he made of a royal personage's engineering project, caused him to lose his chair before his first term expired. He next secured an appointment at Padua, where, under the Venetian government, which jealously asserted its independence of papal authority, there was more intellectual freedom as well as a long tradition of empirical study.

THE SATELLITES OF JUPITER

In 1609 Galileo heard of a toy invented by a Dutchman—a toy that, by the use of lenses fitted in a tube, brought faraway objects near. Galileo knew enough optics to construct such an instrument for himself, and he could think of better things to do with it than to amuse himself and his employers. Galileo's account of his discoveries, published in a work called *The Sidereal Messenger*, caused a sensation, for his observations were much more dramatic than Copernicus' speculations.

> It would be altogether a waste of time to enumerate the number and importance of the benefits which this instrument may be expected to confer, when used by land or sea. But without paying attention to its use for terrestrial objects, I betook myself to observations of the heavenly bodies. . . .
>
> On the 7th day of January in the present year, 1610, . . . the planet Jupiter presented itself to my view, and . . . I noticed . . . that three little stars, small but very bright, were near the planet; and although I believed them to belong to the number of the fixed stars, yet they made me somewhat wonder, because they seemed to be arranged exactly in a straight line, parallel to the ecliptic, and to be brighter than the rest of the stars, equal to them in magnitude. The position of them with reference to one another and to Jupiter was as follows:
>
> ORI.   ★   ★   ○   ★   OCC.
>
> When on January 8th, led by some fatality, I turned again to look at the same part of the heavens, I found a very different state of things, for there were three little stars all west of Jupiter, and nearer together than on the previous night, and they were separated from one another by equal intervals, as the accompanying figure shows.
>
> ORI.   ○ ★ ★ ★   OCC.

22 Galileo did not get around to designing such a clock until late in life.

At this point, . . . my surprise began to be excited, how Jupiter could one day be found to the east of all the aforesaid fixed stars when the day before it had been west of two of them. . . . I therefore waited for the next night with the most intense longing, but I was disappointed of my hope, for the sky was covered with clouds in every direction.

But on January 10th the stars appeared in the following position with regard to Jupiter, the third, as I thought, being hidden by the planet. They

ORI.   ★ ★ ○   OCC.

were situated just as before, exactly in the same straight line with Jupiter, and along the Zodiac. . . .

On January 11th I saw an arrangement of the following kind:

ORI.   ★   ★   ○   OCC.

DEDUCTIONS *from the previous observations concerning the orbits and periods of* JUPITER'S SATELLITES

In the first place, since they are sometimes behind, sometimes before Jupiter, at like distances, and withdraw from this planet towards the east and towards the west only within very narrow limits of divergence, and since they accompany this planet alike when its motion is retrograde and direct, it can be a matter of doubt to no one that they perform their revolutions about this planet, while at the same time they all accomplish together orbits of twelve years' length about the centre of the world. . . . Moreover, it may be detected that the revolutions of the satellites which describe the smallest circles round Jupiter are the most rapid, for the satellites nearest to Jupiter are often to be seen in the east, when the day before they have appeared in the west, and contrawise. . . . Besides, we have a notable and splendid argument to remove the scruples of those who can tolerate the revolution of the planets round the Sun in the Copernican system, yet are so disturbed by the motion of one Moon about the Earth, while both accomplish an orbit of a year's length about the Sun, that they consider that this theory of the universe must be upset as impossible: for now we have not one planet only revolving about another, while both traverse a vast orbit about the Sun, but our sense of sight presents to us four[23] satellites circling about Jupiter, like the Moon about the Earth, while the whole system travels over a mighty orbit about the Sun in the space of twelve years.[s]

KEPLER'S REACTION TO GALILEO'S DISCOVERY

Kepler at once realized the importance of Galileo's discovery. He wrote enthusiastically to Galileo:

---

23 [On January 13 Galileo had observed a fourth satellite—AUTHOR.]

I immediately began to think how there could be any addition to the number of the planets without overturning my Cosmographic Mystery,[24] according to which Euclid's five regular solids do not allow more than six planets round the sun. . . . I am so far from disbelieving the existence of the four circumjovial planets, that I long for a telescope, to anticipate you, if possible, in discovering two round Mars, as the proportion seems to require, six or eight round Saturn, and perhaps one each round Mercury and Venus.[t]

It is instructive to contrast Kepler's reaction to Galileo's discovery with that of some of Galileo's colleagues at Padua. When invited by Galileo to look through the newly invented telescope and see for themselves the satellites of Jupiter, they refused. They *knew* that Jupiter could not have satellites; hence what Galileo reported that he saw could only be witchcraft or sleight of hand. After all, the whole universe demonstrated again and again the importance that God had assigned to the number seven. It was therefore sacrilegious and against all reason to suppose that there could be more than seven heavenly bodies.

There are seven windows given to animals in the domicile of the head. . . . From this and many other similarities in nature, such as the seven metals, etc., which it were tedious to enumerate, we gather that the number of planets is necessarily seven. Moreover these [alleged] satellites of Jupiter are invisible to the naked eye, and therefore can exercise no influence on the earth, and therefore would be useless, and therefore do not exist. Besides, [from the earliest times, men] have adopted the division of the week into seven days, and have named them after the seven planets. Now, if we increase the number of the planets, this whole and beautiful system falls to the ground.[u]

But because Kepler was imbued with what has here been called the empirical spirit, he took for granted that one has to accept the facts. The facts, that is, whatever has been empirically ascertained, are the starting point; one has to respect them and go on from there, constructing hypotheses that (hopefully) fit the facts, not rejecting those facts that disconcertingly disconfirm prized theories. The professors at Padua ignored the facts because the facts seemed neither as certain nor as important as deductions derived from the theological premises of the Christian religion. They could make this choice because they lived in an intellectual world in which the primary fact about things was not simply that they *are*, but rather that they symbolize those sacerdotal meanings that were the fundamental realities of the religious man's experience.

Another point to observe is that because Kepler's theory was based on *number*, it was flexible. If one formula would not do, he could try another. In his letter one sees Kepler's mind leaping ahead to another possibility—the number of satellites may vary with the order of the planets' positions in relation

24 [See p. 95—AUTHOR.]

to the sun. But, by contrast, a theory based on numerology is incapable of modification. If seven has some magical virtue, obviously it cannot be abandoned.

THE CHURCH'S REACTION TO GALILEO'S DISCOVERY

The Sidereal Messenger naturally caused great alarm in the conservative camp. Though many enlightened ecclesiastics, some in very high places, supported the new views, the dangers to which the Church had been exposed in the preceding century, and the general hardening of doctrine that had occurred as a result, had produced a very different situation from that in which Copernicus had launched his speculations. Moreover, Galileo's attitude was quite different from Copernicus': Instead of humbly awaiting the Church's verdict, Galileo campaigned vigorously for the new view, even making a trip to Rome (in 1615) to argue with the theologians. The result was what a less optimistic mind would have expected. Instead of winning the Church over, he merely consolidated the opposition. The new view was condemned as "absurd in philosophy and formally heretical, because expressly contrary to Holy Scripture," Copernicus' book was suspended until it could be "corrected," and teaching the new theory was strictly forbidden unless the teacher stated clearly that he was presenting a piece of speculation that was untrue in fact.

On this occasion Galileo himself seems to have been let off with a severe warning, but in 1632, after the publication of his *Dialogue on the Two Principal Systems of the World*,[25] he was haled before the Inquisition for the second time, interrogated under threat of torture,[26] and required to abjure on his knees "the false doctrine that the sun is the central point of the universe and that the earth is in motion." The popular legend that, as he rose from his knees, he whispered to a friendly cleric, "But it *does* move!" has no basis in fact. Galileo was seventy, broken in health and in spirit, and not disposed to jest in so dangerous a situation. He has sometimes been unfavorably compared with Socrates, who was likewise an old man when he refused to compromise his convictions in order to save his skin. Since the only men who have a right to criticize Galileo are those who are sure that, in the same position, they would choose as Socrates did, we may dispense with moral appraisals of Galileo's conduct. Let us note instead that, had Socrates been a Galileo, Plato would not have been inspired to write the *Apology*, the *Phaedo*, the *Crito*, or, probably, any other of his dialogues, and, similarly, had Galileo been a Socrates, he would not have lived to write one

25 Galileo tried to protect himself by stating that he was not advocating the heretical views described in this work. But there was no doubt as to where his sympathies lay, especially since he assigned the defense of the traditional view to one Simplicio, whose name was an ironical reference to the author's opinion of the view in question.

26 There is no evidence that Galileo was physically tortured, but the reader must judge for himself whether the line between the actual pain of the rack and the mental and moral anguish of months of threats and interrogations is not rather finely drawn.

of the most important contributions to the development of the new science—the *Dialogues Concerning Two New Sciences.*

DIALOGUES CONCERNING TWO NEW SCIENCES

This monumental work, composed during Galileo's old age,[27] when he was in what would now be called "protective custody," analyzed certain ranges of the behavior of bodies on the earth—(1) resistance to fracture, (2) causes of cohesion, (3) uniform motion, (4) naturally accelerated motion, and (5) violent motions. The fundamental thesis was that, just as there is a simple pattern underlying the motion of the planets (as Copernicus and Kepler had found), so there is a pattern of uniformity in various phases of local motion here on the earth.

Galileo began his *Dialogues* by contrasting the ingenuity of skilled mechanics with their inability to explain why their rule-of-thumb methods are so successful. The significant point here is that Galileo believed that an explanation is possible—that is, that a rationale underlies the regularities discovered by empirical observation.

> SALVIATI.[28] The constant activity which you Venetians display in your famous arsenal suggests to the studious mind a large field for investigation, especially that part of the work which involves mechanics; for in this department all types of instruments and machines are constantly being constructed by many artisans. . . .
>
> SAGREDO. You are quite right. . . . At times also I have been put to confusion and driven to despair of ever explaining something for which I could not account, but which my senses told me to be true. [The] current opinion [among these mechanics is that] one cannot argue from the small to the large, because many devices which succeed on a small scale do not work on a large scale. [But] since mechanics has its foundation in geometry, where mere size cuts no figure, I do not see that the properties of circles, triangles, cylinders, cones and other solid figures will change with their size. . . .
>
> SALVIATI. Imperfections in the material . . . are not sufficient to explain the deviations observed between machines in the concrete and in the abstract. . . . The mere fact that it is matter makes the larger machine, built of the same material and in the same proportion as the smaller, correspond with exactness to the smaller in every respect except that it will not be so strong or so resistant against violent treatment; the larger the machine, the greater its weakness. Since I assume matter to be unchangeable and always the same, it is clear that we are no less able to treat this constant and invariable property in a rigid manner than if it belonged to simple and

---

27 In order to get the *Dialogues* published, Galileo had to send them to the Netherlands and to pretend that they were printed without his knowledge.

28 [The characters in this dialogue—Salviati, Sagredo, and Simplicio—are the same as those in the earlier *Dialogue on the Two Principal Systems of the World*—AUTHOR.]

> pure mathematics. . . . We can demonstrate by geometry that the large
> machine is not proportionately stronger than the small. . . .
>   SAGREDO. I am quite convinced of the facts of the case, but I do not
> understand why the strength and resistance are not multiplied in the same
> proportion as the material. . . .
>   SALVIATI. I wish to convince you by demonstrative reasoning rather than
> to persuade you by mere probabilities.[v]

We shall have to pass over the detailed analysis of fracture and cohesion
in order to concentrate on the discussion of uniform and naturally accelerated
motions. But it is clear enough from the passage just quoted that the *general*
assumption of a rationale underlying the behavior of bodies has become a *specific*
assumption that this rationale is *geometric* in character. Now, geometry is a
deductive science, a system of theorems logically derivable from the axioms
and definitions that are its starting point. That is to say, Galileo held that, since
there is a correspondence between the geometric axioms and empirically obser-.
vable properties of moving bodies, the theorems deduced from these axioms
apply to the empirical facts of motion. This means that physics can be an exact
science: There is an explanation, geometrical in character, of the regularities
observed and used by the ingenious artisans in the Venetian arsenal.

> My purpose is to set forth a very new science dealing with a very ancient
> subject. There is, in nature, perhaps nothing older than motion, concerning
> which the books written by philosophers are neither few nor small; neverthe-
> less I have discovered by experiment some properties of it which are worth
> knowing and which have not hitherto been either observed or demonstrated.
> Some superficial observations have been made, as, for instance, that the free
> motion of a heavy falling body is continuously accelerated; but to just what
> extent this acceleration occurs has not yet been announced; for so far as
> I know, no one has yet pointed out that the distances traversed, during equal
> intervals of time, by a body falling from rest, stand to one another in the
> same ratio as the odd numbers beginning with unity. . . .
>   But this and other facts . . . I have succeeded in proving; and what I
> consider more important, there have been opened up to this vast and most
> excellent science, of which my work is merely the beginning, ways and means
> by which other minds more acute than mine will explore its remote corners.[w]

In this passage we should not fail to note the (in this case, at any rate,
well-merited) sense of novelty and achievement—the *leitmotif*, as it were, of the
century; nor should we overlook the key words here, "observe and demonstrate."

THE GEOMETRICAL REPRESENTATION OF MOTION

Leaving for a moment the question of observation, let us see what is involved
in the "demonstration by geometry" of the properties of moving bodies. To

Galileo, this meant the application of geometrical theorems in the determination of the laws of motion. Before this is possible, it is necessary to *represent* motion geometrically; that is, we must find geometrical correlates for the physical properties that interest us. Now, the possibility of representing motion geometrically could occur only to someone accustomed to thinking of the empirical facts quantitatively. As long as one merely observes moving bodies (no matter how carefully), one will never see any correspondence between moving bodies and those relations with which geometry is concerned. But if one is prepared to ignore the material the moving objects are made of; if one is prepared to ignore whether they are handsome or ugly, shining or dull; if, in short, one is prepared to ignore everything about the empirically observed motion except its velocity, one can arrive at properties that lend themselves to geometrical representation. And because such properties are capable of geometrical representation, the application of geometrical theorems to the behavior of physical things becomes possible.

The advantages of demonstration are evident in the following example. If you drive a car at 60 miles per hour for ten hours, how far will you have traveled? Everyone knows ("intuitively," as some would say) how to work this out: Multiply time by velocity (10 × 60) to obtain the total number of miles. But not everyone can demonstrate this, that is, prove it—and prove it not merely empirically (by taking the car out and driving it for ten hours at 60 miles per hour) but in the general form, $d = vt$. In a word, to use the terminology of Galileo's *Dialogues*, there is a difference between "explaining something" and merely using it as a rule of thumb "of which one cannot give an account." Accordingly, let us see how a geometrical representation of motion makes it possible to explain, that is, to demonstrate, some of the "properties" of motion, such as the fact that distance equals velocity multiplied by time.

As regards a geometrical representation of time, it is easy to represent time by a line with direction, say, the line *AB*, on which we can mark off equal units of time—a unit of length representing a unit of time.

A similar procedure can be used for velocity and units of velocity. Combining these lines, we get the following:

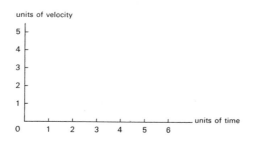

Then, if a body moves for four time units (say, minutes) at a uniform velocity of three units (say, miles per hour), we can indicate the distance it has covered in the following way:

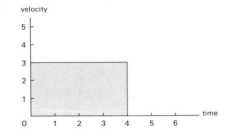

Because the distance through which the body has moved is representable as a rectangle, any geometrical theorem that is true of rectangles will be true of uniform motion. For instance, the area of a rectangle is obtained by multiplying the lengths of two adjacent sides. But here the area of the rectangle represents the distance, and the sides represent the time and the velocity. Hence, $d = vt$.

Or again, suppose that, instead of traveling at a uniform velocity, a body travels with a constantly increasing velocity. The car that traveled at 60 m.p.h. for ten hours had to begin from rest (0 m.p.h.) and take some time (however short) to reach 60 m.p.h. It was at *this* point that we began to consider its motion analytically in our previous example. Is a similar analysis possible for the stage of accelerated motion? Let us suppose that we are dealing with uniform acceleration. Of course, we are not, for no driver, however evenly he applies the accelerator pedal, makes an absolutely smooth start. But this assumption only corresponds to the assumption, made in the first case, of uniform velocity.

How, then, can uniform acceleration be represented? At time 0 the velocity is 0 (the body is at rest); at time 1 (taking the time interval to be as short or as long as one likes) the body has attained a certain velocity 1 (however much or little one likes). Since the acceleration is constant, at the end of another time interval equal to the first, the velocity will be twice the velocity at the end of the first time interval, or at time 2 the body will have 2 units of the original velocity. At time 3, it will have 3 units, and so on. Hence we get the following relationships on our velocity-time coordinate system:

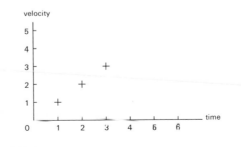

Obviously, since we can take the time intervals to be as small as we like (for we have supposed a uniformly accelerating motion), the diagram of the body's velocity is a straight line, and the distance it travels during any time *t* is a triangle.

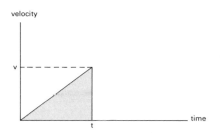

This triangle is one-half of the rectangle *vt*, or the distance the body would have traveled had it proceeded at a *uniform* velocity *v* for time *t*. It follows that the distance a body travels at a *constantly accelerating* velocity during any time interval is equal to one-half of the distance it would have traveled during that same time interval had it traveled at a uniform velocity equal to the maximum velocity attained; or, more succinctly, $d = vt/2$, where v = maximum velocity and t = time from rest.

This method of reasoning is clearly very different from the syllogistic type of reasoning that underlay medieval science, the type of reasoning that, as we have seen, Bacon assumed would continue to be used. Syllogistic reasoning proceeds by determining relations of *class inclusion* or *class exclusion*. For instance:

> All those who enter here are thoughtful and eager.
> All students of this college enter here.
> _____
> Therefore: All students of this college are thoughtful and eager.
>   No thoughtful, eager student fails a course.
> _____
>   Therefore: No student of this college fails a course.

And so on.

The relations asserted in these syllogisms are quite different from those asserted in the geometric reasoning that Galileo used: The velocity of a falling body, for instance, is not included in, or excluded from, the class "time." Ratio, which is the kind of relation Galileo was establishing, is not a relationship between classes and subclasses. Hence it can be said that, while the empirical spirit was reforming the notion of relevance, the mathematical spirit was expanding the notion of validity. The result was a new method capable, or so it seemed to its first users, of disclosing all the secrets of nature.

EXPOSITION OF UNIFORMLY ACCELERATED MOTION

Enough has now been said by way of introduction. Let us proceed to Galileo's own exposition of uniformly accelerated motion:

> *Definition.* A motion is said to be equally or uniformly accelerated when, starting from rest, its momentum receives equal increments in equal times.

Sagredo at once objected:

> Although I can offer no rational objection to this or indeed to any other definition, devised by any author whomsoever, since all definitions are arbitrary, I may nevertheless without offense be allowed to doubt whether such a definition as the above, established in an abstract manner, corresponds to and describes that kind of accelerated motion which we meet in nature in the case of freely falling bodies.[x]

To this, Galileo replied in effect that the best test of the relevance of any hypothesis is to deduce some theorems and check them against the facts. He clearly saw that one advantage of the new method, as compared with Scholasticism, was that it contained a built-in procedure for rejecting hypotheses that fail to "correspond to and describe" the facts.

One more possible misunderstanding had to be cleared up. Galileo pointed out that he was describing the behavior of moving bodies, not discussing the possible causes of the motions:

> At present it is the purpose of our Author merely to investigate and to demonstrate some of the properties of accelerated motion (whatever the cause of this acceleration may be)—meaning thereby a motion, such that the momentum of its velocity goes on increasing after departure from rest.[y]

Galileo's point was that he was concerned not with the *why* but with the *how*. The rationale he was seeking was not a "reason," in the sense of some purpose, or end, that the motion was fulfilling; nor was it a "cause," in the sense of some earlier occurrence that brought about the motion in question. The rationale was simply a description of the motion itself—a description that consisted in certain theorems deduced from a set of axioms. But he believed that the axioms referred to a real state of affairs and that he could show that the theorems also applied to that state of affairs.

Having settled these preliminaries, Galileo proceeded to demonstrate a series of propositions of ever increasing complexity. As an illustration of his method, the proof of one of the simplest is cited here.

> *Theorem II, Proposition II*
>
> The spaces described by a body falling from rest with a uniformly accelerated motion are to each

other as the squares of the time-intervals employed in traversing these distances.

Let the time beginning with any instant A be represented by the straight line AB in which are taken any two time-intervals AD and AE. Let HI represent the distance through which the body, starting from rest at H, falls with uniform acceleration. If HL represents the space traversed during the time-interval AD, and HM that covered during the interval AE, then the space MH stands to the space LH in a ratio which is the square of the ratio of the time AE to the time AD; or we may say simply that the distances HM and HL are related as the squares of AE and AD.

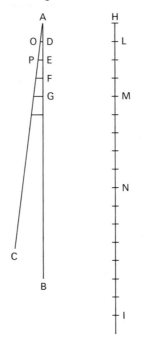

Draw the line AC making any angle whatever with the line AB; and from the points D and E, draw the parallel lines DO and EP; of these two lines, DO represents the greatest velocity attained during the interval AD, while EP represents the maximum velocity acquired during the interval AE. But it has just been proved that so far as distances traversed are concerned it is precisely the same whether a body falls from rest with a uniform acceleration or whether it falls during an equal time-interval with a constant speed which is one-half the maximum speed attained during the accelerated motion. It follows therefore that the distances HM and HL are the same as would be traversed, during the time-intervals AE and AD, by uniform velocities equal to one-half those represented by DO and EP respectively. If, therefore, one can show that the distances HM and HL are in the same ratio as the squares of the time-intervals AE and AD, our proposition will be proven.

But in the fourth proposition of the first book . . . it has been shown that the spaces traversed by two particles in uniform motion bear to one another a ratio which is equal to the product of the ratio of the velocities by the ratio of the times. But in this case the ratio of the velocities is the same as the ratio of the time-intervals (for the ratio of AE to AD is the same as that of $\frac{1}{2}$ EP to $\frac{1}{2}$ DO or of EP to DO). Hence the ratio of the spaces traversed is the same as the squared ratio of the time-intervals.

Q.E.D.

Evidently then the ratio of the distances is the square of the ratio of the final velocities, that is, of the lines EP and DO, since these are to each other as AE to AD.

Corollary I

Hence it is clear that if we take any equal intervals of time whatever, counting from the beginning of the motion, such as AD, DE, EF, FG, in which the spaces HL, LM, MN, NI are traversed, these spaces will bear to one another the same ratio as the series of odd numbers, 1, 3, 5, 7; for this is the ratio of the differences of the squares of the lines [which represent time], differences which exceed one another by equal amounts, this excess being equal to the smallest line [namely, the one representing a single time-interval]: or we may say [that this is the ratio] of the differences of the squares of the natural numbers beginning with unity.

While, therefore, during equal intervals of time the velocities increase as the natural numbers, the increments in the distances traversed during these equal time-intervals are to one another as the odd numbers beginning with unity.ᶻ

Since this yields results identical to those obtained by calculating rates of fall,[29] it may be asked why Galileo did not proceed in the latter way (that is, arithmetically, instead of geometrically). Why did he not simply measure some distances, rates of fall, and so forth, and then generalize? Not only would this have been easier, but it would have given him actual velocities, times, and distances, instead of ratios. The answer is that he proceeded the only way he could. It is easy to talk glibly about "measuring the velocity of a freely falling body," but actual measurement requires far more elaborate apparatus than Galileo possessed.

This is why Galileo had to content himself with the hypothesis that distance is proportional to the square of the time. But how, if he lacked facilities for measurement, could he check this hypothesis against the facts, as he so emphatically held that it is necessary to do? How could he show that the hypothesis, however logically watertight it might be, was relevant?

29 See pp. 88–89.

THE PROBLEM OF EMPIRICAL VERIFICATION

Empirical verification is a problem because one can seldom simply read off the results one wants. It is necessary first to construct a situation in which it is possible to observe whatever it is that one needs to observe in order to verify (or disverify) the hypothesis. Galileo believed that, providing he made a single assumption, he could construct an experimental situation in which, even with the instruments available to him, the ratios deduced in accordance with the theory could be checked against the facts. It is instructive to see how scrupulous he was in stating this assumption. We should also observe how impossible the experimental stage would have been without a guiding hypothesis furnished by logical analysis. If Galileo had not already had an hypothesis that he wanted to check, it would never have occurred to him to set up his inclined plane and roll balls down it. And even if, in the course of pursuing Bacon's recommendation to collect every possible instance, it *had* occurred to him to carry out this particular experiment, it would have meant nothing, for it would have been merely one of thousands of instances of motion. Before the movement of the ball down the inclined plane could be significant, Galileo had to know what he was looking for. This suggests that one of the differences between mere observation and experiment is that in the latter we observe only after we have constructed a situation with a particular hypothesis in mind.

In the present case, the hypothesis is (1) that there is a regularity in the motion of freely falling bodies and (2) that this regularity consists in a certain proportion between the distance fallen through and the duration of the fall. If it is assumed that the motion of a body rolling down an inclined plane conforms to the same *pattern* as the motion of a body falling freely through space, there is a way of checking the deductive system. For it is easy (by taking a sufficiently gentle incline) to get a movement sufficiently slow to permit measurement with even the crude instruments available to Galileo, and so to determine, not *what* the velocity of a freely falling body is, but whether the distance fallen through is proportional to the square of the time.

But is the assumption (that is, that the relation between distance and time is the same whether the body rolls down an incline or falls freely) true? Galileo thought it possible to show that this assumption is reasonable. If the relation is the same, it is clear that the *terminal* velocity from a given height will not vary with the angle of fall. That is, though the *time* required to roll down a gentle slope is longer than the time required to roll down a steep one, the *velocity* acquired at the end of the fall will be the same in both cases. Hence, if it could be shown that the terminal velocities are the same in all cases, this would support the basic assumption (of identity of pattern) underlying the experimental proof.

Accordingly, Galileo set out to show experimentally that "the speeds acquired by one and the same body moving down planes of different inclination are equal when the heights of the planes are equal."

Imagine this page to represent a vertical wall, with a nail driven into it; and from the nail let there be suspended a lead bullet of one or two ounces by means of a fine vertical thread, *AB*, say from four to six feet long; on this wall draw a horizontal line *DC*, at right angles to the vertical thread *AB*, which hangs about two finger-breadths in front of the wall. Now bring the thread *AB* with the attached ball into the position *AC* and set it free; first it will be observed to descend along the arc *CBD*, to pass the point *B*, and to travel along the arc *BD*, till it almost reaches the horizontal *CD*, a slight shortage being caused by the resistance of the air and the string; from this we may rightly infer that the ball in its descent through the arc *CB* acquired a momentum on reaching *B*, which was just sufficient to carry it through a similar arc *BD* to the same height. Having repeated this experiment many times, let us now drive a nail into the wall close to the perpendicular *AB*, say at *E* or *F*, so that it projects out some five or six finger-breadths in order that the thread, again carrying the bullet through the arc *CB*, may strike upon the nail *E* when the bullet reaches *B*, and thus compel it to traverse the arc *BG*, described about *E* as center. From this we can see what can be done by the same momentum which previously starting at the same point *B* carried the same body through the arc *BD* to the horizontal *CD*. Now, gentlemen, you will observe with pleasure that the ball swings to the point *G* in the horizontal, and you would see the same thing happen if the obstacle were placed at some lower point, say at *F*, about which the ball would describe the arc *BI*, the rise of the ball always terminating exactly on the line *CD*. But when the nail is placed so low that the remainder of the thread below it will not reach to the height *CD* (which would happen if the nail were placed nearer *B* than to the intersection of *AB* with the horizontal *CD*) then the thread leaps over the nail and twists itself about it.

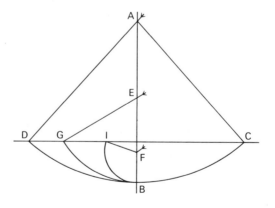

This experiment leaves no room for doubt as to the truth of our supposition; for since the two arcs *CB* and *DB* are equal and similarly placed, the momentum acquired by the fall through the arc *CB* is the same as that gained by fall through the arc *DB*; but the momentum acquired at *B*, owing to fall through *CB*, is able to lift the same body through the arc *BD;* therefore, the momentum acquired in the fall *BD* is equal to that which lifts the same body through the same arc from *B* to *D;* so, in general, every momentum acquired by fall through an arc is equal to that which can lift the same body through the same arc. But all these momenta which cause a rise through the arcs *BD*, *BG*, and *BI* are equal, since they are produced by the same momentum, gained by fall through *CB*, as experiment shows. Therefore all the momenta gained by fall through the arcs *DB*, *GB*, *IB* are equal.[a]

Since the momentum acquired in all these cases is the same, and since what determines it is the height from which the object falls, it seems "reasonable" (as Sagredo said) to conclude that the *terminal* velocity is not affected by the incline of the plane—providing, of course, that we eliminate "outside resistances" by making the planes "hard and smooth" and the "figure of the moving body perfectly round."

In the following experiment, Galileo tried to meet these conditions.

SALVIATI. A piece of wooden moulding or scantling, about 12 cubits long, half a cubit wide, and three finger-breadths thick, was taken; on its edge was cut a channel a little more than one finger in breadth; having made this groove very straight, smooth, and polished, and having lined it with parchment, also as smooth and polished as possible, we rolled along it a hard, smooth, and very round bronze ball. Having placed this board in a sloping position, by lifting one end some one or two cubits above the other, we rolled the ball, as I was just saying, along the channel, noting, in a manner presently to be described, the time required to make the descent. We repeated this experiment more than once in order to measure the time with an accuracy such that the deviation between two observations never exceeded one-tenth of a pulse-beat. Having performed this operation and having assured ourselves of its reliability, we now rolled the ball only one-quarter the length of the channel; and having measured the time of its descent, we found it precisely one-half of the former. Next we tried other distances, comparing the time for the whole length with that for the half, or with that for two-thirds, or three-fourths, or indeed for any fraction; in such experiments, repeated a full hundred times, we always found that the spaces traversed were to each other as the squares of the times, and this was true for all inclinations of the plane, i.e., of the channel, along which we rolled the ball. We also observed that the times of descent, for various inclinations of the plane, bore to one another precisely that ratio which, as we shall see later, the Author had predicted and demonstrated for them.

For the measurement of time, we employed a large vessel of water placed in an elevated position; to the bottom of this vessel was soldered a pipe of small diameter giving a thin jet of water, which we collected in a small glass during the time of each descent, whether for the whole length of the channel or for a part of its length; the water thus collected was weighed, after each descent, on a very accurate balance; the differences and ratios of these weights gave us the differences and ratios of the times, and this with such accuracy that although the operation was repeated many, many times, there was no appreciable discrepancy in the results.

SIMPLICIO. I would like to have been present at these experiments; but feeling confidence in the care with which you performed them, and in the fidelity with which you relate them, I am satisfied and accept them as true and valid.[b]

The New Science and the New Philosophy

When Galileo died in 1642 the Western world differed radically from the world Thomas had known, and the outlines of modern culture were already plainly drawn. The national territorial state and the capitalistic type of economy had long since emerged; the colonization of America was beginning on a large scale; the old conception of a single unified Christendom was shattered. The new-model man who at once fashioned this new culture and was fashioned by it was an enterprising personality—a man "on the make." As a result of the loosening of the old social structure, he had become an individualist, alert to the possibilities for self-improvement. "Self-improvement" he might understand in many ways—as a closer union with a personal savior through faith in Jesus, as a revival of the Greek ideal of all-round development, or, simply, as the acquisition of power and wealth. But however he looked at it, this new man had a sense of standing on the threshold of a new age. His sense of what he had already achieved made him proud; his sense of what he had still to do made him serious; his sense of what he believed he had in him to accomplish made him optimistic.

THE EFFECT OF SCIENTIFIC METHOD ON THE NEW PHILOSOPHY

It is obvious that the metaphysical system that had satisfied the Middle Ages would not satisfy this new man, and that both the questions Scholastic philosophy had asked and the answers it had found would now seem trivial or meaningless. Indeed, at first sight it may appear surprising that philosophical thought did not respond more rapidly to the immense cultural changes that were occurring. Criticism of the past, as we have seen, appeared early and was vociferous. But attacks on Scholasticism do not constitute a new philosophy. Nor could the not very original formulations of the Humanists or the religious quarrels of the theologians be properly described as a new philosophy. These were rather raw materials that would have to be incorporated, along with other cultural novelties, into any new synthesis that might eventually be worked out.

It is highly suggestive, therefore, that as soon as the new scientific method was formulated, metaphysical speculation began again on a great scale. The new science acted as a stimulus to philosophy because the new ideal of knowledge entailed a new conception of reality, a new metaphysics; and this novel conception of the nature of things was at once seen to be the pivot around which a new synthesis would emerge.

SCIENTIFIC CONCEPT OF REALITY

What was the reality that physics disclosed? To the early modern scientists and philosophers the answer seemed obvious. The new physics, they supposed, revealed that physical reality consists of matter in motion. "Matter" was the name they gave to what the physicists measured; it was extended, that is, it occupied space, and it moved about from one part of space to another. Its dimensions, its weight, and its velocity were what were measured in physics, and the result of these measurements showed that its behavior conformed to simple mathematical "laws." For the qualitative and teleological conception of nature with which men of the Middle Ages had operated, there was thus substituted a quantitative and mechanical one.

But what about God and the precious human soul that God had made in His image? How are these entities related to the material universe? How, for instance, can we men be responsible for our actions if all that happens in the physical world (which of course includes our bodies) is completely determined in accordance with the mechanistic laws of motion discovered by the new physics? In such a universe it would seem impossible either for the soul to direct the body or for God Himself to exercise providential care.

And what about the sensuous world of colors, smells, tastes, and sounds, the world that ordinary men—and even physicists and philosophers of science— experience? If reality is identified with what is capable of analysis by means of the new scientific method, if reality consists of matter in motion, it follows that colors, smells, tastes, and sounds are not real. What, then, are they? The answer that suggested itself to the early modern metaphysicians was that they are merely "appearances" that arise in our minds when quantitatively describable stimuli affect our sense organs and, via the nervous system, our brains. Objects outside us are not red and not sweet; nor are our sense organs. Red and sweet are the subjective effects in our conscious minds of colorless, tasteless bits of extended matter. The "objective" qualities of material things (those qualities really located in the objects) are exclusively the quantitative characteristics of position, shape, size, mass, and velocity—that is, the characteristics with which the new physics could deal.

This distinction between objectively real characteristics and those held to be only subjective appearances was stated with great clarity by Galileo:

> I feel myself impelled by the necessity, as soon as I conceive a piece of matter or corporal substance, of conceiving that in its own nature it is bounded and figured in such and such a figure, that in relation to others it is large or small, that it is in this or that place, in this or that time, that it is in motion or remains at rest, . . . that it is single, few or many; in short

by no imagination can a body be separated from such conditions: but that it must be white or red, bitter or sweet, sounding or mute, of a pleasant or unpleasant odour, I do not perceive my mind forced to acknowledge it necessarily accompanied by such conditions; so if the senses are not the escorts, perhaps the reason or the imagination by itself would never have arrived at them. Hence I think that these tastes, odours, colours, etc., on the side of the object in which they seem to exist, are nothing else but mere names, but hold their residence solely in the sensitive body; so that if the animal were removed, every such quality would be abolished and annihilated.[c]

It will be seen that this distinction between objective physical properties and subjective appearances interprets a valuational distinction (quantitative knowledge is "better," "more precise," "more useful," than qualitative knowledge) as an ontological one ("reality" contrasted with "appearances").

It is easy to understand why the early modern metaphysicians made this assumption. Beginning with Plato, there was ample precedent for identifying "higher" (valuational scale) with "more real" (ontological scale). Further, Scholastics like Thomas had made this identification a cornerstone of their philosophy and had "proved" it by elaborate arguments. Indeed, it had become so embedded in the thought of the West that to the new philosophers it must have seemed a part of the "nature of things." Therefore it never occurred to them that they were incorporating into their new metaphysics the vestigial remains of an older way of thought.

Moreover, and apart from this metaphysical survival, another line of thought with which the early modern thinkers were well acquainted led to the same conclusion. It was natural for these thinkers to feel a certain kinship with Democritus;[30] though he had overlooked the crucial importance of mathematization, he *had* held that it is the essence of reality to be extended and to move in space. All that was needed to bring Democritus up to date was to measure the quantitative real that his scheme provided. Hence it was plausible to look in Democritus for a clue about how to deal with the qualitative sense world; when one looked, one found that he relegated it to "appearance," to the subjective world of mind.

Thus everything in the existing climate of opinion pointed inevitably toward an interpretation of the distinction between qualities and quantities in ontological terms, as a distinction between appearance and reality.

These were a few of the problems that confronted the early modern philosophers. As has been noted, most of these thinkers sought to solve them by one version or another of dualism. That is, they tried to provide a sphere, a domain, of immaterial reality outside and beyond the material reality that (as they held)

---

30 So, Bacon, for instance: "The school of Democritus went further into nature than the rest"— *Novum Organum*, I, 51.

the new physics was rapidly exploring. In this sphere they proposed to locate God and the human soul. But at least one of these philosophers adopted a different course: Hobbes was a monist; he rejected the notion of immaterial reality. Whatever in the traditional account of religion and ethics could not be reinterpreted in materialistic terms was relegated by Hobbes to "appearance," that is, to one's subjective experience of one's own brain states, in exactly the way in which the sense world—colors, smells, tastes, and sounds—had been relegated to appearance. If experiences of values are as dependent on physiological states as are experiences of colors and smells, it follows that any comparison of values, except in terms of private preferences, is impossible. Just as the red that I see is *my* red and the red that you see is *your* red (because in each case the experienced red is conditioned on each individual's retina, optic nerve, and cortex), so my value experiences are mine and yours are yours. If values exist only in the experience of different individuals, there is no public realm of value. It seems to follow, then, that objective values—not to mention objective truths and an objectively existing God—cannot be reconciled with materialism.

For these reasons an examination of Hobbes's theories makes a good starting point for our study of modern philosophy. When we see the radical consequences that his monistic theory entailed for religion and for ethics, and when we see how deeply entangled it became in difficulties over the status of "appearance," we will be able to understand better why other philosophers made the move to dualism and why they clung to it despite all the paradoxes it involved.

CHAPTER 4

Hobbes

Life

Thomas Hobbes (1588–1679) was educated at Oxford, where he went through
the regular course of Scholastic logic still in vogue there. Though he found this
irksome and was later to say harsh things about university education, and Oxford
in particular, he did well enough to be recommended as a tutor for the young
son of the head of the great Cavendish family. Hobbes became the young lord's
"page and rode a hunting and a hawking with him and kept his privy purse."
But such aristocratic activities did not keep him from his studies. When they
were in town, he read in the lobby "while his lord was making visits." Hobbes
spent almost the whole of his long life with the Cavendishes, seeing successive
generations through their grand tours and becoming a friend and adviser to

them as they grew older. This position gave him leisure for thought and reflection; and through the Cavendishes, he made the acquaintance at one time or another of most of the leading thinkers in England and on the Continent.

As a young man he knew Francis Bacon and assisted the great Lord Chancellor in translating several of his essays into Latin. Bacon liked to converse with him, and it is pleasant to read that "his Lordship [who] was a very contemplative person . . . was wont to contemplate in his delicious walks at Gorhambury and to dictate . . . to his gentlemen that attended him with ink and paper ready to set down presently his thoughts. His Lordship would often say that he better liked Mr. Hobbes's taking his thoughts than any of the others, because he understood what he wrote."[1]

During this period Hobbes was, however, more interested in literary studies than in philosophy. It was not until he was forty that he was introduced to the charms of mathematical certainty. According to Aubrey,

> Being in a gentleman's library, Euclid's *Elements* lay open, and 'twas the 47th [theorem of Book I]. He read the proposition. "By God," said he, "this is impossible. . . ." So he reads the demonstration of it which referred him back to such a proposition: which proposition he read. That referred him back to another, which he also read. [And so back to the self-evident axioms, when] at last he was demonstratively convinced of that truth. This made him in love with geometry.[a]

Just how early he became acquainted with Galileo's writings on physics is not known, but it was certainly before 1633, when he was trying to get a copy of the newly published *Dialogues*. In any event, about this time it dawned on him that all changes are changes in motion, and he saw the possibility of constructing a systematic philosophy on this basis.

While Hobbes's intellectual development was proceeding apace, the political situation in England was worsening, and so we come to the second major influence on his thought—the Civil War.[2] Hobbes had no sympathy with Parliament's struggle against the Crown's invasion of "ancient rights," nor with the religious sentiments of the Puritans. His diagnosis of the cause of the constitutional crisis was simple: The political and religious freedoms about which the Parliamentarians and the Puritans shouted were merely so many disguises by which they cloaked their own selfish interests. The Parliamentarians, for instance, were not in the least concerned with "liberty and justice" for the people, but with getting a grip on the supreme power, which they would then use to further

1 Aubrey, to whom we are indebted for this story, presumably got it from the modest Hobbes.
2 The Civil War, which broke out in 1642, had its roots in long-standing dissatisfaction, reaching back into the preceding reign, with the Crown's attempt to rule dictatorially and with its religious policy. Several years of fighting won Parliament a victory, and Charles I was executed in 1649. After a period of confusion, Oliver Cromwell established a strong personal government that survived until his death. Eighteen months later, in 1660, the monarchy was revived under Charles II.

the interests of their own group. If the Crown had acted prudently, it could have prevented the situation from coming to a head; having allowed the divisive elements in society to get out of hand, the Crown's position (Hobbes must soon have seen) was hopeless. The solution, he concluded, lay in waiting as patiently as possible until, out of the conflict that ensued, some new power, strong enough to impose its will on all the others, emerged.

In moving to France well before the Civil War broke out, Hobbes was only acting on Hobbesian principles of enlightened self-interest. What he saw as he watched the struggle only confirmed him, we may be sure, in his conviction that the inhumanity of man to man made an all-powerful government essential.

In Paris, Hobbes was briefly mathematical tutor to the Prince of Wales, the future Charles II. But the publication of *Leviathan* in 1651 made his position at the exiled English court intolerable, it being alleged that this "father of atheists" was poisoning the mind of his royal pupil. Nor were Hobbes's attacks on religion any more palatable to Catholic France, which had the power—as the exiled Anglican bishops did not—to hurt him. Accordingly, Hobbes returned home, where there was much in Cromwell's authoritarian government of which he could approve, though basically he and the pious, God-fearing men currently in power had little in common.

Hobbes wisely kept aloof from politics during the closing years of the Protectorate, and after the Restoration Charles remembered his erstwhile tutor affectionately and treated him generously. To his great enjoyment, he was able to spend his last years engaging in controversy on a variety of subjects, ranging from free will to circle-squaring.

Philosophy: Its Method and Scope

Although in outlook Hobbes was almost wholly a man of the new mold, he inherited from the Middle Ages a disposition to think systematically and to view the function of philosophy as the construction of a unified world view, in which all the special sciences are derived from one supreme science, and in which the answers to all questions that can be asked are ultimately statable in terms of a single formula. Aquinas and Hobbes, that is, agreed that all differences in behavior are differences of degree rather than of kind, and hence that a single account of all behavior is possible. But whereas Thomas held that the model of all behavior everywhere in the universe is the purposive behavior we know (or think we know) in ourselves, Hobbes held that the model of all behavior is the falling body's conformity to mechanical law. Accordingly, instead of a universe moved by love of God, Hobbes's universe was one in which everything that happens is reducible to the behavior of material particles moving in accordance with simple mechanical laws. The task of philosophy, as Hobbes conceived it, was to work out social, political, and ethical theories consistent with this account of the nature of reality.

> The *subject* of Philosophy, or the matter it treats of, is every body of which we can conceive any generation, and which we may, by any consideration thereof, compare with other bodies, or which is capable of composition and resolution; that is to say, every body of whose generation or properties we can have any knowledge. . . . Therefore it excludes *Theology,* I mean the doctrine of God, eternal, ingenerable, incomprehensible, and in whom there is nothing neither to divide nor compound, nor any generation to be conceived.
>
> It excludes the doctrine of *angels,* and all such things as are thought to be neither bodies nor properties of bodies; there being in them no place neither for composition nor division, nor any capacity of more and less, that is to say, no place for ratiocination. . . .
>
> It excludes all such knowledge as is acquired by Divine inspiration, or revelation, as not derived to us by reason, but by Divine grace in an instant, and, as it were, by some sense supernatural. . . .
>
> The principal parts of philosophy are two. For two chief kinds of bodies, and very different from one another, offer themselves to such as search after their generation and properties; one whereof being the work of nature, is called a *natural body,* the other is called a *commonwealth,* and is made by the wills and agreement of men. And from these spring the two parts of philosophy, called *natural* and *civil.* But seeing that, for the knowledge of the properties of a commonwealth, it is necessary first to know the dispositions, affections, and manners of men, civil philosophy is again commonly divided into two parts, whereof one, which treats of men's dispositions and manners, is called *ethics;* and the other, which takes cognizance of their civil duties, is called *politics,* or simply *civil philosophy.* In the first place, therefore (after I have set down such premises as appertain to the nature of philosophy in general), I will discourse of *bodies natural;* in the second, of the *dispositions and manners of men;* and in the third, of the *civil duties of subjects.*[b]

Hobbes did not succeed in completing this grandiose scheme of a universal philosophy, partly because of the magnitude of the task, partly because of the time-consuming controversies to which his vigorously expressed opinions gave rise. But he did leave a number of separate works,[3] and so it is possible to give a reasonably complete outline of what the finished work would have been. This account of Hobbes's views will therefore be divided into sections that correspond to the three divisions he proposed.

---

3 Besides *Leviathan,* already mentioned, his principal writings on philosophical subjects were *Human Nature* and the *Elements of Law* (published in 1650 but written earlier) and the *Elements of Philosophy* (1655), which sets out the basic theorems of his physics.

Body

HOBBES'S CONCEPTION OF REALITY

Reality, according to Hobbes, consists of body, or "matter," which he defined as "that which having no dependence upon our thought, is co-extended with some part of space." Besides having quantity, body everywhere is either at rest or in motion. Motion can be defined as the occupancy of different parts of space in successive times, and rest as the occupancy of the same part of space during a time interval. To understand Hobbes's conception of reality we must clear our minds completely of ordinary notions of material things—those thick, rich "bodies" of sense experience. These so-called bodies are but impressions produced in us by the action of real bodies, and the former are not remotely like the latter. To repeat, real bodies have quantity and are capable of motion; that is all.

But in saying that motion and quantity are the universal and generic properties of bodies, Hobbes did not mean that there is anywhere in the world motion-in-general or quantity-in-general. Every actual body has some determinate magnitude and is either at rest or moving at some determinate velocity. Physics and the other special sciences are variously concerned with ascertaining the laws of the behavior of bodies of determinate size moving at determinate velocities. There remain, nevertheless, certain very general theorems that can be deduced from the nature of quantity and motion as such, and that are thus true of *all* actual bodies. Such a study Hobbes called "first philosophy." In his view, physics and the other special sciences are merely the application of these elementary principles to determinate motions of one sort or another.

"FIRST PHILOSOPHY"

First philosophy had been discussed by almost all philosophers since Aristotle. For these earlier thinkers it had been an account of the nature of ultimate reality. So it was for Hobbes as well. But Aristotle and Augustine and Thomas had started from the assumption that ultimate reality must somehow be perfect, and they had proceeded by asking themselves what perfection implies. Hobbes, for his part, assumed that ultimate reality is "body determinate." Consequently, for him first philosophy was simply the exposition of the most general properties of bodies (that is, those properties true of all particular bodies everywhere) and everything said on the subject of first philosophy by earlier philosophers was either erroneous or meaningless.

> Every object is either a part of the whole world, or an aggregate of parts. The greatest of all bodies, or sensible objects, is the world itself; which we behold when we look round about us from this point of the same which we call the earth. Concerning the world, as it is one aggregate of many

parts, the things that fall under inquiry are but few; and those we can determine, none. Of the whole world we may inquire what is its magnitude, what its duration, and how many there be, but nothing else. . . . The questions concerning the magnitude of the world are whether it be finite or infinite, full or not full; concerning its duration, whether it had a beginning, or be eternal. . . . But the knowledge of what is infinite can never be attained by a finite inquirer. Whatsoever we know that are men, we learn it from our phantasms;[4] and of infinite, whether magnitude or time, there is no phantasm at all; so that it is impossible either for a man or any other creature to have any conception of infinite. And though a man may from some effect proceed to the immediate cause thereof, and from that to a more remote cause, and so ascend continually by right ratiocination from cause to cause; yet he will not be able to proceed eternally, but wearied will at last give over, without knowing whether it were possible for him to proceed to an end or not. . . . I cannot therefore commend those that boast they have demonstrated, by reasons drawn from natural things, that the world had a beginning. They are contemned by idiots, because they understand them not; and by the learned, because they understand them; by both deservedly. For who can commend him that demonstrates thus? "If the world be eternal, then an infinite number of days, or other measures of time, preceded the birth of Abraham. But the birth of Abraham preceded the birth of Isaac; and therefore one infinite is greater than another infinite, or one eternal than another eternal; which," he says, "is absurd." This demonstration is like his, who from this, that the number of even numbers is infinite, would conclude that there are as many even numbers as there are numbers simply, that is to say, the even numbers are as many as all the even and odd together. . . . From this absurdity therefore they run into another, being forced to call eternity *nunc stans*, a standing still of the present time, or an abiding now; and, which is much more absurd, to give to the infinite number of numbers the name of unity. But why should eternity be called an abiding now, rather than an abiding then? Wherefore there must either be many eternities, or *now* and *then* must signify the same.[c]

Thus, for Hobbes, the traditional metaphysics—with its concept of a perfect, eternal, and immutable reality—was nonsense. Since for him the only reality was "body determinate," the concept of reality-as-a-whole became simply the concept of all the bodies that are, and the only possible or meaningful metaphysics was the new mechanics.

The first thing that can be said of reality-as-a-whole is simply that it is full. All its parts are "contiguous to one another, in such manner as not to admit of the least empty space between."[d] The other basic theorems of Hobbes's first philosophy simply state properties that are true of all parts of this plenum. To derive these theorems Hobbes required some definitions. These should be contrasted with the more metaphysical definitions, often of the same terms, that

4 [See pp. 128–29—AUTHOR.]

Aristotle and the Scholastics had given for the basic concepts of *their* first philosophies. Notice, too, the short shrift Hobbes gave to such venerable and ethically important notions as freedom and individuality.

Hobbes's account of causality and identity will be given here. In both cases, let us look first at his definition and then at a few of the theorems that he demonstrated.

CAUSALITY

A body is said to work upon or *act,* that is to say, *do* something to another body, when it either generates or destroys some accident in it: and the body in which an accident is generated or destroyed is said to *suffer,* that is, to have something *done* to it by another body; as when one body by putting forwards another body generates motion in it, it is called the AGENT; and the body in which motion is so generated, is called the PATIENT. . . .

An agent is understood to *produce* its determined or certain effect in the patient, according to some certain accident or accidents, with which both it and the patient are affected; that is to say, the agent hath its effect precisely such, not because it is a body, but because such a body, or so moved.[5] For otherwise all agents, seeing they are all bodies alike, would produce like effects in all patients. . . . A CAUSE simply, or *an entire cause, is the aggregate of all the accidents both of the agents how many soever they be, and of the patient, put together; which when they are all supposed to be present, it cannot be understood but that the effect is produced at the same instant; and if any one of them be wanting, it cannot be understood but that the effect is not produced.* . . .

An entire cause is always sufficient for the production of its effect, if the effect be at all possible. For let any effect whatsoever be propounded to be produced; if the same be produced it is manifest that the cause which produced it was a sufficient cause; but if it be not produced, and yet be possible, it is evident that something was wanting either in some agent, or in the patient, without which it could not be produced; that is, that some accident was wanting which was requisite for its production; and therefore, that cause was not *entire,* which is contrary to what was supposed.

It follows also from hence, that in whatsoever instant the cause is entire, in the same instant the effect is produced. For if it be not produced, something is still wanting, which is requisite for the production of it; and therefore the cause was not entire, as was supposed.

And seeing a necessary cause is defined to be that, which being supposed, the effect cannot but follow; this also may be collected, that whatsoever effect is produced at any time, the same is produced by a necessary cause. . . .

But here, perhaps, some man may ask whether those future things, which

5 [In other words, the special sciences are all concerned with determinate bodies. This is what distinguishes them from first philosophy, which is concerned with indeterminate body, or body-in-general—AUTHOR.]

are commonly called *contingents,* are necessary. I say, therefore, that generally all contingents have their necessary causes [as has just been shown]; but are called contingents in respect of other events, upon which they do not depend; as the rain, which shall be tomorrow, shall be necessary, that is, from necessary causes; but we think and say it happens by chance, because we do not yet perceive the causes thereof, though they exist now; for men commonly call that *casual* or *contingent,* whereof they do not perceive the necessary cause; and in the same manner they used to speak of things past, when not knowing whether a thing be done or no, they say it is possible it never was done.

Wherefore, all propositions concerning future things, contingent or not contingent, as this, *it will rain tomorrow,* or this, *tomorrow the sun will rise,* are either necessarily true, or necessarily false; but we call them contingent, because we do not yet know whether they be true or false; whereas their verity depends not upon our knowledge, but upon the foregoing of their causes.[e]

IDENTITY

Two bodies are said to *differ* from one another, when something may be said of one of them, which cannot be said of the other at the same time.

And, first of all, it is manifest that no two bodies are the *same;* for seeing they are two, they are in two places at the same time; as that, which is the *same,* is at the same time in one and the same place. All bodies therefore differ from one another in *number,* namely, as one and another; so that the *same* and *different in number,* are names opposed to one another by contradiction. . . .

The same body may at different times be compared with itself. And from hence springs a great controversy among philosophers about the *beginning of individuation,* namely, in what sense it may be conceived that a body is at one time the same, at another time not the same it was formerly. For example, whether a man grown old be the same man he was whilst he was young, or another man; or whether a city be in different ages the same, or another city. Some place *individuity* in the unity of *matter;* others, in the unity of *form.* . . . According to the first opinion, he that sins, and he that is punished, should not be the same man, by reason of the perpetual flux and change of man's body. . . . According to the second opinion, two bodies existing both at once, would be one and the same numerical body. For if, for example, that ship of Theseus, concerning the difference whereof made by continual reparation in taking out the old planks and putting in new, the sophisters of Athens were wont to dispute, were, after all the planks were changed, the same numerical ship it was at the beginning; and if some man had kept the old planks as they were taken out, and by putting them afterwards together in the same order, had again made a ship of them, this, without doubt, had also been the same numerical ship with that which was at the beginning; and so there would have been two ships numerically the same, which is absurd. . . .

But we must consider by what name anything is called, when we inquire concerning the *identity* of it. . . . Whensoever the name, by which it is asked whether a thing be the same it was, is given it for the matter only, then, if the matter be the same, the thing also is *individually* the same; as the water, which was in the sea, is the same which is afterwards in the cloud; and any body is the same, whether the parts of it be put together, or dispersed; or whether it be congealed, or dissolved. Also, if the name be given for such form as is the beginning of motion, then, as long as that motion remains, it will be the same *individual* thing; as that man will be always the same, whose actions and thoughts proceed all from the same beginning of motion, namely, that which was in his generation; and that will be the same river which flows from one and the same fountain, whether the same water, or other water, or something else than water, flow from thence; and that the same city, whose acts proceed continually from the same institution, whether the men be the same or no.[f]

In short, Hobbes begged leave to differ with Juliet. "What's in a name?" may be all very well for lovesick girls, but philosophers know better. Names are, in fact, of the greatest consequence, and their misuse has created apparently insoluble problems. For instance, once it is realized that the "principle of individuation" is merely a matter of what definition is assigned to the name "same," this great metaphysical question, which so taxed the medieval mind, becomes merely the problem of getting others to agree to use "same" as we do.

But to continue Hobbes's exposition of the basic principles of first philosophy, let us now turn to what can be said about motion.

MOTION

First, I define ENDEAVOUR *to be motion made in less space and time than can be given;* that is, *less than can be determined or assigned by exposition or number;* that is, *motion made through the length of a point, and in an instant or point of time.* . . .

Secondly, I define IMPETUS, *or quickness of motion, to be the swiftness or velocity of the body moved, but considered in the several points of that time in which it is moved. In which sense impetus is nothing else but the quantity or velocity of endeavour. But considered with the whole time, it is the whole velocity of the body moved taken together throughout all the time, and equal to the product of a line representing the time, multiplied into a line representing the arithmetically mean impetus or quickness.* . . .

Thirdly, I define RESISTANCE *to be the endeavour of one moved body either wholly or in part contrary to the endeavour of another moved body, which toucheth the same.* . . .

Sixthly, I define FORCE *to be the impetus or quickness of motion multiplied either into itself, or into the magnitude of the movement, by means whereof the said movement works more or less upon the body that resists it.*

Having premised thus much, I shall now demonstrate, first, that if a point moved come to touch another point which is at rest, how little soever the impetus or quickness of its motion be, it shall move that other point. For if by that impetus it do not at all move it out of its place, neither shall it move it with double the same impetus. For nothing doubled is still nothing; and for the same reason it shall never move it with that impetus, how many times soever it be multiplied, because nothing, however it be multiplied, will for ever be nothing. Wherefore, when a point is at rest, if it do not yield to the least impetus, it will yield to none; and consequently it will be impossible that that, which is at rest, should ever be moved.

Secondly, that when a point moved, how little soever the impetus thereof be, falls upon a point of any body at rest, how hard soever that body be, it will at the first touch make it yield a little.[g]

THE SPECIAL SCIENCES

This is perhaps enough to indicate how Hobbes treated what he called "motion and magnitude in the abstract." Next, we come to his doctrine "concerning motions and magnitudes of the bodies which are parts of the world real and existent," or what he also called "the phenomena of nature." That is to say, we are now ready to turn from first philosophy to astronomy, physics, and the other special sciences that deal with bodies of determinate magnitude moving at determinate velocity (the planets, of course, are prime examples of bodies of this sort).

But all our knowledge of the determinate motions of real and existent bodies is derived from the changes that these bodies cause in our own. Hence, understanding the laws of the changes of these bodies (for example, the law of falling bodies, or Kepler's third law) entails knowing the ways in which these changes produce changes in us.

In fact, Hobbes believed that all these physical laws could be reformulated in terms of those changes that occur in our bodies as a result of the fall of stones or the circling of the planets. Thus the special sciences concerned with what we call the outer world are projections from physiology, and physiology itself is merely the physics of those regions of the plenum that are called brains. This view, it may be pointed out, is not subjective in the ordinary sense. Hobbes did not reduce the world to states of the self; he merely held that study of the objective, material plenum is tied down, as it were, to a certain region of the plenum, and that whatever we know about what is happening in *other* regions is always an inference from what is happening in *this* region, which is caused (in a way that is purely mechanical) by what is happening in those other regions.

It follows that Hobbes could at once pass from a study of body in general to the study of "man"—those particular bodies that occupy the second section of his tripartite philosophy.

Man

Man, of course, is nothing but body; each individual man is simply a certain region of the material plenum, and what distinguishes this region from other regions is only the motions occurring there. Two sorts of motions occur in those parts of the plenum that are men—the motions involved in (experienced as) knowing, and those involved in willing. All these motions, which are nothing but changes in the spatial relations of the parts of human bodies, conform to the laws of motion already laid down; all are completely determined by antecedent events in time—by other changes either in the region we call ourselves or in regions contiguous to us.

COGITATING MOTIONS

Where, it may well be asked, in the kind of situation that Hobbes believed to exist, is there any place for the knower who knows that only motions exist? Do motions know motions? To answer these questions Hobbes introduced elements that he called "phantasms" as the knowers of motions. But what is a phantasm? It is a sensation; it is the way in which certain motions, occurring in the brain, are experienced. What the determinate bodies out there cause in the determinate body called my brain is nothing but motion; yet these motions are not experienced by me as motions. They are experienced as "things" and "qualities." The moon, for instance, is a determinate body; it has a certain magnitude and moves at a certain velocity through a certain region of space. As it moves it presses the ether nearest it, and this displacement is communicated successively to other parts of the ether and eventually, via that body called my eye, to that other body, my brain. This moon ("the real and existent" body that is one of the subjects of study in astronomy) is nothing but a magnitude of determinate size moving at a determinate velocity; it is not itself brightly colored, nor has it any dark shading. And what happens here in my cortex is not really brightly colored with dark shadows; it is nothing but the displacement of a body of a determinate magnitude moving at a determinate velocity. Nevertheless, the movement of this noncolored body here is *experienced* as a small round disk somewhere out there in sensuous space (which is, of course, quite different from the objective externality in which that real and existent body is moving).

This, then, is the doctrine of phantasms. Does it answer the questions raised above? That depends on what sort of answer one wants. The doctrine certainly does not account for the fact that sensations occur, if "account for" is taken to mean "deduce their character from the principles of first philosophy." Why a motion should be experienced as a sensation at all, and why one motion is experienced as middle C and another as red, are, and remain, complete mysteries as far as first philosophy goes. Since Hobbes's goal was to explain everything by deducing it from the principles of first philosophy, his attempt to establish a *purely* mechanical philosophy breaks down almost at the outset.

And there is an even graver problem. Hobbes's position is that a motion in my brain is experienced as some color, smell, or taste. Experienced by whom? By me? So it would seem. But I am only matter in motion. Hence there is not merely a puzzle about why a motion should be experienced as what it is not (a sensation) instead of what it is (a motion). There is also a puzzle about how it gets experienced at all. Hobbes disguised this difficulty from himself by covertly introducing an observer; but since he explicitly maintained that only matter is real, he is reduced to the very odd position that one motion somehow experiences another motion. Clearly, experience implies consciousness, and Hobbes's system cannot admit consciousness—either as an "accident" of matter or, still less, as the activity of an immaterial reality, mind.

There are still further difficulties. Hobbes had to maintain that the data of sense are the bases from which "all the knowledge we have is derived."[h] But how can this be? Though Hobbes naturally wished to hold, in agreement with common sense, that the phantasm somehow *knows* the world and reports truly about its nature, it follows from his basic thesis that what the phantasm thinks it knows is actually only "a tumult of the mind, raised by external things that press the organical parts of man's body."[i] Thus perception, far from being knowledge, is sheer delusion to the extent that men are taken in by it: "*Whatsoever accidents* or qualities our senses make us think there be in the *world*, they be *not* there, but are *seeming* and *apparitions* only; the things that really *are* in the world without us, are those *motions* by which these seemings are caused. And this is the *great deception of sense*."[j]

There is even worse to follow. How can it be known that what sense reports is an illusion, that is, that the real is a motion here in this region caused by a motion out there in that region? Hobbes went on, in the passage just quoted, to say that the great deception of sense "is by sense *corrected:* for as sense telleth me, when I see *directly,* that the colour seemeth to *be* in the object; so also sense telleth me, when I see by *reflection,* that colour is not in the object." But this is quite unsatisfactory. It is true that *isolated* deceptions of sense are "by sense corrected." For instance, the illusory perception of a stick in water as bent is corrected by other sense perceptions of the stick—I lift it out of the water, or I run my hand along it as it lies in the water. Indeed, to say that some sense perceptions are deceptive is to say that they fail to cohere with, to fit in with, other sense perceptions. But Hobbes was not talking about particular illusions, such as mistaking a reflection in a mirror for the object reflected there or mistaking a moonbeam on a curtain for a ghost. What he was talking about was a generic, universal deception. Since it was supposed to infect all experience whatever, it could never be corrected, or even detected, by sense experience. To put this differently, it is an empirical fact that some sense experiences are deceptive: We discover that they are deceptive by means of sense experience itself. But it is not an empirical fact that sense experience as such is deceptive, and this fact—if it were a fact—could never be ascertained by means of sense experience. Indeed, it is not a fact; it is an inference from another theory—the theory that all reality is matter in motion.

SENSATION

Let us now leave these puzzles about how bodily movements can correct their mistakes about what they know, and the even more fundamental question of how they can know at all, and pass on to Hobbes's account of the movements themselves.

According to the traditional philosophy, the mind has various powers—it perceives, thinks, imagines, remembers, and so on. According to Hobbes, these are all simply motions in our bodies. The most elementary of these motions is perception (or "sense"). The rest are "derived from that original."

Imagination, for instance, is "decaying sense." We are said to *see* (to sense, to perceive) the moon when it causes motions experienced as "bright round disk." We are said to *imagine* the moon when the object that caused these motions is no longer present. How can the motions in question occur if the object that caused them is not also present? Of course, the motions would not occur in imagination if the object had never been present (we would never experience "bright round disk" in the first place if "moon" were not originally present and acting causally on our bodies). But it follows from the principle of inertia that

> When a body is once in motion, it moveth, unless something else hinder it, eternally; and whatsoever hindereth it, cannot in an instant, but in time, and by degrees, quite extinguish it; and as we see in the water, though the wind cease, the waves give not over rolling for a long time after: so also it happeneth in that motion, which is made in the internal parts of a man, then, when he sees, dreams, &c. For after the object is removed, or the eye shut, we still retain an image of the thing seen, though more obscure than when we see it. . . .
>
> The decay of sense in men waking, is not the decay of the motion made in sense; but an obscuring of it, in such manner as the light of the sun obscureth the light of the stars; which stars do no less exercise their virtue, by which they are visible, in the day than in the night. But because amongst many strokes, which our eyes, ears, and other organs receive from external bodies, the predominant only is sensible; therefore, the light of the sun being predominant, we are not affected with the action of the stars. And any object being removed from our eyes, though the impression it made in us remain, yet other objects more present succeeding, and working on us, the imagination of the past is obscured, and made weak, as the voice of a man is in the noise of the day. From whence it followeth, that the longer the time is, after the sight or sense of any object, the weaker is the imagination. For the continual change of man's body destroys in time the parts which in sense were moved: so that distance of time, and of place, hath one and the same effect in

us. . . . This *decaying sense*, when we would express the thing itself, I mean *fancy* itself, we call *imagination*, as I said before: but when we would express the decay, and signify that the sense is fading, old, and past, it is called *memory*. So that imagination and memory are but one thing which for divers considerations hath divers names. . . .

The imaginations of them that sleep are those we call *dreams*. And these also, as all other imaginations, have been before, either totally or by parcels, in the sense.[k]

ASSOCIATION OF IDEAS

There is, then, a regularity to the way in which various phantasms succeed one another; what is more, phantasms that succeed one another in sense tend to succeed one another in imagination.

When a man thinketh on any thing whatsoever, his next thought after, is not altogether so casual as it seems to be. Not every thought to every thought succeeds indifferently. But as we have no imagination, whereof we have not formerly had sense, in whole, or in parts; so we have no transition from one imagination to another, whereof we never had the like before in our senses. The reason whereof is this. All fancies are motions within us, relics of those made in the sense: and those motions that immediately succeeded one another in the sense, continue also together after sense: insomuch as the former coming again to take place, and be predominant, the latter followeth, by coherence of the matter moved, in such manner, as water upon a plane table is drawn which way any one part of it is guided by the finger. But because in sense, to one and the same thing perceived, sometimes one thing, sometimes another succeedeth, it comes to pass in time, that in the imagining of any thing, there is no certainty what we shall imagine next; only this is certain, it shall be something that succeeded the same before, at one time or another. . . .

[For instance,] in a discourse of our present civil war, what could seem more impertinent, than to ask, as one did, what was the value of a Roman penny? Yet the coherence to me was manifest enough. For the thought of the war, introduced the thought of the delivering up the king to his enemies; the thought of that, brought in the thought of the delivering up of Christ; and that again the thought of the thirty pence, which was the price of that treason; and thence easily followed that malicious question, and all this in a moment of time; for thought is quick.[l]

This acute account of what later came to be called "association of ideas" was the beginning of empirical psychology. Hobbes was well aware of how different it was from the psychology taught in the "philosophy-schools of the universities of Christendom." "Intelligible species" and "sensible species," he pointed out, explain nothing, being merely impressive-sounding names for "seeing" and "understanding"; they only serve to demonstrate the regrettable "frequency of insignificant speech" at institutions of higher learning.[m]

Hobbes, it is clear, was attempting to observe the behavior of thoughts, just as Gilbert had observed the behavior of magnets or Tycho Brahe the behavior of planets in their paths, in order to find the "laws" of their behavior. And one such law, Hobbes said in effect, is that if the sense experience of A has been followed by the sense experience of B, the thought of A on another occasion tends to be followed by the thought of B. Doubtless Hobbes's account was deficient in many respects; conscious life is more like a stream than a series of hard, self-enclosed units that have to be compounded or separated, as the case may be.

Here Hobbes was misled by the mechanistic analogy—a mistake, perpetuated by his followers, that has plagued psychology almost to our own day. But even if association cannot be accepted as a complete account of the relations among our thoughts, Hobbes certainly pointed out an important fact about our mental life. And more important than the results of his observation was the fact of observation and the conviction underlying it—that patterns exist in men's thoughts as well as in things.

Incidentally, it should be noted that the "law" of association is an empirical generalization, not a theorem deduced in mechanics. The relata are not quantities but phantasms, and the law of their connection is not formulated in mathematical terms. The extent to which Hobbes departed from his mechanism and adopted a new set of ultimates will be clear if we look at what the law of association implies about the doctrine of cause and effect. Far from being a necessary relation, causality becomes merely an expectation on man's part, growing out of the tendency of human thoughts to associate. "When a man hath *so often* observed like antecedents to be followed by like consequents, that *whensoever* he seeth the antecedent, he looketh again for the consequent . . . then he calleth both the antecedent and the consequents, *signs* one of another. . . ." If, for instance, a man has "always seen the day and night to follow one another hitherto," he will expect the present day to be followed by night. But this is merely because, as a result of the law of association, the thought of day is followed by the thought of night. We cannot "thence conclude they shall do so, or that they have done so eternally."[n]

THOUGHT DISTINGUISHED FROM SENSATION

So far discussion has centered on sensation and its laws, and it is clear that as yet nothing that has been said is uniquely true of man. All bodies "fit for retaining of such motions as is made in them" are capable of sensation. And many bodies possess this property (looked at physiologically) of retaining motion, or (looked at on the felt side) of remembering experiences. A dog, for instance, who "understands the call or the rating of his master" does so because he "remembers" the call (that is, "associates" call and food). What, then, distinguishes men from dogs? Not some special spiritual power that reaches into things and collects their intelligible species; still less an immortal soul made in God's image. The distinguishing mark of thought, in contrast to sensation, is the capacity to give names "or other voluntary signs" to the felt states, and this capacity itself conforms to the law of association.

Names have, indeed, a twofold use: They help our memory, and they enable us to communicate with others. This is possible because, as a name becomes associated with a given phantasm, it serves to call this phantasm up again, either in the silence of our own thoughts or in the minds of others. Just as thought of day calls up thought of night, so the name "red" calls up the phantasm red. The only difference is that whereas day is a natural sign, "red" is an arbitrary sign. Accordingly, Hobbes defined a name as

> . . . *a word taken at pleasure to serve for a mark, which may raise in our mind a thought like to some thought we had before, and which being pronounced to others, may be to them a sign of what thought the speaker had, or had not before in his mind.* . . .
>
> Of names, some are *common* to many things, as *a man, a tree;* others *proper* to one thing, as *he that writ the Iliad, Homer, this man, that man.* And a common name, being the name of many things severally taken, but not collectively of all together (as man is not the name of all mankind, but of every one, as of Peter, John, and the rest severally) is therefore called an *universal name;* and therefore this word *universal* is never the name of any thing existent in nature, nor of any idea or phantasm formed in the mind, but always the name of some word or name; so that when *a living creature, a stone, a spirit,* or any other thing, is said to be *universal,* it is not to be understood, that any man, stone, &c. ever was or can be universal, but only that these words, *living creature, stone, &c.* are *universal names,* that is, names common to many things. . . .
>
> A *true* proposition is that, whose predicate contains, or comprehends its subject, or whose predicate is the name of every thing, of which the subject is the name; as *man is a living creature* is therefore a true proposition, because whatsoever is called *man,* the same is also called *living creature;* and *some man is sick,* is true, because *sick* is the name of *some man.* That which is not true, or that whose predicate does not contain its subject, is called a *false* proposition, as *man is a stone.* . . .
>
> And from hence it is evident, that truth and falsity have no place but amongst such living creatures as use speech. . . .
>
> From hence also this may be deduced, that the first truths were arbitrarily made by those that first of all imposed names upon things, or received them from the imposition of others. For it is true (for example) that *man is a living creature,* but it is for this reason, that it pleased men to impose both those names on the same thing.°

SCIENTIFIC KNOWLEDGE

At this point, Hobbes was in a position to give an account of "reason and science." Reasoning is "nothing but *reckoning,* that is adding and subtracting, of the consequences of general names,"[p] and science is the name of the kind of knowledge obtained as a result of reasoning.

It follows that scientific knowledge, though certain, is conditional, for it is only knowledge of the consequences of such-and-such definitions. Thus we know that "*if* the figure shown be a circle, then any straight line through the centre shall divide it into two equal parts." This we know certainly, for it can be derived from the definition of "circle." But science cannot tell us whether this figure is a circle. For that we need "sense and memory," or, as Hobbes also called it, "knowledge of fact."

> No discourse whatsoever, can end in absolute knowledge of fact, past, or to come. For, as for the knowledge of fact, it is originally, sense; and ever after, memory. And for the knowledge of consequence, which I have said before is called science, it is not absolute, but conditional. No man can know by discourse, that this, or that, is, has been, or will be; which is to know absolutely: but only, that if this be, that is; if this has been, that has been; if this shall be, that shall be: which is to know conditionally; and that not the consequence of one thing to another; but of one name of a thing, to another name of the same thing.[q]

Hobbes's own account of first philosophy is an application of this doctrine. Starting from such-and-such definitions of cause and identity, he proceeded to develop the consequences of these definitions, taking care, as he said, to affirm "nothing . . . which hath not good coherence with the definitions I have given; that is to say, which is not sufficiently demonstrated to all those, that agree with me in the use of words and appellations; for whose sake only I have written the same."[r]

If Hobbes had started with another set of definitions (say, those of Aristotle or Thomas), he would have obtained a different set of theorems. The advantage of his own definitions, in Hobbes's view, lay in the fact that the theorems derived from them enabled men to exert more effective control over their environment. For instance, men want to be able to generate fire—not to have to wait until a bolt of lightning ignites a tree. Accordingly, it is desirable to know the causes of fire, that is, the conditions under which it is generated. And it is obviously advantageous to be able to state the causes of fire in the most general possible terms—not to know merely that "striking a flint causes fire" or that "rubbing sticks together causes fire," but to find the generic accidents that are operating both when sticks are rubbed and when flints are struck. Moreover, it is desirable to have an account of the causes of fire that will be "agreeable to the rest of the phenomena."[s] Just as it is advantageous to give a single generic account of the generation of fire, one that includes all the particular causes of fire, so it will be advantageous to have a still more generic account: one that includes the accounts of all kinds of cause or generation whatever.

In Hobbes's view, the justification of his doctrine of motion and of the definitions on which it was based was that it provided a general framework from which it was possible to deduce formulas for the production of any and all combinations of states of affairs. Of course, this justification was still only a claim, not a fact. It had not yet been demonstrated in detail. But when it was worked out in detail, this general framework, or unified world view, would not only be intellectually satisfying but would give man immense power over nature.

Hobbes's way of putting this was to say that the test of any theory is its capacity to "salve the appearances," that is, to bring a hodgepodge of facts into intelligible relation to one another by means of some deductive system. But, of course, there may be other deductive systems that, if they were known, would also "salve" this set of facts. Hence one must never say that he has demonstrated "the true cause of the phenomena," only that he has demonstrated a cause "sufficient to produce them." From the pragmatic point of view this may be satisfactory, but Hobbes's position will hardly satisfy those who hope to obtain absolutely certain factual knowledge.

Now, the age in which Hobbes lived had a very deep urge for certainty. For centuries men had been comforted by the assurance that God was in His heaven and that He had revealed Himself through His Church on earth. As they lost their belief in the validity of this revelation, they sought elsewhere for a corresponding certainty. Those who rejected the authority the Church had imposed felt that they had to find a new authority. This, most of them believed, they had found in "reason" as it was applied in the method of science.

But, in Hobbes's view, the new science did not give an insight into the nature of reality; it was merely a science of the consequences of names. Whereas most of his contemporaries supposed that reason yields knowledge that is at the same time certain and about facts, Hobbes distinguished sharply between (1) "experience," which yields knowledge of facts but "concludes nothing universal," and (2) "reason," which is a "certain and infallible art" but yields only conditional truths of an "if . . . then" type. Hence, though he shared the prevailing enthusiasm about the utility of the new science, he could not accept the optimistic opinion that it was a satisfactory instrument for ascertaining objective truth and the final authority to replace faith. In his view, that final authority had to be the secular arm—the temporal sovereign. The ultimate ground for accepting one set of definitions instead of another is not that the former gives a better account of the phenomena (for we cannot be *sure* that it does), but that he who holds supreme power in the state commands us to accept it.

This is a very drastic conclusion. The following considerations may help to explain why Hobbes reached it. In the first place, he overlooked the part experimentation plays in the acquisition of scientific knowledge. In the actual practice of scientists, the relation between hypothesis and experiment is intimate and organic. Because Hobbes supposed that the scientist first draws up a number of arbitrary definitions and then deduces their consequences in isolation from any knowledge of facts, he exaggerated the possibility of there being other, equally arbitrary definitions that would have done as well. If he had understood that the knowledge of facts by which the consequences of definitions are tested is itself the product of prior definings and testings, Hobbes would have seen that the scientist's conclusions, though admittedly provisional, are less sheerly arbitrary than he supposed.

A second reason for Hobbes's antirationalism was his extreme nominalism. How this affected his conclusions can be seen if Hobbes's position is briefly compared with that of a realist like Plato. The *Republic* opened with a playful dispute between Socrates and his friends about the use of force and the use of reason. When Socrates pointed out that reason is an alternative to force as an instrument for securing agreement, his friends teasingly threatened not to listen to his arguments. This was because they all assumed that there is a rationale in the nature of things, a rationale that the mind cannot but follow if it listens at all. There is, they believed, a compulsion in reason that makes force unnecessary, at least among the rational elite. This is so because, according to their view, when the mind thinks correctly, it traverses, and accommodates itself to, an objectively real order. Truth is not a matter of the agreement of certain names with other, arbitrarily chosen names; it is a matter of the agreement of man's thoughts with reality.[6]

But according to Hobbes, there is no reason in the universe; there is only body in motion. Reasoning is merely the manipulation of "marks," that is, verbal symbols; and any correspondence between the conclusions of such reckoning and the behavior of the real is a happy coincidence that we accept because of its "advantages." Whereas Socrates and Glaucon and Adeimantus believed themselves to be living in an intellectual community constituted by the fact that their minds were in contact with a common and rational real, Hobbes held that there is a chasm between every individual mind and every other individual mind, and between all minds and material reality. Hence, whereas Socrates and his friends were confident that reason would lead them to agreement, Hobbes maintained that men need a sovereign with unlimited powers to compel their agreement.[7] Thus, according to Hobbes, "good" is whatever the sovereign says is good; "lawful" is whatever he says is lawful; "true" is whatever he says is true.

Finally, Hobbes may not have realized how radical his position was. He may, quite inconsistently, have exempted his own theory from his general conclusions about theory, believing it to be "really" true—not merely true by decree of some sovereign, as he held other theories to be.

However this may be, Hobbes anticipated views that were not to win wide acceptance until our own day. Like Hobbes, many people today believe that the certainty of mathematical reasoning results from the fact that it is merely a "computation" of the consequences of definitions; hence they agree with him in denying that there is any "necessary knowledge of facts." But not everyone

---

6 Of course, for purposes of communication men use names, and the names they use are arbitrary. One says "horse" if one is communicating in English, "equus" if in Latin, "hippos" if in Greek. But, according to this view, the *form* one is talking about is what it is, regardless of the language one is speaking.

7 See pp. 144–52 for the development of this thesis in Hobbes's political theory.

is as bold and as frank as Hobbes in facing up to the ethical, political, and epistemological consequences of this extreme antirationalism.

VOLUNTARY MOTIONS

This brings us to voluntary motions, the second of the two types of motion that occur in the part of the plenum that is called man. The human body naturally makes all sorts of movements, many of which (for example, falling) differ in no way from those made by inanimate bodies. But some are peculiar to animate bodies. These, which are studied in physiology and psychology, are the interior movements of the parts of that complex whole that we call an animal. Some of these movements are caused exclusively by the movements of other parts (for example, the circulation of the blood). Some are caused by those other movements that are called phantasms. It is the latter class of movements that is voluntary.

There be in animals, two sorts of *motions* peculiar to them: one called *vital;* begun in generation, and continued without interruption through their whole life; such as are the *course* of the *blood,* the *pulse,* the *breathing,* the *concoction, nutrition, excretion,* &c., to which motions there needs no help of imagination: the other is *animal motion,* otherwise called *voluntary motion;* as to *go,* to *speak,* to *move* any of our limbs, in such manner as is first fancied in our minds. That sense is motion in the organs and interior parts of man's body, caused by the action of the things we see, hear, &c.; and that fancy is but the relics of the same motion, remaining after sense, has been already said in the first and second chapters. And because *going, speaking,* and the like voluntary motions, depend always upon a precedent thought of *whither, which way,* and *what;* it is evident, that the imagination is the first internal beginning of all voluntary motion. And although unstudied men do not conceive any motion at all to be there, where the thing moved is invisible; or the space it is moved in is, for the shortness of it, insensible; yet that doth not hinder, but that such motions are. For let a space be never so little, that which is moved over a greater space, whereof that little one is part, must first be moved over that. These small beginnings of motion, within the body of man, before they appear in walking, speaking, striking, and other visible actions, are commonly called ENDEAVOUR.

This endeavour, when it is toward something which causes it, is called APPETITE, or DESIRE. . . . And when the endeavour is fromward something, it is generally called AVERSION. . . .

And because the constitution of a man's body is in continual mutation, it is impossible that all the same things should always cause in him the same appetites, and aversions: much less can all men consent, in the desire of almost any one and the same object.

But whatsoever is the object of any man's appetite or desire, that is it which he for his part calleth *good:* and the object of his hate and aversion, *evil;* and of his contempt, *vile* and *inconsiderable.* For these words of good, evil, and contemptible, are ever used with relation to the person that useth them:

there being nothing simple and absolutely so; nor any common rule of good and evil, to be taken from the nature of the objects themselves; but from the person of the man, where there is no commonwealth; or, in a commonwealth, from the person that representeth it; or from an arbitrator or judge, whom men disagreeing shall by consent set up, and make his sentence the rule thereof. . . .

When in the mind of man, appetites, and aversions, hopes, and fears, concerning one and the same thing, arise alternately; and divers good and evil consequences of the doing, or omitting the thing propounded, come successively into our thoughts; so that sometimes we have an appetite to it; sometimes an aversion from it; sometimes hope to be able to do it; sometimes despair, or fear to attempt it; the whole sum of desires, aversions, hopes and fears, continued till the thing be either done, or thought impossible, is that we call DELIBERATION. . . .

This alternate succession of appetites, aversions, hopes and fears, is no less in other living creatures than in man: and therefore beasts also deliberate.

Every *deliberation* is then said to *end*, when that whereof they deliberate, is either done, or thought impossible; because till then we retain the liberty of doing, or omitting; according to our appetite, or aversion.

In *deliberation*, the last appetite or aversion, immediately adhering to the action, or to the omission thereof, is that we call the WILL.; the act, not the faculty, of *willing*. . . . *Will* therefore *is the last appetite in deliberating*.[t]

Since Hobbes defined a voluntary act as a change caused by a phantasm, all the ambiguities in his doctrine of phantasms infect his psychology of volition. Here is an instance of so-called voluntary motion. While sitting in my chair, I remember that my pipe is on the mantel. I get up, walk over to the mantel, and pick up the pipe. All these complex movements supposedly occur in accordance with simple mechanical laws. The memory of pipe-on-mantel is decaying sense, and sense is motion (the visual percept surviving as a motion in the cortex). What is the difference between these motions and an involuntary motion like the circulation of the blood? Hobbes's answer was that in the voluntary motion a phantasm (remembering the pipe) is operative, whereas in the involuntary motion no phantasm operates.

But what, exactly, is the phantasm "remembering the pipe," and how does it produce a bodily change? If the phantasm is merely a spatial change in my cortex, then the only difference between voluntary and involuntary motion is a difference in the location of the cause. If the cause occurs in the cortex, the change is a volition; otherwise, it is involuntary. But surely a voluntary act (fetching my pipe from the mantel) does not differ from an involuntary act (yawning or jerking my knee when a physician taps it) merely, or even chiefly, in having its cause located in a different region of space. Voluntary acts have a different and more complex structure, and they have this structure because they are *intended*. Intention is an aspect of behavior that Hobbes's theory cannot take into account.

In any case, it seems that Hobbes did not hold the phantasm to be merely the change in the cortex; rather, he held it to be the way this change is experienced.[8] But what does this mean, and how can a way-change-is-experienced produce a change in the position of some material particle? Since, on Hobbes's view, all motion is occasioned by contact, it is not plausible to say that a phantasm (conceived of as an experience, not as a motion in the cortex) could make contact with the nerves that energize my leg muscles.

Passing over these puzzles, let us grant for the sake of argument that somehow or other phantasms produce motions—sometimes motion toward the body of which one is having the phantasm, sometimes motion away from that body. Why should a toward-motion be felt as pleasurable and a fromward-motion as painful? There are two questions here: (1) Why should any motion be felt at all, except as what it is, a motion? (2) Why should one motion be felt as pleasure and another as pain? The theory does not account for these facts in the way in which the theory claims to account for all facts, namely, by deducing the characteristics in question from the principles of first philosophy. The connections between "pleasure" and "toward" and between "pain" and "fromward" are just new facts introduced *ab extra* at this point.

Further, what is already implausible at the level of a simple act like fetching my pipe from the mantel if I happen to think of its being there becomes even more implausible when applied to action following reflection or deliberation. According to Hobbes's view, when I deliberate, a succession of phantasms pass across my mind (the pipe on the mantel, the can of beer in the refrigerator, the warm sunshine outside, the unfinished chapter on my desk, and so on). Suddenly, one of these phantasms energizes the appropriate muscles—I go to the mantel, to the kitchen, to the front door, or to my study, depending on whichever phantasm happens to be before my mind at this moment. Of course, the one that happens to be there is there as a result of a complicated series of movements in the plenum, all completely determined by purely mechanical law.

Though Hobbes can thus account for the obvious fact that action after deliberation is affected by what occurs during the period of deliberation, it does not appear that what happens after deliberation is the mechanical combination of forces that it must be if Hobbes's theory is correct. If the theory is correct, the process of deliberation is equivalent to what occurs on a billiard table. It is possible to say, though it sounds odd, that what happens to ball A after its collision with balls B and C is a product of A's "deliberation" with B and C; A's subsequent movement is different from what it would have been had A not deliberated with B and C. But behavior that results from desire, aversion, reflection, and will looks very different from the deliberation of billiard balls. No outsider observing the behavior of billiard balls and of men would confuse what goes on among the balls with what goes on among three friends who are discussing Hobbes's theories or trying to decide how to spend the evening.

8 See pp. 128–29.

RELATION BETWEEN PHYSICS AND PSYCHOLOGY

Unless Hobbes's theory can explain these observed differences, it is fair to conclude that his attempt to base psychology on physics failed. And though Hobbes himself, of course, would not have admitted it, the sign of his failure is the fact that he in effect made a wholly new start at this point, introducing material derived from his observations of men and their affairs, without even making a pretense of deducing it from the principles of mechanics. But before we turn to this second account of human nature, let us note several important ways in which Hobbes's initial attempt to derive psychology from mechanics affected his conclusions about motivation and behavior.

For one thing, he concluded that values are subjective—we do not aim at something because it is good; we call it good because we move toward it. Of course, on some subsequent occasion we may aim at the thing in question because we remember that it was good (that is, because we have a phantasm of it as having produced a toward-movement felt as pleasurable). It also follows that everyone aims exclusively at his own good: When, for instance, a man cooperates with others or makes gifts to them, what he is aiming at is simply the pleasure he expects to feel on making these movements.

Again, it follows that the particular objects toward which men move (and which they call their "good") vary with the states of men's bodies. Nevertheless, since human bodies are quite similar, men will usually make their toward-movements toward the same sort of objects. This means that an empirical science of psychology is possible. It will simply be a description of the types of objects that men find good, that is, a description of the types of objects toward which the generality of men are observed to move.

> Felicity of this life consisteth not in the repose of a mind satisfied. For there is no such *finis ultimus*, utmost aim, nor *summum bonum*, greatest good, as is spoken of in the books of the old moral philosophers. Nor can a man any more live, whose desires are at an end, than he, whose senses and imaginations are at a stand. Felicity is a continual progress of the desire, from one object to another; the attaining of the former, being still but the way to the latter. The cause whereof is, that the object of man's desire, is not to enjoy once only, and for one instant of time; but to assure for ever, the way of his future desire. . . .
>
> So that in the first place, I put for a general inclination of all mankind, a perpetual and restless desire of power after power, that ceaseth only in death. And the cause of this, is . . . that a man . . . cannot assure the power and means to live well, which he hath present, without the acquisition of more. . . .
>
> Nature hath made men so equal, in the faculties of the body, and mind; as that though there be found one man sometimes manifestly stronger in body, or of quicker mind than another; yet when all is reckoned together, the difference between man, and man, is not so considerable, as that one

man can thereupon claim to himself any benefit, to which another may not pretend, as well as he. . . .

And as to the faculties of the mind, setting aside the arts grounded upon words, and especially that skill of proceeding upon general, and infallible rules, called science; which very few have, and but in few things; as being not a native faculty, born with us; nor attained, as prudence, while we look after somewhat else, I find yet a greater equality amongst men, than that of strength. . . .

From this equality of ability, ariseth equality of hope in the attaining of our ends. And therefore if any two men desire the same thing, which nevertheless they cannot both enjoy, they become enemies; and in the way to their end, which is principally their own conservation, and sometimes their delectation only, endeavour to destroy, or subdue one another. . . .

And from this diffidence of one another, there is no way for any man to secure himself, so reasonable, as anticipation; that is, by force, or wiles, to master the persons of all men he can. . . .

Again, men have no pleasure, but on the contrary a great deal of grief, in keeping company, where there is now power able to over-awe them all. For every man looketh that his companion should value him, at the same rate he sets upon himself: and upon all signs of contempt, or undervaluing, naturally endeavours, as far as he dares (which amongst them that have no common power to keep them in quiet, is far enough to make them destroy each other), to extort a greater value from his contemners, by damage; and from others, by the example.

So that in the nature of man, we find three principal causes of quarrel. First, competition; secondly, diffidence; thirdly, glory.

The first, maketh men invade for gain; the second, for safety; and the third, for reputation. The first use violence, to make themselves masters of other men's persons, wives, children, and cattle; the second, to defend them; the third, for trifles, as a word, a smile, a different opinion, and any other sign of undervalue, either direct in their persons, or by reflection in their kindred, their friends, their nation, their profession, or their name.

Hereby it is manifest, that during the time men live without a common power to keep them all in awe, they are in that condition which is called war; and such a war, as is of every man, against every man. For WAR consisteth not in battle only, or the act of fighting; but . . . in the known disposition thereto, during all the time there is no assurance to the contrary. All other time is PEACE.

Whatsoever therefore is consequent to a time of war, where every man is enemy to every man; the same is consequent to the time, wherein men live without other security, than what their own strength, and their own invention shall furnish them withal. In such condition, there is no place for industry, because the fruit thereof is uncertain: and consequently no culture of the earth; no navigation, nor use of the commodities that may be imported by sea; no commodious building; no instruments of moving, and removing, such things as require much force; no knowledge of the face of the earth; no account of time; no arts; no letters; no society; and which is worst of all, continual fear, and danger of violent death; and the life of man, solitary, poor, nasty, brutish, and short. . . .

And thus much for the ill condition, which man by mere nature is actually placed in; though with a possibility to come out of it, consisting partly in the passions, partly in his reason.[u]

If, as Hobbes maintained, competition, diffidence, and glory are the basic human drives, he was correct in concluding that men are unfit to live in communities. But the fact is that men do, and must, live communally. Hence the central problem that Hobbes sought to solve in his political theory—how to create conditions in which men can live together peacefully in societies, when temperamentally they are wholly unfit to do so. Before turning to Hobbes's solution of this problem, let us examine his account of religion, one of those drives that, if undirected, make a stable social life difficult to achieve but that, manipulated by a competent sovereign, can help keep a people in disciplined obedience.

RELIGION

Though religion is not a primary drive like sex, sleep, and elimination, it is a very powerful one. It is peculiar to men, and its roots can be traced to a combination of fear and egoism.

Seeing there are no signs, nor fruit of *religion*, but in man only; there is no cause to doubt, but that the seed of *religion*, is also only in man; and consisteth in some peculiar quality, or at least in some eminent degree thereof, not to be found in any other living creatures.

And first, it is peculiar to the nature of man, to be inquisitive into the causes of the events they see, some more, some less; but all men so much, as to be curious in the search of the causes of their own good and evil fortune.

Secondly, upon the sight of anything that hath a beginning, to think also it had a cause, which determined the same to begin, then when it did, rather than sooner or later.

Thirdly, whereas there is no other felicity of beasts, but the enjoying of their quotidian food, ease, and lusts; as having little or no foresight of the time to come, . . . man observeth how one event hath been produced by another; and remembereth in them antecedence and consequence; and when he cannot assure himself of the true causes of things, (for the causes of good and evil fortune for the most part are invisible), he supposes causes of them, either such as his own fancy suggesteth; or trusteth the authority of other men, such as he thinks to be his friends, and wiser than himself.

The two first, make anxiety. For being assured that there be causes of all things that have arrived hitherto, or shall arrive hereafter; it is impossible for a man, who continually endeavoureth to secure himself against the evil he fears, and procure the good he desireth, not to be in a perpetual solicitude of the time to come; so that every man, especially those that are over provident, . . . hath his heart all the day long, gnawed on by fear of death, poverty, or other calamity; and has no repose, nor pause of his anxiety, but in sleep.

This perpetual fear, always accompanying mankind in the ignorance of causes, as it were in the dark, must needs have for object something. And therefore when there is nothing to be seen, there is nothing to accuse, either of their good, or evil fortune, but some *power*, or agent *invisible*. . . .

In these four things, opinion of ghosts, ignorance of second causes, devotion towards what men fear, and taking of things casual for prognostics, consisteth the natural seed of *religion;* which by reason of the different fancies, judgments, and passions of several men, hath grown up into ceremonies so different, that those which are used by one man, are for the most part ridiculous to another. . . .

From the propagation of religion, it is not hard to understand the causes of the resolution of the same into its first seeds, or principles; which are only an opinion of a deity, and powers invisible, and supernatural; that can never be so abolished out of human nature, but that new religions may again be made to spring out of them, by the culture of such men, as for such purpose are in reputation.

For seeing all formed religion, is founded at first, upon the faith which a multitude hath in some one person, whom they believe not only to be a wise man, and to labour to procure their happiness, but also to be a holy man, to whom God himself vouchsafeth to declare his will supernaturally; it followeth necessarily, when they that have the government of religion, shall come to have either the wisdom of those men, their sincerity, or their love suspected; or when they shall be unable to show any probable token of divine revelation; that the religion which they desire to uphold, must be suspected likewise; and, without the fear of the civil sword, contradicted and rejected.

That which taketh away the reputation of wisdom, in him that formeth a religion . . . is the enjoining of a belief of contradictories: for both parts of a contradiction cannot possibly be true: and therefore to enjoin the belief of them, is an argument of ignorance. . . .

That which taketh away the reputation of sincerity, is the doing or saying of such things, as appear to be signs, that what they require other men to believe, is not believed by themselves. . . .

That which taketh away the reputation of love, is the being detected of private ends: as when the belief they require of others, conduceth or seemeth to conduce to the acquiring of dominion, riches, dignity, or secure pleasure, to themselves only, or specially.[v]

Hobbes intended this shrewd, even if one-sided, analysis of the causes of the Protestant Reformation as an object lesson for princes and for all supporters of the status quo: Above all else, the prince must not let the religion with which he is allied become suspect in any of these four ways. The only safe course, therefore, is to maintain rigid control over "opinions and doctrines"[w] and to prevent would-be reformers from upsetting the superstitions of the masses. These reformers are either deluded fools or cynics who hope to use the religious passions of the masses to further their own private ends. In any case, their reforms, far from doing good, could only cause civil war, anarchy, and misery. Therefore, for the good of everyone concerned, they should be suppressed.

According to Hobbes, religion is distinguished from other fears only by the fact that it happens to be a completely irrational one. Fear is rational when the object feared (fire, earthquake, pestilence) is really dangerous. But the object feared in religion is completely imaginary. Since there is no religious truth—no objective state of affairs in terms of which rival religions can be evaluated—the only criterion for choosing between religions is subjective preference. It would be possible, of course, to allow each individual to express his own subjective preference. But, human nature being what it is, everyone would promptly try to impose his preference on others, and chaos would ensue. The only alternative is to let *one* individual's preference (the sovereign's) be decisive. Accordingly, religious "truth" is whatever the sovereign decrees it to be. "*Fear* of power invisible, feigned by the mind, or imagined from tales publicly allowed, [is called] RELIGION; not allowed [is called] SUPERSTITION."[x] There is thus no *real* difference between religion and superstition; all religion is sheer superstition. And the only meaningful difference between religions is political.

Nothing could show more dramatically the contrast between the typically medieval and the typically modern conception of the world than Hobbes's approach to religion. For him religion was not distinctive in any way; it was just another human drive and just as much a neutral object of study as digestion or elimination. What of the values religious men experience, the insights they believe to be true and important? Since the new method was not equipped to deal with such aspects of the situation, they either dropped wholly out of the picture or remained as "subjective" feelings. And the fact that men feel differently when they are praying from the way they feel when they are digesting their dinner was (for the new science) simply another fact.

Thus Hobbes's account of religion illustrates the general doctrine already described—that man's nature is singularly ill adapted for the social life he leads. Religion is but one of the many drives in human nature that makes it necessary for men to accept an omnipotent sovereign. This brings us to the third, and last, section of Hobbes's system.

The State

A state is as much a natural phenomenon as a billiard ball or a man; it is merely a larger and more complicated segment of the material plenum. Theoretically, therefore, the behavior of societies ought to be capable of the same rigorous prediction as the behavior of billiard balls on a billiard table, and it ought to be in accordance with precisely the same laws.

> Nature, the art whereby God hath made and governs the world, is by the *art* of man, as in many other things, so in this also imitated, that it can make an artificial animal. For seeing life is but a motion of limbs, the beginning whereof is in some principal part within; why may we not say, that all *automata* (engines that move themselves by springs and wheels as doth a watch) have an artificial life? For what is the *heart,* but a *spring;* and the *nerves,* but so many *strings;* and the *joints,* but so many *wheels,* giving motion to the whole body, such as was intended by the artificer? *Art* goes yet further, imitating that rational and most excellent work of nature, *man.* For by art is created the great LEVIATHAN called a COMMONWEALTH, or STATE, in Latin CIVITAS, which is but an artificial man.[y]

It might be expected that, in accordance with his general scheme, Hobbes would attempt to deduce the properties of the state from the laws of motion. But he started instead from that black view of human nature that has just been sketched. His contention was that, given such stupidity and selfishness as men habitually display, the only way to prevent them from destroying themselves was to concentrate all power in the hands of a single individual, the sovereign. The argument is in two stages: (1) If men were to follow such-and-such rules (which Hobbes chose to call "laws of nature"), they could live together peacefully. (2) Since they will not follow these rules of their own volition (being too shortsighted to see where their own greatest good lies), they need an all-powerful sovereign to compel them to do so.

THE LAWS OF NATURE

Hobbes began by pointing out that some of the characteristics giving rise to competition and dissension also give rise to a desire for peace and a willingness to accept any rule that offers security. Thus, so far as men try to get the better of those who have the power to harm them, fear of death leads to competition; but it can also incline men to surrender themselves up to one who guarantees to protect their lives. Again, love of "commodious living" inclines men to competition; but it can also incline them to take an easier course and resign themselves to having less than they would like, for the sake of holding on to what they already have.

On the basis of these drives, Hobbes proceeded to set down certain "convenient articles of peace upon which men may be drawn to agreement." All these "laws of nature" are based upon an original "right," the right of every man to preserve "his own life and of doing any thing, which in his own judgment, and reason, he shall conceive to be the aptest means thereunto." The laws of nature are simply those acts that Hobbes believed to be the aptest means toward this end.

A LAW OF NATURE, *lex naturalis*, is a precept or general rule, found out by reason, by which a man is forbidden to do that, which is destructive of his life, or taketh away that means of preserving the same; and to omit that, by which he thinketh it may be best preserved. . . .

And because the condition of man, as hath been declared in the precedent chapter, is a condition of war of every one against every one: in which case every one is governed by his own reason; and there is nothing he can make use of, that may not be a help unto him, in preserving his life against his enemies; it followeth, that in such a condition, every man has a right to every thing; even to one another's body. And therefore, as long as this natural right of every man to every thing endureth, there can be no security to any man, how strong or wise soever he be, of living out the time, which nature ordinarily alloweth men to live. And consequently it is a precept, or general rule of reason, *that every man, ought to endeavour peace, as far as he has hope of obtaining it; and when he cannot obtain it, that he may seek, and use, all helps, and advantages of war.* The first branch of which rule, containeth the first, and fundamental law of nature; which is, *to seek peace, and follow it.* The second, the sum of the right of nature; which is, *by all means we can, to defend ourselves.*

From this fundamental law of nature, by which men are commanded to endeavour peace, is derived this second law; *that a man be willing, when others are so too, as far-forth as for peace, and defense of himself he shall think it necessary, to lay down this right to all things; and be contented with so much liberty against other men, as he would allow other men against himself.* . . .

Right is laid aside, either by simply renouncing it; or by transferring it to another. . . . And when a man hath in either manner abandoned, or granted away his right; then is he said to be OBLIGED, or BOUND, not to hinder those, to whom such right is granted, or abandoned, from the benefit of it: and that he *ought*, and it is his DUTY, not to make void that voluntary act of his own: and that such hindrance is INJUSTICE, and INJURY, as being *sine jure;* the right being before renounced, or transferred. So that *injury*, or *injustice*, in the controversies of the world, is somewhat like to that, which in the disputations of scholars is called *absurdity.* For as it is there called an absurdity, to contradict what one maintained in the beginning: so in the world, it is called injustice, and injury, voluntarily to undo that, which from the beginning he had voluntarily done. . . .

Whensoever a man transferreth his right, or renounceth it; it is either in consideration of some right reciprocally transferred to himself; or for some other good he hopeth for thereby. For it is a voluntary act: and of the voluntary acts of every man, the object is some *good to himself.* And therefore there be some rights, which no man can be understood by any words, or other signs, to have abandoned, or transferred. As first a man cannot lay down the right of resisting them, that assault him by force, to take away his life; because he cannot be understood to aim thereby, at any good to himself. . . .

The mutual transferring of right, is that which men call CONTRACT. . . .

From that law of nature, by which we are obliged to transfer to another, such rights, as being retained, hinder the peace of mankind, there followeth a third; which is this, *that men perform their covenants made:* without which, covenants are in vain, and but empty words; and the right of all men to all things remaining, we are still in the condition of war.

And in this law of nature, consisteth the fountain and original of JUSTICE. For where no covenant hath preceded, there hath no right been transferred, and every man has right to every thing; and consequently, no action can be unjust. But when a covenant is made, then to break it is *unjust:* and the definition of INJUSTICE is no other than *the not performance of covenant.* And whatsoever is not unjust, is *just.*

But because covenants of mutual trust, where there is a fear of not performance on either part . . . are invalid; therefore before the names of just and unjust can have place, there must be some coercive power, to compel men equally to the performance of their covenants, by the terror of some punishment, greater than the benefit they expect by the breach of their covenant; . . . and such power there is none before the erection of a commonwealth.[z]

For Aquinas and other medieval thinkers, the laws of nature were God's decrees for the universe, that is, they were both the way things *do* behave and the way things *ought* to behave. For Hobbes, the laws of nature were merely a number of recommendations based on observed factual and causal relationships among things. If today I say, "You ought to drink orange juice," I am not saying that you have a moral duty to do so, derived from a divine decree about the universe. I believe that you want to be healthy and I also believe that there is a causal relation between vitamin C deficiency and a tendency toward respiratory infection. In saying that you ought to drink orange juice, I am offering you a bit of advice based on these beliefs; that is all. Similarly, when Hobbes talked about the natural law of contracts, he meant no more than that the way for a man to preserve his life, assuming that he wants to preserve it, is to keep contracts. In other words, the Hobbesian "ought" is derived from an alleged causal relation: Given the nature of human drives, a particular effect (preservation of life) will result from a particular cause (keeping contracts).

And just as for Hobbes "law of nature" was only a utilitarian calculation ("a theorem concerning what conduceth to men's conservation and defense"), so "right" meant only "is capable of." In the Hobbesian state there is no nonsense about whether the sovereign is just or unjust or about whether civil rights are being invaded. "Justice" and "right" are whatever the sovereign permits his subjects; "injustice" and "wrong" are whatever the sovereign forbids.[9]

Hobbes thus ignored a question that was central for medieval thinkers and

9 Under a weak sovereign, the people have "rights" that they lack under a strong sovereign, but this means merely that they are capable of taking advantage of their sovereign's incompetence.

that has remained central even to this day for political theorists of the traditional school: What is the moral justification for the use of force? There has been much earnest debate as to when the sovereign is morally justified in using his power—when he is using it to save souls? to kill infidels and heretics? to implement natural law? to promote the greatest good for the greatest number? In Hobbes's view, this whole discussion is pointless. It may be to the sovereign's advantage to have his subjects *believe* that he is doing some, or all, of these things, for many people are taken in by claptrap about a "moral justification" of the use of force. But in reality the only thing that matters to the sovereign is the fact of power; it needs no justification, for there are no moral justifications for anything.

It is clear, then, that there is little relation between the laws of nature as Hobbes understood them and as they have been understood in the Western tradition. There is, indeed, but one similarity between the two types of law: Both claim to be eternal and immutable—the traditional laws of nature because they are supposedly God's decrees, and the Hobbesian laws of nature because they supposedly follow from the nature of fundamental human drives. Now, granting the presuppositions of traditional theory, the argument for eternal validity seems sound. But Hobbes's utilitarian maxims can hardly have the same status. Is it really true, for instance, that the best way to preserve one's life is to keep contracts? In a society in which everyone else was keeping contracts, it is possible that it would be to my advantage to do so. But it is more likely that a shrewd man in such a society would find it to his profit to violate contracts while others kept them. Hence it is far from clear that Hobbes's maxims *are* the ones that egoists would follow if they were enlightened enough to see where their long-range interests really lay. And, even granting that their long-range interests did lie in acting on these maxims, this would be so only if all other egoists were acting on the same maxims. For it would not be to my advantage to keep my end of a contract if the other party might break it. And how am I going to be sure that other men *are* being as enlightened about their long-range interests as I am?

NECESSITY FOR A SOVEREIGN

In other words, Hobbes's laws of nature are neither moral *prescriptions* (like St. Thomas') nor *descriptive* natural laws (like Galileo's $d = vt/2$). Now, though Hobbes would not have wanted to admit this (for, as we have seen, he wanted to hold that his laws of human nature had the universality and necessity of physical laws), the next step in his argument requires precisely this admission. For, obviously, if men were enlightened enough to adopt Hobbes's maxims of their own accord, and if following these maxims did lead to peace and security, no absolute sovereign would be necessary. On the contrary, the best state would be a complete *laissez-faire* democracy. Hobbes's position was that, though the scheme is perfectly logical for enlightened egoists and though we are all certainly egoists, we are not enlightened enough to follow it of our own accord. Hence we need a sovereign who will have sufficient power to make us follow it. This brings us to the second stage in his argument:

> The final cause, end, or design of men, who naturally love liberty, and dominion over others, in the introduction of that restraint upon themselves, in which we see them live in commonwealths, is the foresight of their own preservation, and of a more contented life thereby; that is to say, of getting themselves out from that miserable condition of war, which is necessarily consequent, as hath been shown [pp. 140–42], to the natural passions of men, when there is no visible power to keep them in awe, and tie them by fear of punishment to the performance of their covenants, and observation of those laws of nature [just] set down. . . .
>
> For the laws of nature, as *justice, equity, modesty, mercy*, . . . of themselves, without the terror of some power, to cause them to be observed, are contrary to our natural passions, that carry us to partiality, pride, revenge, and the like. And covenants, without the sword, are but words, and of no strength to secure a man at all. . . .
>
> Nor is it the joining together of a small number of men, that gives them this security; because in small numbers, small additions on the one side or the other, make the advantage of strength so great, as is sufficient to carry the victory, and therefore gives encouragement to an invasion. . . .
>
> And be there never so great a multitude; yet if their actions be directed according to their particular judgments, and particular appetites, they can expect thereby no defense, nor protection, neither against a common enemy, nor against the injuries of one another. For being distracted in opinions concerning the best use and application of their strength, they do not help but hinder one another; and reduce their strength by mutual opposition to nothing. . . .
>
> The only way to erect such a common power, as may be able to defend them from the invasion of foreigners, and the injuries of one another, and thereby to secure them in such sort, as that by their own industry, and by the fruits of the earth, they may nourish themselves and live contentedly; is, to confer all their power and strength upon one man, or upon one assembly of men, that may reduce all their wills, by plurality of voices, unto one will: which is as much as to say, to appoint one man, or assembly of men, to bear their person; and every one to own, and acknowledge himself to be author of whatsoever he that so beareth their person, shall act, or cause to be acted, in those things which concern the common peace and safety; and therein to submit their wills, every one to his will, and their judgments, to his judgment. This is more than consent, or concord; it is a real unity of them all, in one and the same person, made by covenant of every man with every man, in such manner, as if every man should say to every man, *I authorize and give up my right of governing myself, to this man, or to this assembly of men, on this condition, that thou give up thy right to him, and authorize all his actions in like manner.* . . . This is the generation of the great LEVIATHAN, or rather, to speak more reverently, of that *mortal god,*

to which we owe under the *immortal God,* our peace and defense. For by
this authority, given him by every particular man in the commonwealth,
he hath the use of so much power and strength conferred on him, that by
terror thereof, he is enabled to perform the wills of them all, to peace at
home, and mutual aid against their enemies abroad. . . .

And he that carrieth this person, is called SOVEREIGN, and said to have
sovereign power; and every one besides, his SUBJECT.[a]

Hobbes's argument, taken as a whole, amounts to this: All men want peace
and security. By doing such-and-such things they could attain this end. Unfortunately, they are not rational enough to do these things on their own
initiative. If, however, they contract together to appoint an all-powerful
sovereign, he will be in a position to compel them to do these things. Therefore
it is sensible to appoint such a sovereign.

There are many difficulties in this line of reasoning. In the first place, subjects
contract with one another, not with their sovereign. It would be ridiculous, on
Hobbes's premises, to ask the sovereign to agree to abide by the laws of nature.
He might "promise" to do so, but such a promise would be meaningless. It
could not be binding, for contracts are meaningful only *inside* the power system
that he creates and enforces. Nor is it plausible to argue that the sovereign
would, as a matter of fact, abide by the laws of nature because it would be
to his advantage to do so, just as (according to the argument) it is to our advantage
to do so. For there is no reason to suppose that the sovereign would be more
enlightened than his subjects, and, as we have seen, the whole argument for
the institution of a sovereign rests on the premise that men are not sufficiently
enlightened to conform to the laws of nature of their own accord. Hence the
institution of a Hobbesian sovereign would be a gamble in which the odds would
probably be against the prospective subjects: They certainly could not count
on the sovereign's using the power they grant him to produce the state of affairs
for which they grant him this power.

Let us allow, however, for the sake of argument, that the situation of men
without a Hobbesian sovereign is so desperate that it is worth this gamble. That
is, let us allow that, given the viciousness of human nature that Hobbes supposed,
the institution of an absolutely all-powerful sovereign is desirable. Hobbes still
has not proved his point. He must show not only (1) that men would actually
be better off under an absolute sovereign but also (2) that they would see that
they would be better off and that, seeing this, they would agree to institute
such a sovereign. The trouble is that in order to prove (1), Hobbes had to make
men so vicious and so irrational that they would be unlikely to choose (as the
argument of (2) implies that they would choose) a really long-range good. Or,
to put it the other way around, in order to prove (2), Hobbes had to make
men so enlightened and sensible that they would be unlikely to need (as the
argument of (1) implies that they need) an absolute sovereign. The difficulty
of Hobbes's position is that, whereas other theorists agree that man has some

sort of natural tendency to socialize, he made man a purely self-regarding animal. Hence he could explain the fact of communal living only as the result of an elaborate calculation of long-range interests by a group of egoists. This means that, for all his attack on man's rationality, Hobbes had to attribute to him a remarkable degree of prudence and "calm reason."

CONTRAST BETWEEN DESCRIPTIVE AND NORMATIVE THEORIES

It is sometimes asked whether Hobbes's view is the prototype of modern democratic or of totalitarian political theory. On the one side, in requiring consent, in defending the state on utilitarian grounds, and in denying divine-right doctrines, Hobbes anticipated fundamental theses of democratic theory. On the other side, the all-powerful sovereign of democratic theory is the people as a whole, not an individual or a group to whom they relinquish all their "rights," and the Hobbesian sovereign, once instituted, is a dictator of a surprisingly modern kind. Thus there are elements in Hobbes's theory that could be, and were, developed in widely different directions. But the basic contrast is less between totalitarianism and democracy than between naturalism and moralism. The contrast between sovereignty in the hands of "one, few, or many" (as Aristotle put it) is less fundamental than the contrast (also in Aristotelian language) between a state in which the laws govern and one in which men govern. Thus, as was said a moment ago, in democratic theory "the people as a whole are sovereign." But many democratic theorists would add a condition: The people are sovereign, *subject to fundamental law*—either in the form of a written constitution or in the form of some unwritten but generally recognized "rule of right." From this point of view, in the final analysis, the laws govern; and men implement the laws as far as they are able. On the other hand, there are theorists who hold that what ought to be the case comes into political theory only to the extent that men's beliefs about "ought" influence their conduct; for such theorists political theory is descriptive, not normative.

The chief interest of Hobbes's political theory today results from the fact that he tried to combine a primarily descriptive view with a normative argument. He did not merely ask himself whether men in fact do or do not like an absolute sovereign (the answer would have been that under certain circumstances they seem to; under others they certainly do not). He tried to show that it is sensible (this was what he meant by "ought") for them to do so—and this is a normative, not a factual, question. This attempt to fuse the two types of theories was not successful, but it illustrates one of the major problems with which philosophers of the modern period have been increasingly concerned—the problem, that is, that besets a descriptive (or naturalistic) type of theory when it comes to deal with a normative field like ethics or politics.

For a thinker of the naturalistic type, the business of political theory is simply to describe what occurs in human societies, just as astronomy describes what happens in the solar system (a far simpler society). From this point of view, sovereignty is one of the kinds of motions that occur when particles are grouped in certain complex patterns. To attempt to "justify" this motion (in the sense of trying to show that it is best for the particles that it occur) is meaningless. It is simply a fact that this motion does occur; all that the political theorist can (or should) do is to try to make generalizations about it—that under such-and-such conditions it behaves this way, that under such-and-such other conditions it behaves that way.

If one maintains this point of view consistently, the so-called normative sciences cause no special difficulty; what makes them normative does not even enter the picture. This does not mean, of course, that ethics and politics will not remain more difficult than astronomy. In the first place, the objects they deal with are vastly more complex; in the second place, in these subjects the scientist's feelings cannot help but influence his supposedly neutral inquiries. But in principle there is nothing that prevents politics from being just as objective as mathematics or astronomy.

The question, however, is whether one will really be content with the purely descriptive science of politics that results from this method of inquiry. Hobbes, as we have seen, was not. He wanted not merely to describe sovereignty but to show that sensible men ought to like it. The trouble is that in his attempt to show this he raised a question that, given his descriptive point of view, he could not answer. This question was not "What sorts of states do sensible men think are good?" but "Are their judgments correct?" And this implies the existence of a norm. Thus Hobbes's failure to derive a consent system from the *fact* of a universal desire to live is symptomatic of a much more pervasive problem—the problem of finding a place for value in a world of fact. There is a chasm between the *good* of the subjects and the *facts* of power that his theory cannot bridge. It falls, therefore, into two distinct parts—an account of how power operates, and an attempt to show that it is *desirable* that it operate in this way.

Part of the time, then, Hobbes was a scientist analyzing the phenomena of political life. From this standpoint, it is a matter of complete indifference who has sovereign power and how he uses it. One merely notes what happens when power is present in a society and what happens when it is absent from a society, just as one notes what happens when a particle is uniformly accelerated and what happens when it is violently accelerated. Part of the time, however, Hobbes was a moralist (it is immaterial here whether one accepts or rejects his moral standard). From this standpoint, it matters a great deal who has sovereign power and how he uses it. The state is not a good state unless it produces the peace and security at which men aim and for the sake of which they contract together to submit to their sovereign. But the concept of "good" and the concept of "contract" introduce references foreign to a purely descriptive theory. Movements in the plenum (however complex their mechanistic interrelations) do not conceive ends, act for goods, and enter into contracts; nor are goods, ends, and contracts meaningful concepts in a world in which only matter in motion is real.

Hobbes's Place in the History of Philosophy

Hobbes's views were so antagonistic to the dominant mores of his age that his influence was more negative than positive. Naturally, the bishops attacked him (and he welcomed their criticisms, for he thought that he could show them up as either knaves or fools). But even the advanced minds of the time, whom Hobbes himself could hardly write off as incompetent, drew back from his extreme conclusions. This does not mean, however, that Hobbes's theories are unimportant in the history of Western thought. On the contrary, his views are very important because they served as a warning to other thinkers and as an example of what a successful philosophical synthesis had to avoid. Hobbes is important, that is to say, because of the almost brutal way in which he exposed the crucial problem of finding a place for value in the world of physical fact, the world conceived of as the new science conceived of it.

Of course, it would have been easy to avoid Hobbes's conclusions by rejecting his premises and reverting to the radically different version of first philosophy taught by Scholasticism. But the point is that the premises Hobbes had adopted— especially his commitment to the new scientific method—were precisely those that the other thinkers of the new age wanted to adopt. Their problem was to show how they could accept a physical theory similar to his without being led, as he was, to conclusions that offended men's religious sense and committed them to a purely amoral and secular conception of life. How was it possible, Hobbes's successors had to ask themselves, in the neutral world of matter in motion that physics disclosed, to find a place for the reality of purpose, for the spontaneity of human conduct, for the significance of human life, for the validity of thought?

If we take medieval philosophy as one philosophical extreme, in which, roughly speaking, the scientific view of reality is ignored in favor of concentration on the valuational view, we may take Hobbism as the other extreme, in which the valuational point of view is ignored in favor of concentration on the scientific. The history of philosophy after Hobbes was a series of attempts to find a *via media* between these extremes. Hobbes's importance lies in the fact that, historically speaking, he was a turning point.

CHAPTER 5

Descartes

Life

René Descartes (1596–1650) was born near Tours and was educated at a Jesuit school where he studied Scholastic philosophy and physics, but where he was encouraged to study mathematics as well. After finishing his schooling at the age of seventeen, he went to Paris, where for a brief time he led the life expected of a gentleman of noble birth. He next spent some years in travel and in soldiering as a gentleman volunteer. When (in 1629) he decided to settle down, he chose to live in Holland, where there was greater intellectual freedom than elsewhere in Europe. Though he lived quietly, he soon acquired a reputation on the Continent and attracted the attention of a number of princely dilettantes, who occupied much of his time in correspondence. He died in 1650 at the Swedish court, where he had gone the year before to teach his philosophical system to Queen Christiana.

Much more interesting than the external facts of this uneventful life is the intellectual voyage of discovery described by Descartes in his autobiographical *Discourse on Method*. His account of his quest for certainty should be contrasted, as regards both the nature of the pursuit and its outcome, with Augustine's *Confessions*. Like Augustine, Descartes had a mystical experience. But this experience did not lead to the salvation of his soul; it led to the discovery of a new scientific method. Notice, too, in the statement that follows, Descartes' sense of the novelty of the age in which he lived, his contempt for all past learning (which, however, he expressed more temperately than Bacon or Galileo), and his supreme confidence in the capacity of the human intellect to solve all human problems.

So soon as I had achieved the entire course of study at the close of which one is usually received into the ranks of the learned, . . . I found myself embarrassed with so many doubts and errors that it seemed to me that the effort to instruct myself had no effect other than the increasing discovery of my own ignorance. And yet I was studying at one of the most celebrated Schools in Europe. . . . Along with this I knew the judgments that others had formed of me, and I did not feel that I was esteemed inferior to my fellow-students. . . . And finally our century seemed to me as flourishing, and as fertile in great minds, as any which had preceded. And this made me [conclude] that there was no learning in the world such as I was formerly led to believe it to be. . . .

I knew that the Languages which one learns there are essential for the understanding of all ancient literature; that fables with their charm stimulate the mind and histories of memorable deeds exalt it. . . .

But I considered that . . . those who regulate their conduct by examples which they derive from such a source, are liable to fall into the extravagances of the knights-errant of Romance, and form projects beyond their power of performance.

I esteemed Eloquence most highly and I was enamoured of Poesy, but I thought that both were gifts of the mind rather than fruits of study. . . .

I honoured our Theology and aspired as much as anyone to reach to heaven, but having learned . . . that the revealed truths which conduct thither are quite above our intelligence, I should not have dared to submit them to the feebleness of my reasonings; and I thought that, in order to undertake to examine them and succeed in so doing, it was necessary to have some extraordinary assistance from above and to be more than a mere man.

I shall not say anything about Philosophy,[1] but that . . . it has been cultivated for many centuries by the best minds that have ever lived, and that nevertheless no single thing is to be found in it which is not subject of dispute, and in consequence which is not dubious. . . .

1 [Descartes meant, of course, Scholasticism—AUTHOR.]

This is why, as soon as age permitted me to emerge from the control of my tutors, I . . . resolv[ed] to seek no other science than that which could be found . . . in the great book of the world, [and] employed the rest of my youth in travel, in seeing courts and armies, in intercourse with men of diverse temperaments and conditions, [and] in collecting varied experiences. . . . For it seemed to me that I might meet with much more truth in the reasonings that each man makes on the matters that specially concern him, and the issue of which would very soon punish him if he made a wrong judgment, than in the case of those made by a man of letters in his study touching speculations which lead to no result. . . .

[But I found in] other men . . . almost as much diversity as I had formerly seen in the opinions of philosophers. So much was this the case that the greatest profit which I derived from their study was that . . . I learned to believe nothing too certainly of which I had only been convinced by example and custom. . . . After I had employed several years in thus studying the book of the world and trying to acquire some experience, I one day formed the resolution of also making myself an object of study and of employing all the strength of my mind in choosing the road I should follow. . . .

I was then in Germany, to which country I had been attracted by the wars which are not yet at an end. And as I was returning from the coronation of the Emperor to join the army, the setting in of winter detained me in a quarter where, since I found no society to divert me, while fortunately I had also no cares or passions to trouble me, I remained the whole day shut up alone in a stove-heated room, where I had complete leisure to occupy myself with my own thoughts.[a]

According to Descartes' earliest biographer, it was here, on November 10, 1619, that a great light dawned on him—he "discovered the foundations of a wonderful new science." The following night, "having gone to bed all full of his inspiration and wholly occupied with the thought" of his great discovery, "he was visited by three consecutive dreams, which he believed came from on high." Descartes gave thanks to God and pledged himself to make a pilgrimage to the shrine of the Blessed Virgin at Loretto.

The Method

All these auspicious circumstances[2] seemed to Descartes to guarantee the validity of his idea of a universal and infallible method of reasoning. This method, worked out over a period of years, Descartes formulated in twenty-one *Rules for the Direction of the Mind*. Of these, the most important are

2 In one of his dreams, he had heard a clap of thunder that he believed to be "the Spirit of Truth descending to take possession of him."

Rule III. In the subjects we propose to investigate, our inquiries should be directed, not to what others have thought, nor to what we ourselves conjecture, but to what we can clearly and perspicuously behold and with certainty deduce; for knowledge is not won in any other way. . . .

We shall here take note of all those mental operations by which we are able, wholly without fear of illusion, to arrive at the knowledge of things. Now I admit only two, viz. intuition and deduction.

By *intuition* I understand, not the fluctuating testimony of the senses, nor the misleading judgment that proceeds from the blundering constructions of imagination, but the conception which an unclouded and attentive mind gives us so readily and distinctly that we are wholly freed from doubt about that which we understand. . . . *Intuition* . . . springs from the light of reason alone. . . .

By *deduction* . . . we understand all necessary inference from other facts that are known with certainty. [For] many things are known with certainty, though not by themselves evident, but only deduced from true and known principles by the continuous and uninterrupted action of a mind that has a clear vision of each step in the process. It is in a similar way that we know that the last link in a long chain is connected with the first, even though we do not take in by means of one and the same act of vision all the intermediate links on which that connection depends, but only remember that we have taken them successively under review and that each single one is united to its neighbour, from the first even to the last. . . .

These two methods are the most certain routes to knowledge, and the mind should admit no others. All the rest should be rejected as suspect of error and dangerous. . . .

Rule IV. There is need of a method for finding out the truth. So blind is the curiosity by which mortals are possessed, that they often conduct their minds along unexplored routes. . . . As well might a man burning with an unintelligent desire to find treasure, continuously roam the streets, seeking to find something that a passer by might have chanced to drop. [Yet] this is the way in which most Chemists, many Geometricians, and Philosophers not a few prosecute their studies. . . . It is very certain that unregulated inquiries and confused reflections of this kind only confound the natural light and blind our mental powers. . . . By a method I mean certain and simple rules, such that, if a man observe them accurately, he shall never assume what is false as true, and will never spend his mental efforts to no purpose, but will always gradually increase his knowledge and so arrive at a true understanding of all that does not surpass his powers. . . .

Rule V. Method consists entirely in the order and disposition of the objects towards which our mental vision must be directed if we would find out any truth. We shall comply with it exactly if we reduce involved and obscure propositions step by step to those that are simpler, and then starting with the intuitive apprehension of all those that are absolutely simple, attempt to ascend to the knowledge of all others by precisely similar steps.

. . . .

Rule VI. In order to separate out what is quite simple from what is complex, and to arrange these matters methodically, we ought, in the case of every series in which we have deduced certain facts the one from the other, to notice which fact is simple. . . .

Although this proposition seems to teach nothing very new, it contains, nevertheless, the chief secret of method. . . . For it tells us that all facts can be arranged in certain series . . . in so far as certain truths can be known from others. . . .

We must note first that for the purpose of our procedure, which does not regard things as isolated realities, but compares them with one another in order to discover the dependence in knowledge of one upon the other, all things can be said to be either absolute or relative.

I call that absolute which contains within itself the pure and simple essence of which we are in quest. . . .

But the relative is that which, while participating in the same nature, or at least sharing in it to some degree which enables us to relate it to the absolute and to deduce it from that by a chain of operations, involves in addition something else in its concept which I call relativity. Examples of this are found in whatever is said to be dependent, or an effect, composite, particular, many, unequal, unlike, oblique, etc. . . .

Secondly we must note that there are but few pure and simple essences. . . . These we say should be carefully noticed, for they are just those facts which we have called the simplest in any single series. All the others can only be perceived as deductions from these, either immediate and proximate, or not to be attained save by two or three or more acts of inference. . . . So pronounced is everywhere the inter-connection of ground and consequence, which gives rise, in the objects to be examined, to those series to which every inquiry must be reduced, that it can be investigated by a sure method. . . .

Rule VIII. If in the matters to be examined we come to a step in the series of which our understanding is not sufficiently well able to have an intuitive cognition, we must stop short there. We must make no attempt to examine what follows; thus we shall spare ourselves superfluous labour.[b]

COMMENT ON DESCARTES' METHOD ⟩

The Cartesian method, both in general approach and in detail, reflects Descartes' passionate desire for certainty: "I always had an excessive desire to learn to distinguish the true from the false, in order to see clearly in my actions and to walk with confidence in this life."[c] This desire was natural in an age that had thrown overboard all the authorities on which, for many centuries, the institutions of the West had been grounded. In this connection it should be noted that Descartes followed Scotus and Occam in defining theology as knowledge of revealed truth. In an age of secure faith, insistence on a sharp distinction between philosophy and science had seemed to insure the tenets of religion. But now, in an age of reason, abandonment of the Thomistic notion of a natural theology merely debarred theology from an effective share in the practical affairs of life.

Descartes was a man of his age in believing that the medieval alliance of revelation and Scholasticism must be replaced by a new and, as it were, secular instrument—an instrument that, following the usage of the time, he called "reason." He was also a man of his age in his optimistic belief both in the universality of reason and in its adequacy to perform the tremendous task assigned it.

> Good sense is of all things in the world the most equally distributed. . . . The power of forming a good judgment and of distinguishing the true from the false, which is properly speaking what is called Good sense or Reason, is by nature equal in all men. Hence . . . the diversity of our opinions does not proceed from some men being more rational than others, but solely from the fact that our thoughts pass through diverse channels and the same objects are not considered by all. For to be possessed of good mental powers is not sufficient; the principal matter is to apply them well.[d]

The assumption that there is in all men a native power adequate to know a reality that is fundamentally rational combined the best insights in the Greek and Christian traditions. The Greeks assumed that reason is an adequate power, but they held that it is not equal in all men. The early Christians took little or no account of reason, but they assumed that all men are morally equal before God. By making reason adequate and equal in all men, Descartes laid the intellectual basis for the social and political institutions of democracy. If "the diversity of our opinions" results merely from the fact that we do not all have an opportunity to develop our intellectual powers, education can raise all men to the level of enlightened and responsible citizenship. The American and French Revolutions were among the fruits of these assumptions. In the nineteenth century, however, they came to be questioned and, in many quarters, rejected. Perhaps the most critical problem of contemporary social and political theory is the rehabilitation of this old basis for democracy—or else the discovery of a satisfactory new one.

DESCARTES' MATHEMATICAL MODEL

The fact that almost all the thinkers of the new age talked about "reason" and agreed that it was exemplified in the new scientific method tended to hide how much they differed about its nature. Indeed, Descartes was in agreement with Bacon and Hobbes only in his dissatisfaction with Scholastic science. Whereas Bacon proposed to collect vast tables of empirical data, Descartes proposed to turn the mind inward upon itself so that it could fasten upon some absolutely certain and self-evident truth.

The fact is that, like Hobbes, Descartes had "fallen in love with mathematical certainty."[3] Even in his student days, he had exempted mathematics from his

3 See p. 119.

sweeping condemnation of the sciences: "Most of all was I delighted with Mathematics because of the certainty of its demonstrations and the evidence of its reasoning." Although in those days he had not understood "its true use" and had considered it "of service only in the mechanical arts," even then he had wondered why, "seeing how firm and solid was its basis, no loftier edifice had been reared thereupon." [e]

The great discovery he made in the winter of 1619 was, so he believed, a way of generalizing the method of mathematics so that it could serve as a universal instrument.

> Considering . . . that of all those who have hitherto sought for the truth in the Sciences, it has been the mathematicians alone who have been able to succeed in . . . producing reasons which are evident and certain, I did not doubt that . . . it was requisite that I should borrow all that is best in Geometrical Analysis and Algebra. . . .
>
> [My] Method . . . contains everything which gives certainty to the rules of Arithmetic. . . .
>
> Not having restricted this Method to any particular matter, I promised myself to apply it as usefully to the difficulties of other sciences as I had done to those of Algebra. [f]

But though both Descartes and Hobbes were so impressed by the "certainty of mathematical demonstration" that they modeled their methods on this science, they differed utterly about what "gives it certainty." This difference was reflected in their metaphysics and, indeed, in their whole outlook on life. Descartes believed that there is an objective, rational order in the world, an order that the mind infallibly discerns in its clear and distinct intuitions. Hobbes believed that the certainty of mathematics derives from the fact that it is a knowledge of the consequences of arbitrarily chosen names, from the fact, that is, that the objects judged about are nothing but what we say they are.

Thus, for Descartes, mathematical knowledge was absolute; it was an insight into an objective and rational real (that is, in the terminology that Kant was later to introduce, it was "synthetic"). For Hobbes, it was conditional; it was a manipulation of signs (that is, in Kant's terms, it was "analytic"). For Descartes, mathematical reasoning was the basis on which a great metaphysical structure, including a system of values and a God, could be erected. For Hobbes, mathematical reasoning was merely an instrument by which each man could get clear about his own meanings and discover in what he agreed with, and in what he differed from, others. The difference is obviously fundamental; indeed, it ran through the whole history of early modern philosophy and continues to this day. For instance, among twentieth-century mathematicians, Hermann Weyl holds, in Hobbesian fashion, that

> The sequence of the natural numbers, 1, 2, 3 . . . is our minds' own free creation. It starts with 1, and any number is followed by the next one. That

is all. . . . 2 is the number that follows 1, 3 the number that follows 2, etc. Nothing else. You know very little about Henry VIII when you know that he followed Henry VII on the English throne. But you know all about 8 when you know that it follows 7. . . . Numbers . . . are nothing but marks, and all that is in them we have put into them by the simple rule of straight succession. It is therefore no wonder that we can predict what they do.[g]

On the other hand, G. H. Hardy is a Cartesian:

> There is no sort of agreement about the nature of mathematical reality among either mathematicians or philosophers. Some hold that it is "mental" and that in some sense we construct it, others that it is outside and independent of us. A man who could give a convincing account of mathematical reality would have solved very many of the most difficult problems of metaphysics. . . .
> I believe that mathematical reality lies outside us, and that our function is to discover or *observe* it, and that the theorems which we prove, and which we describe grandiloquently as our "creations," are simply our notes of our observations. This view has been held, in one form or another, by many philosophers of high reputation from Plato onwards.[h]

Mathematicians dispute over this question because it is a philosophical, rather than a strictly mathematical, problem; philosophers dispute over it because it is connected with some very difficult and complex metaphysical and epistemological issues. Thus, though Classical philosophers like Plato and Aristotle did not put the question in quite this way, they would have sided with Descartes and against Hobbes, and so would most of the medieval philosophers. For all these thinkers tended to believe in the reality of universals, to take the principle of contradiction as the final test of truth, to derogate perception in contrast to reason, and to hold that the real is rational. About the only philosophers, before the beginning of the modern period, who would have been sympathetic to the Hobbesian point of view were the medieval nominalists and voluntarists. Because the former held that only particulars are real, they had to deny the possibility of universal and necessary propositions in any field, including mathematics; because the latter held the universe to be an expression, not of God's reason, but of His arbitrary will, they would have come to much the same conclusion.

The issue did not, however, become critical until, with the development of physics in the seventeenth century, mathematics came into sudden prominence. Philosophers like Descartes were in the rationalistic descent from Plato; philosophers of the empirical school were descendants of the medieval voluntarists, at least to the extent that they too emphasized the factuality, rather than the rationality, of the world. This is not, of course, to say that modern empiricists attributed this factuality to God's arbitrary will; they were determined to accept nothing but what they could observe, and what they could observe was mere factuality—coexistence and succession. Hence they threw out God's will along with His reason.

This is enough, perhaps, to suggest some of the complicating interrelations of this question about the nature of mathematical certainty. It is more important for historians of culture to understand the issues involved than to take sides. Let us pass on, therefore, to see how Descartes' decision to model his method of mathematics, and especially his conception of mathematics as synthetic, determined both his philosophical procedure and the nature of the theory that resulted from it.

The Self

DOUBT

The procedure seemed simple. In geometry, according to Rule VI, one first finds some geometric "absolutes" and then arranges in proper order the "relatives" dependent on them. Translating this into more familiar language, Descartes held that in geometry one starts from self-evident and independent truths (such as "A straight line is the shortest distance between two points") and then arranges the various theorems that depend on these truths in proper order. So, in philosophy, Descartes held that one must look first for some metaphysical "absolute" (that is, a self-evident and indubitable principle) and then for the various theorems that, when arranged in proper order, will yield an absolutely certain science of reality. Note that since Descartes held his intuitions to be synthetic, he held that the science so constructed was not a science of names; it was an insight into the nature of an objective and rational reality.

One was to proceed in the search for a metaphysical absolute by challenging every belief, however widely accepted and plausible it might be, in order to see whether it in fact met the test of certainty. Descartes had not turned up any evidence against these beliefs, and he had not really come to doubt them (as a man might come to doubt the integrity of his congressman in the light of the latter's voting record). Descartes' doubt was methodological: He undertook simply to suspend his beliefs until he could prove them conclusively. Given an absolutely certain starting point, he would begin a reconstruction in the course of which his former beliefs would be reinstated as they were deduced in accordance with the new and infallible method that he had derived from his study of geometry.

> As regards all the opinions which up to this time I had embraced, I thought I could not do better than endeavour once for all to sweep them completely away, so that they might later on be replaced, either by others which were better, or by the same, when I had made them conform to the uniformity of a rational scheme.[i]

Some judgments—such as forecasts of the future ("It will rain tomorrow") and estimates of the past ("Homer was the author of the *Iliad*")—are obviously less than certain. Descartes undertook to show that there are serious reasons for doubting even such seemingly indubitable judgments as "This is white paper with printing on it."

[Surely I] cannot reasonably . . . doubt . . . that I am here, seated by the fire, attired in a dressing gown, having this paper in my hands and other similar matters. And how could I deny that these hands and this body are mine, were it not perhaps that I compare myself to certain persons, devoid of sense, whose cerebella are so troubled and clouded by the violent vapours of black bile, that they constantly assure us that they think they are kings when they are really quite poor, or that they are clothed in purple when they are really without covering. . . .

At the same time I must remember that I am . . . in the habit of sleeping, and in my dreams representing to myself the same things or sometimes even less probable things, than do those who are insane in their waking moments. How often has it happened to me that in the night I dreamt that I found myself in this particular place, that I was dressed and seated near the fire, whilst in reality I was lying undressed in bed! . . . On . . . reflection I see . . . manifestly that there are no certain indications by which we may clearly distinguish wakefulness from sleep. . . .

Now let us assume that we are asleep and that all these particulars, e.g. that we open our eyes, shake our head, extend our hands, and so on, are but false delusions; and let us reflect that possibly neither our hands nor our whole body are such as they appear to us to be. At the same time . . . , although these general things, to wit, eyes, a head, hands, and such like, may be imaginary, we are bound . . . to confess that there are at least some other objects yet more simple and more universal, which are real and true. . . .

[Surely] Arithmetic, Geometry and other sciences of that kind which only treat of things that are very simple and very general, without taking great trouble to ascertain whether they are actually existent or not, contain some measure of certainty and an element of the indubitable. For whether I am awake or asleep, two and three together always form five, and the square can never have more than four sides, and it does not seem possible that truths so clear and apparent can be suspected of any falsity.

Nevertheless I have long had fixed in my mind the belief that an all-powerful God existed by whom I have been created such as I am. But how do I know that He has not brought it to pass that . . . I am . . . deceived every time I add two and three . . . ? But possibly God has not desired that I should be thus deceived, for He is said to be supremely good. If, however, it is contrary to His goodness to have made me such that I constantly deceive myself, it would also appear to be contrary to His goodness to permit me to be sometimes deceived, and nevertheless I cannot doubt that He does permit this. . . .

[Moreover, we cannot be certain] that God . . . is supremely good and the fountain of truth. [He may be an] evil genius not less powerful than deceitful, [who] has employed his whole energies in deceiving me; I shall consider that the heavens, the earth, colours, figures, sound, and all other external things [may be] nought but the illusions and dreams of which this genius has availed himself in order to lay traps for my credulity. . . .

At the end I feel constrained to confess that there is nothing in all that I formerly believed to be true, of which I cannot in some measure doubt, and that not merely through want of thought or through levity, but for reasons which are very powerful and maturely considered.[j]

"COGITO ERGO SUM"

But now, in the midst of this seemingly universal doubt, Descartes found one thing that he certainly and infallibly knew—that he doubted. Even supposing the worst—that God is an "evil genius not less powerful than deceitful" who devotes all His "energies to deceiving me"—it is impossible to suppose that He could deceive me about my own existence. He may deceive me about everything else, but the I that is so deceived must exist in order to be deceived and so cannot be a deception. I may doubt that a sheet of paper is now before my eyes; I may even doubt that $2 + 3 = 5$. But if I try to doubt my own existence, this doubt disproves itself. I must surely exist in order to doubt that I exist.

> I suppose, then, that all the things that I see are false; I persuade myself that nothing has ever existed of all that my fallacious memory represents to me. I consider that I possess no senses; I imagine that body, figure, extension, movement and place are but fictions of my mind. What, then, can be esteemed as true? Perhaps nothing at all. . . .
>
> Yet I hesitate, for . . . am I so dependent on body and senses that I cannot exist without these? But I was persuaded that there was nothing in all the world, that there was no heaven, no earth, that there were no minds, nor any bodies: was I not then likewise persuaded that I did not exist? Not at all; of a surety I myself did exist since I persuaded myself of something [or merely because I thought of something]. But there is some deceiver or other, very powerful and very cunning, who ever employs his ingenuity in deceiving me. Then without doubt I exist also if he deceives me, and let him deceive me as much as he will, he can never cause me to be nothing so long as I think that I am something. So that after having reflected well and carefully examined all things, we must come to the definite conclusion that this proposition: I am, I exist, is necessarily true each time that I pronounce it, or that I mentally conceive it.[k]

Descartes' reasoning at this point is similar to Augustine's. But what for Augustine had been merely incidental to certain theological considerations became for Descartes the basis for a whole philosophy. Indeed, the fact that in his quest for absolute certainty Descartes was led to the self, the fact that the existence of the self became the premise of his whole philosophy, was at once a symptom of the enormous change that had already occurred and a foreshadowing of the subsequent course of philosophic thought.

Here, in his certainty of his own existence, Descartes had the "absolute," the indubitable truth, that he needed as a starting point for his science of reality. Accordingly, he proposed to follow his own rules—to arrange his thoughts in "due order" and to advance by a series of simple steps, each of which could be seen to be clearly and distinctly true. The road proved to lead from self to God, and from God to the physical world. Let us see, therefore, how Descartes sought to prove the existence of God and so to retrieve this important belief from the limbo of doubt into which he had provisionally cast it.

God

PROOFS OF GOD'S EXISTENCE

Though Descartes' proof of God's existence is somewhat complicated, the main steps are easily outlined: (1) Everything, including our ideas, has a cause. (2) We have an idea of God. (3) Nothing less than God is adequate to be the cause of our idea of God. Therefore, (4) God exists.

> Now it is manifest by the natural light that there must at least be as much reality in the efficient and total cause as in its effect. For, pray, whence can the effect derive its reality, if not from its cause? And in what way can this cause communicate this reality to it, unless it possessed it in itself? And from this it follows, not only that something cannot proceed from nothing, but likewise that what is more perfect—that is to say, what has more reality within itself—cannot proceed from the less perfect. And this is not only evidently true of those effects which possess actual or formal reality, but also of the ideas in which we consider merely what is termed objective reality.[4] To take an example, the stone which has not yet existed not only cannot now commence to be unless it has been produced by something which possesses within itself, either formally or eminently, all that enters into the composition of the stone. . . . But, further, the idea of . . . a stone cannot exist in me unless it has been placed within me by some cause which possesses within it at least as much reality as that which I conceive to exist in the . . . stone. . . .
>
> Although it may be the case that one idea gives birth to another idea, that cannot continue to be so indefinitely; for in the end we must reach an idea whose cause shall be so to speak an archetype, in which the whole reality which is so to speak objectively in these ideas is contained formally.

4 [This terminology may confuse modern readers. Descartes was distinguishing here between (1) the objects we think about (which Descartes described as having "formal" existence) and (2) the ideas we have of these objects (which Descartes described as having "objective" existence). His point was that everything, including our ideas, must be traced back, ultimately, to some nonideal, or "formal," cause. This may be correct, but it was illegitimate for Descartes to slip such a crucial distinction into the argument. Since he never subjected it to "methodological doubt," he could not know whether it would survive this challenge—AUTHOR.]

Thus the light of nature causes me to know clearly that the ideas in me are like images which can, in truth, easily fall short of the perfection of the objects from which they have been derived, but which can never contain anything greater or more perfect. . . .

But what am I to conclude from [all this]? It is this, that if the objective reality of any one of my ideas is of such a nature as clearly to make me recognise that it is not in me either formally or eminently, and that consequently I cannot myself be the cause of it, it follows of necessity that I am not alone in the world, but that there is another being which exists, or which is the cause of this idea. . . .

But of my ideas, beyond that which represents me to myself, as to which there can here be no difficulty, there is another which represents a God, and there are others representing corporeal and inanimate things, others angels, others animals, and others again which represent to me men similar to myself. . . .

And in regard to the ideas of corporeal objects, I do not recognise in them anything so great or so excellent that they might not have possibly proceeded from myself. . . .

To these it is certainly not necessary that I should attribute any author other than myself. For if they are false, i.e. if they represent things which do not exist, the light of nature shows me that they issue from nought, that is to say, that they are only in me in so far as something is lacking to the perfection of my nature. But if they are true, nevertheless because they exhibit so little reality to me that I cannot even clearly distinguish the thing represented from non-being, I do not see any reason why they should not be produced by myself. . . .

Hence there remains only the idea of God, concerning which we must consider whether it is something which cannot have proceeded from me myself. By the name God I understand a substance that is infinite, [eternal, immutable,] independent, all-knowing, all-powerful, and by which I myself and everything else, if anything else does exist, have been created. Now all these characteristics are such that the more diligently I attend to them, the less do they appear capable of proceeding from me alone; hence, from what has been already said, we must conclude that God necessarily exists.

For although the idea of substance is within me owing to the fact that I am substance, nevertheless I should not have the idea of an infinite substance—since I am finite—if it had not proceeded from some substance which was veritably infinite.

Nor should I imagine that I do not perceive the infinite by a true idea, but only by the negation of the finite . . . ; for, on the contrary, I see that there is manifestly more reality in infinite substance than in finite, and therefore that in some way I have in me the notion of the infinite earlier than the finite—to wit, the notion of God before that of myself. For how would it be possible that I should know that I doubt and desire, that is to say, that something is lacking to me, and that I am not quite perfect, unless I had within me some idea of a Being more perfect than myself, in comparison with which I should recognise the deficiencies of my nature? . . .

But possibly I am something more than I suppose myself to be, and perhaps all those perfections which I attribute to God are in some way potentially in me. . . . I am already sensible that my knowledge increases [and perfects itself] little by little, and I see nothing which can prevent it from increasing more and more into infinitude. . . .

[But] in the first place, although it were true that every day my knowledge acquired new degrees of perfection, . . . nevertheless . . . it can never be actually infinite, since it can never reach a point so high that it will be unable to attain to any greater increase. But I understand God to be actually infinite, so that He can add nothing to His supreme perfection. And finally I perceive that the objective being of an idea cannot be produced by a being that exists potentially only, which properly speaking is nothing, but only by a being which is formal or actual. . . .

I see nothing in all that I have just said which by the light of nature is not manifest to anyone who desires to think attentively on the subject.[1]

CRITICISM OF THIS PROOF

This proof is a revision of Anselm's ontological argument insofar as Descartes too held that the idea of God necessarily has God for its object. But whereas Anselm had maintained that God's existence follows from a purely logical consideration (perfection implies existence), Descartes introduced a causal argument: God is the only possible cause of the idea of God. There are thus two stages in the Cartesian proof, and each of them may be challenged: (1) Do we really have a clear and distinct idea of an infinite and perfect being? (2) Supposing that we do have such an idea, is God its only possible cause?

(1) Many medieval philosophers, among them St. Thomas, denied that man's idea of God is adequate to serve as the basis for an ontological type of argument. But far more drastic criticisms of this first stage in Descartes' proof were made by certain of his contemporaries. It so happened that one of Descartes' friends circulated the manuscript of the *Meditations* among a number of theologians and philosophers. The comments of these readers were forwarded to Descartes and eventually printed (along with Descartes' replies) in conjunction with the *Meditations*. The reply of one of these critics, Hobbes, was in part as follows:

> When I think of a man, I recognize an idea, or image, with figure and colour as its constituents; and concerning this I can raise the question whether or not it is the likeness of a man. . . .
>
> But, when one thinks of an Angel, what is noticed in the mind is now the image of a flame, now that of a fair winged child, and this, I may be sure, has no likeness to an Angel, and hence is not the idea of an Angel. But believing that created beings exist that are the ministers of God, invisible and immaterial, we give the name of Angel to this object of belief, this supposed being, though the idea used in imagining an Angel is, nevertheless, constructed out of the ideas of visible things.
>
> It is the same way with the most holy name of God; we have no image, no idea corresponding to it. . . .

> If there is no idea of God . . . the whole of [Descartes'] argument collapses. Further (if it is my body that is being considered) the idea of my own self proceeds [principally] from sight; but (if it is a question of the soul) there is no idea of the soul. We only infer by means of the reason that there is something internal in the human body, which imparts to it its animal motion, and by means of which it feels and moves; and this, whatever it be, we name the soul, without employing any idea.[m]

Though Hobbes prudently referred here to "the most holy name of God," it is evident that, in his view, "God" was only an empty noise. This follows inevitably from the premise that only body in motion exists.

(2) Even if it be allowed that we have an idea of God, it does not follow that God must exist to be the cause of this idea. In another set of objections to Descartes' proof, a group of theologians maintained that

> We find in our own selves a sufficient basis on which alone to erect [the idea of a supreme being], even though that supreme being did not exist. . . . Do I not see that I, in thinking, have some degree of perfection? . . . Hence I have a basis on which to construct the thought of any number of degrees and so to add one degree of perfection to another to infinity, just as, given the existence of a single degree of light or heat, I can add and imagine fresh degrees up to infinity. Why, on similar reasoning, can I not add, to any degree of being that I perceive in myself any other degree I please, and out of the whole number capable of addition construct the idea of a perfect being? . . . Besides this, how do you know that that idea would have come before your mind if you had not been nurtured among men of culture . . . ? Have you not derived it from reflections previously entertained, from books, from interchange of converse with your friends, etc., not from your own mind alone or from a supreme being who exists? . . . It seems to be shown clearly that that idea springs from previous notions by the fact that the natives of Canada, the Hurons, and other savages, have no idea in their minds such as this. . . . You do not possess the idea of God any more than that of an infinite number or of an infinite line; and though you did possess this, yet there could be no such number. . . . The idea of the unity and simplicity of a sole perfection which embraces all other perfections, is merely the product of the reasoning mind.[n]

To most modern readers this argument will probably seem far more convincing than Descartes'. Recent studies in psychology and the other social sciences have disposed us to be sympathetic to the view that men's ideas grow out of and reflect their social milieu rather than some sort of alleged suprasensible reality. But whether this invalidates Descartes' argument is a difficult question, for Descartes' entire case depends on his belief that there is "at least as much reality in the cause as in the effect."

Here again Descartes made a move that was quite unwarranted in terms of his own announced procedure. Despite his claim to have suspended belief in every opinion that had not survived the challenge of methodological doubt, Descartes never for a moment doubted that the cause contains at least as much reality as the effect. Though he held this proposition to be "manifest by the natural light," it cannot be self-evidently true. If it were, everyone would accept it as soon as the meanings of the terms were understood—as everyone accepts the assertion that cats are felines as soon as the meanings of "cat" and "feline" are understood. The proposition seemed self-evident to Descartes because he unconsciously made a whole cluster of assumptions, including the assumption that reality is rational. But it is not *self*-evident; it depends on those other beliefs for any plausibility it may have.

That this is so will be plain to modern readers, since most of us do not share the assumptions that Descartes unconsciously made. Indeed, the assumptions of modern readers are likely to be so different from those of Descartes that it is difficult for us even to understand what he meant by this proposition, let alone to accept it as "manifest by the natural light." For whereas Descartes thought of causality as a rational relation, many people today think of it as a merely spatiotemporal relation between otherwise unconnected events. But although Descartes' view is not, as he thought, self-evidently true, it is not self-evidently false. Indeed, here, as in the problem of mathematical certainty, we reach a fundamental parting of the ways.

The disagreement between Descartes and his theological friends about the idea of "infinity" is typical. He agreed with them, of course, that no one has ever *perceived* an actually infinite object or quantity; the most that one ever perceives is "very large." But whereas they thought it possible to construct the idea of infinity by adding together experiences of "very large," Descartes maintained that without a priori knowledge of "infinity" men would never even have the sense experience "very large." Descartes' reasoning here was characteristically Platonic: Men, Plato held, must know the form "equality" in order to experience those relative equalities that they encounter in sense perception. Descartes shared with Plato the underlying thesis that knowledge implies the existence of true universals and, ultimately, the existence of a single, supremely real entity, which Plato called the "Form of the Good" and which Descartes called "God."

For Descartes, as for other rationalists, the rationality of reality was demonstrated by the certainty of mathematical knowledge. Since it did not occur to him that mathematics might be merely a knowledge of the consequences of names, it seemed to him evident that there must be a real and rational order of entities that is the object of mathematical thinking. Now, although in Rule VI of his method he distinguished between what he called "absolutes" (which are the indubitable starting points of demonstrations) and "relatives," Descartes' proof of the existence of God depends on every intuition's being the intuition of a "relative." In other words, the "absolutes" of his method turn out to be only "relatively absolute."[5] The assumption underlying the proof of the existence of God is that the intuition of a necessary relation (for example, A implies B) is possible only because the pair of entities in question (A and B) are a part of a much larger whole and because our thought moves within the context of this whole. Hence, any single intuition is true only because there is a system that includes this particular intuited connection. Wherever a man's thought starts, it always starts at some particular "where"; that is, its starting point is always conditioned by something lying outside it. And however far his thought moves, it always remains inside a "more" that is larger than itself.

Consider the intuition of self-existence. Though it appears at first sight to be a kind of absolute, or encapsuled, truth, we see, when we reflect, that its truth (and so our certainty) rests on conditions beyond itself. The recognition that the self is only a relative absolute seems to be the inner meaning of Descartes' insistence that it is the act of thinking and of doubting that affirms the self's existence. On the one hand, it is certain that the self exists; on the other hand, this self that so certainly exists is a doubter. Such a self—so finite, so limited— could not really be the guarantor of its own existence. Hence the certain existence of a doubting self demonstrates that this self is part of, and dependent for its being on, a larger system.

Now, in accordance with a venerable tradition, Descartes named this "rational more" that validates every finite truth "God." Considered from this standpoint— from the standpoint, that is, of a rational reality constituted by "relative" absolutes—Descartes' version of the ontological argument is valid. If the doctrine that the real is rational implies that every individual thought is conditioned by a rational more, and if we choose to call this more "God," then obviously God is real.

But, just as obviously, this proof depends on the doctrine that the real is rational, a doctrine that, in our own empirically oriented age, has come to be widely doubted. Consider once again the Cartesian thesis that there is "at least as much reality in the cause as in the effect." This amounts to equating the causal relation with the relation of implication, so that "cause" is equivalent to "prem- ise," and "effect" is equivalent to "conclusion." Now, whereas Descartes identified implication and causality, we sharply distinguish them. Thus, whereas he might say that being baldheaded is the "cause" of having no hair, and that there is at least as much reality in the cause as in the effect, we would say that being baldheaded "implies" having no hair (since "having no hair" is the definition of "baldheadedness"), and that the "cause" of having no hair is not baldness but such-and-such a condition of the scalp. To say that baldness is the cause of hairlessness is no more meaningful, we feel, than the declaration of the doctor

5 Descartes himself seems, at least part of the time, to have realized this. Thus, in the discussion of Rule VI, in which the notion of "absolutes" was first introduced, he said that "some things are from one point of view more absolute than others, but from a different standpoint more rela- tive."

in Molière's play that the dormitive power of opium causes its soporific quality.

Hence, as with St. Thomas' quite different proofs of the existence of God, Descartes' proof is either obviously true or obviously false, depending on what view one adopts about the nature of reality. Which view is correct? As the history of modern philosophy abundantly illustrates, each view taken by itself gets into almost hopeless difficulties; yet because the various views are so different, it is extremely difficult to see how they can be satisfactorily combined.

DIFFERENCES BETWEEN DESCARTES' AND PLATO'S VIEWS OF KNOWLEDGE

So far, in this account of Descartes' conception of knowledge and its objects, his affinity with Plato has been emphasized. But there are several important differences, one of which is suggested by the fact that whereas Plato called his "rational more" the "Form of the Good," Descartes called it "God." Though there was a mystical side to Plato's thought and though his account of the Form of the Good certainly contained overtones that a later generation developed into a suprarational philosophy, on the whole Plato himself remained a rationalist, regarding reason as self-sustaining and self-validating. For him, what any particular truth required was more rational truth, not divine light.

Descartes' view of reason was much more ambivalent. Like the other men of his age, he wanted to insist on the autonomy of reason, unlimited by ecclesiastical sanctions. "We should never," he insisted, "allow ourselves to be persuaded of anything excepting by the evidence of our reason." Yet, though he held reason to be independent, Descartes did not think of it as the *completely* secular and self-sustaining power that Plato and Aristotle had conceived it to be. It was characteristic of the complex new world that even those who, like Hobbes, made reason wholly secular hesitated to make it self-sustaining. Hobbes saw that, left to their own devices, men will agree that "right reason" is always right but nevertheless quarrel over whose reason is right. The sovereign "must therefore declare" it; whatever the sovereign says is right reason *is* right reason—by definition and by the power the sovereign possesses to enforce his decision.[6] But Descartes was not willing to let reason remain utterly secular. According to him, the "more" that validates our finite reason is not merely *more* reason. There is more reason, it is true; but behind the more reason (and not clearly distinguished from it in Descartes' mind) there lurks a personal and transcendent God.

Descartes' Platonism had a Neoplatonic overlay: Beyond the rational was the suprarational; beyond the "rational more," a "transcendent more." Thus intuition, usually conceived of by Descartes as an active power in us, sometimes became a passive state in which we are illumined from above; and reason, far

---

6 The parallel with the position adopted in the Soviet Union about scientific truth is striking. When Soviet geneticists disputed in an unseemly way, and without reaching definitive conclusions, about the inheritance of acquired characteristics, the state settled the matter.

from being a searchlight that focuses a clear beam on real entities out there in the world beyond us, became a superillumination that fills our souls with transcendent light and truth. Thus, "Intuitive knowledge is an illumination of the mind by which it sees in the light of God those things which it pleases Him to have the mind discover, by a direct impression on our understanding of the divine light. So far, the mind cannot be considered as an agent; it only receives the rays of divinity."

Here rationalism has passed over into religion and must find a higher sanction for itself. Pressed to its conclusion, this would have led Descartes into radically different emphases—emphases that, it cannot be doubted, he would have resisted. After all, one of his major theses was that the physical world exists and that mechanics is a true science. Although the logical outcome of the religious, Neoplatonic strain in Descartes' thought would have been a physical world even less real than Plato's, Descartes' interest in Galilean mechanics required a physical world far more real than Plato's. For Plato's physical world was at best a shadowy imitation of the immaterial forms; insofar as this world had any kind of ontological status, it was of the same kind as the forms, only in much lower degree. Hence it would never have occurred to Plato to ask whether mathematical knowledge applies to the physical world—it obviously does, or so it seemed to him, for physical things "participate" in their forms. By the same token, since physical things participate only inadequately in their forms, physics, according to Plato, is only a likely story.

But Galilean mechanics required a very different way of looking at the relation between mathematics and nature. First, if mechanics is an exact science, mathematics must apply absolutely to the world mechanics knows. Second, the objects of mechanics are bodies, occupying space, moving in time, having an independent existence. The real is truly rational—this Kepler and Galileo believed as firmly as had Plato. But no one who understood Kepler's and Galileo's work could possibly hold that the rational and the real are coextensive. A deductive system based on the hypothesis that the planets' paths are circular and that their velocities vary with the distances traversed is just as rational as the deductive system based on elliptical paths and velocities that vary with the areas swept out. As Galileo indicated, we must not only "demonstrate"; we must "observe" in order to discover whether our demonstrations are relevant to the actual physical world. The world of Galilean mechanics thus has a status in its own right, quite different from that of the physical world in Plato's theory. This added a complication to Cartesianism that must now be examined.

The Physical World

So far, if Descartes' arguments are acceptable, he has established the existence of (1) the self, an imperfect and incomplete being, and (2) God, that *ens per-*

fectissimum that is the completion and fulfillment of this self and of any other beings that may subsequently be proved to exist. We have seen how the proof of God's existence rests on the existence of self.[7] Let us now see how the proof of the existence of the physical world rests on the existence of God.

> Nothing further now remains but to inquire whether material things exist. And certainly I at least know that these may exist in so far as they are considered as the objects of pure mathematics, since in this aspect I perceive them clearly and distinctly. For there is no doubt that God possesses the power to produce everything that I am capable of perceiving with distinctness, and I have never deemed that anything was impossible for Him, unless I found a contradiction in attempting to conceive it clearly. . . .
>
> [Next,] because I know that all things which I apprehend clearly and distinctly can be created by God as I apprehend them, it suffices that I am able to apprehend one thing apart from another clearly and distinctly in order to be certain that the one is different from the other, since they may be made to exist in separation at least by the omnipotence of God. . . . [Now, besides my] clear and distinct idea of myself . . . as . . . a thinking and unextended thing, . . . I possess a distinct idea of body . . . as an extended and unthinking thing. . . .
>
> I observe also in me some other faculties such as that of change of position, the assumption of different figures and such like, [and] it is very clear that these faculties, if it be true that they exist, must be attached to some corporeal or extended substance, and not to an intelligent substance, since in the clear and distinct conception of these there is some sort of extension found to be present, but no intellection at all. There is certainly further in me a certain passive faculty of perception, that is, of receiving and recognising the ideas of sensible things, but this would be useless to me, if there were not either in me or in some other thing another active faculty capable of forming and producing these ideas. But this active faculty cannot exist in me seeing that it does not presuppose thought, and also that those ideas are often produced in me without my contributing in any way to the same, and often even against my will; it is thus necessarily the case that the faculty resides in some substance different from me in which all the reality which is objectively in the ideas that are produced by this faculty is formally or eminently contained. . . . And this substance is either a body, that is, a corporeal nature . . . or it is God Himself. . . . But, since God is no deceiver, it is very manifest that He does not communicate to me these ideas immediately and by Himself. . . . For since He has given me no faculty to recognise that this is the case, but, on the other hand, a very great inclination to believe that they are conveyed to me by corporeal objects, I do not see how He could be defended from the accusation of deceit if these ideas were produced by causes other than corporeal objects. Hence we must allow that corporeal things exist.º

---

7 The *proof* of God's existence depends on the existence of self just because the *being* of self turns out to depend on the existence of God.

Whereas the validation of my own existence and of the truths of mathematics rests on God's nature as a "rational more,"[8] the proof of the existence of the physical world rests on God's goodness and His power—on His will, not His reason. The fact that this proof depends on God's will, instead of on His reason, is a sign that Descartes recognized that there is a distinction between "corporeal nature in so far as it is the object of pure mathematics" and corporeal nature as extended magnitude. The fact that various theorems can be proved true of the geometric entity "triangle" does not establish that any triangular-shaped bits of matter actually exist in the physical world.

Most people today would agree with Descartes in drawing this distinction but would maintain that whether or not physical triangles exist is an empirical, not a theological, question: "Look around, observe, measure," they would say. But what we observe are concrete, sensuous triangles, that is, triangles drawn on paper or cut out of wood or leather. What Descartes wanted to prove was the existence of that abstract, nonsensuous matter, possessing only "length, breadth, and depth," that he conceived to be the cause of our sensations of leather, paper, and wood triangles. Obviously, the existence of this nonsensuous matter could not be proved by reference to sense perception, for we cannot sense the nonsensuous. Hence Descartes appealed to the goodness of a God who would not allow us to be deceived about anything as clear and distinct as the principles of mechanics.

This appeal to God's goodness had another advantage for Descartes. It allowed him to make a place for final causes in a mechanistic universe. If his proof of the existence of matter is valid, the physical world is God's creature, an expression of His providence; yet it runs according to mechanical law and can be completely understood without any further reference to purposes or final causes. In this way, Descartes hoped to preserve the teleologically oriented world of the Middle Ages without interfering with the nonteleological physical theory that scientists were developing.

Descartes' Conception of Substance

So far, we have seen how Descartes attempted to prove the existence of self, God, and matter. But what *are* self, God, and matter? It seemed obvious to Descartes that everything that exists is either a substance or an attribute of a substance. Since self, matter, and God are clearly not attributes, they are substances. The following theorems illustrate Descartes' treatment:

> *Prin. LI. What substance is, and that it is a name which we cannot attribute in the same sense to God and to His creatures. . . .* By substance, we can

8 See p. 171.

understand nothing else than a thing which so exists that it needs no other thing in order to exist. And in fact only one single substance can be understood which clearly needs nothing else, namely, God. We perceive that all other things can exist only by the help of the concourse of God. That is why the word substance does not pertain *univoce* to God and to other things, as they say in the Schools, that is, no common signification . . . which will apply equally to God and to them can be distinctly understood.

Prin. LII. That it may be attributed univocally to the soul and to body, and how we know substance. Created substances, however, whether corporeal or thinking, may be conceived under this common concept; for they are things which need only the concurrence of God in order to exist. But yet substance cannot be first discovered merely from the fact that it is a thing that exists, for that fact alone is not observed by us. We may, however, easily discover it by means of any one of its attributes because it is a common notion that nothing is possessed of no attributes, properties, or qualities. For this reason, when we perceive any attribute, we therefore conclude that some existing thing or substance to which it may be attributed, is necessarily present.

Prin. LIII. That each substance has a principal attribute, and that the attribute of the mind is thought, while that of body is extension. But although any one attribute is sufficient to give us a knowledge of substance, there is always one principal property of substance which constitutes its nature and essence, and on which all the others depend. Thus extension in length, breadth and depth, constitutes the nature of corporeal substance; and thought constitutes the nature of thinking substance. For all else that may be attributed to body presupposes extension, and is but a mode of this extended thing; as everything that we find in mind is but so many diverse forms of thinking.[p]

That substances exist seemed so obvious to Descartes that he held we must "conclude" that a substance is "necessarily present" wherever we encounter a property, even though the substance in question is "not observed by us." Hence it never occurred to him to subject the concept of substance to criticism in accordance with his program of systematic doubt, even though he was prepared to doubt the existence of things that *are* "observed by us." Like Bacon, Descartes illustrates both the characteristic desire of the new age to make an absolutely fresh start and the difficulty—not to say the impossibility—of managing to do so.

Hobbes, naturally, was more critical of the notion of substance: "Do you understand the connexion of *substance* and *incorporeal?* If you do, explain it in English; for the words are Latin. It is something, you will say, that being *without body, stands under*—. Stands under what? . . . *Substance* and *body* signify the same thing; and therefore *substance incorporeal* are words, which when they are joined together, destroy one another, as if a man should say, an *incorporeal body.*"[q] As we shall see, this Hobbesian scepticism about substance was congenial to the empirical criterion of meaning that gradually developed in England. As a result, the whole concept of substance, corporeal and incorporeal, came under attack there.[9] But on the Continent, and, indeed, wherever the ideas of British empiricism did not penetrate, substance for a long time remained a prime metaphysical category. Indeed, the substantival way of thinking is still deeply embedded in Western culture, and many of the traditional values of the West have remained bound up with substance. Accordingly, although much of the history of modern philosophy has been concerned with criticizing this concept, much has been devoted to revising and reinterpreting it.

The Cartesian Compromise

It has been noted that the task of Hobbes's successors was to find a *via media* that would allow them to adopt the principles of the new physics without ending, as Hobbes had done, in a completely secular and amoral view of the universe.[10] Descartes was just as enthusiastic an admirer of the new science as was Hobbes, but, unlike Hobbes, he was a sincerely religious man and a loyal Catholic. He was well aware of the Church's misgivings concerning the implications of the new science, and one of the main motives of his philosophy was to show that these suspicions were ill founded and thus to free physicists from the prohibitions that were interfering with their work.

The basic idea of Descartes' compromise was very simple, and it followed immediately from his belief that in proving the existence of self and matter he had proved each to be an independently existing substance. If mind and body are completely different kinds of things, and if the truths about each follow from the distinct nature of each, it is impossible for the science of minds and the science of bodies to contradict each other. Theologians, therefore, have no reason to interfere with the study of the new physics, and physicists have no reason to claim any special competence regarding spiritual truths. Further, men need never fear, for instance, that minds, as well as bodies, are determined by antecedent events in time; nor is there any danger that free will, moral responsibility, and God will prove to be merely subjective illusions in a materialistic universe. There can be no conflict between science and religion, for each is sovereign in its own sphere and neither has any standing in the sphere of the other. The truths about minds are just as true of minds as the truths about bodies are true of bodies; but the truths about minds are not true of bodies, nor are the truths about bodies true of minds.

This solution may sound reasonable to many people even today. If so, this is testimony to the persistent influence of Cartesianism. But Descartes' solution depends on the validity of the substantival mode of thought that, as has just been noted, was soon to come under heavy criticism. And even for those who accept

9 See pp. 249–51, 281–88, and 304.
10 See p. 153.

the concept of substance, the Cartesian compromise is full of paradoxes. Some of these will be discussed later. For the present, let us see how Descartes proceeded to develop his dual-substance theory.

Nature of Material Things

The physical world, Descartes held, is a material plenum; all change is local motion of various parts of this plenum; since this motion conforms to simple, mathematically statable laws, it is capable of being predicted with complete certainty.

The following theorems illustrate these and other propositions that Descartes believed to be true of the physical world.

> *Prin. IV. That the nature of body consists . . . in . . . extension alone.* . . . The nature of matter or of body in its universal aspect, does not consist in its being hard, or heavy, or coloured, or one that affects our senses in some other way, but solely in the fact that it is a substance extended in length, breadth and depth. . . . If, whenever we moved our hands in some direction, all the bodies in that part retreated with the same velocity as our hands approached them, we should never feel hardness; and yet we have no reason to believe that the bodies which recede in this way would on this account lose what makes them bodies. It follows from this that the nature of body does not consist in hardness. The same reason shows us that weight, colour, and all the other qualities of the kind that is perceived in corporeal matter, may be taken from it, it remaining meanwhile entire: it thus follows that the nature of body depends on none of these.
> . . . .
> *Prin. X-XI. What space or internal place is.* Space or internal place and the corporeal substance which is contained in it, are not different otherwise than in the mode in which they are conceived of by us. For, in truth, the same extension in length, breadth, and depth, which constitutes space, constitutes body; and the difference between them consists only in the fact that in body we consider extension as particular and conceive it to change just as body changes; in space, on the contrary, we attribute to extension a generic unity. . . .
> Extension which constitutes the nature of body [and] space [do not] differ, excepting as the nature of the genus or species differs from the nature of the individual.
> . . . .
> *Prin. XIII. What external place is.* . . . The words place and space signify nothing different from the body which is said to be in a place, and merely designate its magnitude, figure, and situation as regards other bodies. . . . For example, if we consider a man seated at the stern of a vessel when it is carried out to sea, he may be said to be in one place if we regard the parts of the

vessel . . . : and yet he will be found continually to change his position, if regard be paid to the neighbouring shores. . . . But if at length we are persuaded that there are no points in the universe that are really immovable, as will presently be shown to be probable, we shall conclude that there is nothing that has a permanent place except in so far as it is fixed by our thought.

. . . .

Prin. XVI. That it is contrary to reason to say that there is a vacuum or space in which there is absolutely nothing. . . . It is evident that [a vacuum] cannot exist, because the extension of space or internal place, is not different from that of body. . . .

Prin. XVII. That a vacuum, in the ordinary sense, does not exclude all body. And when we take this word vacuum in its ordinary sense, we do not mean a place or space in which there is absolutely nothing, but only a place in which there are none of those things which we expected to find there. Thus because a pitcher is made to hold water, we say that it is empty when it contains nothing but air.

. . . .

Prin. XXI. That extension of the world is . . . indefinite. We likewise recognise that this world, or the totality of corporeal substance, is extended without limit, because wherever we imagine a limit we are not only still able to imagine beyond that limit spaces indefinitely extended, but we perceive these to be in reality such as we imagine them, that is to say that they contain in them corporeal substance indefinitely extended. For, as has been already shown very fully, the idea of extension that we perceive in any space whatever is quite evidently the same as the idea of corporeal substance.

. . . .

Prin. XXIII-V. That all the variety in matter, or all the diversity of its forms, depends on motion. There is therefore but one matter in the whole universe, and we know this by the simple fact of its being extended. All the properties which we clearly perceive in it may be reduced to the one, viz. that it can be divided, or moved according to its parts. . . .

But motion (i.e. local motion, for I can conceive no other kind, and do not consider that we ought to conceive any other in nature), . . . is the *transference of one part of matter or one body from the vicinity of those bodies that are in immediate contact with it . . . into the vicinity of others.* . . .

Prin. XXVI. That more action is not required for movement than for rest.

. . . .

Prin. XXXVI. That God is the First Cause of movement and that He always preserves an equal amount of movement in the universe.

Prin. XXXVII. The first law of nature: that each thing as far as in it lies, continues always in the same state.

. . . .

Prin. XXXIX. The second law of nature: that all motion is of itself in a straight line; and thus things which move in a circle always tend to recede from the centre of the circle that they describe.

Prin. XL. The third law: that a body that comes in contact with another stronger than itself, loses nothing of its movement; if it meets one less strong, it loses as much as it passes over to that body.[r]

The net result of Descartes' identification of material substance with extension and of extension with space was to make physics an absolutely certain science. For by means of this double identification, geometry, which is the absolutely valid science of the properties of space, becomes the instrument by which the nature of material things is to be investigated. As Descartes said, "I do not accept or desire any other principle in Physics than in Geometry or abstract Mathematics, because all the phenomena of nature may be explained by their means, and sure demonstrations can be given of them."[8]

This identification of physics with geometry neatly avoids the Hobbesian chasm between "science" and "knowledge of fact." What was only a pragmatically justified assumption for Hobbes—that there is a rationale in the physical world and that this rationale is geometric in character—was *proved*, Descartes thought, by the fact that God created material substance and endowed it exclusively with geometric properties. Thus—such was the ingenuity of Descartes' scheme—it was by an appeal to religion that the Hobbesian chasm between theory and fact was bridged and the validity of physics was assured.

But, according to Descartes, though the physical world is God's creature, it behaves as if it were not. Material objects do not, for instance, seek "the Divine likeness"; they merely move on impact with other bodies. Hence physics does not investigate final causes or study the forms of things; it formulates the various laws of motion. The reason physicists can thus dispense with the study of final causes is that, once God created the material plenum and put a "quantity of motion" in it, He obligingly withdrew. (Of course, though He has since abstained from active intervention, He remains conveniently in the background to see to it that the quantity of motion remains constant and that motion is communicated from one part of the plenum to another in regular ways.) Descartes recognized, of course, that since "each body is affected by many others at the same time," exact prediction of the motions in the plenum will be "difficult." But he believed it at least theoretically possible to ascertain exactly "how much the movement of any bodies is altered by impact of other bodies," and so to construct a certain and complete science of physical nature, not only for relatively simple bodies like the planets but even for complex organisms.

Thus, according to Descartes, animals are thoroughgoing machines. What is called their learning is not a coming-to-know; it is merely mechanical adjustment.[11] Their behavior is as much determined by the stimuli that reach their bodies from other bodies as the behavior of one billiard ball is determined by the "stimuli" it receives from another. Since the behavior of animals is determined by antecedent events in time, it would be possible, if enough were known about

---

11 Descartes would have been pleased with Pavlov's "conditioned reflex" experiment. Though we say, speaking loosely, that the dog has "learned" that the bell means that food is on the way, we do not suppose that the dog thinks, "Ah ha! dinner's coming; I will get ready by starting to salivate." We suppose that a connection has been developed in the dog's cortex, so that a new stimulus now initiates the familiar response. The dog *does* nothing; learning *happens* in his body.

the laws of motion, to predict with absolute precision what any animal would do at any time.

Nature of Mind

As we have seen, everything in the created universe that is not a body is a mind, or self. Since each of us is a self, we know the nature of mind much better than we know the nature of body, and we "observe many more qualities in our mind than in any other thing." All these qualities—willing, imagining, desiring, thinking, hoping, doubting, perceiving, and so on—are, however, modes of one or the other of two basic powers, "one of which consists in . . . the operation of the understanding, and the other in volition, or the operation of the will."† Let us examine these powers, starting with volition.

VOLITION

Religious and moral considerations made it seem essential to Descartes to establish the freedom of the will.

> *Prin. XXXIX.* It is so evident that we are possessed of a free will that . . . this may be counted as one of the first and most ordinary notions that are found innately[12] in us. We had before a very clear proof of this, for at the same time as we tried to doubt all things . . . , we perceived in ourselves a liberty such that we were able to abstain from believing what was not perfectly certain and indubitable. But that of which we could not doubt at such a time is as self-evident and clear as anything we can ever know.
> . . . .
> *Prin. XLI. How the freedom of the will may be reconciled with Divine pre-ordination.* . . . We shall have no trouble at all if we recollect that our thought is finite, and that the omnipotence of God . . . is infinite. In this way we may have intelligence enough to come clearly and distinctly to know that this power is in God, but not enough to comprehend how He leaves the free action of man indeterminate; and, on the other hand, we are so conscious of the liberty and indifference which exists in us, that there is nothing that we comprehend more clearly and perfectly. For it would be absurd to doubt that of which we inwardly experience and perceive as existing within ourselves, just because we do not comprehend a matter which from its nature we know to be incomprehensible.
> *Prin. XLII. How, although we do not will to err, we yet err by our will,* . . . There is a great deal of difference between willing to be deceived

12 [See pp. 182–83—AUTHOR.]

.and willing to give one's assent to opinions in which error is sometimes found. For although there is no one who expressly desires to err, . . . it frequently happens that . . . the very desire for knowing the truth . . . causes those who are not fully aware of the order in which it should be sought for, to give judgment on things of which they have no real knowledge and thereby to fall into error.⁸

UNDERSTANDING

This brings us to understanding, the power by which men seek truth. In his method Descartes formulated rules for the right employment of this power; what concerns us here is his examination of its nature. First, he distinguished between (1) thinking, which is cognition of the world as it is, namely, a universe of unextended minds and of material substances possessing only "length, breadth, and depth," and (2) sensing, which is perception of a world of colored, sounding, and odorous bodies.

The main problem in connection with Descartes' account of understanding, both at the level of thought and at the level of perception, results from that substantival dualism that seemed to him necessary in order to maintain the autonomy of theology and physics. For if a mind and its objects are different substances, how does a mind come to know its objects? It cannot go out in the world to study it *in situ,* nor can the world, conceived of as matter in motion, come into the mind. A cognitive link between mind and world was thus needed. This link, which Descartes called an "idea," is a state of the mind, and a true idea represents in the mind the object out there that is its cause.

[Ideas are] so to speak, images of the things . . . ; examples are my thought of a man or of a chimera, of heaven, of an angel, or of God. . . .

Now . . . the principal error and the commonest which we may meet with in them, consists in my judging that the ideas which are in me are similar or conformable to the things which are outside me; for without doubt if I considered the ideas only as certain modes of my thoughts, without trying to relate them to anything beyond, they could scarcely give me material for error.

But among these ideas, some appear to me to be innate, some adventitious, and others to be formed [or invented] by myself; for, as I have the power of understanding what is called a thing, or a truth, or a thought, it appears to me that I hold this power from no other source than my own nature. But if I now hear some sound, if I see the sun, or feel heat, I have hitherto judged that these sensations proceeded from certain things that exist outside of me; and finally it appears to me that sirens, hippogryphs, and the like, are formed out of my own mind. But again I may possibly persuade myself that all these ideas are of the nature of those which I term adventitious, or else that they are all innate, or all fictitious: for I have not yet clearly discovered their true origin.

> And my principal task in this place is to consider, in respect to those ideas which appear to me to proceed from certain objects that are outside me, what are the reasons which cause me to think them similar to these objects.[v]

DOCTRINE OF INNATE IDEAS

As long as ideas are regarded as the mental links between minds and their world, it is necessary to distinguish between (1) the cause of the truth of an idea, (2) the cause of anyone's having the idea at all, and (3) the cause of someone's having the idea now. According to the doctrine that ideas represent things, the cause of the truth of an idea will always be some real, nonideal thing to which the idea corresponds. Suppose I have an idea that my typewriter is at my office. The cause of its truth, if it proves to be true, is the presence of the typewriter at my office. The cause of my having the idea now is my desire to illustrate a point about Descartes' doctrine of innate ideas. But what is the cause of my having this idea at all? Maybe it is a memory of the typewriter in the office on an earlier occasion. But then again, I may be mixing together a memory of my desk at the office and a memory of my typewriter in the study at home.

Now what about the idea "triangle"? The cause of my thinking about it at this moment may be some sense perception, for example, a figure drawn on a blackboard. But this sense perception, Descartes held, cannot be the cause of the truth of my idea, for the interior angles of the drawn figure do not exactly equal 180°. Nor can the sense perception be the cause of my thinking of "triangle" in the first place, for I could not identify the drawn figure as a triangle unless I was *already* acquainted with the idea "triangle."

Where, then, do I obtain the idea "triangle"? Descartes' answer was that God has implanted it in me. I can be sure that a beneficent God would not let me be deceived about anything whose nature I understand so clearly and distinctly. Now, notice the complication that has arisen in Descartes' theory of knowledge as a result of the dual-substance theory. Since, in his account of the new method, he was not thinking in terms of metaphysically distinct substances, he assumed that the mind is immediately in the presence of its real and rational object. What the mind contemplates is "simple natures," that is, the real essences themselves, not the mind's ideas of the real essences. But when Descartes recalled the dual-substance theory, he saw that the mind knows only its own states and that there is nothing about any of these states to guarantee that it represents its object adequately. This problem did not arise, of course, in connection with ideas of colors, sounds, and odors, for these do not, he held, represent the real world adequately. But his whole position depended on the assertion that our ideas of simple natures (for example, of mathematical entities) are adequate; and he could make sure of their adequacy only by claiming that our ideas of simple natures have been implanted in us by God, that is, that they are innate.

All these complications reflect a radically new orientation in philosophy. The distinctions that had characterized earlier philosophical thinking, such as those

between form and matter and between universal and particular, had been distinctions between classes of the mind's objects. For, until Galilean mechanics
and matter in motion appeared on the scene, there had been no reason to assert
a radical difference between minds and their objects. On the contrary, it had
always been assumed that mind and its objects have an affinity for each other,
and this affinity was precisely the basis of all earlier accounts of knowledge. Thus
both Plato and Aristotle had held that what the mind knows is reality itself,
whether this was understood to be a "form" or an "essence" or whatever. For
in this Aristotle was as much a realist as Plato: Even though he did not agree
that the universals are separate from the particulars, even though he held that
they had to be known in and through the particulars, he still held that what
the mind knows is the universal itself; it is not an *idea* of the universal.

Consider, for instance, the contrast between Descartes' doctrine of innate
ideas and Plato's doctrine of reminiscence. There are obvious similarities; but
whereas Plato could hold that the forms are present to our minds and that sense
perception reminds us of them, Descartes had to hold that sense perception only
reminds us of our ideas of mathematical entities and other simple natures. These
ideas require further authentication by an omnipotent, all-good power. And if
the ideas of simple natures are implanted by God, we do not need sense perception even as a "reminder" of the simple entities. Hence Descartes minimized
the role of sense perception even more than Plato did. This not only caused
Descartes to oversimplify the method of modern science (which, as we have seen,
involves an empirical element); it also brought him into conflict with Church
doctrine. Thomas, following Aristotle's lead, had held that all our knowledge,
even knowledge of the most generic of universals, is "collected" by the mind
from the particulars of sense. From the point of view of Thomism (which was
the predominant theory in the Church), Descartes was guilty of the sin of
intellectual pride in attributing to man a knowledge of the kind that can be had
only by angels, who are unlimited by "body." [13] It would seem that the Church
was right to suspect this position; for the eighteenth-century rationalists, who
agreed with Descartes that the human mind has direct access to an absolute and
eternal truth, rejected the Church's claim to be the sole channel by which God
communicates His message to man. These rationalists were like the medieval
mystics in this respect, though of course they held that the proper method for
approaching God was, not prayer and ascetic discipline, but "reason."

PERCEPTION

So much for cognition. If perception caused Descartes less trouble than did
cognition, it was only because he took perception less seriously. Assuming as
he did that the real world is truly known in physics and that what physics knows

---

13 This was one reason for the adverse comment made by Descartes' theological friends on his
proof of the existence of God. See pp. 167–68.

is extension, he inevitably concluded that the objects of sense perception are less than real. Indeed, in his view, "objects of sense perception," as they have just been called, are only adventitious ideas in us—products of the action on our sense organs of the material bodies of Galilean physics.

Now, some people are more convinced of the objective reality of the world of sense perception than of the objective reality of the world of Galilean bodies in motion. In fact, they might even say that the latter are only "abstractions" from the former. Descartes, of course, was too deeply committed to the new mechanics to accept such a suggestion. Though "nature" had taught him to believe in the truth of adventitious ideas, he thought he could distinguish between this kind of "spontaneous inclination" and the "natural light" that made him recognize the truth of his innate ideas.

> These two things [the spontaneous inclination and the natural light] are very different; for I cannot doubt that which the natural light causes me to believe to be true, as, for example, it has shown me that I am from the fact that I doubt, or other facts of the same kind. And I possess no other faculty whereby to distinguish truth from falsehood, which can teach me that what this light shows me to be true is not really true, and no other faculty that is equally trustworthy. But as far as natural impulses are concerned, I have frequently remarked . . . that they often enough led me to . . . error.ʷ

From Descartes' point of view, the main trouble with perception is simply that men tend to take it at face value. They ignore the distinction just pointed out, and, "perverting the order of nature," they assume that the senses yield information about "the essence of the bodies which are outside" them. If, however, men learn not to expect more of perception than it can give, they will find that, *for the purposes of ordinary life,* it is not a bad guide. For we are not disembodied minds eternally contemplating that "corporeal nature which is the object of pure mathematics." We are men, with "a head, hands, feet, and all other members" of a body, and this body is "placed amidst many others, from which it is capable of being affected in many different ways, beneficial and hurtful."

Thus, though my perceptions tell me nothing about the real nature of these bodies outside me, they do tell me about the beneficial or hurtful effects that these bodies are likely to have on my own body. The real corporeal nature of fire is not at all similar to my perception of fire; nevertheless, I know from perception that "in approaching fire I feel heat, and [that] in approaching it a little too near I even feel pain."ˣ Hence I can take the sensation of heat as a signal warning me not to move any closer. Perception is thus a system of signs, like the signals on a railroad track. These tell us nothing about the real nature of the train on the track ahead, for example, whether it is a freight or a passenger train, but they do tell us that a train is there and that we must proceed with caution.

Unfortunately, even as a system of signs, perception is far from perfect. How, then, are we to explain the fact that the good God who never allows us to be mistaken about our innate ideas often allows us to be mistaken about our adventitious ideas, even though the latter have perhaps a more direct bearing on the conduct of life than the former?

Descartes' answer was that whereas innate ideas are directly implanted in us by God, adventitious ideas are the products of corporeal nature "out there" acting on our bodies. My experience of heat, for instance, usually comes from something outside setting up a motion of such-and-such a specific kind in my body. But if it should happen that some internal change in my body produces the same motion, I will mistakenly suppose myself in the presence of that outside thing.

> When I feel pain in my foot, my knowledge of physics teaches me that this sensation is communicated by means of nerves dispersed through the foot, which, being extended like cords from there to the brain, when they are contracted in the foot, at the same time contract the inmost portions of the brain which is their extremity and place of origin, and then excite a certain movement which nature has established in order to cause the mind to be affected by a sensation of pain represented as existing in the foot. But because these nerves must pass through the tibia, the thigh, the loins, the back and the neck, in order to reach from the leg to the brain, it may happen that although their extremities which are in the foot are not affected, but only certain ones of their intervening parts, this action will excite the same movement in the brain that might have been excited there by a hurt received in the foot, in consequence of which the mind will necessarily feel in the foot the same pain as if it had received a hurt. And the same holds good of all the other perceptions of our senses. . . .
>
> From this it is quite clear that, notwithstanding the supreme goodness of God, the nature of man, inasmuch as it is composed of mind and body, cannot be otherwise than sometimes a source of deception.[y]

Thus, in a well-constructed house the ringing of the bell in the kitchen is a signal that someone is at the front door. But, if something goes wrong with the electrical system (for example, if rats gnaw through the cable), an identical signal will be produced in the kitchen, and the maid who goes to the door will be deceived. This is not the fault of the architect who designed the house; it is just one of the things that happen when an electric cable is used. The only way to prevent its happening is to leave out the bell system. But it is surely handier for the owners of the house to have a front-door bell that occasionally deceives them than not to have a front-door bell at all.

Unfortunately, as Descartes saw, this explains only a special class of errors. In general, the source of error, he thought, is men's tendency to rush into decisions before they have sufficient evidence to make an adequate judgment. If men were to proceed in accordance with the rules of Descartes' method, if they were to withhold judgment until they saw the conclusion clearly and distinctly, they would never fall into error. But the method is slow, and men are impatient. Error results, that is to say, from a disparity between the unlimited human thirst for knowledge and the limited human capacity for satisfying this thirst. But men must not blame this disparity on God. It is the consequence of an inevitable difference between human intellect and human will. Intellect is a power that varies in degree, and on an intellectual scale human minds are immeasurably below God's. But a will must be either free or not-free. Since the human will is free, it is as perfect (in respect to its freedom) as is God's. Hence their infinite will constantly takes men beyond the grasp of their finite intellect.

> The perception of the understanding only extends to the few objects which present themselves to it, and is always very limited. The will, on the other hand, may in some measure be said to be the infinite, because we perceive nothing which may be the object of some other will, even of the immensity of the will that is in God, to which our will cannot also extend, so that we easily extend it beyond that which we apprehend clearly. And when we do this there is no wonder if it happens that we are deceived. . . .
>
> And although God has not given us an understanding which is omnipotent, we must not for that reason consider that He is the originator of our errors. For all created understanding is finite, and it is of the nature of finite understanding not to embrace all things.[z]

Interaction

Mind and matter are, as we have seen, completely distinct substances. Yet sense perception can be explained only by presupposing their interaction. It is as a result of changes in my body (for example, changes in the nerve connecting my foot and my brain) that my mind feels pain, experiences pressure, and so on. Nor is it only in perception that interaction between mind and body occurs. Descartes' study of the passions led him to conclude that their causes are "not in the brain alone, but also in the heart, the spleen, the liver, and in all the other portions of the body in as far as they serve for the production of the blood and consequently of the spirits." The passions in their turn cause certain physiological changes (for example, changes in rate of pulse); accordingly, these changes can be taken as the external signs of love, hatred, hope, jealousy, and the other passions. For instance,

> Sadness, . . . in contracting the orifices of the heart, causes the blood to flow more slowly in the veins, and, becoming colder and thicker, the blood requires less space there, so that, retreating into those that . . . are nearest to the heart, it leaves the more remote; and since the most conspicuous of these are in the face, this causes it to become pale and sunk, more especially when the sadness . . . supervenes quickly, as we see in sudden fright when the surprise increases the action which constricts the heart.[a]

This analysis is a good example of the stimulus imparted by the new physics to the other sciences. Instead of passing moral judgments on the emotions, Descartes concentrated on the connection between private mental states and public bodily states, thus laying the basis for the future development of physiological psychology.

But how is it possible, within the framework of Descartes' thought, to account for the alleged fact of interaction on which his procedure here rested? If mind and body are the two distinct substances that the Cartesian compromise required them to be, how can they interact in sense perception and emotion?

According to Descartes, interaction occurs in the pineal gland, which is located between the two hemispheres of the brain.

> Nature[14] also teaches me . . . that I am not only lodged in my body as a pilot in a vessel, but that I am very closely united to it, and so to speak so intermingled with it that I seem to compose with it one whole. For if that were not the case, when my body is hurt, I, who am merely a thinking thing, should not feel pain, for I should perceive this wound by the understanding only, just as the sailor perceives by sight when something is damaged in his vessel. . . .
>
> [Nevertheless] there is a great difference between mind and body, inasmuch as body is by nature always divisible, and the mind is entirely indivisible. . . .
>
> [It follows] that the soul is really joined to the whole body, and that we cannot, properly speaking, say that it exists in any one of its parts to the exclusion of the others, because it is one and in some manner indivisible, . . . and because it is of a nature which has no relation to extension, nor dimensions, nor other properties of the matter of which the body is composed, but only to the whole conglomerate of its organs. . . .
>
> It is likewise necessary to know that although the soul is joined to the whole body, there is yet in that a certain part in which it exercises its functions more particularly than in all the others. . . . In examining the matter with care, it seems as though I had clearly ascertained that [this] part . . . is . . . a certain very small gland which is situated in the middle of [the brain] and so suspended above the duct whereby the animal spirits in its anterior cavities have communication with those in the posterior, that the slightest movements which take place in it may alter very greatly the course of these spirits; and reciprocally that the smallest changes which occur in the course of the spirits may do much to change the movements of this gland.[b]

In this discussion Descartes obviously failed to follow his own rule about suspending judgment until the truth is seen clearly and distinctly: He had no evidence at all that the pineal gland is the locus of interaction. Indeed, the

14 [This "nature" is Descartes' "spontaneous inclination," not his "natural light." See p. 184 —AUTHOR.]

problem at this point in his argument is to see how *any* organ can be the locus of something that is not extended. How can the mind, which is immaterial, cause changes in body, which by definition moves only on contact? How can body, which causes changes only on contact, cause changes in something it cannot touch? No answer to these questions is possible in Cartesian terms.

But the major problem that Descartes faced was not how to explain interaction; it was how to save the Cartesian compromise. For interaction, if it were a fact, brought the mind back into the mechanistic world of nature and so seemed to subject it to the fate that Hobbes had foreseen. As long as it was possible to forget about interaction, the Cartesian compromise had a specious plausibility. Minds, according to the dual-substance theory, are completely free and spontaneous. Since they are unextended, the laws of motion do not apply to them. Minds contemplate eternal truths; they enjoy and cultivate values. Bodies, on the other hand, being parts of the material plenum, are machines; their behavior is completely predictable in accordance with the laws of motion. Since these two substances, mind and body, are absolutely distinct, and since the truths about each follow from the distinct nature of each, the science of minds and the science of bodies cannot conflict. Body is body and mind is mind, and never the twain shall meet.

Unfortunately for Descartes, they meet at one point at least—in man. A man's mind acts on his body and his body acts on his mind. But the assertion that a completely free mind produces changes in its body is ultimately fatal for the Cartesian compromise. I will to move my finger, and it moves. Did my will freely move it? If so, my soul has disrupted the mechanical sequence of causes in the material universe. Did my will not move it? Then the causality of will (except perhaps in the internal world of mind) is an illusion, and man is as much a machine as is an animal—doubtless a more complicated machine, but still a machine.

If the soul is an immaterial, spontaneous cause, then, insofar as it brings about changes in its body, and through its body in the other Galilean bodies out there, the behavior of the material universe is not determined by antecedent events in time. On the other hand, if the material universe is the completely deterministic system that the new science seems to require it to be, man must be (as Hobbes held) only so much more matter in motion, and his free will is an illusion.

Thus the neat substantival dualism that was intended to segregate mind from body fails to prevent a conflict between the presuppositions of the theologians and the presuppositions of the physicists. If the theologians are correct, physics is not a universal and necessary science of bodies; if the physicists are correct, man is a machine, the soul is not immortal, and God is merely a local condition in a part of the plenum.

The same difficulty arises with respect to thought. Just as Descartes was willing to allow that "passion" is entangled in the material universe because he believed that he could exempt "will" from this involvement, so he was willing to allow that perception is entangled in the material universe because he believed that he could reserve thought as a pure activity of soul, uncontaminated by interaction with body. It is easy to show, however, that thought goes along with perception, just as will goes along with desire. Something presumably occurred in Descartes' cortex when he was intuiting his timeless essences and simple natures, just as something occurred there when he sensed red or middle C. Hence his thought was not a pure spiritual act. If we shut up thought in the mind, how does it come to know reality? If we let it loose in the world, how does it preserve its virginity? If the world were what Descartes' thought reported it to be, the thought that knew this could not be the kind of activity that Descartes took it to be.

Significance of Descartes

We must conclude, then, that the Cartesian compromise failed. But this should not blind us to the virtues of Descartes' theory. The breakdown occurred because of his determination to work out a theory that would make a place for both the religious and the scientific views of life. He saw that a satisfactory modern synthesis must do justice both to our sense of human freedom and to the claims of universal mechanism. It must concern itself with the actual and existent while undertaking to rise above the here and now. It must recognize that thought is rooted in perception and perception in body, yet it must find a way for thought to reach a rational truth.

Thus, if Descartes did nothing else, he made clear the formidable task that faced his successors. But, as a matter of fact, he did much more. His formulation of the basic question confronting philosophy seemed so sensible that it determined the course of philosophical development for more than a century and left its mark on the whole subsequent history of philosophy. All his immediate successors took it more or less for granted, at least as a starting point, that there is a material world and that there is a self that knows this world while remaining immune to its vicissitudes and to its mechanism. Even those who were not happy about all Descartes' conclusions tended to start with the Cartesian compromise and to work out *ad hoc* solutions for each of the problems that emerged as they proceeded. Thus, in the course of time, theories were developed that were very different from Cartesianism in their detailed conclusions and that even contradicted it completely, though they all started out from a Cartesian basis. And this continued until it occurred to Kant that the root of the trouble was the common Cartesian starting point. This was certainly, in a way, a very simple idea, but like most really simple ideas, it was exceedingly hard to come around to. Kant himself would never have tried to think the question through had the situation of philosophy not become almost a public scandal as a result of all the difficulties encountered in trying to patch up Cartesianism.

Let us see, then, how the ground was prepared for Kant. First, let us consider a group of thinkers known in the history of philosophy as "the Continental Rationalists." They are called "Rationalists" because, like Descartes (and Plato and a great many other people), they insisted on certainty in knowledge and because they believed that mathematical reasoning was the ideal of certain knowledge. They are called "Continental" because they happened to live on the continent of Europe.

Parallelism

Before we examine the views of the leading Continental Rationalists, a brief discussion of the first and simplest revision of Cartesianism must be given. A considerable group of Descartes' supporters believed that interaction was the major (it was certainly the most obvious) problem that his theory faced. They reasoned as follows: If mind and body interact, they are not metaphysically distinct substances; if they are metaphysically distinct substances, they cannot interact. Since all these thinkers agreed with Descartes that the dual-substance theory was essential to preserve the independence of physics and theology, they set themselves to explain away interaction. But if mind and body really do not interact, they certainly seem to do so. How, then, can this apparent interaction be accounted for?

Mind and body, these thinkers replied, are utterly distinct substances whose behavior patterns are precisely parallel. I will to move my finger, and it moves. This certainly happens, but it is a mistake to suppose either that my act of will causes my finger to move or that my act of will has no causal efficacy at all. The truth is that there is a whole series of mental causes and effects,

$$A \rightarrow B \rightarrow C \rightarrow D \rightarrow E \rightarrow F \rightarrow$$

and, exactly parallel to this, a whole series of physical causes and effects,

$$a \rightarrow b \rightarrow c \rightarrow d \rightarrow e \rightarrow f \rightarrow$$

I happen to be aware of mental event C (willing to move my finger) and of physical event d (movement of my finger), which happen to be the outstandingly noticeable events in their particular series at this time. Since physical event d always follows mental event C, I assume that d is C's effect. Actually, however, there are antecedent mental events, A and B, too obscure for me to be aware of, that bring it about that I now will to move my finger, and there are subsequent mental events, E and F, that are the effects of this act of will. There are also antecedent bodily events, a and b, too obscure for me to be aware of, that move my finger.

This is a very ingenious solution of a specific difficulty, and a good example of an *ad hoc* hypothesis constructed to meet a particular emergency. It does what it is intended to do: It keeps mind and body separate and so prevents any conflict between science and religion. Indeed, it provides an opportunity for assigning God even greater importance in the universe of physical substances, for it is plausible to argue either that God decreed this parallelism from the beginning of time (for who but God could possibly have foreseen all this immense detail and constructed two such neatly parallel series?) or that God intervenes in the operation of the universe from moment to moment (thus, each time that I will to move my finger, He sees to it that my finger moves). In both versions, the system of physical laws is no longer autonomous; it is merely an arrangement worked out by a provident deity for the advantage of his favorite creature, man.

Though the hypothesis of parallelism accounts for the observed facts without having to introduce interaction, it is so far-fetched that almost any other hypothesis that accounts for the facts would be preferable. Moreover, there are a great many difficulties in Cartesianism that parallelism does not touch. Chief among these perhaps is the problem of obtaining mathematical certainty (which the theory demands) about matters of fact. Parallelism's revision of Cartesianism only makes this more difficult: Not content to shut the mind up in itself, parallelism seals it in. Nevertheless, the doctrine of parallelism was so useful in disposing of the troublesome problem of interaction that all the Continental Rationalists resorted to it.

CHAPTER 6

Spinoza

Life

The first thinker to undertake a more thoroughgoing "correction" of Cartesianism than that proposed by the Parallelists was Benedictus de Spinoza (1632–77).[1] Spinoza was a Jew born in the Netherlands, where his family had found refuge from persecution in Spain. Although the Netherlands was at that time an oasis of liberty compared to the rest of Europe, Spinoza was hounded all his life by those who were offended by his opinions. He early broke with the Jewish

---

1 Spinoza would probably not have regarded himself as a Cartesian, and certainly many other strains of thought, including the Talmud, medieval Jewish philosophy, and Scholasticism, entered into his theory.

orthodoxy in which he had been brought up; when he was twenty-four he was expelled from the synagogue and banished from Amsterdam. He lived for some years in a nearby village, earning his living by polishing lenses, and eventually settled in The Hague, where he continued to live in a modest and unobtrusive way.

Obscurity did not, however, free him from persecution. The sale of his *Treatise on Theology and Politics* (published anonymously in 1670) was prohibited both by Protestants and by Catholics. He was almost mobbed by a Dutch crowd who suspected him of being a French spy. Because of the intense opposition, publication of his magnum opus, the *Ethics,* was put off until after his death. But none of this affected him. He was indifferent to poverty or neglect; he cared nothing for wealth or success. His motives were utterly different from those set forth by Hobbes as the basic human drives.

Spinoza was in many ways similar to Socrates. Like Socrates he was accused of atheism, because, being a far more deeply religious man than his persecutors, he was not satisfied with the outer forms that contented them. Like Socrates he was a mystic who was also a rationalist, and though he was indifferent to the things most men prize, he was no ascetic. Like Socrates he conceived of philosophy as not just a theoretical exercise but a way of life. No man has ever lived closer to what he taught.

Spinoza's Assumptions

Spinoza's starting point was similar to that of other thinkers of the new age. He sought certainty; he considered mathematics to be the best example of certain knowledge; he was impressed by Galileo's successful application of mathematics to the study of nature. And, as with Descartes, the desire for certainty caused Spinoza to concentrate on "demonstration" (which was, of course, certain) and to neglect the other half of Galileo's dictum—"observe." Hence Spinoza failed to see that in Galileo's method the transition from nature to geometry was effected by measurement and guaranteed by experiment. Further, Spinoza assumed (again with Descartes and in opposition to Hobbes) that mathematical knowledge is an insight into an objectively existing reality, not merely a knowledge of the consequences of names. Finally, Spinoza assumed, as had Descartes, that substance is a prime metaphysical concept.

What Spinoza did was to draw, much more explicitly and consistently than had Descartes, the logical consequences of these assumptions. To many people today, these consequences will seem odd and paradoxical. Indeed, for these people, Spinoza's philosophizing serves primarily to demonstrate that something was radically wrong with at least some of the assumptions from which he began.

The Geometric Method

The first consequence of Spinoza's greater consistency in developing Descartes' assumptions was the application of geometry to metaphysics. If geometry is the model science, reality must consist in entities connected by the kind of relation cognized in geometry. This is the relation of implication—for instance, being a triangle implies having three sides. It follows that reality must consist in a set of entities every one of which is implicatorily related to various other entities. As a consequence, the mind moves from some entity A to some other entity B, which is implied by A. When the mind is in the presence of these two entities, A and B, it infallibly sees that A implies B. It then moves on to C, implied by B, and so on. The whole problem is to arrange our thinking about these entities in such a way that our minds traverse these relations in due order, that is, that we move from A to C, via B.

All this, of course, is what Descartes had laid down in his *Rules* and carried out (though in an incomplete way) in his own philosophizing. Spinoza simply proposed, quite logically, a systematic application of this procedure. He would begin with self-evident metaphysical truths and develop an absolutely certain science of reality by demonstrating successively the various theorems implied by these truths:

DEFINITIONS

I. By that which is *self-caused*, I mean that of which the essence involves existence, or that of which the nature is only conceivable as existent.

II. A thing is called *finite after its kind*, when it can be limited by another thing of the same nature. . . .

III. By *substance*, I mean that which is in itself, and is conceived through itself in other words, that of which a conception can be formed independently of any other conception.

IV. By *attribute*, I mean that which the intellect perceives as constituting the essence of substance.

V. By *mode*, I mean the modifications of substance, or that which exists in, and is conceived through, something other than itself.

VI. By *God*, I mean a being absolutely infinite—that is, a substance consisting in infinite attributes, of which each expresses eternal and infinite essentiality. . . .

VII. That thing is called free, which exists solely by the necessity of its own nature, and of which the action is determined by itself alone. . . .

VIII. By *eternity*, I mean existence itself, in so far as it is conceived necessarily to follow solely from the definition of that which is eternal. . . .

AXIOMS

I. Everything which exists, exists either in itself or in something else.

II. That which cannot be conceived through anything else must be conceived through itself.

III. From a given definite cause an effect necessarily follows; and, on the other hand, if no definite cause be granted, it is impossible that an effect can follow.

IV. The knowledge of an effect depends on and involves the knowledge of a cause.

V. Things which have nothing in common cannot be understood, the one by means of the other; the conception of one does not involve the conception of the other.

VI. A true idea must correspond with its ideate or object.

VII. If a thing can be conceived as non-existing, its essence does not involve existence.

PROPOSITIONS

Prop. I. Substance is by nature prior to its modifications.

Proof.—This is clear from Deff. iii. and v.

Prop. II. Two substances, whose attributes are different, have nothing in common.

Proof.—Also evident from Def. iii. For each must exist in itself, and be conceived through itself; in other words, the conception of one does not imply the conception of the other.

Prop. III. Things which have nothing in common cannot be one the cause of the other.

Proof.—If they have nothing in common, it follows that one cannot be apprehended by means of the other (Ax. v.), and, therefore, one cannot be the cause of the other (Ax. iv.). Q.E.D.

Prop. IV. Two or more distinct things are distinguished one from the other either by the difference of the attributes of the substances, or by the difference of their modifications.

Proof.—Everything which exists, exists either in itself or in something else (Ax. i.),—that is (by Deff. iii. and v.), nothing is granted in addition to the understanding, except substance and its modifications. Nothing is, therefore, given besides the understanding, by which several things may be distinguished one from the other, except the substances, or, in other words (see Ax. iv.), their attributes and modifications. Q.E.D.

Prop. V. There cannot exist in the universe two or more substances having the same nature or attribute.

Proof.—If several distinct substances be granted, they must be distinguished one from the other, either by the difference of their attributes, or by the difference of their modifications (Prop. iv.). If only by the difference of their attributes, it will be granted that there cannot be more than one with an identical attribute. If by the difference of their modifications—as substance is naturally prior to its modifications (Prop. i.),—it follows that setting the modifications aside, and considering substance in itself, that is truly (Deff. iii. and vi.), there cannot be conceived one substance different from another,—

> that is (by Prop. iv.), there cannot be granted several substances, but one substance only. Q.E.D.
>
> . . . .
>
> *Prop. VII.* Existence belongs to the nature of substance.
> *Proof.*—Substance cannot be produced by anything external, . . . it must, therefore, be its own cause—that is, its essence necessarily involves existence.ª

This is perhaps enough to indicate how Spinoza proceeded. Assuming, for the sake of argument, that the whole set of theorems (some two hundred and fifty in all) has been correctly deduced, what has Spinoza accomplished? According to Spinoza himself, the result is knowledge of reality—reality is one, eternal, necessary, and so on. But according to Hobbes, Spinoza has only shown the consequences of his arbitrarily chosen definitions. If "cause" is defined in such-and-such a way, "eternity" in such-and-such a way, "substance" in such-and-such a way, it can be shown that substance is self-caused and eternal. But if these terms are defined differently (in, for instance, the words Hobbes himself used in his first philosophy), then another set of consequences follows. That is all. Why did Hobbes prefer his own definitions and theorems? Because these theorems enable us to control our physical environment (for instance, to predict the rate of fall of a freely falling body at the nth second), whereas Spinoza's theorems, in Hobbes's opinion, enable us to control nothing.

If we are to make any sense of Spinoza, we must see that he wholly denied this Hobbesian nominalism. From the generally realistic premises he adopted in common with Plato, Descartes, and many other philosophers, it follows that when the mind knows, it is traversing and communing with objective reality. Knowledge, Spinoza held, means knowledge *of* something; the possibility of an absolutely certain knowledge proves the existence of an absolutely real object. The correct procedure for ascertaining the nature of reality is therefore to analyze the nature of knowledge and to show what it implies about the nature of reality. Although everyone must allow the appropriateness of this general line of procedure, many people would hold Spinoza's conclusions to be invalidated because he virtually identified knowledge with mathematical thinking. Hence, though he supposed that his analysis was exposing the nature of reality, it was at best only making clear what is implied by the mathematical factor in scientific method.

God

It was fairly easy, from the definitions, axioms, and theorems already discussed, for Spinoza to prove that there is but one substance and that this substance is God.

PROOFS OF GOD'S EXISTENCE

In order to proceed regularly with the demonstration, we must premise:—

1. The true definition of a thing neither involves nor expresses anything beyond the nature of the thing defined. From this it follows that—

2. No definition implies or expresses a certain number of individuals, inasmuch as it expresses nothing beyond the nature of the thing defined. For instance, the definition of a triangle expresses nothing beyond the actual nature of a triangle: it does not imply any fixed number of triangles.

3. There is necessarily for each individual existent thing a cause why it should exist.

4. This cause of existence must either be contained in the nature and definition of the thing defined, or must be postulated apart from such definition.

It therefore follows that, if a given number of individual things exist in nature, there must be some cause for the existence of exactly that number, neither more nor less. For example, if twenty men exist in the universe . . . and we want to account for the existence of these twenty men, it will not be enough to show the cause of human existence in general . . . . For the true definition of man does not involve any consideration of the number twenty. Consequently, the cause for the existence of these twenty men . . . must necessarily be sought externally to each individual. Hence we may lay down the absolute rule, that everything which may consist of several individuals must have an external cause. And, as it has been shown already that existence appertains to the nature of substance, existence must necessarily be included in its definition; and from its definition alone existence must be deducible. But from its definition . . . we cannot infer the existence of several substances; therefore it follows that there is only one substance of the same nature. Q.E.D.

. . . .

Prop. XI. God, or substance, consisting of infinite attributes, of which each expresses eternal and infinite essentiality, necessarily exists.

Proof.—If this be denied, conceive, if possible, that God does not exist: then his essence does not involve existence. But this (by Prop. vii.) is absurd. Therefore God necessarily exists.

Another proof.—Of everything whatsoever a cause or reason must be assigned, either for its existence, or for its non-existence. . . . This reason or cause must either be contained in the nature of the thing in question, or be external to it. For instance, the reason for the non-existence of a square circle is indicated in its nature, namely, because it would involve a contradiction. . . .

But the reason for the existence of a triangle or a circle does not follow from the nature of these figures, but from the order of universal nature in extension. From the latter it must follow, either that a triangle necessarily exists, or that it is impossible that it should exist. So much is self-evident. It follows therefrom that a thing necessarily exists, if no cause or reason be granted which prevents its existence.

If, then, no cause or reason can be given, which prevents the existence of God, or which destroys his existence, we must certainly conclude that he necessarily does exist. If such a reason or cause should be given, it must either be drawn from the very nature of God, or be external to him—that is, drawn from another substance of another nature. For if it were of the same nature, God, by that very fact, would be admitted to exist. But substance of another nature could have nothing in common with God (by Prop. ii.), and therefore would be unable either to cause or to destroy his existence.

As, then, a reason or cause which would annul the divine existence cannot be drawn from anything external to the divine nature, such cause must perforce, if God does not exist, be drawn from God's own nature, which would involve a contradiction. To make such an affirmation about a being absolutely infinite and supremely perfect, is absurd; therefore, neither in the nature of God, nor externally to his nature, can a cause or reason be assigned which would annul his existence. Therefore, God necessarily exists. Q.E.D.

. . . .

Prop. XIV. Besides God no substance can be granted or conceived.

Proof.—As God is a being absolutely infinite, of whom no attribute that expresses the essence of substance can be denied (by Def. vi.), and he necessarily exists (by Prop. xi.); if any substance besides God were granted it would have to be explained by some attribute of God, and thus two substances with the same attribute would exist, which (by Prop. v.) is absurd; therefore, besides God no substance can be granted, or, consequently, be conceived. . . . Q.E.D.[b]

COMMENT ON THESE PROOFS

The first proof restates the ontological argument. The second is a revision of Descartes' causal argument. Like Descartes, Spinoza did not distinguish between something's being deducible and its being real. Anything that is true (that is, deducible) *is* real, for there is no other way (not by means of sense perception, for instance) to establish a thing's reality. In a wholly rational world, in other words, everything that *is* (that is, is true) can be demonstrated by being deduced from something else (that is, some other truth) that implies it. This is what Spinoza meant by saying that everything that exists has a cause or reason why it exists, and that everything that does not exist has a cause or reason why it does not exist. The cause of its existence (or nonexistence) is the reason (or, as we would say, "ground") from which its truth or falsity can be deduced.[2] Thus, the cause of a triangle (or, as we would say, the grounds from which the various theorems about triangles can be deduced) is "the order of universal nature in extension" (or, as we would say, the definitions and axioms of Euclidean geometry).

It is fairly obvious, then, on the assumption that the real is rational, that everything that is has a cause or reason for its existence. It is a little more difficult to see why a thing must exist unless there is a cause or reason for its not existing.

2 Compare Descartes' identification of "cause" with "imply" (p. 170).

But this, too, follows from the assumption that the real is rational. In a wholly rational universe, everything is necessarily what it is; everything, that is, that is real (that is, true) can be deduced from something else, and this from something else, and so on until some self-evident truth (or reality) is ultimately reached. But if everything is necessarily what it is, a merely *possible* something is as much a contradiction (and so as much an impossibility) as a square circle. Now, if the possible is ruled out, the only alternatives are the impossible and the necessary. Hence, if it can be shown that a thing is not impossible (that is, if it can be shown that there is no cause or reason that makes it impossible), then it is necessary.

The next question is: Can there be any cause or reason that makes God (as defined by Spinoza) impossible? Any such cause or reason would have to be either outside God or inside God. But nothing outside God could make God impossible, for anything outside God, being different from God, would have nothing in common with Him. And things that have nothing in common cannot contradict each other. (It is a contradiction to say that some entity A is a square circle; it is not a contradiction to say that A is a square and that B is a circle.) Well, then, if there is a reason for God's nonexistence, it must be inside God. But it is absurd to hold that the concept of a perfect being contains a contradiction (for it would not be perfect if it contained a contradiction). Therefore there is *no* reason for God's nonexistence. Therefore God exists.

GOD THE WHOLE

But the God whose existence Spinoza believed he had proved is very different from the Christian God. He is not transcendent; He is the totality of everything that is. He is that rational system whose existence Spinoza held to be guaranteed by the certainty of mathematical knowledge. Also, the conclusion that God is the totality of everything that is follows from a rigidly logical application of the traditional definition of substance. A substance, it was widely agreed, does not depend on anything outside it; it *is,* independently of its environment. This is the difference between a substance and an attribute. An attribute cannot stand alone; it depends for its being and existence on something else, namely, on a substance.

On this definition of substance, as Spinoza pointed out, the so-called finite substances, of whose reality almost all other philosophers were convinced, are a contradiction in terms. Even Thomas and Descartes had had to allow that the infinite substance they called God and the various dependent beings they called finite substances were not "univocally" substantial.[3] For Thomas and Descartes both held (as every Christian must) that the finite beings were created and so are dependent on God, their creator. If they are dependent, they are not independent; if they are not independent, they are not substances. Why call them

3 See pp. 174–75.

substances, Spinoza asked, when your own argument shows that they are not substances? Spinoza believed the explanation to be that these Christian philosophers wanted to eat their cake and have it too. Dogmatic considerations required that everything be dependent on God, but these thinkers nevertheless wanted some of these dependent beings to have individuality and, as it were, personality in their own right. They did not want creature to be absorbed into creator. Hence they called their dependent beings "finite substances"—"finite" as a mark of dependence, "substance" as a mark of independence. But, Spinoza held, this is equivocation and confusion.

There is nothing in this line of reasoning that makes it necessary that there be but one substance. There might be several (or, indeed, many), providing only that each is complete in itself and independent of all the others. Why, then, did Spinoza insist that only one substance exists? The answer is that, though dogmatic considerations did not require him to hold that everything is dependent on a creator god, his analysis of the nature of knowledge led him to conclude that there can be but one substance and that this substance is the totality of everything that is. If there was a plurality of independent substances, there would be not one universe but several. And this, he thought, was absurd. According to Spinoza's view of the nature of knowledge, to understand anything is to be able to deduce it from something else, and in order to be deduced, the thing in question must stand in an implicatory relation to that other thing. Hence either several allegedly independent substances are implicatorily related (in which case they are not independent substances) *or* the universe contains entities that are *in principle* incomprehensible. Since this second alternative conflicted with one of Spinoza's deepest convictions, he concluded that nothing, except the one whole, stands alone, and that this whole is a single implicatorily related system.

It is instructive to contrast Spinoza's reasoning here with St. Thomas' proofs of the existence of God. Thomas agreed with Spinoza, of course, that there is but one universe. However, he held that this universe is finite, not infinite. Because it is finite, Thomas reasoned, it is necessary, in order to understand it, to pass beyond it to a transcendent creator god. Spinoza, on the other hand, maintained that we cannot pass outside the universe and that, since it is infinite, we do not need to.

Was Thomas correct? Or was Spinoza? Historically speaking, of course, Christian thinkers, whether Catholic or not, have tended to support the Thomistic thesis that there must be a transcendent Other to support the rational system. Since these thinkers proceed to identify the transcendent Other with God,[4] they have, or so they think, a logical argument for the existence of God. They hold that the rationalists' assumption that reason is enough leads, by a series of necessary steps whose validity rationalists themselves must acknowledge, to the conclusion that reason is not enough. That Spinoza in effect denied the logic

---

4 Actually, of course, it is not at all easy to get from a transcendent Other to the Person to whom the Christian prays.

of this argument helps to explain why his views caused such intense wrath in theological circles.

Whatever one thinks about the theologians' logic, there may be a contradiction in Spinoza's own reasoning. The argument that led him to a single, all-inclusive substance seems to entail, as a corollary, that nothing finite (no part of the whole) is ever wholly true. But his geometric method presupposed absolutely self-evident, axiomatic starting points. The conflict here about the nature of proof corresponds exactly to Descartes' shift, in *his* proof of the existence of God, from the "absolutes" of Rule VI to merely "relative absolutes." The question at issue here reflects the ambivalence about the nature and status of reason that, as we have seen, ran through the whole age. Whether knowledge is atomistic, so that the mind can rest here and there in a complete grasp of truth, or whether knowledge is continuous and expansive, so that every truth we attain is conditional on something beyond it, is perhaps another major parting of the ways in philosophy.

A further consequence of Spinoza's reasoning is that God, being an infinite system of implicatory truths, is not the Person of Christian tradition.

> Some assert that God, like a man, consists of body and mind, and is susceptible of passions. How far such persons have strayed from the truth is sufficiently evident from what has been said. . . .
>
> For intellect and will, which should constitute the essence of God, would perforce be as far apart as the poles from the human intellect and will, in fact, would have nothing in common with them but the name; there would be about as much correspondence between the two as there is between the Dog, the heavenly constellation, and a dog, an animal that barks. This I will prove as follows: If intellect belongs to the divine nature, it cannot be in nature, as ours is generally thought to be, posterior to, or simultaneous with the things understood, inasmuch as God is prior to all things by reason of his causality.[5] On the contrary, the truth and formal essence of things is as it is, because it exists by representation as such in the intellect of God. Wherefore the intellect of God, in so far as it is conceived to constitute God's essence, is, in reality, the cause of things, both of their essence and of their existence. . . . As, therefore, God's intellect is the sole cause of things, namely, both of their essence and existence, it must necessarily differ from them in respect to its essence, and in respect to its existence. For a cause differs from a thing it causes, precisely in the quality which the latter gains from the former. . . .
>
> The reasoning would be identical in the case of the will, as anyone can easily see.[c]

For instance, when we men determine on something, the end that we seek is something as yet outside us, and the plan that we follow in attempting to

---

5 [This is proved by Proposition XVI, which has not been quoted here—AUTHOR.]

realize it is conditioned by our environment. Suppose that a man wants a house to live in. The house he settles for reflects limitations in the external environment over which he has no control—the availability of housing in the particular community, his own income, his credit status, and so on. To hold that God wills, that He acts for ends as men do, that He is limited as men are by an external environment, is not only the baldest anthropomorphism; it also ignores the fact, which Spinoza believed himself to have proved, that God is perfect and so lacks nothing, that God is the totality of everything that is and so could not work within an environment that limits Him.

It follows that God has not created the universe, and that He is not a loving and providential Father. According to Spinoza, all the attributes with which Christian piety has endowed God are illusions, projections of our own ignorance and insecurity.

But was it not arbitrary of Spinoza to apply the name "God" to a system of implicatorily related truths? Any sense of the strangeness of this identification is in part, of course, a reflection of a Christian preoccupation with a transcendent, personal, and creative God; there is a very long tradition, far older than Christianity and going back far beyond Plato, that identifies God with ultimate reality and truth. Spinoza's usage accords with this tradition. He believed that he had discovered what ultimate reality is—a system of implicatorily related truths—and he held that he had conclusively demolished the arguments purporting to show that ultimate reality is a Person. From his point of view, he and the Christian philosophers were discussing the same reality, with the important difference that what he was saying about it was true, whereas much that they were saying about it (not all, of course) was false. Thus, he agreed with the Christian philosophers that God (ultimate reality) is the guarantor of all finite truth and the source of whatever reality the finite parts have. In fact, Spinoza's nexus of truths performs exactly the same metaphysical and epistemological functions in his system as Thomas' transcendent substance does in his.

But from the Christian point of view the religious function of God is far more important than His metaphysical and epistemological functions. Can one worship a system of truths? This is perhaps a psychological, rather than a philosophical, question. Certainly, Spinoza himself seems to have felt the same way about his God that Christians feel about theirs. He experienced the same reverence for his system-of-truths-that-completes-our-finite-truth that the Christian experiences for his loving Father. Doubtless, for the ordinary man, the Spinozistic system of truths would be a cold abstraction; the strongest appeal of Christianity rests precisely on those personal qualities that Spinoza rejected. But is this a valid criticism of Spinozism? Spinoza would have held that it is not. The truth, he would have said, is what it is. It is unfortunate if the truth fails to satisfy the ordinary man's religious needs, but that cannot be helped. Metaphysics is the attempt to ascertain the truth about reality. It is not designed to comfort the ignorant or to assuage the fears of the superstitious, and it should not be judged by such emotional criteria.

The World

So far we have been considering God's nature, conceived of as the totality of everything that is. In turning from God to the world we do not pass (as we would in a Christian philosophy) to something different from God. We merely leave off considering the totality as it is in itself and begin considering it under different aspects or from different points of view.

Every part of God is necessarily what it is. Only God, that is, the totality of everything that is, is free. And, of course, God is not free in the sense of having a free will (whatever that may mean); He is free merely in the sense that, because He is the totality, His nature is not limited by anything outside it. Everything else (everything that is less than the totality) is limited by other parts of the totality, that is, is implicatorily related to other things in such a way that its existence and nature can be deduced from those other things. This necessity is not physical necessity (whatever that may mean); it is logical necessity—the sort of necessity that makes it necessarily true that if anyone is completely baldheaded, then he has no hair on his head.

But now, side by side with this account of the universe as a system of implicatorily related propositions (a vast geometry), Spinoza gave an account of it in the traditional terms of substance and property. According to this line of reasoning, what is not substance must be a property of a substance. Since there is but one substance, every part of the whole must be a property of that substance. Accordingly, we find Spinoza saying that everything that is not God is either an "attribute" or a "mode" of God.[6] But what does it mean to call a part of an implicatorily related whole "an attribute"? And what is the difference between a property that is an attribute and one that is a mode? No aspect of Spinoza's theory has given rise to more widely varying interpretations than this distinction between attributes and modes. For, unfortunately, the notion of reality as a nexus of implicatorily related entities (or truths) and the notion of it as a substance possessing properties do not fuse neatly. It is not surprising that Spinoza failed to realize this; indeed, the substantial way of thought was so deeply embedded in the culture of his time that it was natural and inevitable to record all novel insights in its terms.

Let us begin by asking what happens, in Spinoza's view, to Descartes' material and thinking substances? They become attributes of the one whole substance. And what happens to Thomas' innumerable individual substances, each an amalgam of matter and form? They become modes of this one substance. Mind and body are, as it were, basic determinations of substance; modes are particular, local specifications of these basic determinations. Thus your individual body is a mode of the one substance *qua* body (that is, under the aspect or determination of body); your mind is a mode of the one substance *qua* mind. Spinoza took

---

6 This follows from Definitions III, IV, and V, and Axiom I.

the wholeness of reality very seriously; calling the parts of his reality "modes" reinforced for him this sense of reality's oneness. However, the relation of subordination in which a property stands to the substance that supports it is altogether different from the relation in which one truth stands to the truth that implies it. In other words, although in a monistic philosophy like Spinoza's all differences in kind reduce ultimately to differences in degree, it does not follow that they must be (or, indeed, can be) *adjectives* of one substance.

If a mode is, then, a part of reality, what is an attribute—a larger part? No; mind and body do not *divide* reality. It is not that some of the whole's modes are minds and that others are bodies; the whole of reality is body, the whole of reality is mind. It was noted above that your mind is a mode of substance under the attribute of mind, and your body is a mode of substance under the attribute of body. Though your body is not your mind, they do not differ substantively. Indeed, there is a sense in which they are the same mode; the mode that is your body *is* the mode that is your mind. Further, Spinoza held that the attributes of mind and body are not the only attributes of reality. It is ("has," "contains") an infinite number of attributes—mind and body just happen to be the only attributes *we* can know. Hence the same mode appears under the aspect of an infinite variety of attributes—one of these being mind, another being body, and the others being unknown to us.

This is certainly very obscure. Perhaps it will be helpful to ask what Spinoza hoped to gain by involving himself in such complex distinctions. They were designed to get around the difficulties of interaction. Like Descartes, Spinoza took for granted that there are "ideas" and that ideas and their objects are different. "A circle," he said, "is different from the idea of a circle." It follows that neither can be used to explain the other, for explanation means deduction, that is, discovering the implicatory relation between the thing to be explained and something else; and such a relation could never be found between things radically distinct. Hence the *idea* of a circle can be explained only if there are other ideas from which it can be deduced, and (eventually) a whole system of ideas; and the circle itself can be explained only if there is a whole system of entities of which *it* is a part. Each of these systems must be complete and closed. But does this not amount to a substantial dualism like that of the Parallelists? No, for Spinoza believed he had proved there can be only *one* whole. Hence each subsystem must be an attribute—it *is* the whole under one aspect.

But even if we now understand Spinoza's reasons for introducing modes and attributes into his philosophy, the distinction between them may remain unclear. Since the difference between two attributes is not unlike the difference between two languages, an analogy may be helpful. The word *city* and the word πολις can be thought of as being the same "mode" in two languages. πολις is the Greek mode, *city* is the English mode, just as "circle" is the physical mode and "idea of circle" is the mental mode. Neither πολις nor *city* is more fundamental than the other; neither is derivative from the other. Moreover, there must be other Greek words to "explain" πολις and other English words to "explain" *city*. And, of course, the words that explain πολις must be explained by other Greek words, and the words that explain *city* must be explained by other English words, so that, ultimately, the existence of πολις and *city* requires two closed systems of words (two dictionaries), the one in Greek and the other in English. Nor is there any reason why there may not be other dictionaries in other languages, and indeed an infinity of languages, each of which is a closed system, such that to every word in any one of the dictionaries there corresponds a word in every other dictionary. The words in any one dictionary cause (that is, define) each other, and there is no causality between dictionaries. Nevertheless, even though there is no causality between words in different dictionaries, the fact of correspondence enables us to infer from what is going on in one dictionary what is going on in another. Corresponding to the definition of πολις in the Greek dictionary, there will be a definition of *city* in the English dictionary.

To put this another way, let us define reality as whatever-can-be-said. Now, there are an indefinitely large number of languages, of which we happen to know but two, in which the whatever-can-be-said can be said. None of these languages says anything more about the whatever-can-be-said than any other language, for each language is capable of saying *all* that can be said. In each of them, that is, the *whole* of whatever-can-be-said can be said. Now, when we claimed to know two languages—Greek and English—we did not mean we knew them both perfectly. As a matter of fact, we do not know all the words in either language, so that what we actually say about the whatever-can-be-said is a mixture of Greek and English. We piece out with English whenever Greek words fail us, and with Greek words when English words fail us. But it would be absurd, because we have to resort to this kind of patchwork, to say either (1) that English and Greek are the same language or (2) that each would not be entirely adequate (providing we knew all the vocabulary) to say *all* there is to say about the whatever-can-be-said.

Some such conception (which is certainly not free from difficulties, though we cannot go into them here) seems to have been Spinoza's way of relating attributes to each other and to substance.[7] This conception had the advantage of emphasizing that the differences between mind and body, though real, are not ultimate. Thus, there is a difference between a circle and a thought about a circle, just as there is a difference between πολις and *city*. But instead of conceiving this to be a substantive difference, as Descartes had done, with the ensuing impossibility of explaining how we ever know that our ideas are true of their objects, Spinoza maintained that the distinction between idea and object, like the distinction between πολις and *city*, is merely a distinction between two ways of *talking* about, or experiencing, the same thing. If we are thinking in Greek, we think πολις; if we are thinking in English, we think *city*. The problem

7 In this linguistic analogy, a mode would be a particular configuration (or determination) of the attributes, that is, an English sentence to which there would correspond, point for point, a Greek sentence.

of getting from idea to object is exactly like the problem of getting from πολις to *city*—the chasm is linguistic, not substantival. Here we are, looking at an object. If we are in a Greek frame of reference, we say we are looking at a πολις. If we are in an English frame of reference, we say we are looking at a *city*. But we do not suppose ourselves on this account to be seeing double. So is it when, as we say, we are "thinking about a circle." From one point of view we say we are entertaining the thought of a circle; from the other point of view we say that it is a circle we are thinking about. Ideas are ideas-of-objects, and objects are objects-for-ideas.

Ideas and Their Objects

Are all ideas then true? It looks as if Spinoza solved Descartes' problem about determining how any idea is true only by creating a Spinozistic problem about how any idea can be false. In a sense, all ideas *are* always true, according to Spinoza. They are always about their objects, because the object of an idea, as we have just seen, is simply another aspect (attribute) of the cognitive situation. Nonetheless, error is possible, for men sometimes suppose the object to be different from what it is. Suppose a person has an idea that there is a pink rat on his hearthrug. This is an error, for there is no pink rat on his hearthrug. But this does not mean that the idea "pink rat" has no object; as a matter of fact, the object of this particular idea is a quantity of alcohol in that person's blood stream, and his error consists in failing to realize that this is the real object.

This may seem an odd way of describing the situation. Today most people would probably say that the alcohol is the cause of the idea, not its object. But according to Spinoza's viewpoint, "alcohol" is in one self-contained language and the idea "pink rat" is in another. From this point of view, the sentence "The alcohol in his stomach causes him to think that there is a pink rat in his room" is a confused mixture of two languages. The cognitive situation that is called (in the idea-language) "sensing a pink rat" is correctly described (in the object-language) as "so-and-so many ounces of alcohol in the blood stream." If someone thinks that it is described in the object-language as "pink rat," he is mistaken, just as, if someone thinks that the situation described in Greek as πολις is described in English as *horse*, he is mistaken.

Spinoza may well have been right about this. It would appear that many seemingly profound metaphysical puzzles are the result of linguistic muddles and that, in the present case, there are two different languages in which a straightforward account of what has occurred can be given— a physicalistic language in which one talks about a quantity of alcohol and a mentalistic language in which one talks about seeing pink rats. Metaphysical difficulties emerge only when one shifts in midstream from one language to the other.

However, there is one consequence of Spinoza's way of dealing with this matter that few philosophers would accept today: It follows that perception is always inadequate. In perception, according to Spinoza, the object of my idea is never a body-out-there, as it appears to be; it is always a state-of-my-body-caused-by-a-body-out-there. For instance, when I say that I see a kitten on my hearthrug, what is really happening is that a body out there (the kitten) is causing a change in my body (retina, optic nerve, cortex, and so on). But instead of having an idea of what is *really* happening—instead of having an idea of the change in my cortex—I have an idea of a kitten on my hearthrug. Hence, according to Spinoza, *all* perception is inadequate—and the difference between what most people would call a veridical perception (kitten on hearthrug) and an hallucinatory perception (pink rat on hearthrug) is the difference between being confusedly aware of an *externally* caused change in the state of the body and being confusedly aware of an *internally* caused change in its state. In both cases, and in all cases, perception is confused.

If all ideas of perception are inadequate, what is an adequate idea? According to Spinoza, an adequate idea of the perception "kitten on hearthrug" would be knowledge of the changes in the optic nerve and cortex—and such knowledge is not perception. The only adequate ideas, in a word, are those that form parts of some deductive system, or science: The perceptual kitten must be replaced by either a science of the perceiver's body or a science of the kitten's body, depending on whether what interests us is perception of the kitten or the kitten itself.

> A mode of extension and the idea of that mode are one and the same thing, though expressed in two ways. This truth seems to have been dimly recognized by those Jews who maintained that God, God's intellect, and the things understood by God are identical. For instance, a circle existing in nature, and the idea of a circle existing, which is also in God, are one and the same thing displayed through different attributes. . . .
>
> God is the cause of an idea—for instance, of the idea of a circle—in so far as he is a thinking thing; and of a circle, in so far as he is an extended thing. . . . So long as we consider things as modes of thinking, we must explain the order of the whole of nature, or the whole chain of causes, through the attribute of thought only. And, in so far as we consider things as modes of extension, we must explain the order of the whole of nature through the attribute of extension only. . . . Wherefore of things as they are in themselves God is really the cause. . . . I cannot for the present explain my meaning more clearly.[d]

An adequate idea, then, is an idea of reality; it is an idea in which the mind is tracing out some of those implicatory relations whose totality is the universe. Hence, ultimately, since reality is one whole, there will be but one wholly adequate idea, and this will be a nexus of implicatorily related ideas exactly reflecting the nexus of implicatorily related objects. And, because ideas and objects are, after all, simply two ways of talking about the same reality, this wholly adequate idea and the object of which it is the idea turn out to be identical. It is a matter of indifference whether reality is described as a nexus of entities or as a nexus of truths.

Physics

For Spinoza, physics was the science of the attribute of extension (just as psychology was the science of the attribute of thought). He never asked himself, as Descartes had done,[8] how he could be sure that the extended matter studied in physics has those properties that are clearly and distinctly cognized in geometry. On the assumption that the real is rational and the rational is real, this was a meaningless question. Here, as so often, Spinoza was more consistent than Descartes in drawing the logical consequences of Descartes' own assumptions. If the real is rational, what more can be wanted to show that something is real than to show that it is free from inconsistency? Yet surely Descartes' inconsistency was rooted in the sound feeling, wholly ignored by Spinoza, that there is something more to being real than being rational.

Hence, whereas Descartes had appealed to God's goodness to establish the geometric character of the physical world, and whereas an empiricist would rely on empirical observation, Spinoza simply took for granted that the laws of physics are a set of theorems whose implicatory relations reflect the necessary properties (under the attribute of extension) of a rational-real. This rational-real, he held, is infinite and continuous. All distinctions in it, that is, distinctions between its parts, are ultimately unreal.

> Assuredly it is not less absurd to assert that extended substance is made up of bodies or parts, than it would be to assert that . . . a line [is made up] of points. . . . For if extended substance could be so divided that its parts were really separate, why should not one part admit of being destroyed, the others remaining joined together as before? . . . Surely in the case of things, which are really distinct one from the other, one can exist without the other, and can remain in its original condition. . . .
>
> If anyone asks me the further question, Why are we naturally so prone to divide quantity? I answer, that quantity is conceived by us in two ways; in the abstract and superficially, as we imagine it; or as substance, as we conceive it solely by the intellect. . . . This will be plain enough to all, who make a distinction between the intellect and the imagination, especially if it be remembered, that matter is everywhere the same, that its parts are not

8 See pp. 172–74.

distinguishable, except in so far as we conceive matter as diversely modified, whence its parts are distinguished, not really, but modally.[e]

All this follows, of course, from Spinoza's view that only reason, not perception, is adequate. That is, the conclusion here depends on the assumption that reality is rational. The real properties of extension are not those that we perceive but those that we deduce it to have. To suppose that extension is made of extended parts is like supposing a surface to be put together out of lines. We can "mark out" on a surface various plane figures, and we can arrange them in ways that will "fill up" the surface. But the surface is not composed of the figures. On the contrary, it is the logical presupposition of all such figures. As "plane" figures, they presuppose a "plane." Or, to give another example, the relation of space (extension) to its parts is exactly the same as the relation of an argument to its steps. Steps can be distinguished, but they do not exist as independent entities, that is, if you took one step out, you would not have an argument with a gap in it; you would not have an argument at all. The reality that is rational is a single whole.

It follows that bodies are distinguished from each other not "in respect of substance," but solely "in respect of motion and rest." Moreover, every body is

> . . . determined to motion or rest by another body, which other body has been determined to motion or rest by a third body, and that third again by a fourth, and so on to infinity. . . .
> Hence it follows, that a body in motion keeps in motion, until it is determined to a state of rest by some other body; and a body at rest remains so, until it is determined to a state of motion by some other body. This is indeed self-evident. . . .
> So far we have been speaking only of the most simple bodies. . . . We now pass on to compound bodies.
> *Definition.*—When any given bodies of the same or different magnitude are compelled by other bodies to remain in contact, . . . so that their mutual movements should preserve among themselves a certain fixed relation, we say that such bodies are in union, and that together they compose one body or individual, which is distinguished from other bodies by this fact of union.[f]

Now, the human body is such a compound body, that is, it is a complex of motions of different velocities maintaining a relatively stable pattern among themselves. The science of physiology is the set of theorems that formulate the necessary relations holding among such patterns of motions. Physiology is therefore simply a department of physics. It is the mechanics of a particular subclass of movements.[9]

---

9 Spinoza did not try to deduce any of these theorems.

Psychology

According to Spinoza, just as a man's body is a finite mode of God under the attribute of extension, so his mind is a finite mode of God under the attribute of thought. A man's mind may be defined as the idea of his body, just as his body is the extension of his mind. But though there is this general correspondence between mind and body, ideas have one property that bodies lack: Ideas are reflexive. Perhaps the easiest way to understand what Spinoza meant here is to note that, whereas one can have an idea of an idea, it does not make sense to talk about a body of a body. Without this reflexive power, every idea would remain bound to the particular body to which it corresponds (that is, of which it is the idea). There would be a universe of ideas and a universe of bodies (like the English and Greek dictionaries), but no idea ever would be able to know more of the corresponding material universe than the particular body of which it happened to be the idea. Hence, it is this reflexive power that makes knowledge, science, and philosophy possible.

All men start, whether they recognize it or not, with more or less fragmentary ideas of their own bodies. And this is where inanimate objects and very simple organisms remain. If men advance beyond this level of awareness, it is only by not staying where they began. Even as children we find that our bodies are in a world containing other bodies. Gradually we realize that the mode we call our body is not merely "in" the world, but that it is tied by necessary connections to other bodily modes, and these to others, and so on. And to understand this is to *be* it: Insofar as I really understand the interrelations in which my body stands to other bodies, my mind is enlarged; it loses the limitations that made it uniquely mine. The bodies whose interrelations are understood are nothing but the ideas that understand them. It is a confusion to suppose that I stay here and have ideas about the world. My ideas of the attribute of extension, insofar as they are adequate, are not different from yours. For adequate ideas do not belong to me or to you. Insofar as they can be said to belong to anything, they belong to the bodies of which they are the adequate ideas. Just as my idea of my body is not different from my body, but the same mode under a different aspect (πολις is not different from *city*, but the same thing under a different aspect), so my idea of the solar system (if adequate) is not different either from your idea of the solar system or from the solar system itself. This means that insofar as I think adequately, my mind *is* everything that I think about.

Here again an analogy may be helpful. Suppose *city* to be reflexive, that is, to be capable of having an idea of itself, and let it set out to understand itself. It consults the dictionary and discovers itself defined as "incorporated municipality," whereupon it has to look up "municipality" and "incorporated." It finds that "municipality" is "self-governing community," that "community" is "people living in an organized group," and so on. Thus *city*, which doubtless started out by supposing itself a neat, "bounded" thing, soon finds that it is nothing of the kind. Meanwhile, of course, *group* is inquiring about itself and finds, to its surprise, that it is *city*. Of course, city and group are not *sheerly* identical; each is more than just the other. But they *are* identical, and the "more than" for each consists of other identities.

Accordingly, personal uniqueness is an illusion. One's sense of uniqueness is—sense; it is confused thinking. At the level of perception (that is, in introspection), each of us feels himself to be a distinct individual; at the level of thought, each of us knows himself to be all the others.

Thus Spinoza's analysis of the nature of knowledge led him to a conclusion about the human mind that corresponded exactly with the conclusion he had already reached, as a result of his analysis of the nature of extension, about the human body. Being exactly parallel aspects, what is true of the one must be true of the other. Neither a man's body nor his mind is the autonomous, independent entity that it seems to be; each is only a finite mode, the one of the attribute of extension, the other of the attribute of thought.

Nevertheless, according to Spinoza, it is a mistake to conclude that because everything is ultimately one, all distinctions fade into nothingness. Though city and group are identical, they are not an undifferentiated unity. And the same is true of you and me. Every element in reality, that is to say, has an inner nature that, though only partial, is real as far as it goes. As body, its partial nature is, as we have seen, inertia—the tendency to persist in a present state (motion or rest) and to require the application of force (another motion) to cause a modification of this state. As idea, this fragmentary nature is (and, when it is reflexive, is *felt* as) a drive to preserve one's own identity. There is, then, an endeavor, or appetite, in all things. This endeavor is the basis of the science of psychology, as motion and rest are the basis of the science of physics. Just as the various states of motion follow each other with an absolute necessity, so do the various states of desire or appetite. The causes and effects of any desire or appetite are other desires and appetites, just as the causes and effects of any motion are other motions. And, in both sciences, when Spinoza said "causes and effects," he of course meant that structure of implicatory relations that he took reality to be. The characteristics of mental life can be deduced from the nature of the mind with the same necessity as that with which the properties of a triangle (for example, having interior angles equal to 180°) are deduced from the nature of a triangle. Spinoza's psychology, like his physics, was a purely deductive science.

We cannot now examine Spinoza's attempt, in the *Ethics*, to demonstrate this geometric psychology. Rather, let us confine ourselves to noting a few main points. The various emotions are, as it were, reflections of the success or failure of the drive to self-preservation. What defeats this drive causes sorrow; what supports it causes joy. There is no distinction between intellect and will, and no such psychic state as the suspension of judgment that Descartes, for instance, thought he practiced. All psychic states, as successive phases in the movement of this drive to self-preservation, are at once judgings *and* desirings—they are at once recognizings and affirmings (or rejectings) of what is recognized. The changes in inner tone from one such phase to another—from joy to sorrow or to any other felt state—are completely determined by antecedent psychic states. Psychic states do not cause changes in the body; nor do bodily states cause changes in the psychic flow. What men call "will" and suppose to be the initiation of a change in some bodily state is an illusion resulting from ignorance of (1) the implicatory system of which this psychic state is a part and (2) the implicatory system of which the bodily state (the movement of some muscle or organ) is a part.

Much of this has a very modern sound. In his denial of separate "faculties" of will and intellect, in his insistence on the basic fact of activity, of a drive to self-affirmation, and the relation of feeling states to this drive, Spinoza was far ahead of his time. But this is only one side of the picture. Spinoza's approach was completely unempirical; the whole scheme was dominated by a geometric ideal, and he believed it possible to begin with "self-evident" axioms and deduce the nature of the mental life.

Ethics

Psychology was important to Spinoza only as a basis for ethics, and we now come to what was the culmination of his whole system. For Spinoza, science was to provide (was, in fact, to *be*) a way of life. But though this new way of life satisfied Spinoza's own lofty standards, it was at many points in conflict with the traditional ethics of the West.

We have already seen what Spinozism did to the personal Deity on whose authority so many of the imperatives of traditional morality had been grounded. We have also seen, at least by implication, what Spinozism did to the freedom of choice that most philosophers have held to be the basis of responsibility. In Spinoza's rigorously deterministic and monistic system, freedom of choice is an illusion stemming from our ignorance of our own natures and of their complete dependence on the universal system of things. And it is an illusion, too, to suppose that in experiencing and comparing values we are dealing with an objective state of affairs. Every man's values are his own, since they reflect his attitudes and drives. If men happen to agree about values, this results from the fact that their bodies are similar and are being affected by similar environments.

> When a man has purposed to make a given thing, . . . his work will be pronounced perfect, not only by himself, but by everyone who rightly knows, or thinks that he knows, the intentions and aim of its author. For instance, suppose anyone sees a work (which I assume to be not yet completed), and knows that the aim of the author of that work is to build a house, he will call the work imperfect; he will, on the other hand, call it perfect, as soon

as he sees that it is carried through to the end, which its author had purposed for it. . . . Such seems to be the primary meaning of these terms.

But, after men began to form general ideas, to think out types of houses, buildings, towers, &c., and to prefer certain types to others, it came about, that each man called perfect that which he saw agree with the general idea he had formed of the thing in question, and called imperfect that which he saw agree less with his own preconceived type, even though it had evidently been completed in accordance with the idea of its artificer. This seems to be the only reason for calling natural phenomena, which, indeed, are not made with human hands, perfect or imperfect; for men are wont to form general ideas of things natural, no less than of things artificial, and such ideas they hold as types, believing that Nature . . . has them in view, and has set them as types before herself. . . . Thus we see that men are wont to style natural phenomena perfect or imperfect rather from their own prejudices, than from true knowledge of what they pronounce upon. . . .

As for the terms *good* and *bad*, they indicate no positive quality in things regarded in themselves, but are merely modes of thinking, or notions which we form from the comparison of things one with another. Thus one and the same thing can be at the same time good, bad, and indifferent. For instance, music is good for him that is melancholy, bad for him that mourns; for him that is deaf, it is neither good nor bad.[g]

But all this, Spinoza would have held, is true only at that level of confused thought at which most men live most of the time. There is a way (by scientific knowledge) of coming to know and to enjoy a real, objective good. This good is God, the totality of everything that is.

Prop. XXVIII. The mind's highest good is the knowledge of God, and the mind's highest virtue is to know God.

Proof.—The mind is not capable of understanding anything higher than God, that is (I. Def. vi.), than a Being absolutely infinite, and without which (I. xv.) nothing can either be or be conceived; therefore (IV. xxvi. and xxvii.),[10] the mind's highest . . . good is the knowledge of God. Again, the mind is active, only in so far as it understands, and only to the same extent can it be said absolutely to act virtuously. The mind's absolute virtue is therefore to understand. Now, as we have already shown, the highest that the mind can understand is God; therefore the highest virtue of the mind is to understand or to know God. Q.E.D.[h]

What Spinoza meant seems to be the following. First, "knowing God" means knowing the whole nexus of implicatory relations of which each man is a finite part; it means, therefore, understanding one's place in the universe. Second, this knowledge, insofar as a man attains it, radically alters the whole emotional tone

10 [These propositions have not been quoted here—AUTHOR.]

of his life, the way he feels about the world. Third, it alters the way men behave. As long as a man lives at the level of perception, he sees himself as a unique self with a private good. At this level, therefore, his drive to self-affirmation is in competition with the drive to self-affirmation in every other part of the whole; each man envies and fears his fellows. This life of supposed freedom is actually one of hopeless bondage. It is inevitably doomed to defeat, for men are mistaken, of course, about the supposed separateness of their "selves," about the autonomy of their acts and the objectivity of the values they prize.

Accordingly, as a man rises from the level of confused thought to a recognition of the true state of affairs and of his relation to it, both his outer behavior and his inner experience change. Naturally, he still experiences the drive to self-affirmation (for, as we have seen, self does not dissolve into the whole), but his notions about the "self" that is being affirmed, and about the means by which its affirmation is to be achieved, are radically altered.

Happiness still consists in the preservation of one's own being; the basic right, the fundamental moral law, is still to love one's self and seek one's own profit. Virtue does not lie in self-sacrifice, but in self-affirmation, in acting in accordance with the laws of one's own nature. But the laws of a man's nature are a part of a pervasive rational scheme, and his own profit is a part of that universal order. Here Spinoza passed beyond the egocentric utilitarianism of Hobbes, who held that the way for a man to get his own good is to help others get theirs. "Their" good, Spinoza believed, turns out to be really "his," and his theirs. For the self he calls his and the self he calls theirs are both elements in an all-inclusive whole.

It follows, too, that the values a man prized at the level of confused thought are seen at the level of scientific knowledge to be merely ephemeral aspects of the universal order of things. The so-called "goods and ills of fortune" he will no longer take personally, as affronts to, or triumphs of, his small personality, for he will have come to understand that they are totally inconsequential. He will no longer complain, no longer struggle, for he will see that everything that happens is part of a necessary order.

Since this necessary order is rational, men do not have to take it on faith. They can *understand* it; their acceptance, and the peace acceptance brings, will be based on evidence that is as satisfactory as a geometric proof. And this rational acceptance of the necessary nature of things is experienced on its inner side as a cheerfulness and contentment readily distinguishable from the titillations of the senses that ignorant men call pleasure.

This "intellectual love of God," as Spinoza called it—this rational certainty that "in God we live and move and have our being"—is man's true good. But can any man ever come to *know* the whole? Not if men are limited to passage from one demonstration to another, for the whole, considered as a system of such linkages, is indefinitely large and cannot be encompassed by any finite intellect. But just as rational, demonstrative knowledge surpasses perception, so there is an intuitive knowledge that surpasses rational knowledge. Intuition,

Spinoza believed, is a grasping all at once of connections that, in rational knowledge, can be understood only one after the other. Insofar as a man attains this kind of knowledge, everything falls into its place and he views the whole as it might view itself, *sub specie aeternitatis*.

Spinoza described man's true good in moving terms. But since the order of the universe is necessary, how can men take any steps to achieve their good? How can they do anything to improve their condition? Spinoza dealt with this difficult question in Part V of the *Ethics*. It treats "of the power of the reason, showing how far the reason can control the emotions, . . . what is the nature of Mental Freedom or Blessedness, [and] how much more powerful the wise man is than the ignorant." The exposition begins with an attack on Descartes' conception that the will, by acting on the pineal gland, can intervene in the body's behavior and regulate its emotions.

> What does he understand, I ask, by the union of the mind and the body? What clear and distinct conception has he got of thought in most intimate union with a certain particle of extended matter? . . . In truth, as there is no common standard of volition and motion, so is there no comparison possible between the powers of the mind and the power or strength of the body; consequently the strength of one cannot in any wise be determined by the strength of the other.[i]

In contrast to Descartes, Spinoza of course maintained that a mental state is not the cause of a bodily state; it *is* that bodily state (this follows from the fact that mind and body are attributes, not substances). More particularly, the mental state that is called "coming to understand" *is* (not "is the cause of") a change in the tone of one's psychic life from relative unhappiness to relative happiness.

> *Prop. II.* If we remove a disturbance of the spirit, or emotion, from the thought of an external cause, and unite it to the other thoughts, then will the love or hatred toward that external cause, and also the vacillations of spirit which arise from these emotions, be destroyed.
> *Proof.*—That which constitutes the reality of love or hatred, is pleasure or pain, accompanied by the idea of an external cause (Def. of the Emotions, vi. and vii.[11]); wherefore, when this cause is removed, the reality of love or hatred is removed with it; therefore these emotions and those which arise therefrom are destroyed. Q.E.D.
> *Prop. III.* An emotion, which is a passion, ceases to be a passion, as soon as we form a clear and distinct idea thereof.
> *Proof.*—An emotion, which is a passion, is a confused idea (by the general Def. of the Emotions). If, therefore, we form a clear and distinct idea of a given emotion, that idea will only be distinguished from the emotion, in so

11 [These propositions and those cited in the following proofs have not been quoted here—AUTHOR.]

far as it is referred to the mind only, by reason (II. xxi. and note); therefore (III. iii.), the emotion will cease to be a passion. Q.E.D.

Corollary.—An emotion therefore becomes more under our control, and the mind is less passive in respect to it, in proportion as it is more known to us.

Prop. IV. There is no modification of the body, whereof we cannot form some clear and distinct conception. . . .

Corollary.—Hence it follows that there is no emotion, whereof we cannot form some clear and distinct conception.

. . . .

Prop. VI. The mind has greater power over the emotions and is less subject thereto, in so far as it understands all things as necessary. . . .

Note.—The more this knowledge, that things are necessary, is applied to particular things, which we conceive more distinctly and vividly, the greater is the power of the mind over the emotions, as experience also testifies. For we see, that the pain arising from the loss of any good is mitigated, as soon as the man who has lost it perceives, that it could not by any means have been preserved. So also we see that no one pities an infant, because it cannot speak, walk, or reason, or lastly, because it passes so many years, as it were, in unconsciousness. Whereas, if most people were born full-grown and only one here and there as an infant, everyone would pity the infants; because infancy would not then be looked on as a state natural and necessary, but as a fault or delinquency in Nature; and we may note several other instances of the same sort.[j]

To generalize, any limitations with respect to the cognitive side of our life (ignorance) are reflected in similar limitations in our psychic life (unhappiness), for will and intellect are not separate faculties, but aspects of the whole. It follows that the more we understand, the happier we are. To understand the whole (that is, God) is therefore to be supremely happy—to attain blessedness. This is a high and difficult doctrine. Spinoza was not writing a handbook on self-improvement, or on how to be happy. Most men, he knew, will never attain to an understanding of themselves, no matter what they do, no matter what is done or said to them. But some—a few saints, a few stoic sages here and there—appear actually to have attained blessedness. The theorems of Part V of the *Ethics* are not the exposition of a program about how "you too may become blessed." Rather, Part V tells what it *means* to be blessed—and it tells this, not in the language of ecstasy or mystic vision, but in the language of the geometric method.

Prop. XLII. Blessedness is not the reward of virtue, but virtue itself; neither do we rejoice therein, because we control our lusts, but, contrariwise, because we rejoice therein, we are able to control our lusts.

Proof.—Blessedness consists in love toward God (V. xxxvi. and note), which love springs from the third kind of knowledge[12] (V. xxxii. Coroll.); therefore

12 [The third kind of knowledge is intuition—AUTHOR.]

this love (III. iii. and lix.) must be referred to the mind, in so far as the latter is active; therefore (IV. Def. viii.) it is virtue itself. This was our first point. Again, in proportion as the mind rejoices more in this divine love or blessedness, so does it the more understand (V. xxxii.); that is (V. iii. Coroll.), so much the more power has it over the emotions, and (V. xxxviii.) so much the less is it subject to those emotions which are evil; therefore, in proportion as the mind rejoices in this divine love or blessedness, so has it the power of controlling lusts. And, since human power in controlling the emotions consists solely in the understanding, it follows that no one rejoices in blessedness, because he has controlled his lusts, but, contrariwise, his power of controlling his lusts arises from this blessedness itself. Q.E.D.

Note.—I have thus completed all I wished to set forth touching the mind's power over the emotions and the mind's freedom. Whence it appears, how potent is the wise man, and how much he surpasses the ignorant man, who is driven only by his lusts. For the ignorant man is not only distracted in various ways by external causes without ever gaining the true acquiescence of his spirit, but moreover lives, as it were unwitting of himself, and of God, and of things, and as soon as he ceases to suffer, ceases also to be.

Whereas the wise man, in so far as he is regarded as such, is scarcely at all disturbed in spirit, but, being conscious of himself, and of God, and of things, by a certain eternal necessity, never ceases to be, but always possesses true acquiescence of his spirit.

If the way which I have pointed out as leading to this result seems exceedingly hard, it may nevertheless be discovered. Needs must it be hard, since it is so seldom found. How would it be possible, if salvation were ready to our hand, and could without great labour be found, that it should be by almost all men neglected? But all things excellent are as difficult as they are rare.[k]

Estimate of Spinoza's Position

Many strands come together in Spinozism—rationalism, naturalism, determinism, mysticism. How much more inclusive it is than Hobbism, how much more subtle and coherent than Cartesianism, should be plain. But from the point of view of many people today, the inclusiveness and coherence are likely to seem artificial and unreal. To those who do not agree with Spinoza that the real is rational without remainder, Spinozism seems a dream philosophy—a magnificent, even inspiring, edifice, but still a dream. In a culture that has grown steadily more empirically minded—more concerned with facts, with the concrete, with the practical, with the thickness and the here-and-nowness of the actual—Spinozism can have only a limited appeal. Thus, for most people today, Spinoza's physics and psychology are caricatures. Because he completely separated the rational thought and the empirical observation that were united in Galileo's method, he ended with a set of universal truths off by themselves in a cloud and a perceptual awareness that he wrote off as confused thinking, and no way of getting from one to the other.

This central difficulty in Spinozism may be illustrated by considering briefly how Spinoza would have dealt with what has been called the central problem of modern philosophy—the problem of finding a place for value in a world of fact. Spinoza would have held this to be a pseudo-problem, occurring only at the level of confused thought at which most of us live. Ultimate reality, he would have said, is at once fact *and* value. Not only is there no conflict between science and value, but the life of science (of knowing the system of implicatorily related truths) *is* the only real value. For knowing the truth is knowing God.

If one is prepared to accept Spinoza's definitions of fact and value, this seems correct. The trouble is that the definitions are rather odd. The world of "fact" in which it was easy for him to find a place for value is not the spatiotemporal world of modern science; it is a world of logically related, abstract entities. And the value Spinoza found there is too high a doctrine for ordinary men to live by. Hence, though Spinozism solves the problem technically, both facts and values, as they are ordinarily understood, disappear in the process of solution. It is all very well to say that our problem exists only at the level of confused thought. But unless Spinoza was correct in identifying the rational with the real, the problem is not a pseudo-problem, for the thought in question is not confused.

These objections, of course, would not have touched Spinoza. His mind moved on another plane, and the criteria most of us use for distinguishing the real from the unreal seemed to him trivial. Today many people may write him off as a "mere" visionary, but in the whole history of Western culture, there have been a great many—a very great many—first-rate minds who have agreed with Spinoza and who have held that what we may be disposed to call his "blind spot" for the actual was not blindness at all, but acute vision. Here, then, we come once again to a fundamental parting of the ways; whether to take the ideal or the actual as the real is not so much a question to be settled by philosophy as it is a starting point for philosophical systems.

A question that *can* be dealt with, however, is whether, starting from the real-is-rational presupposition that Spinoza took over from Descartes, it is possible to avoid the Spinozistic version of God, self, and value. Must the consistent rationalist conclude with Spinoza that the only real value consists in recognizing that values are subjective attitudes and that the only real freedom consists in realizing that everything we do is infallibly determined? Must he admit that self disappears into God and that God is merely the rationale that validates our thought? Is religion reconciled with science only by making a religion of science? Leibniz held that these are not the inevitable consequences of rationalism. Let us therefore examine his views before leaving Continental Rationalism. They constitute one more attempt to correct Cartesian dualism from within, and to correct it in a rationalistic spirit.

Leibniz

Life

Leibniz was born in Germany in 1646, just as the Thirty Years' War was coming to an end, four years before Descartes' death and four years after Galileo's. Hobbes was still in exile in France, and Locke was a schoolboy. Leibniz died in 1716, as the new century, full of confidence drawn from the immense achievements of the preceding century, was beginning. It is no wonder that Leibniz thought he lived in "the best of all possible worlds."

Like everyone else for still some time to come, Leibniz was educated in the Scholastic tradition, but he did not react as sharply against it as had Hobbes or even Descartes. He studied law in preparation for what we would call the civil service, a field in which he had a distinguished career. He was in fact not so much a philosopher as a universal genius who interested himself in philosophy as in every other branch of knowledge. He was a first-rate mathematician and the inventor, along with Newton, of the infinitesimal calculus.[1] He was an early student of semantics and sought to develop a complete and uniform scientific language to replace "words of vague and uncertain meanings" by "fixed symbols" and so permit arguments to be settled by "simple calculation." He was an able diplomatist and administrator, first in the service of the Elector of Mainz and subsequently in the service of the Duke of Hanover, who employed him as librarian, archivist, and historian of the ducal family as well. He undertook the formidable task of reconciling Catholicism and Protestantism and also sought to mend the breach that divided the various Protestant sects. In the midst of all these activities he found time to travel widely and to carry on an immense correspondence with, it is said, more than a thousand persons.

Philosophy, then, was hardly more than an avocation for Leibniz. He tended to deal separately with single problems as they occurred to him, and since much of what he wrote was designed for a circle of royal dilettantes, what we have in his work is a number of exceedingly acute and stimulating suggestions that have not been thought through to a unified system and that are not always mutually consistent. Leibniz, in fact, approached philosophy as a diplomatist— seeking for each specific crisis a formula on which divergent parties could be brought to agree. But the disputants whose agreement he sought were all rational- ists; the "empirics," as Leibniz scornfully called them, were left outside the fold and permitted to enter, if at all, only on his terms. It never occurred to him to criticize the concept of substance or the doctrine that mathematics is the ideal of knowledge. He simply thought that the conclusions Spinoza had reached from this Cartesian starting point were unsound. For Leibniz, Spinoza had made quite unnecessary concessions to "science" (understood, of course, as all the rationalists understood it, as a body of demonstrative truths). The monism, naturalism, and pantheism that seemed to Spinoza the logical conclusions of Cartesian rationalism were unpalatable to Leibniz, who set himself to find a place in the new rational- ism for a transcendent and creative God, for real individuals, and for objective purposes. In other words, he saw that Cartesianism was inadequate as it stood, yet he really wanted to get back to the Cartesian kind of compromise—a compromise that took the orthodox conception of God and the notion of a teleological universe seriously and that sought to show that the new scientific world view was compatible with these traditional beliefs.

Physics

But what, exactly, *was* the scientific world view? What metaphysics did physics entail? Leibniz thought that both Descartes and Spinoza had gone wrong here.

---

1 Each suspected the other of stealing his ideas, and this led to an acrimonious quarrel among prideful nationalists on both sides.

Both had assumed that mechanics was about something they called "extension," or "matter," or "body." They reasoned that since physics investigates the properties of extension, extension must be real; the only question (for them) was about its status and its relation to mind. Descartes thought that extension must be a substance, but since substances are independent by definition, it followed, as the Parallelists pointed out, that it was out of relation to every other real, including mind. Accordingly, Spinoza said that extension was only an "attribute" of substance, but in Leibniz's opinion this did not help; extension remained a completely closed, irreducible system.

In a word, as long as the subject matter of physics (something called "extension") was conceived to be utterly different from the subject matter of the moral sciences (something called "mind"), it did not matter much whether extension was a substance or an attribute. The world was hopelessly divided. But what if, appearances to the contrary, extension were not an ultimate? What if analysis showed that extension was a derivative concept and that the really basic concept in physics was a psychic concept? In this event, there would be a way of reconciling physics and the moral sciences.

FORCE

Leibniz thought it easy to show that, even if extension were *an* ultimate, it was certainly not *the* ultimate, physical concept. Descartes himself had had to introduce a "quantity of motion" (supposedly put into the system by God), which he held to be constant. Leibniz thought he could show that Descartes' reasoning here was fallacious and that the principles of physics required "force," not motion, to be constant.

> It is not the quantity of . . . movement, but that of the force which I conserve. . . . It is by way of a new approach which has taught me that not only is the force conserved but also the very quantity of kinetic action which is different from that of the motion [momentum], as you are going to see through [the following] line of reasoning . . . : In the uniform motion of a single body (1) the action of traversing two leagues in two hours is double the action of traversing one league in one hour (for the first action contains the second exactly twice), (2) the action of traversing one league in one hour is double the action of traversing one league in two hours (for the actions producing the same effect are to each other as their speeds). Therefore, (3) the action of traversing two leagues in two hours is four times the action of traversing one league in two hours. This demonstration shows that a moving body receiving a double or triple speed in order to be able to produce a double or triple effect in the same time, receives an action four or nine times as great. Whence actions are to one another as the squares of the speeds. Now that happens most fortunately to agree with my estimate [that] forces are to one another as the heights from which heavy bodies might descend in order to acquire their speeds. And as the force is always conserved in order

to raise something finally to the same height or to produce some other effect, it follows that there is also conserved the same quantity of kinetic action in the world; that is to say, in order to get it straight, there is in one hour as much kinetic action in the universe as there is in any other hour whatsoever. So the purpose of our philosophers, and particularly of the late M. Descartes, was good in conserving action and in estimating the force by the action; but they have taken a *quid pro quo* by taking what they call the quantity of motion [momentum] for the quantity of kinetic action [energy].[a]

THE CONTINUUM

Leibniz's conception of substance as force, rather than as matter in motion, can be approached by way of his work in mathematics on infinitesimals. Galileo's mechanics had dealt with such concepts as a continuously increasing velocity, that is, a velocity such that, no matter how small the time interval taken, one never comes to a point at which the velocity has suddenly jumped ahead. Everywhere in mechanics (in the Newtonian theory of gravitational action, for instance) it soon appeared that the physicist has to deal with such continuously divisible quantities—with infinitesimal times and distances. Leibniz (and Newton) developed the infinitesimal calculus precisely to deal with this newly discovered feature of the physical world, and Leibniz, at least, saw that it put physics in a wholly new light. The physical world, he realized, is not a collection of discrete entities, but a continuum. Is it a continuum of motions? No, Leibniz thought; for no matter how small a section of motion one takes, it has been artifically cut off, as it were, from the "next" section. What the physicist studies, whatever it is, is not made up of very small sections "next" to one another. This means that it cannot be motion, for motion implies a span—a section, however small. Someone might, indeed, want to say that it is *potential* movement; but whatever it is called, it is something more ultimate than motion—it is a kind of flow, a thrust or drive that carries the motion from any section into the "next." In a word, what the physicist has to deal with is not, as Descartes thought, gross motions; it is infinitely small units of force.[2] As Leibniz remarked, this concept of force was the "Ariadne thread" that led him out of the "labyrinth of the continuum."

> Now this is the axiom which I utilize, *namely, that "no event takes place by a leap."* This proposition flows, in my view, from the laws of order and rests on the same rational ground by virtue of which it is generally recognized that *motion does not occur by leaps,* that is, that a body in order to go from one place to another must pass through definite intermediate places. . . .
> I do not believe extension alone constitutes substance, since its conception is incomplete. . . . For we can analyze it into plurality, continuity and co-existence (that is, simultaneous existence of parts). Plurality has to do with

2 Though they are called here, provisionally, "units" of force, they are not spatially extended. If they were, they would not be infinitely small—and they would be motion, not force.

number, and continuity with time and motion; co-existence, on the contrary, is the only thing that approaches extension. . . . Hence I believe that our thought of substance is perfectly satisfied in the conception of force and not in that of extension. Besides, there should be no need to seek any other explanation for the conception of power or force than that it is the attribute from which change follows and its subject is substance itself. . . . I am convinced that any unity of extended things exists only in abstraction, so long as we neglect the inner motions of the parts through which each and every part of matter is actually analyzed into different parts. . . .

We have elsewhere explained that there was contained in material things something which has to be added to mere extension, and is really prior to it, viz., a natural *force* implanted by the Creator in all things. It . . . is characterized by an effort (*conatu*) or nisus which, were it not limited by a contrary effort, would also come to complete realization. This tendency is often apparent directly to the senses, and also, even if not apparent to sensation, is, in my judgment, known everywhere in matter by means of reason. . . . Since *activity* is the characteristic mark of substances, extension on the contrary affirms nothing other than the continual reiteration or propagation of an already presupposed effort and counter-effort, that is, resistant substance, and therefore, extension cannot possibly constitute substance itself. . . .

Motion just like time, when reduced by analysis to its elements, has no existence as a whole so long as it possesses no co-existing parts. And thus there is nothing real in motion itself apart from the reality of the momentary transition which is determined by means of force and a nisus for change. In that force, therefore, consists whatever there is in material nature apart from its also being the object of geometry or extension. In this way, finally, we take into account the truth as well as the teachings of the ancients. . . . We . . . attain here an understanding of the traditional Aristotelian doctrine of the forms or entelechies—which was justifiably regarded as puzzling and appeared scarcely to be understood by the authors themselves. Accordingly, we believe that this philosophy, which has been accepted for centuries, is not to be discarded in general, but only stands in need of an elucidation which may make it consistent as far as possible. We shall . . . develop it with new truths.[b]

This is a good example of the spirit of compromise that animated Leibniz's philosophy. Far from rejecting traditional approaches, he argued that the new physics itself required a concept drawn from Aristotelian-Scholastic philosophy. Quite apart from theological considerations, he held that any attempt to give a "rigorously systematic" account of the principles of physics takes us beyond "a purely geometrical concept of matter" and "purely geometric laws of motion" and requires us to "introduce certain metaphysical axioms"—axioms about, for instance, "cause and effect [and] activity and passivity." Only if, in this way,

> . . . we unite metaphysical laws with the laws of extension, do we obtain the *systematic* rules of motion, as I might call them. . . . A body which pushes

another along must therefore always suffer a retardation such that neither more nor less force is contained in the effect than in the cause. Since this law cannot be derived from the merely geometrical concept of mass, there must then be another basic principle immanent in bodies, viz., the force itself which is always preserved in the same quantity, although it is divided among different bodies. From this, then, I drew the conclusion that we must, in addition to purely mathematical principles . . . , recognize metaphysical ones.[c]

So far we have been considering Leibniz's correction of Cartesian physics. If Leibniz was right, the concept of "unit of force" provides a sounder basis for physics than the concept of matter in motion. So far so good. But Leibniz also believed that "unit of force" could serve as the basis of a unified world view, a view "which equally satisfies religion and science."

Monads

Leibniz called the basic element in his unified world view a "monad," which may be defined as a center of psychic activity. How did Leibniz get from "unit of force" to "monad"? The first step was to ask whether a unit of force is a substance or an attribute of a substance. (To many people today this will seem a red herring, or worse; but it was an inevitable question for the rationalists, who held that everything that is, is either a substance or an attribute of a substance.) Leibniz agreed with Spinoza that the logic of substance requires substance to stand alone, and that this means that it must enter into no relations. Since Spinoza held that things do not stand alone, he concluded that there is but one substance; since Leibniz wanted to avoid Spinoza's all-embracing substance, he had no alternative but to make each unit of force a substance in its own right.

The next question is, "How do all these individual substances differ from one another?" They cannot differ in size or in space occupancy, for these concepts imply extension; extension cannot be used to explain force, since force, as we have seen, is a more basic concept than extension. The only other way they could differ would be in respect of thought, or in the quality of their psychic life.

Leibniz derived this conclusion from the general Cartesian principle that everything that is not body is mind: If a monad is not a body, it must be a mind. Moreover, Leibniz believed that this was confirmed in experience: What we experience in ourselves as "being alive" is nothing but that drive or thrust that, as we have seen, Leibniz held it necessary to presuppose as the basis of physical movement and change.

The net result of these considerations was a universe consisting of a vast assemblage of individual lives.

Substance is a being capable of action. It is simple or compound. *Simple substance* is that which has no parts. *Compound* substance is the collection of simple substances or *monads*. *Monas* is a Greek word which signifies unity, or that which is one. . . .

Simple substances, lives, souls, spirits are unities. . . . Consequently all nature is full of life.

Monads, having no parts, cannot be formed or decomposed. They cannot begin or end naturally; and consequently last as long as the universe, which will be changed but will not be destroyed. They cannot have shapes; otherwise they would have parts. And consequently a monad, in itself and at a given moment, could not be distinguished from another except by its internal qualities and actions, which can be nothing else than its *perceptions* (that is, representations of the compound, or of what is external, in the simple), and its *appetitions* (that is, its tendencies to pass from one perception to another), which are the principles of change. . . .

There is also no way of explaining how a monad can be altered or changed in its inner being by any other creature, for . . . the monads have no windows through which anything can enter or depart. The accidents cannot detach themselves nor go about outside of substances, as did formerly the sensible species of the Schoolmen. Thus neither substance nor accident can enter a monad from outside.

Nevertheless, the monads must have some qualities, otherwise they would not even be entities. . . .

It is necessary, indeed, that each monad be different from every other. For there are never in nature two beings which are exactly alike and in which it is not possible to find an internal difference, or one founded upon an intrinsic quality (*dénomination*).

I take it also for granted that every created being, and consequently the created monad also, is subject to change, and even that this change is continuous in each.

If follows from what has just been said, that the natural changes of the monads proceed from an *internal principle,* since an external cause could not influence their inner being.

But, besides the principle of change, there must be an individuating *detail of changes,* which forms, so to speak, the specification and variety of the simple substances.

This detail must involve a multitude in the unity or in that which is simple. For since every natural change takes place by degrees, something changes and something remains; and consequently, there must be in the simple substance a plurality of affections and of relations, although it has no parts.

The passing state, which involves and represents a multitude in unity or in the simple substance, is nothing else than what is called *perception,* which must be distinguished from apperception or consciousness, as will appear in what follows. Here it is that the Cartesians especially failed, having taken no account of the perceptions of which we are not conscious. It is this also which made them believe that . . . there are no souls of brutes or of other entelechies. . . .

The action of the internal principle which causes the change or the passage from one perception to another, may be called *appetition;* it is true that desire cannot always completely attain to the whole perception to which it tends, but it always attains something of it and reaches new perceptions.

We experience in ourselves a multiplicity in a simple substance, when we find that the most trifling thought of which we are conscious involves a variety in the object. Thus all those who admit that the soul is a simple substance ought to admit this multiplicity in the monad. . . .

Whence we see that there is a world of creatures, of living beings, of animals, of entelechies, of souls, in the smallest particle of matter.

Each portion of matter may be conceived of as a garden full of plants, and as a pond full of fishes. But each branch of the plant, each member of the animal, each drop of its humors is also such a garden or such a pond. . . .

Therefore there is nothing fallow, nothing sterile, nothing dead in the universe, no chaos, no confusion except in appearance; somewhat as a pond would appear from a distance, in which we might see the confused movement and swarming, so to speak, of the fishes in the pond, without discerning the fish themselves.

We see thus that each living body has a ruling entelechy, which in the animal is the soul; but the members of this living body are full of other living beings, plants, animals, each of which has also its entelechy or governing soul.[d]

AN INNER PRINCIPLE OF CHANGE

Quite apart from its principal merit, which was that it resolved the conflict between science and religion,[3] this scheme had, Leibniz believed, many advantages. Consider, for instance, the old problem of change. A created substance, as Leibniz said, must change; only God is immutable. But what can cause a substance to change? Not something outside it, for then it would not be independent—it would not, in fact, be a substance. In every created substance there must therefore be an inner principle of change. There must be an identity that produces changing states while yet preserving its own unity. Leibniz believed that he had found this identity in the conscious life of the self. That is to say, he conceived of thought as the holding together of a diversity in unity. There is unity in that the thought is *my* thought; there is diversity in that my thought is always the thought of another—of an object, a not-me.

My perceptions, my thoughts, change; yet they are all my thoughts. And introspection also reveals the "principle" of their change. What causes my perceptions and thoughts to change is appetition, or desire. Naturally, desire does not always attain to the whole of the perception that it seeks, but it always attains some of it, and insofar as it does, we advance to fresh perceptions.

What is true of the psychic life of men is true, in varying degrees, throughout the whole universe. For the principle of continuity, which Leibniz introduced in connection with his revision of Cartesian physics, enabled him to formulate a doctrine of degrees of consciousness and so to project the unity-in-diversity we know in ourselves into a general metaphysical law. Consciousness, that is to say, is not just a peculiarity of human minds. Consciousness is a continuum, and every monad is a focus of sentient experience (a feeling, a life) at some particular level in this continuum. Though there are monads at many different levels of consciousness (both below our minimum and above our maximum), every monad is a real individual just because, at whatever level of consciousness it operates, its experience is its own.

HIERARCHY OF MONADS

If there were not these different degrees of consciousness, there would not be a variety of individual monads. For there is nothing about one monad to make it different from others except perceptual difference. Hence, if there were two monads with exactly the same degree of consciousness, they would be the same monad, which is absurd. Reality, accordingly, is a collection of psychic centers, or lives, each of which is an individual distinguished from all other individuals precisely by the fact that no other monad is conscious of its experience to just the same degree. Leibniz also held, as another consequence of the principle of continuity, that there are no gaps in the series of monads. *Every* possible degree of consciousness exists. Hence reality is not merely a collection of monads; it is a hierarchy.

This conception of a hierarchy of individual substances is of course reminiscent of St. Thomas, especially since, as with Thomas, each of these substances contains (is) a drive to completion. But whereas Thomas had associated this drive with the actualization of form (the process by which, for example, an acorn becomes an oak), Leibniz's emphasis was not on the terminus, not on what a thing *becomes,* but on *what* becomes. This was not only an expression of the individualism of the new age; it also ruled out the investigation of final causes in natural science.

Spinoza had also appropriated Thomas' drive to completion and had also reinterpreted it as self-fulfillment. But Spinoza held the drive to self-fulfillment to be the distinguishing mark of modes; Leibniz held it to be the essence of substance. Moreover, Leibniz did not conceive of the drive under the aspect of various metaphysically distinct attributes, including "mind" and "body," all equally real and equally complete. In Leibniz's view, the drive is just what it is—an unfolding of perceivings and desirings. What Spinoza held to be completely distinct languages, Leibniz held to be simply different levels of awareness in the monad itself.

REPRESENTATION

The next question for Leibniz was the nature of causality. If a monad is a distinct substance, it cannot (as Leibniz pointed out) be in causal interaction with other monads. In fact, for Spinoza's complete and closed attributes, Leibniz simply substituted the complete and self-contained lives of the various individual monads. And, like Spinoza, he explained away causality by presupposing a kind of parallelism. Naturally, however, Leibniz's was a parallelism among monads instead of between attributes.

> All nature is a *plenum*. There are everywhere simple substances, separated in effect from one another by activities of their own which continually change their relations; and each important simple substance, or monad, which forms the centre of a composite substance (as, for example, of an animal) and the principle of its unity, is surrounded by a *mass* composed of an infinity of other monads, which constitute the body proper of this central monad; and in accordance with the affections of its body the monad represents, as in a *centre*, the things which are outside of itself. . . . Each monad is a living mirror, or endowed with internal activity, representative according to its point of view of the universe, and as regulated as the universe itself. . . . Thus there is a perfect *harmony* between the perceptions of the monad and the motions of bodies, pre-established at the beginning between the system of efficient causes and that of final causes. . . .
>
> The creature is said to *act* externally in so far as it has perfection, and to be *acted on* by another in so far as it is imperfect. Thus *action* is attributed to the monad in so far as it has distinct perceptions, and *passivity* in so far as it has confused perceptions. . . .
>
> For since a created monad can have no physical influence upon the inner being of another, it is only in this way that one can be dependent upon another.
>
> And hence it is that the actions and passive reactions of creatures are mutual. For God, in comparing two simple substances, finds in each one reasons which compel him to adjust the other to it, and consequently that which in certain respects is active, is according to another point of view, passive; *active* in so far as that what is known distinctly in it, serves to account for that which takes place in another; and *passive* in so far as the reason for what takes place in it, is found in that which is distinctly known in another. . . .
>
> Thus, although each created monad represents the entire universe, it represents more distinctly the body which is particularly attached to it, and of which it forms the entelechy.[e]

PREESTABLISHED HARMONY

Every monad, whatever level of awareness it happens to possess, represents, or mirrors, the whole universe of monads. Since every monad is "windowless," its whole past and its whole future are contained in its own life. If we (or it) knew enough about its past, we would be able to predict everything that would ever happen to it. And we would be able to do this without reference to anything outside this individual monad. On the other hand, how much can be told about the *rest* of the universe from any one monad's life is a function of that monad's level of consciousness. Most monads exist and operate at such a low level of consciousness that their lives tell only about their immediate environment—about those monads that we call their "body."

The universe is therefore like a great number of clocks that all keep perfect time because a very skillful watchmaker has made them and regulated them. Or, better, it is like a symphony orchestra playing in perfect harmony. What the first violins, for instance, play at any given moment is determined by what they played (that is, by what was written for them to play) in their past. The present of the first-violin score unfolds out of its past, and the same is true for the woodwinds and the other instruments. But though the score for each instrument is distinct, all the separate scores fit together harmoniously as the scores for such-and-such a symphony. When the woodwinds enter against the violins, it may sound to the uninitiated listener as if the violins called them into sound; but this is because what the violins are doing at this point in their score is harmonically (not causally) related to what the woodwinds are doing at the same point in *their* score.

The Existence of God

Just as the dovetailing of the various instruments playing together in an orchestra implies that a musician has composed each score with the others in mind, so the harmony of the monads implies that a mind, and clearly a supreme one, has arranged their orchestration. Though Leibniz believed that this consideration is enough to show that God exists, he offered other proofs of the existence of God, including a version of the ontological argument:

> If there is a reality in essences or possibilities or indeed in the eternal truths, this reality must be founded in something existing and actual, and consequently in the existence of the necessary being, in whom essence involves existence, or with whom it is sufficient to be possible in order to be actual.
>
> Hence God alone (or the necessary being) has this prerogative, that he must exist if he is possible. And since nothing can hinder the possibility of that which possesses no limitations, no negation, and, consequently, no contradiction, this alone is sufficient to establish the existence of God *a priori*. [God's existence can be] proved . . . also *a posteriori*, since contingent beings exist, which can only have their final or sufficient reason in a necessary being who has the reason of his existence in himself. . . .
>
> Now, as there is an infinity of possible universes in the ideas of God, and as only one of them can exist, there must be a sufficient reason for the choice of God, which determines him to select one rather than another.
>
> And this reason can only be found in the *fitness*, or in the degrees of perfection, which these worlds contain, each possible world having a right to claim existence according to the measure of perfection which it possesses.
>
> And this is the cause of the existence of the Best; namely, that his wisdom

makes it known to God, his goodness makes him choose it, and his power makes him produce it.

Now this *connection*, or this adaptation, of all created things to each and of each to all, brings it about that each simple substance has relations which express all the others, and that, consequently, it is a perpetual living mirror of the universe.

And as the same city looked at from different sides appears entirely different, and is as if multiplied *perspectively;* so also it happens that, as a result of the infinite multitude of simple substances, there are as it were so many different universes, which are nevertheless only the perspectives of a single one, according to the different *points of view* of each monad.

And this is the way to obtain as great a variety as possible, but with the greatest possible order; that is, it is the way to obtain as much perfection as possible.

Moreover, this hypothesis (which I dare to call demonstrated) is the only one which brings into relief the grandeur of God. [My critics have] raised objections . . . that I attributed too much to God and more than is possible. But [they] can state no reason why this universal harmony, which brings it about that each substance expresses exactly all the others through the relations which it has to them, is impossible.[f]

Teleology and Mechanism

Thus the universe in its ultimate nature is a teleological system, not merely in the Cartesian sense that God created it in accordance with His plan, but also in the sense that *every* element in the universe is itself a miniature teleological system, a reflection of the universe as a whole. Between monads there is no causality, but only a reciprocity resulting from God's preestablished harmony. Within every monad there is real causality, and this is of the nature of appetition, or desire. Hence the basic relation in the universe is not mechanical but purposive. These considerations permitted Leibniz to give an account of morality and religion in the traditional sense, according to a means-end scheme.

MATTER AND EXTERNALITY

But what about physics? Could Leibniz make a place for physics in this teleological universe? It is clear that, according to his view, the Galilean bodies in motion are not real, for only monads are real, and no monad or aggregate of monads is a body. But it does not follow, because the bodies of physics are not ultimately real, that they are sheer illusion. What is called body is the way in which certain monads represent (or mirror) aggregates of other monads. From a distance a cloud of dust *looks* continuous and solid, though it is in fact composed of tiny particles. So a relatively low-level monad (or a higher-level monad during a period of low-level awareness) represents the universe of monads as bodies in space. As the monad's consciousness rises, it comes to represent the universe more adequately; when and if it passes from the "confused thought" of perception to the clear and distinct thought of rationalism, it represents the universe more nearly as it is. That is, it comes to understand that what men call "bodies" are aggregates of monads of the same nature as it experiences itself to be.

Thus, according to Leibniz, externality is a confused awareness of otherness. Insofar as a monad is capable of any degree of self-awareness at all, it distinguishes self from not-self (How could it be aware of self except insofar as it is also aware of something else that it is not?). Self, that is to say, is felt to exclude what is not-self, and this exclusiveness is represented (at this level of awareness) as spatial externality. As men gain a clearer knowledge of the world, they come to understand that the real exclusiveness of self is not spatial, but rather, the exclusiveness of a unique experience. In other words, a monad is not distinguished from other things by being spatially outside them (for no monad is really in space), but by being a different life, a different focus of experience, a different perspective on the universe.

SCIENCE

On this basis Leibniz could give an account of science that both validated it as far as it goes and showed that it requires supplementation by theology. Every monad represents the universe in its own way, which is a reflection of its particular level of consciousness. At human levels of consciousness various types of representation occur, ranging from perception to what is called science. Each level of representation reflects the order of the universe with a certain degree of adequacy. The higher the level of consciousness, the more adequate the representation, and hence the more precise the information obtainable at that level. At the relatively low level of perception, men form empirical generalizations—"water freezes," "fire burns," "friction causes heat." At higher levels of representation, the generalizations become firmer, more precise, better coordinated. But generalizations are possible even at the level of perception, because our representations are the representations of an objectively existing and harmoniously arranged whole, a preestablished harmony of coordinated lives. Of course, "fire burns" is only the most rudimentary kind of knowledge. Science, properly speaking, emerges only when a level is reached at which the representations form a deductive system, such as mechanics. Though the concepts and theorems of mechanics are far more adequate representations than the sensuous "fire" of perception, they are still only phenomena, only representations. Hence physics is not the final explanation of the universe. It only tells (with much greater precision, of course, than perception's "fire burns") *what* is happening; it does not tell *why* it is happening.

Hence, though mechanics is adequate in the sense that the information it yields is useful, reliable, and true, it is also limited. It is possible, for instance, to give a complete mechanistic account of Socrates sitting in prison about to drink the hemlock. This would show how Socrates' bodily movements were related to those of his jailors, to those of his friend Crito, and so on. Theoretically, at least, such an account could be just as complete as an account of the causes of a billiard ball's "imprisonment" in the pocket of a billiard table, though the former, involving more complex bodies, would be immensely more complicated. But when this mechanistic description was complete, Socrates' question would remain—"Why am I not in Megara?" Physics cannot answer this question. To answer *it*, one must get at that unfolding flow of perceivings and desirings that is the *inner* life of Socrates' soul monad. In other words, it is necessary to know what Socrates hoped to achieve by rejecting Crito's offer to arrange his escape— and only Socrates himself could tell us this. Indeed, what *he* could tell us about it would depend on the level of self-conscious awareness that his soul monad had achieved.

Socrates—and, of course, every other object of behavior—is an aggregation of monads, the various lives of which form a preestablished harmony. Every such object may be looked at from the outside (as by an external observer) or from the inside (if one or more of the monads that constitute this aggregate happen to be self-conscious). Looked at from the outside, these various lives appear as a sequence of mechanically related bodily states. But this mechanism is nothing but the means by which the ends of the aggregated monads are realized. Observation of the mechanism itself and of the relations between its various parts will never reveal the desires of the monads. Any outside observer will find only related parts interacting according to simple, mathematically statable laws, for the desirings are *inside* the individual parts of the machine, that is, they constitute the inner lives (whether or not these lives are consciously aware of themselves is immaterial) of these parts.

> *Perception* and that which depends on it *are inexplicable by mechanical causes*, that is, by figures and motions. And, supposing that there were a machine so constructed as to think, feel and have perception, we could conceive of it as enlarged and yet preserving the same proportions, so that we might enter it as into a mill. And this granted, we should only find on visiting it, pieces which push one against another, but never anything by which to explain a perception. This must be sought for, therefore, in the simple substance and not in the composite or in the machine. Furthermore, nothing but this (namely, perceptions and their changes) can be found in the simple substance. It is also in this alone that all the *internal activities* of simple substances can consist.[g]

There is no difference in principle between Socrates and a billiard ball. The only difference between them is that the billiard ball's dominant monad is not self-conscious. Therefore it can give no reports of its inner life. If it could report, however, it would tell us about the goods it perceives and the ends it aims at, just as Socrates does. We would see that the movements across the billiard table, which we describe mechanistically from the outside, fulfill a desire, expressed in the unfolding inner life of the dominant monad and reflected in the unfolding inner lives of its aggregate. Getting into the pocket would be just as much an end, in terms of the billiard ball's system of values, as staying in prison was for Socrates. In both, the bodily mechanism is merely the outer expression of an inner harmony of the various desirings of some aggregate of monads.

Further, just as any particular bodily machine with its particular sequences is the expression of some particular purpose, so the mechanistic type of explanation, as such, is grounded in purposive behavior. Just as we can ask, "Why did Socrates refuse to escape to Megara?" so we can ask, "Why are mechanical accounts of behavior possible?" The significant point is that Leibniz thought this an intelligible question. Here he differed from both Descartes and Spinoza, who had held that mechanics is self-explanatory. As we have seen, they derived physics from geometry; holding as they did that the real is rational, they thought it as meaningless to ask "Why?" about mechanics as it would be to ask "Why?" about, say, the principle of contradiction. But since Leibniz held that the principles of mechanics cannot be deduced from the geometric properties of extension, he held that an additional, "metaphysical principle" is necessary. In his view, that is to say, the real is a rational structure, but it requires something more than reason to explain it.

GOD'S CHOICE OF THE BEST

Mechanics, Leibniz believed, is certainly a rational and demonstrative science, but an infinite number of equally rational and demonstrative sciences are possible. Why, of all these equally possible rational sciences, does Galilean mechanics happen to be the one that is real, that is, the one that is true of the world? The reason cannot be a rational one, for there is no rational basis for distinguishing between equally rational alternatives.

Up to this point, Leibniz's reasoning coincides in a curious way with Hobbes's. Here, however, the two thinkers part company, for Hobbes concluded that since there is no rational way of distinguishing, decision must be left to the arbitrary will of the sovereign, who has the power to enforce his decree. Leibniz, for his part, rejected the notion that there is no reason, that there is only brute, inexplicable fact. He argued that since there is a reason, and since it is not rational, it must be a purpose. Specifically, he held that the reason Galilean mechanics is the true science lies in God's intention to choose what is best for men. Of all the possible and equally rational systems that God might have chosen, He chose mechanics because it "is the way to obtain as great a variety as possible, but with the greatest possible order."[4,h]

The inverse square law is an example. What could be simpler than the formula that bodies attract each other directly with their masses and inversely with the

4 For the whole passage, see pp. 229–30.

square of their distances? And yet this simple formula comprehends an immense range of phenomena; tides, planets, billiard balls, apples falling on Newton's head—all conform to this law. God, in other words, *could* have organized the lives of the monads according to any one of an infinite variety of equally rational schemes, all of which were present to His infinite mind and considered by Him at the moment of creation. He chose mechanics as the principle of organization, not because it was more rational than the other schemes, but because it was more useful to man. Thus Leibniz believed that he had once again demonstrated the goodness and wisdom of God and His providential concern for man.

TWO PRINCIPLES OF EXPLANATION

It follows that two principles of explanation are necessary. If reality were merely rational, we would need only one principle—the principle of contradiction. But since the rational is only the possibly-real, a second principle is needed. So far, most people today would agree with Leibniz; but we would probably think of this second principle in empirical terms and use observation and experiment to distinguish between what is real and what is only possibly real. Because Leibniz held that what makes the possibly-real real is God's choice of the best, his second principle was teleological. He called it the "principle of sufficient reason."

The principle of contradiction yields what Leibniz described as "truths of reason"; the principle of sufficient reason, "truths of fact." The two principles, and the truths derived from them, supplement each other; any satisfactory account of things involves the use of both. Truths of reason are implicatory propositions like those of arithmetic and geometry, and they are absolutely necessary. When the mind understands the proposition "the interior angles of a triangle equal two right angles," it is intuiting an eternal and objective relation between essences. But, unlike Spinoza, Leibniz held that this order, though eternal and objective, is not as such real; it is only possible. The theorem only states that *if* anything is a triangle, then its interior angles equal two right angles. Some other principle is needed to determine whether Euclidean triangles exist— whether, that is to say, out of all the equally possible geometries (considered as closed systems of implicatory propositions), Euclidean geometry is real. There is nothing *logically necessary* about the fact that the real world is Euclidean.[5] Some other geometry might just as well apply. Nevertheless there must be *some* reason why the real world is Euclidean rather than non-Euclidean. Since this reason cannot be rational, it must be teleological.

5 To follow Leibniz here, it is necessary to bear in mind that, in his view, "necessary" means "is implied by." "Contingent" does not mean "not determined"; it means "not implied by." "The interior angles of a triangle equal two right angles" is "necessary" because it can be deduced from definitions and axioms that imply it. But it is not necessary that real figures be Euclidean, for there is nothing that implies *this*. Hence the theorems of Euclidean geometry are, taken individually, necessary; the Euclidean system (the theorems taken collectively) are contingent.

Just as we need a dual explanation of the basic characteristics of the universe as a whole, so we need a dual explanation of any particular occurrence in it. A purely mechanistic account of an occurrence is suspended, for what mechanics shows about Socrates is merely that *if* there is a body of such-and-such a size moving at such and such a velocity and impinged on by such-and-such other bodies, it will do thus-and-so—sit in prison in Athens, instead of escaping to Megara. It does not show *why* there is a body of this size moving at this velocity and so on. A teleological account of Socrates' behavior explains *why* he did what he did; specifically, it shows that, of all the various possible things he might have done, staying in prison was the best possible. But this teleological account, taken by itself, does not show *how* the movements that occurred produced the end that Socrates was seeking.

A *complete* account combines the why and the how. Because it must give both the ultimate reason and the connective tissue of motions, a complete account always has the form, "If A is B, then C is D. But A *is* B; therefore C is D." The "if A is B, then C is D" part of such an account consists in truths of reason; it is a system of implicatory propositions that enables us to understand the various movements (for example, those of Socrates' body) as a part of a whole system of movements. The "but A *is* B" part of the account consists in truths of fact; it is a system of purposes terminating in a final purpose that is good in itself. Without the former, the account lacks logical structure; without the latter, it is merely about the possible, not about the actual.

By showing that mechanics and teleology, far from conflicting, actually supplement each other, Leibniz believed he had demonstrated that the theory of monads "equally satisfies both science and religion." This metaphysical scheme also solved, he thought, a number of other problems that had long perplexed believers in the transcendent, all-good God of Christianity. Consider, for instance, the problem of evil. God, according to Leibniz, had an infinite variety of possible worlds to choose from, and He chose the best of them. Since He had an infinite variety to choose from, His choice was unrestricted; since He chose the best, the imperfection of the actual world is not incompatible with His goodness. Because both His power and His knowledge are unlimited, His goodness is wholly preserved. Or consider the problem of freedom. Though what men do is completely determined (the present of every monad is "big with its future"), human conduct is not necessary. It is contingent, because it depends on a free choice of the best.

Limitations of Leibniz's View

Though it is impossible not to admire the ingenuity of this scheme, there are not many Leibnizians today. Why? One reason is that the theory does not so much bring opposing views into real agreement as it allows them to go on differing. It is like an ingenious diplomatic formula that everyone can accept because everyone understands it in his own way. Thus, for instance, the solution of the problem of freedom depends on the special meanings Leibniz chose to give to "necessity" and "contingency." And not even diplomacy resolves some of the theological dilemmas. Is God a monad? Apparently so. What, then, is His relation to the created monads? Is not the whole universe to be conceived of as God's body? Yes, it would seem that the universe of created monads are grouped around God as their dominant monad, just as man's body monads are grouped around his soul monad. But this comes dangerously close to pantheism.

These divergences from orthodoxy are relatively minor points. A more serious problem is connected with Leibniz's belief in the existence of other monads. Leibniz never really tried to prove their existence; he just took it for granted. He started from the Cartesian assumption that there are minds and bodies. Then, having worked out the notion of a monad, he concluded that the Cartesian bodies must "really" be monads. Here is but another example of the way in which the basic Cartesian formula underlay the whole philosophic development that followed—the way in which it was assumed in principle even while being rejected in detail.

Again, Leibniz assumed that a plurality of monads exists, just as Descartes had assumed that a plurality of bodies exists. But Leibniz also held that monads are substances, that substances are independent, and hence that every monad is windowless, a closed life. It follows that the only monad I know is "me"—my own soul monad, which knows itself. How, then, can I know that its states represent other monads? If I knew on independent grounds that other monads exist, I might argue that, by means of a preestablished harmony, I represent those others adequately. Preestablished harmony, in a word, does not prove that representation occurs; it only proves, assuming that representation does occur, that it is adequate. But how, shut forever inside myself by the exigencies of the substance doctrine, could I ever hope to find evidence for the existence of other monads or to show that my states represent anything at all? It would seem, then, that Leibniz really ended, like Spinoza, with one substance, the only difference being that whereas Spinoza's "one" was a self-transcending whole, Leibniz's was a whole-consuming self. But whether we have a world that has swallowed the self or a self that has swallowed the world seems almost a matter of indifference. In both cases, we are a long way from the kind of real world that the physicists supposed themselves to be investigating.

Leibniz has, in fact, turned Spinozism upside down, but a dream turned on end is still a dream. The Leibnizian real, chosen by God from among all those possible-rationals, is still a purely intelligible order—still suspended, still out of contact with the concrete facts of experience. And the failure to make contact is still justified by shrugging off those concrete facts as the products of confused thought. The Leibnizian actual is in fact a Pickwickian actual—it is actual by decree, and the test of its reality, once it has been decreed into existence, is still rationality. Leibniz wanted to argue, in opposition to Spinoza, that something more is involved in scientific knowledge than pure deduction. But in place of the empirical element that we found in Galileo, the element that ties theory down to the actual, he offered, instead, a teleological "fact." It is this "instead" that causes the trouble. We may grant that there is a teleological factor, which Galileo and Spinoza had overlooked, and that Leibniz's revival of it was an important contribution toward effecting a synthesis between the traditional view, which was teleological in character, and the new mechanical view. But even so, Leibniz's account of scientific knowledge and of the world view it implies is inadequate.

CHAPTER 8

Locke

Life and Times

John Locke (1632–1704) was educated at Oxford, where, like Hobbes before him, he was "perplexed with obscure terms and useless questions" and where he found the Scholastic type of instruction, with its emphasis on formal disputations, "invented for wrangling and ostentation rather than to discover the truth."[a] He seems to have intended for some time to take holy orders—a move that would have been natural in view of his deep religious and moral convictions. But his theological views were probably already too broad for the Church of England, and he finally decided on medicine as a career.

In 1666 Locke met Lord Ashley (later Earl of Shaftesbury) and in 1667 became his personal physician, friend, and confidant. Residence in London with Shaftesbury introduced him to "the wisest men and the greatest wits" of the age. Locke's relation to Shaftesbury was, indeed, not unlike that of Hobbes to the Cavendishes, with the difference that, since Shaftesbury was a leading politician, Locke found himself adviser to a Minister of State. It was in this capacity, for instance, that he helped to draft (in 1669) a constitution for the colony of Carolina, a document in which he embodied his ideas on toleration.

Shaftesbury, one of the earliest politicians in the modern sense, exercised his power through a party machine, rather than by reliance on the king's support. His attempt to exclude James from the succession on the grounds that this prince's avowed Catholicism was incompatible with the Restoration settlement and the Protestant basis of the kingdom, resulted in a rash of plots and counterplots. He was eventually dismissed and fled to Holland.

Though Locke cannot have had much sympathy with some of the means Shaftesbury used, he was in entire accord with his friend's effort to preserve parliamentary rights against the royal prerogative. The king was naturally suspicious of him as an intimate of Shaftesbury's, and in 1683 (the year in which Shaftesbury died) Locke too went into exile in Holland. There he made the acquaintance of Prince William and Princess Mary of Orange; when this couple was called to the British throne following the bloodless revolution in 1688 that overthrew James, Locke returned home in the entourage of the new queen. He was now favorably placed to argue in support of his favorite ideas—freedom of the press, religious toleration, improvement in the poor law, new methods of education, and new approaches to managing the economy of the kingdom.

A flood of writings, the fruit of reflection during the years of exile, now poured from his pen. The chief of these were the *Two Treatises on Government* and the *Essay Concerning Human Understanding* (both appeared in 1690), which made him famous. His views, especially in the field of theology, were bitterly attacked by the divines, and a long exchange of "replies" and "vindications" followed. But Locke's temper was too well balanced to take acrimonious criticism to heart. Indeed, as he grew older, his thoughts turned more and more to religion, and he spent his last years studying the Epistles of St. Paul. He died in 1704, surrounded by devoted friends to whom he declared that he left this world "in perfect charity with all men and in sincere communion with the whole church of Christ, by whatever names Christ's followers call themselves."[b]

Basic Assumptions

We have seen that while the new scientific method actually involved both an empirical element and a mathematical element, the inferences that philosophers drew about the nature of knowledge were seriously distorted by the fact that they all exaggerated the role of one of these two elements and minimized the role of the other. Thus Descartes, Spinoza, and Leibniz tended to emphasize the mathematical element, to take mathematical certainty as their ideal, and to formulate their criterion of truth and reality in terms of the principle of contradiction. On the other hand, Locke and his followers tended to rely on sense perception for obtaining knowledge about the world, to emphasize experimental verification, and to be sceptical about the possibility of achieving absolute certainty in most fields of human inquiry.

This empirical emphasis was partly, perhaps, an inheritance from Bacon, but it was partly a deliberate answer to the Continental Rationalists. Locke aimed at a "common sense" philosophy, in contrast to the "speculative theories" (terms of opprobrium among the Empiricists) in vogue on the Continent. Locke's theory was in fact the response of a temperament exactly the opposite of Spinoza's to the dilemmas of Cartesianism and to the problem of accommodating the new science and the traditional philosophy to each other. Whereas Spinoza preferred the indubitable and the rational and the ideal, Locke preferred the concrete and practical and was deeply suspicious of neat and tidy, but abstract, schemes.

Locke's starting point was typical of this empirical disposition: Before men begin to philosophize about ultimate realities, he said, they ought to find out what kind of instrument the human mind is and whether it is at all fitted for such metaphysical inquiries. In the winter of 1670–71, he spent some time, with five or six philosophically minded friends, in discussing the subject that most interested him—"the principles of morality and revealed religion." But he and his friends found themselves "quickly at a stand, by the difficulties that rose on every side. After we had awhile puzzled ourselves, without coming any nearer a resolution of those doubts which perplexed us, it came into my thoughts that we took a wrong course; and that before we set ourselves upon inquiries of that nature, it was necessary to examine our own abilities, and see what *objects* our understandings were, or were not, fitted to deal with."[c]

Locke was, of course, anything but unique in this emphasis on making a fresh start. The men of the seventeenth century were acutely aware that most (some said "all") of what past ages had taken for knowledge was ignorance and superstition that had to be cleared away in order to provide a firm basis for progress. "Reason" was the name they used to describe the new method that was to replace the dogmatism of the past. For the men of this age, "reason" had rich emotive-conative overtones: It stood for "cool" objectivity (as opposed to "passion"), for impartiality (as opposed to prejudice), for intellection (as opposed to revelation). They held it to be a property with which all men were endowed, and the instrument by which they were to fashion for themselves a better life. In this broad, honorific sense of the term, Locke was as much a rationalist as Descartes. They shared the Enlightenment outlook that man is competent to cure all his ills, cognitive as well as moral, by the use of his natural powers.[1]

---

1 The estimate of Locke's mind by his friend Lady Masham provides a good example of this broad, inexact use of the term "reason"—"He was always, in the greatest and in the smallest affairs of human life, as well as in speculative opinions, disposed to follow reason, whosoever it were that suggested it: he being ever a faithful servant, I had almost said, a slave to truth; never abandoning her for anything else, and following her for her own sake purely."

But whereas Descartes took as the prototype of reason that abstract *vis cognoscens* that seemed to him to be at work in mathematical reasoning, Locke took as the prototype of rational thought the kind of thinking he employed as a physician. How, for instance, was he to treat an "internal abscess" from which Shaftesbury was suffering? It is all very well to say "wait until you have achieved mathematical certainty about the correct treatment." But if you wait, the patient will die. Accordingly, you decide on surgery, even though you are not sure what you will find or what you will do when you find it. To prepare yourself, though you know that no two cases are exactly alike, you consult as many other physicians as you can. Then you operate, and finding that the abscess has been discharging internally, you insert a silver tube into the incision to draw off the discharge. The patient lives—well and good. You have kept detailed notes; these may be of use to other doctors.[2]

The real world, for Locke, was the here-and-now world of abdominal incisions, discharging abscesses, and emergency operations, not an ideal world of mathematically certain relations. Though reasoning about this world of concrete occurrences does not yield absolute certainty, we should not (Locke held) scorn it; it is the best we can expect in this life, and it is a great deal better than anything we would get by trying to apply the geometric method to concrete problems.

The latter might "amuse our understanding with fine and useless speculations," but it would only divert

> . . . our inquiries from the true and advantageous knowledge of things. . . . He that in physic shall lay down fundamental maxims, and, from thence drawing consequences and raising disputes, shall reduce it into the regular form of a science, has indeed done something to enlarge the art of talking and perhaps laid a foundation for endless disputes; but if he hopes to bring men by such a system to the knowledge of . . . the constitution, nature, signs, changes, and history of diseases . . . [he] takes much [the same] course with him that should walk up and down in a thick wood, overgrown with briars and thorns, with a design to take a view and draw a map of the country.[d]

Descartes and the Continental Rationalists had assumed that the a priori method of mathematics can be used satisfactorily in other fields, especially in that most obscure of all fields, metaphysics. The result was a series of speculative flights into the unknown.

The contradictions into which these philosophers fell are therefore not in the least grounds for "suspecting either that there is no such thing as truth at all, or that mankind hath no sufficient means to attain a certain knowledge of it." There is nothing wrong, Locke was convinced, with reason itself. Providing

---

2 Locke's notes on this case are summarized in Fox Bourne, *The Life of John Locke*, Vol. I, pp. 200–01.

we know how to employ it and do not demand too transcendent a truth from it, it is an entirely adequate instrument for ascertaining what we need to know. It is "the candle of the Lord set up by himself in men's minds," and without it we are plunged into "Egyptian darkness." Truly, therefore, it "must be our last judge and guide in everything."[e]

Locke initially believed that clearing the ground for a proper use of the understanding would be easy. To his surprise, he found the study of the powers of the understanding so complicated that it was nearly twenty years before he felt ready to publish—and even the large volume he finally issued was far from the last word on the matter. For, despite his intention to remain neutral on all metaphysical issues until he had ascertained the mind's capacity, he unconsciously assumed a metaphysical position that determined the course of his epistemological inquiry. This assumption was the familiar Cartesian belief that the world consists of two different kinds of things, minds and bodies; that minds know only their own states (which, like Descartes, Locke called "ideas"); and that ideas somehow "represent" the external world of bodies.

Now, because he assumed that what the mind knows are its ideas, his proposal to study the extent of the human understanding seemed to Locke to mean investigating the nature and origin of ideas. Suppose, for instance, that I have an idea of a centaur. Before I make any judgments employing this idea (such as "Centaurs do not take kindly to the saddle"), surely I ought to find out whether there *are* any centaurs to judge about. And how can I ascertain whether centaurs exist? Obviously, by tracing this idea back to its origin. If I find its origin in sense perception—if, for instance, I find centaurs cavorting in my garden—the idea is certified as fit to be employed in judgments. If I cannot find its origin in sense perception, it must have originated in imagination, and so it is unfit to be employed in judgments about the real world. Similarly, the fact that I have an idea of a monad does not mean that monads exist; perhaps, like centaurs, they originated in imagination, not in sense perception. Hence metaphysical speculation that employs the idea of monads is idle, and may be dangerous, until I have tracked this idea back to its source.

Attack on Innate Ideas

Everyone, Locke believed, allows that *some* ideas originate in experience—such ideas as "green," "hot," "angry." But the "received opinion" was that we start life with a certain number of "native ideas and original characters," and that these ideas, "being in our minds from their first beginnings, are antecedent to all experience and must have been implanted in them by God himself." Locke probably had in view, as the holders of the "received opinion," teachers like those he had known in his own university—"Scholastic men," whether Catholic or Protestant in their theology, who used the doctrine of innate ideas to silence criticism. They argued (1) that innate ideas, because of their allegedly divine origin, are sacrosanct and above the kind of scrutiny that Locke held to be an indispensable preliminary to philosophical speculation, and (2) that, again because of their divine origin, these ideas have a transcendent importance that makes them particularly well suited to be the axiomatic starting points for metaphysical system-building.

Against such obscurantism, Locke was very effective. No one, he said, has yet discovered a new truth or advanced the sciences a jot by starting out from "What is, is," or from "It is impossible for the same thing to be and not to be." This was not the way "Mr. Newton [proceeded] in his never enough to be admired book. [He] demonstrated several propositions, which are so many new truths, before unknown to the world, and are further advances in mathematical knowledge: but, for the discovery of these, it was not the general maxims, 'what is, is'; or 'the whole is bigger than a part,' or the like, that helped him." [f]

Further, Locke argued, most supposedly "innate" ideas are not self-evident (if sterile) maxims such as these. The dogmatists call all their pet ideas innate, hoping thereby to induce us to accept them uncritically. Though they claim that criticism of the doctrine of innateness destroys "the foundations of knowledge and certainty," it is their own dogmatism that is destructive of knowledge.

> We may as rationally hope to see with other men's eyes, as to know by other men's understandings. So much as we ourselves consider and comprehend of truth and reason, so much we possess of real and true knowledge. The floating of other men's opinions in our brains, makes us not one jot the more knowing, though they happen to be true. . . .
>
> When men have found some general propositions that could not be doubted of as soon as understood, it was, I know, a short and easy way to conclude them innate. This being once received, it eased the lazy from the pains of search, and stopped the inquiry of the doubtful concerning all that was once styled innate. And it was of no small advantage to those who affected to be masters and teachers, to make this the principle of principles,—*that principles must not be questioned.* For, having once established this tenet,— that there are innate principles, it put their followers upon a necessity of receiving *some* doctrines as such; which was to take them off from the use of their own reason and judgment, and put them on believing and taking them upon trust without further examination: in which posture of blind credulity, they might be more easily governed by, and made useful to some sort of men, who had the skill and office to principle and guide them. [g]

Unfortunately, this eminently sound criticism of dogmatism led Locke to adopt a very naïve conception of the relation of the mind to its experiences. It seems that some of the "Scholastic men" whose views he was attacking had illustrated their position by a rather crude metaphor—that of a closet well stocked with canned goods, whose superior contents were guaranteed by the trademark of the manufacturer. Instead of pointing out that the mind is not a closet and that the metaphor is misleading, Locke accepted the metaphor and argued that the closet is empty.[3] In language reminiscent of Bacon,[4] he declared that the mind at birth is a "blank tablet" on which experience subsequently writes. These metaphors were to have far-reaching consequences.

When Leibniz read Locke's attack on innate ideas, he concluded that this was directed against Descartes, and in his *New Essays* he refined the Cartesian view to escape these criticisms. As might be expected, Leibniz's reformulation reflected his doctrine of a continuum of degrees of consciousness. Whereas Locke argued that "no proposition can be said to be in the mind which it never yet knew, which it was never yet conscious of,"[5] Leibniz pointed out that one can know a proposition (say, the axiom that the whole is greater than the part) without being able to state it formally.

Thus Leibniz admitted that Descartes' own formula is ambiguous. The term "originate" can mean either (1) "is the occasion for our coming to know" or (2) "is the source of the truth of." Descartes meant the latter when he denied that certain ideas "originate in perception." Locke supposed him to mean the former and criticized him on that basis. Thus, when Descartes denied that mathematical ideas originate in perception, he meant that measuring the perceptual triangle is not a proof (or a disproof) of the theorem about interior angles equaling two right angles. But this is not to deny that the perceptual triangle *suggests* the theorem.

Again, as Leibniz pointed out, the real question is not whether everyone *recognizes* certain universal truths, but whether there *are* any universal truths. Locke did not want to deny the latter—in fact, he insisted on it;[h] no one, Leibniz thought, wanted to hold the former. There was, therefore, no real dispute. There only appeared to be one because Locke had confused a psychological question (Under what conditions does such-and-such a mind think such-and-such a thought?) with an epistemological question (What are the conditions that determine whether such-and-such a thought is true?).

Leibniz willingly acknowledged that, as Locke maintained, all our knowledge "begins in particulars and spreads itself by degrees to generals." But this is merely a statement about the psychological order of coming to know; it in no way affects the fact that "the generals" must be true in order for the particulars to be recognized. Our knowledge, Leibniz pointed out, does indeed begin in experience; and there is nothing in our minds other than their several experiences—nothing, that is, *except the mind itself*. In this way, Leibniz characteristically presented a compromise formula that, it might be thought, Locke could accept. But about the nature of this mind that knows the experiences, the two thinkers

---

3 "Methinks the understanding is not much unlike a closet wholly shut from light, with only some little openings left, to let in . . . ideas of things without"—*An Essay Concerning Human Understanding* (Fraser), II, xi, 17

4 See p. 76.

5 In this argument (*Essay*, I, i, 5), Locke was following Descartes, who also supposed that all knowledge is self-conscious awareness. In criticizing this thesis, Leibniz reached a much more mature conception of innate truths than either the Platonic doctrine of reminiscence or the Cartesian version of innate ideas.

were poles apart. For Leibniz assumed that the real is rational; hence he believed that the mind must be the kind of thing that can know this universal rational order. Locke, on the other hand, assumed that the real is actual, that the test of truth is experience, and that the mind, accordingly, is simply a surface on which experience writes.

From Leibniz's point of view, Locke arbitrarily assumed that the mind is an illuminated surface and then triumphantly discovered that the surface is unmarked prior to experience. Leibniz's position was, in effect, that the mind has depth as well as surface. Locke, for his part, held the Leibnizian assumption of unconscious depths to be but a springboard to a speculative and uncritical metaphysics. We should, he thought, make *no* assumptions about the nature of the mind, but wait to discover its nature, like the nature of everything else, in experience.

Thus the basic question was not whether there are innate truths (whether there are canned goods in the closet), but what sort of thing the mind must be to know (as everyone, including Locke, acknowledged that it *does* know) universal truths. Put in this way, it is clear that, though both Locke and Leibniz saw the mote in the other's eye, neither was aware of the beam in his own.

The "Historical Plain Method": All Ideas Derive from Experience

For his part, Locke concluded that his "historical plain method," as he called it, had been established. That is, he believed he had proved that there are no innate ideas, that "at its beginning" the mind is an empty surface, and hence that all its ideas come from experience, there being no other source from which they *could* come. But Locke did not clearly distinguish between this psychological doctrine and the epistemological thesis that experience is the test of truth. Hence the historical plain method was not only the procedure of tracing ideas to their origins in experience; it was also the fundamental thesis of empirical epistemology: Only experience can confirm or disconfirm our beliefs.

NATURE OF EXPERIENCE

Experience, Locke thought, is either inner or outer, either the data of external sense—colors, sounds, smells, and so forth; or the data of introspection—our awareness of the operations of our mind as it organizes these sensations.

> *All ideas come from sensation or reflection*—Let us then suppose the mind to be, as we say, white paper, void of all characters, without any ideas:—How comes it to be furnished? . . . Whence has it all the *materials* of reason and knowledge? To this I answer, in one word, from EXPERIENCE. In that all our knowledge is founded; and from that it ultimately derives itself. Our observa-

tion employed either about external sensible objects, or about the internal operations of our minds perceived and reflected on by ourselves, is that which supplies our understandings with all the *materials* of thinking. These two are the fountains of knowledge, from whence all the ideas we have, or can naturally have, do spring.

The objects of sensation one source of ideas.—First, our Senses, conversant about particular sensible objects, do convey into the mind several distinct perceptions of things, according to those various ways wherein those objects do affect them. And thus we come by those *ideas* we have of *yellow, white, heat, cold, soft, hard, bitter, sweet,* and all those which we call sensible qualities; which when I say the senses convey into the mind, I mean, they from external objects convey into the mind what produces there those perceptions. This great source of most of the ideas we have, depending wholly upon our senses, and derived by them to the understanding, I call SENSATION.

The operations of our minds, the other source of them.—Secondly, the other fountain from which experience furnisheth the understanding with ideas is,—the perception of the operations of our own mind within us, as it is employed about the ideas it has got;—which operations, when the soul comes to reflect on and consider, do furnish the understanding with another set of ideas, which could not be had from things without. And such are *perception, thinking, doubting, believing, reasoning, knowing, willing,* and all the different actings of our own minds;—which we being conscious of, and observing in ourselves, do from these receive into our understandings as distinct ideas as we do from bodies affecting our senses. . . . I call this REFLECTION, the ideas it affords being such only as the mind gets by reflecting on its own operations within itself. . . .

All our ideas are of the one or the other of these.—The understanding seems to me not to have the least glimmering of any ideas which it doth not receive from one of these two. . . .

Let any one examine his own thoughts, and thoroughly search into his understanding; and then let him tell me, whether all the original ideas he has there, are any other than of the objects of his senses, or of the operations of his mind, considered as objects of his reflection. And how great a mass of knowledge soever he imagines to be lodged there, he will, upon taking a strict view, see that he has not any idea in his mind but what one of these two have imprinted;—though perhaps, with infinite variety compounded and enlarged by the understanding, as we shall see hereafter.[i]

THE DISTINCTION BETWEEN SIMPLE AND COMPLEX IDEAS

Locke next drew a distinction, which looks innocent and straightforward but which proved to be very tricky, between simple and complex ideas:

> The better to understand the nature, manner, and extent of our knowledge, one thing is carefully to be observed concerning the ideas we have; and that is, that some of them are *simple* and some *complex*.

Though the qualities that affect our senses are, in the things themselves, so united and blended, that there is no separation, no distance between them; yet it is plain, the ideas they produce in the mind enter by the senses simple and unmixed. For, though the sight and touch often take in from the same object, at the same time, different ideas,—as a man sees at once motion and colour; the hand feels softness and warmth in the same piece of wax: yet the simple ideas thus united in the same subject, are as perfectly distinct as those that come in by different senses. The coldness and hardness which a man feels in a piece of ice being as distinct ideas in the mind as the smell and whiteness of a lily; or as the taste of sugar, and smell of a rose. And there is nothing can be plainer to a man than the clear and distinct perception he has of those simple ideas; which, being each in itself uncompounded, contains in it nothing but *one uniform appearance, or conception in the mind*. . . .

When the understanding is once stored with these simple ideas, it has the power to repeat, compare, and unite them, even to an almost infinite variety, and so can make at pleasure new complex ideas. But it is not in the power of the most exalted wit, or enlarged understanding, by any quickness or variety of thought, to *invent* or *frame* one new simple idea . . . : nor can any force of the understanding *destroy* those that are there. . . . I would have any one try to fancy any taste which had never affected his palate; or frame the idea of a scent he had never smelt: and when he can do this, I will also conclude that a blind man hath ideas of colours, and a deaf man true distinct notions of sounds.[j]

Simple ideas may originate either in sensation or in reflection. Simple ideas of sensation may enter the mind either through a single sense or through several. "Solidity" is an example of a simple idea that originates in a single sense organ. This idea "arises from the resistance which we find in body to the entrance of any other body into the place it possesses, till it has left it." "Solidity" is an ultimate datum, incapable of analysis. "If any one asks me, *What this solidity is*, I send him to his senses to inform him. Let him put a flint or a football between his hands, and then endeavour to join them, and he will know."[k]

On the other hand, our ideas of space, figure, rest, and motion are simple ideas that originate in more than one sense, "for these make perceivable impressions, both on the eyes and touch; and we can receive and convey into our minds the ideas of [them] both by seeing and feeling." Examples of simple ideas of reflection are discerning, reasoning, judging, willing.[l]

Complex ideas originate in three different ways. (1) The mind can unite several simple ideas. Examples of ideas derived in this way are "beauty, gratitude, a man, an army, the universe."[m] (2) The mind can take two ideas (whether simple or complex) and "set them by one another, so as to take a view of them at once, without uniting them into one." This operation is the source of our ideas of relation. (3) The mind can separate one idea from all those that accompany it in its real existence. This operation is called "abstraction: and thus all its *general ideas* are made."[6]

Complex ideas of the first type are formed either by joining together two or more identical simple ideas or by joining together two or more different simple ideas. An example of the former is the idea of immensity. Here we start with the simple idea of a distance (perceived through sight or through touch) between two bodies, or between two parts of the same body. We can then repeat this idea to ourselves as often as we like, and so "enlarge [our] idea of space as much as [we] please. The power of repeating or doubling any idea we have of any distance, and adding it to the former as often as we will, without being ever able to come to any stop or stint, let us enlarge it as much as we will, is that which gives us the idea of *immensity*."[n]

Now, from reflecting on this "power we observe in ourselves of repeating without end our own ideas," we obtain the idea of *infinity*.

> Whatsoever *positive* ideas we have in our minds of any space, duration, or number, let them be ever so great, they are still finite; but when we suppose an inexhaustible remainder, from which we remove all bounds, and wherein we allow the mind an endless progression of thought, without ever completing the idea, there we have our idea of infinity: which . . . seems to be pretty clear when we consider nothing else in it but the negation of an end.[o]

It follows that *infinity of space* is to be distinguished from *space infinite*.

> For, as our idea of infinity being, as I think, *an endless growing idea*, but the idea of any quantity the mind has, being at that time *terminated* in that idea, (for be it as great as it will, it can be no greater than it is,)—to join infinity to it, is to adjust a standing measure to a growing bulk. . . . The idea of the infinity of space . . . is nothing but a supposed endless progression of the mind, over what repeated ideas of space it pleases; but to have actually in the mind the idea of a space infinite, is to suppose the mind already passed over, and actually to have a view of *all* those repeated ideas of space which an *endless* repetition can never totally represent to it.[p]

This analysis is a good example of how the historical plain method helps clarify men's ideas. It shows that "infinite space" is only a name, not an idea. It is no wonder, therefore, that we are "so easily confounded when we come to argue and reason about infinite space or duration."

6 Obviously, the only compound ideas, strictly speaking, are those produced by the first type of operation; for ideas of relation ("sensation A sweeter than sensation B") are not compounded of the sweetness of A plus the sweetness of B, and abstraction is a process of decompounding rather than of compounding.

THE IDEA OF SUBSTANCE

Before we turn to comment on Locke's account of the origin of ideas, it will be useful to examine his analysis of another idea that has long perplexed metaphysicians—the complex idea of substance.

Ideas of particular substances, how made.—The mind being, as I have declared, furnished with a great number of the simple ideas, conveyed in by the senses as they are found in exterior things, or by reflection on its own operations, takes notice also that a certain number of these simple ideas go constantly together; which being presumed to belong to one thing, and words being suited to common apprehensions, and made use of for quick dispatch, are called, so united in one subject, by one name; which, by inadvertency, we are apt afterward to talk of and consider as one simple idea, which indeed is a complication of many ideas together: because, as I have said, not imagining how these simple ideas *can* subsist by themselves, we accustom ourselves to suppose some *substratum* wherein they do subsist, and from which they do result, which therefore we call *substance.*

Our obscure idea of substance in general.—So that if any one will examine himself concerning his notion of pure substance in general, he will find he has no other idea of it at all, but only a supposition of he knows not what *support* of such qualities which are capable of producing simple ideas in us; which qualities are commonly called accidents. If any one should be asked, what is the subject wherein colour or weight inheres, he would have nothing to say, but the solid extended parts; and if he were demanded, what is it that solidity and extension adhere in, he would not be in a much better case than the Indian . . . who, saying that the world was supported by a great elephant, was asked what the elephant rested on; to which his answer was—a great tortoise: but being again pressed to know what gave support to the broad-backed tortoise, replied—*something, he knew not what.* . . . The idea . . . to which we give the *general* name substance [is] nothing but the supposed, but unknown, support of those qualities we find existing, which we imagine cannot subsist *sine re substante,* without something to support them. . . .

Of the sorts of substances.—An obscure and relative idea of *substance in general* being thus made we come to have the ideas of *particular sorts of substances,* by collecting *such* combinations of simple ideas as are, by experience and observation of men's senses, taken notice of to exist together; and are therefore supposed to flow from the particular internal constitution, or unknown essence of that substance. Thus we come to have the ideas of a man, horse, gold, water, &c.; of which substances, whether any one has any other *clear* idea, further than of certain simple ideas co-existent together, I appeal to every one's own experience. It is the ordinary qualities observable in iron, or a diamond, put together, that make the true complex idea of those substances, which a smith or a jeweler commonly knows better than a philosopher; who, whatever *substantial forms* he may talk of, has no other idea of those substances, than what is framed by a collection of those simple ideas which are to be found in them. . . .

As clear an idea of spiritual substance as of corporeal substance.—The same thing happens concerning the operations of the mind, viz. thinking, reasoning, fearing, &c., which we concluding not to subsist of themselves, nor apprehending how they can belong to body, or be produced by it, we are apt to think these the actions of some other *substance*, which we call *spirit*; whereby . . . supposing a substance wherein thinking, knowing, doubting, and a power of moving, &c., do subsist, we have as clear a notion of the substance of spirit, as we have of body; the one being supposed to be (without knowing what it is) the *substratum* to those simple ideas we have from without; and the other supposed (with a like ignorance of what it is) to be the *substratum* to those operations we experiment in ourselves within.[q]

Further, according to Locke, the complex idea of substance contains the idea of power. "He that will examine his complex idea of gold will find several of the ideas that make it up to be only powers: as the power of being melted, but not of spending itself in the fire, of being dissolved in *aqua regia*, are ideas as necessary to make up our complex idea of gold as its colour and weight." In other words, besides thinking of substance as a substratum that "holds up" a number of qualities, men think of it as a causal agent that produces changes in other things. Since this analysis of the idea of substance has led us to the idea of cause, we must investigate the source of this idea.

Locke saw that men do not get the idea of "cause," but only the idea of "alteration," from what they experience in sensation. For instance, when we see one billiard ball strike another, we experience only the transfer, not the *production*, of motion. Where, then, do we get the idea of agency, or active power? From introspection, Locke believed. "The idea of the *beginning* of motion we have only from reflection on what passes in ourselves; where we find by experience, that, barely by willing it, barely by a thought of the mind, we can move the parts of our bodies, which were before at rest."[r]

But even this does not exhaust the idea of cause. For to say that x causes y is not only to say that x has an active power (like the power we experience when we will) that produces y; it is also to say that x *always* produces y.

> The mind [takes] notice how one [thing] comes to an end, and ceases to be, and another begins to exist which was not before; . . . and [concludes] from what it has so constantly observed to have been, that the like changes will for the future be made in the same things, by like agents, and by the like ways, . . . and so comes by that idea which we call *power*.[s]

The idea of substance finally stands revealed in all its complexity. The idea of any particular substance (for example, gold) contains (1) simple ideas of certain properties, or accidents ("yellow," "hard," and so forth); (2) the "confused" idea of a "somewhat" that supports these properties; and (3) the idea of cause—which is itself analyzable into (a) the idea of succession, or "alteration," derived from sensation, (b) the idea of agency, derived from reflection, and (c) the idea of necessity, which is not given in experience but "concluded" from it.

COMMENT ON ACCOUNT OF ORIGIN OF IDEAS

Here, then, is an example of the historical plain method at work. What is wrong with it? The basic trouble is Locke's assumption that the originals of all our ideas are simple elements. Because of this assumption, Locke's method became a search for simple units of sensation (or reflection). But do we start with the ideas "red," "sweet," "spherical," and compound them to get the idea "apple"? Or do we see an apple and then, by a process of selective attention, note that it is red, spherical, and so on? Surely, the latter. The world of ordinary experience is a world of objects, and Locke's simple ideas, far from being starting points of experience, are terminals.

As William James said,

> No one ever had a simple sensation by itself. Consciousness, from our natal day, is of a teeming multiplicity of objects and relations, and what we call simple sensations are results of discriminative attention, pushed often to a very high degree. It is astonishing what havoc is wrought in psychology by admitting at the outset apparently innocent suppositions, that nevertheless contain a flaw. The bad consequences develop themselves later on, and are irremediable, being woven through the whole texture of the work. The notion that sensations, being the simplest things, are the first things to take up in psychology is one of these suppositions.[t]

Locke's critique of innate ideas confused a psychological question with an epistemological question, asking "What are the causes of our ideas?" instead of "What is the test of their truth?" Here, Locke made the opposite error. Instead of the historical order (from complex to simple), he gave the logical order (from simple to complex). But since he supposed himself to be giving the historical order, he had to invent various complicated mental processes to reconstruct the world of experience.

It seems likely that in this instance Locke was influenced by a physical parallel. Psychology, he thought, must correspond to physics. If the latter accounts for the behavior of gross bodies by showing that they are "composed" of particles in local motion, the former must deal with atomic sensations and account for psychic behavior in terms of various mechanical combinings and separatings of thought-elements.

Though such compoundings might conceivably account for such complex ideas as "centaur," "gold mountain," or "glass slipper," they obviously cannot account for ideas like "substance," which, as Locke's own analysis made clear, are not aggregates of elementary sensations. Thus, if the idea of necessity is, as Locke said, a "conclusion," it is manifestly not an original element. It would seem that in using such vague terms as "collect," "suggest," "infer," and "conclude," Locke covertly introduced elements found neither in sensation nor in reflection.[7] This does not mean that "necessity" and "cause," for instance, are innate ideas, in either the Cartesian or the Leibnizian sense. On the contrary, it suggests (as has already been pointed out) that the dispute over how ideas get "into" the mind was a red herring, and that the relation between the mind and its ideas must be conceived of in an altogether different way.

Theory of Knowledge

What sort of world, Locke next asked himself, is this about which we have ideas? The "Scholastic men" who still taught at Oxford and Cambridge supposed it to consist of various substances, each of which owns certain attributes; the new physicists supposed it to consist of bodies in motion; Leibniz held it to consist of "monads." Who was right? The historical plain method was supposed to inform us. After all, Locke undertook his study of our ideas' originals only in order to ascertain whether, and to what extent, they are cognitively adequate.

DEGREES OF COGNITIVE ADEQUACY

There are, according to Locke, three degrees of cognitive adequacy. First, there is *intuitive* knowledge, which is immediately certain and cannot be doubted. Here the mind simply "sees" a necessary connection. Second, there is *demonstrative* knowledge, which is "less easy" and "less clear." It is the kind of knowledge we have of a connection that we do not immediately "see" but that we can come to see by finding a series of subconnections each of which *is* immediately seen. The only difference between intuitive knowledge and demonstrative knowledge is that the former consists in a single intuition, the latter in a chain of intuitions. The latter is "less easy" because we require "sagacity" to discover the intermediate linkages; it is "less clear" because in a long series of intuitions, though each is certain in itself, error may somewhere creep in.

Third, there are many ideas between which there are no necessary relations to be seen. Here we are limited to *sensitive* knowledge. In fact, since Locke (following Descartes' usage) held that knowledge is the clear and distinct apprehension of a necessary relation, he maintained that this state of mind ought to be called "faith or opinion" rather than knowledge.

---

7 Compare, for instance, "Whatever change is observed, the mind must collect a power somewhere able to make that change"—*Essay,* II, xxi, 4.

THE OBJECTS OF KNOWLEDGE

Turning now from the question of degrees of knowledge to the question of the objects of knowledge, let us recall that Locke's official position was that the mind knows nothing but its own states.

> Since the mind, in all its thoughts and reasonings, hath no other immediate object but its own ideas, which it alone does or can contemplate, it is evident that our knowledge is only conversant about them. *Knowledge* then seems to me to be nothing but *the perception of the connexion of and agreement, or disagreement and repugnancy of any of our ideas.*[u]

But the qualification in the phrase "no immediate object" suggested to Locke the possibility of our somehow getting outside the circle of our ideas. Accordingly, he listed "real existence" as one of the "four sorts" of agreement and disagreement that occur between ideas. But, of course, a relation between an idea and a "real existent" is clearly not a relation between ideas. Locke thus innocently by-passed a major problem: If the mind knows only its own states, how can it know to what real existents, if any, its ideas are related? This is, of course, the problem Descartes had sought to solve by appealing to God's goodness, which he supposed to guarantee the existence of a real world corresponding to our innate ideas. Since Locke had rejected the doctrine of innateness, he could not adopt this solution, and it must be confessed that, instead of trying to find a better one, he usually ignored the whole difficulty and assumed that our ideas do, as a matter of fact, give us information about real existents. Let us therefore pass over this formidable dilemma and ask, "What sorts of real existents did he believe to exist and what degrees of knowledge did he hold it possible for men to have of them?" We will return later to Locke's account of knowledge and of the relations of ideas.[8]

KNOWLEDGE OF REAL EXISTENCE

There are, in Locke's view, three types of real existents: selves, God, and bodies—in other words, the three sorts of substances of Cartesianism. Of our own existence, Locke believed, each of us has an intuitive knowledge; of God's, a demonstrative knowledge; of other selves and physical things, only a sensitive knowledge.

> Nothing can be more evident to us than our own existence. I think, I reason, I feel pleasure and pain: can any of these be more evident to me than my own existence? If I doubt of all other things, that very doubt makes me perceive my own existence, and will not suffer me to doubt of that. For if

8 See pp. 257–58.

I know I feel pain, it is evident I have as certain perception of my own existence, as of the existence of the pain I feel: or if I know I doubt, I have as certain perception of the existence of the thing doubting, as of that thought which I *call doubt*. Experience then convinces us, that we have an *intuitive knowledge* of our own existence, and an internal infallible perception that we are. In every act of sensation, reasoning, or thinking, we are conscious to ourselves of our own being; and, in this matter, come not short of the highest degree of certainty.[v]

In the next place, man knows, by an intuitive certainty, that bare *nothing can no more produce any real being, than it can be equal to two right angles*. . . . If, therefore, we know there is some real being, and that nonentity cannot produce any real being, it is an evident demonstration, that *from eternity there has been something;* since what was not from eternity had a beginning; and what had a beginning must be produced by something else.

And that eternal Being must be most powerful.—Next, it is evident, that what had its being and beginning from another, must also have all that which is in and belongs to its being from another too. All the powers it has must be owing to and received from the same source. This eternal source, then, of all being must also be the source and original of all power; and *so this eternal Being must be also the most powerful.*

. . . .

And therefore God.—Thus, from the consideration of ourselves, and what we infallibly find in our own constitutions, our reason leads us to the knowledge of this certain and evident truth,—*That there is an eternal, most powerful, and most knowing Being;* which whether any one will please to call God, it matters not. The thing is evident; and from this idea duly considered, will easily be deduced all those other attributes, which we ought to ascribe to this eternal Being. . . .

From what has been said, it is plain to me we have a more certain knowledge of the existence of a God, than of anything our senses have not immediately discovered to us. Nay, I presume I may say, that we more certainly know that there is a God, than that there is anything else without us.[w]

As regards other selves and physical things, Locke posed two questions: (1) Do other things and selves exist while we are experiencing them? (2) Do they exist when we are not experiencing them? These questions will seem absurd unless we recall that what we experience (in Locke's view) are not the things themselves, but our ideas of them. Suppose you are now having an experience of a piece of paper with printing on it. This is your experience, a state of your mind. Locke's first question was whether, while you are having this experience, you can know that something exists outside you that is the cause of your having it. Supposing this question to be answered affirmatively, Locke's second question was whether you can know that this thing exists even when it is not causing you to have an experience.

Locke's answer to the first question was that, though the existence of things while we see and feel them cannot be *demonstrated,* "nobody can in earnest be so sceptical as to be uncertain" of their existence. His answer to the second was that their continued existence is "highly probable."

> The having the idea of anything in our mind, no more proves the existence of that thing, than the picture of a man evidences his being in the world, or the visions of a dream make thereby a true history.
>
> *Instance: whiteness of this paper.*—It is therefore the *actual receiving* of ideas from without that gives us notice of the existence of other things, and makes us know, that something doth exist at that time without us, which causes that idea in us . . . v.g., whilst I write this, I have, by the paper affecting my eyes, that idea produced in my mind, which, whatever object causes, I call *white*; by which I know that that quality or accident (i.e. whose appearance before my eyes always causes that idea) doth really exist, and hath a being without me. And of this, the greatest assurance I can possibly have, and to which my faculties can attain, is the testimony of my eyes, which are the proper and sole judges of this thing . . . which is a certainty as great as human nature is capable of, concerning the existence of anything, but a man's self alone, and of God. . . .
>
> *This certainty is as great as our condition needs.* . . . The certainty of things existing in *rerum natura* when we have the testimony of our senses for it is not only as great as our frame can attain to, but as our condition needs. For, our faculties being suited not to the full extent of being, nor to a perfect, clear, comprehensive knowledge of things free from all doubt and scruple; but to the preservation of us, in whom they are; and accommodated to the use of life: they serve to our purpose well enough, if they will but give us certain notice of those things, which are convenient or inconvenient to us. . . . So that this evidence is as great as we can desire, being as certain to us as our pleasure or pain, i.e. happiness or misery; beyond which we have no concernment, either of knowing or being. Such an assurance of the existence of things without us is sufficient to direct us in the attaining the good and avoiding the evil which is caused by them, which is the important concernment we have of being made acquainted with them.
>
> *But reaches no further than actual sensation.*—In fine, then, when our senses do actually convey into our understandings any idea, we cannot but be satisfied that there doth something *at that time* really exist without us, which doth affect our senses, and by them give notice of itself to our apprehensive faculties, and actually produce that idea which we then perceive: and we cannot so far distrust their testimony, as to doubt that such *collections* of simple ideas as we have observed by our senses to be united together, do really exist together. But this knowledge extends as far as the present testimony of our senses, employed about particular objects that do then affect them, and no further. For if I saw such a collection of simple ideas as is wont to be called *man*, existing together one minute since, and am now alone, I cannot be certain that the same man exists now, since there is no *necessary connexion* of his existence a minute since with his existence now: by a thousand ways he may cease to be, since I had the testimony of my senses for his existence. And if I cannot be certain that the man I saw last to-day is now in being, I can less be certain that he is so who hath been longer

removed from my senses, and I have not seen since yesterday, or since the last year: and much less can I be certain of the existence of men that I never saw. And, therefore, though it be highly probable that millions of men do now exist, yet, whilst I am alone, writing this, I have not that certainty of it which we strictly call knowledge; though the great likelihood of it puts me past doubt, and it be reasonable for me to do several things upon the confidence that there are men (and men also of my acquaintance, with whom I have to do) now in the world: but this is but probability, not knowledge.[x]

Some of the time, Locke assumed that *all* our simple ideas are caused by existents that they resemble. Thus, when I sense red, the red-in-here is caused by a red-out-there. But since, like everyone else, he took Galilean mechanics seriously, his considered view had to be more complex: The continuing existent out there that causes red-in-here is not red-out-there, but body-in-motion-out-there. Bodies out there thus cause two kinds of ideas in us: (1) ideas that truly resemble them—for instance, "ideas of solidity, extension, figure, and mobility," for the Galilean bodies out there are "truly possessed" of these qualities; and (2) ideas that do not in the least resemble them—for instance, ideas of "sweet" and "red," for the bodies out there are not sweet and red. This distinction corresponds roughly to the Cartesian distinction between innate and adventitious ideas, but according to Locke *both* kinds of ideas are adventitious; the distinction is between adventitious ideas that do resemble, and adventitious ideas that do not resemble, their causes.

Now, consider solidity, figure, motion, and the other characteristics (or, as Locke called them, "primary qualities") of bodies. Is there more to body than these qualities? Descartes had held that these qualities inhere in an "extended substance." In view of Locke's ironic references to the "poor Indian philosopher" and his scorn for the Scholastic men "who suppose that real essences exist,"[9] it might be expected that he would deny this. But instead, he maintained in a Cartesian fashion that every object "has a real internal but unknown constitution whereon its discernable qualities depend." What is more, "all the properties flow" from this essence, so that, if only we could discover it, we could deduce these properties, just as we can deduce the properties of a triangle from *its* essence (which happens, of course, to be knowable).[y]

No wonder Locke's critics inquired whether his concept of substance was "grounded upon true reason or not." Locke simply refused to face up to the alternatives these critics were trying to force on him. There was little point in holding onto essences while denying that they can ever be known; indeed, if they are unknowable, how could Locke claim to know that they exist? Nonetheless, Locke wanted to retain the concept of substance. Most of the things that both he and his critics conceived to be important—God, self, values, for instance—had been interpreted for centuries in terms of substantival modes of

9 See pp. 242–43 and 249–50.

thought; to throw out substance seemed equivalent to rejecting them all. More-over, Locke wanted a basically rational real. Even though the historical plain method, which was supposed to be the test of truth and reality, revealed only sequences and groupings of simple sense experiences, Locke wanted to hold onto the view of his critics that this empirical order is somehow or other "grounded upon true reason."

KNOWLEDGE OF RELATIONS

So far we have been considering Locke's account of knowledge of real existence. It will be recalled that, besides this alleged knowledge of an external world, men are capable, according to Locke, only of a knowledge of the agree-ment and disagreement of their ideas.[10] Let us now examine his analysis of this kind of knowledge. Here, instead of compounding two or more ideas, men merely bring them together "so as to take a view of them at once, without uniting them into one." Of the types of agreement and disagreement detected when ideas are thus brought together, the most important are (1) identity and diversity and (2) coexistence.

(1) An example of "knowledge of identity and diversity" is the knowledge that "blue is not yellow." This kind of knowledge, Locke believed, is basic. Insofar as the mind knows anything at all about "blue" and "yellow," it knows that "blue is not yellow." For knowing that "blue is blue" involves knowing that "blue is not-yellow."

> It is the first act of the mind, when it has any sentiments or ideas at all, to perceive its ideas; and so far as it perceives them, to know each what it is, and thereby also to perceive their difference, and that one is not another. This is so absolutely necessary, that without it there could be no knowl-edge . . . at all. By this the mind clearly and infallibly perceives each idea to agree with itself, and to be what it is; and all distinct ideas to disagree.[z]

"Men of art" (the Scholastic men of Book I of Locke's *Essay*) have generalized this kind of knowledge into rules—"What is, is"; "It is impossible for the same thing to be and not to be." But these general rules, properly understood, are only shorthand ways of stating that "blue is not yellow," that "red is not green," that "square is not circle," that "sweet is not sour," and so on. Since the rules *mean* only particular identities and diversities, and since all the particular identities and diversities are agreements and disagreements of ideas, it seemed obvious to Locke that such maxims could never be the basis for a metaphysical knowledge of reality.[11]

(2) An example of "knowledge of coexistence" is the knowledge that "iron is susceptible of magnetic attraction." What we know of "iron," that is to say,

10 See p. 253.
11 See p. 243.

is not its alleged real essence, but only a collection of coexisting simple ideas of vision, touch, and so forth. Among these is the perception of movement toward a magnet. Hence "Iron is susceptible of magnetic attraction" means "In our experience the idea 'moving-toward-magnet' accompanies (belongs to the same set as) the idea 'turns-brown-in-presence-of-oxygen,' the idea 'does-not-melt-in-ordinary-flame,' and so on." Experience also shows that this set of secondary qualities (or qualitative ideas) is related to (belongs to the same set as) certain primary qualities—for example, that the idea "turns-brown-in-presence-of-oxygen" accompanies the ideas (which might be experienced under experimental conditions) of the movement of "certain minute and visible parts" of the iron and the oxygen. But this is still merely to report the coexistence in experience of such-and-such ideas.

Hence, in Locke's view, a "science of bodies" in the sense in which the Continental Rationalists understood science (as a body of demonstratively certain propositions) is impossible. They supposed a demonstrative science to be possible because they mistakenly held that we know the real essences of things. And they supposed themselves to know the real essences of things because they were confused about the status of names.

NAMES

Locke regarded the confusions arising from the misuse of names to be so serious that he devoted the whole of Book III of the *Essay* to this subject. A name, he maintained, is simply a device to "abridge discourse." It always stands for either (1) a group of coexisting ideas or (2) one of such a coexisting group. When a group of coexisting ideas recurs frequently, we give it a name to avoid the inconvenience of enumerating all the coexisting ideas each time we want to talk about it. Thus we learn to say "apple" instead of "red-spherical-sweet." The name is merely an indication, or sign, of the fact that these ideas happen to coexist frequently in our experience. There is nothing else in our experience— that is, there is no essence or substantial form—of which "apple" is the name.

We give names not only to groups of coexisting ideas but also to the single ideas that can be isolated from such groups. For instance, the collections of coexisting ideas that we call, respectively, "cherry," "orange," "apple," all contain the idea "edible-pulpy-matter-surrounding-seeds." To this idea we give the name "fruit." A name like "apple" differs from a name like "fruit" merely in that the former is the name of a group of ideas that actually coexist in experience, whereas the latter is the name of an idea that is isolated from the others with which it coexists. Ideas of the latter type are called "abstract ideas"— not because the idea in question is any less a particular, concrete datum of experience, but because it is abstracted, or isolated, from its context.[12]

12 The power by which Locke supposed the mind to isolate an idea from its context is, of course, the third basic mental operation—"abstraction"—which has already been enumerated but has not yet been described (see pp. 247–48).

A general name, then, is merely the name for some specific experience that occurs repeatedly in combination with other specific experiences. The name "man," for instance, is merely the name of what is common to Peter, James, Mary, and Jane, with what is particular to each of them left out. The name "animal" is not the name of some new experience; it is merely the name of what is common to Peter, James, Mary, and Jane after further exclusions have been made. Here, in fact, we leave out "the shape, and some other properties signified by the name man, and retain only a body, with life, sense, and spontaneous motion."[a]

Locke's historical plain method is at its best in such attacks on empty verbalism. Pressed to its logical conclusion, it might lead further than Locke himself would have liked, but it was an immensely powerful weapon against the obscurantism and dogmatism—what Bacon had called the "frivolous distinctions"—that for centuries had passed as learning and science.

Ethical Theory

Locke's theory of knowledge, it will be recalled, was in his own view a purely preliminary undertaking, designed to "see what objects our understandings were or were not fitted to deal with." The net result of this inquiry was to show that our understandings were not fitted to deal with the metaphysical inquiries that had consumed so much of the energy of earlier philosophers. This limitation did not in the least distress Locke, for he thought that the traditional metaphysics was not only useless but positively harmful, both because it distracted men from more important matters and because, more often than not, it resulted in scepticism. But ethics and politics were fields of inquiry in which Locke *was* deeply interested. Let us see how the historical plain method equipped him to deal with them.

THE GOOD

Medieval philosophers like St. Thomas had held the good to be a knowledge of God. According to Locke, it is pleasure.

> Things are good or evil only in reference to pleasure or pain. That we call *good*, which is apt to cause or increase pleasure, or diminish pain in us; or else to procure or preserve us the possession of any other good or absence of any evil. And, on the contrary, we name that *evil* which is apt to produce or increase any pain, or diminish any pleasure in us.[b]

Everyone, Locke believed, knows what pleasure and pain are. For, though they are simple ideas (like "blue"), and so unanalyzable and undefinable, they constantly occur in all men's experience. No idea of sensation or of reflection is ever experienced "barely in itself"; every such idea is "accompanied with pain or pleasure."

The ethical problem is thus simply the problem of ascertaining which, of all the acts open to us in any given situation, will be productive of the "greatest positive good." Locke realized, of course, that this is not always easy to ascertain, and that even when we have ascertained it, we do not always act on our information. "Let a drunkard see that his health decays, his estate wastes; discredit and diseases, and the want of all things, even of his beloved drink, attends him in the course he follows: yet the . . . habitual thirst after his cups . . . drives him to the tavern. . . . It is not want of viewing the greater good: for he sees and acknowledges it."[c]

THE BAD WILL

Here is the problem that so taxed Paul and Augustine and the other early Christians—the problem of the bad will. Characteristically, Locke's treatment of it was psychological rather than theological.

> Though . . . all good be the proper object of desire in general; yet all good, even seen and confessed to be so, does not necessarily move every particular man's desire; but only that part, or so much of it as is considered and taken to make a necessary part of *his* happiness. . . .
>
> The reason whereof is evident from the nature of our happiness and misery itself. All present pain, whatever it be, makes a part of our present misery: but all absent good does not at any time make a necessary part of our present happiness, nor the absence of it make a part of our misery. . . . All uneasiness therefore being removed, a moderate portion of good serves at present to content men; and a few degrees of pleasure, in a succession of ordinary enjoyments, make up a happiness wherein they can be satisfied. If this were not so, there could be no room for those indifferent and visibly trifling actions, to which our wills are so often determined, and wherein we voluntarily waste so much of our lives. . . .
>
> As to *present* happiness and misery, when that alone comes into consideration, and the consequences are quite removed, a man never chooses amiss: he knows what best pleases him, and that he actually prefers. Things in their present enjoyment are what they seem: the apparent and real good are, in this case, always the same. For, the pain or pleasure being just so great and no greater than it is felt, the present good or evil is really so much as it appears. And therefore were every action of ours concluded within itself, and drew no consequences after it, we should undoubtedly never err in our choice of good: we should always infallibly prefer the best. Were the pains of honest industry, and of starving with hunger and cold set together before us, nobody would be in doubt which to choose: were the satisfaction of a lust and the joys of heaven offered at once to anyone's present possession, he would not balance, or err in the determination of his choice.

But since our voluntary actions carry not all the happiness and misery that depend on them along with them in their present performance, but are the precedent causes of good and evil, which they draw after them, and bring upon us, when they themselves are past and cease to be; our desires look beyond our present enjoyments, and carry the mind out to *absent good*, according to the necessity which we think there is of it, to the making or increase of our [present] happiness. It is our opinion of such a necessity that gives it its attraction: without that, we are not moved by absent good. For, in this narrow scantling of capacity which we are accustomed to and sensible of here, wherein we enjoy but one pleasure at once, which, when all uneasiness is away, is, whilst it lasts, sufficient to make us think ourselves happy, it is not all remote and even apparent good that affects us.[d]

The question of why men choose a lesser good in preference to a greater is thus, from Locke's point of view, a purely psychological one. His answer was that a kind of foreshortening causes the lesser, present good to *seem* greater than the more remote good, in the way that a child standing near us seems larger than a man a long distance away. If I put off going to the dentist, it is because the present pleasure of avoiding the drill is greater than the present pain of the future toothache. My mistake is not about present pleasures and pains, but about future ones. The pain of the toothache, when I experience it six months from now, will be greater than the pain of the drill would have been today.

LAW

Of course, to some extent our own past experience helps us counteract this foreshortening. But we also need the assistance of other men. Some of this help takes the form of private advice from friends and family; some of it has been condensed into maxims, or laws, that provide more formal guidance concerning the things that really produce the "greatest positive good." The main difference between advice and law lies in the fact that a penalty is attached to the violation of the latter.

> Good and evil, as hath been shown, are nothing but pleasure or pain, or that which occasions or procures pleasure or pain to us. *Moral good and evil,* then, is only *the conformity or disagreement of our voluntary actions to some law, whereby good or evil is drawn on us, from the will and power of the law-maker;* which good and evil, pleasure or pain, attending our observance or breach of the law by the decree of the law-maker, is what we call *reward* and *punishment.*
>
> Of these moral rules or laws . . . there seem to me to be *three sorts,* with their three different enforcements, or rewards and punishments. For, since it would be utterly in vain to suppose a rule set to the free actions of men, without annexing to it some enforcement of good and evil to determine his will, we must, wherever we suppose a law, suppose also some reward or punishment. . . .

The laws [are] these three: 1. The *divine* law. 2. The *civil* law. 3. The law of *opinion* or *reputation*, if I may so call it. By the relation they bear to the first of these, men judge whether their actions are sins or duties; by the second, whether they be criminal or innocent; and by the third, whether they be virtues or vices.[e]

Let us take the third type first.

Men everywhere . . . give the name of virtue to those actions, which amongst them are judged praiseworthy; and call that vice, which they account blameable. . . . Thus the measure of what is everywhere called and esteemed virtue and vice is this approbation or dislike, praise or blame, which, by a secret and tacit consent, establishes itself in the several societies, tribes, and clubs of men in the world: whereby several actions come to find credit or disgrace amongst them, according to the judgment, maxims, or fashion of that place. . . .

And though perhaps, by the different temper, education, fashion, maxims, or interest of different sorts of men, it fell out, that what was thought praiseworthy in one place, escaped not censure in another; and so in different societies, virtues and vices were changed: yet, as to the main, they for the most part kept the same everywhere.[f]

A "law of *opinion* or *reputation*" is, in a word, an empirical generalization summarizing the experience of some particular society concerning the best means to happiness—for example, "Honesty is the best policy." The only sanction of such a law is, of course, the pressure of public opinion, but "he who imagines commendation and disgrace not to be strong motives to men to accommodate themselves to the opinions and rules of those with whom they converse, seems little skilled in the nature or history of mankind: the greatest part whereof we shall find to govern themselves chiefly, if not solely, by this *law of fashion*."[g]

The distinction between the law of opinion and the civil law is that, whereas the former is enforced only by public opinion, the latter, being "set by the commonwealth," is enforced by the courts and the police. The law of opinion and the civil law naturally tend to coincide, for any action that is strongly disapproved by public opinion is likely sooner or later to get written into the statutes as a criminal offense.

Divine law, in contrast, is

. . . that law which God has set to the actions of men,—whether promulgated to them by the light of nature, or the voice of revelation. That God has given a rule whereby men should govern themselves, I think there is nobody so brutish as to deny. He has a right to do it; we are his creatures: he has goodness and wisdom to direct our actions to that which is best: and he has power to enforce it by rewards and punishments of infinite weight and duration in another life; for nobody can take us out of his hands. This is the only true touchstone of moral rectitude; and, by comparing them to this law, it is that men judge of the most considerable moral good or evil of their actions; that is, whether, as duties or sins, they are like to procure them happiness or misery from the hands of the ALMIGHTY.[h]

There are thus two quite distinct criteria for evaluating conduct. One is the test of pleasure: Of the various acts open to us, we ought to do the one that maximizes pleasure. The other is the test of conformity to divine law: Of the various acts open to us, we ought to do the one that most closely corresponds with "the unchangeable rule of right and wrong which the law of God hath established."

Locke, of course, would have maintained that these two tests yield the same result, for he held that God established the divine law with men's best interests (their long-range "greatest positive good") in mind. Ideally, then, both the law of opinion and the civil law should be brought into correspondence with divine law. If this correspondence were effected, the chances for men's happiness would be greatly enhanced, since all three types of sanctions would exert pressures in a single direction. Therefore, for Locke, the function of political theory was to discover what kind of state organization is most likely to bring civil law into conformity with divine law.[13]

ETHICS A DEMONSTRABLE SCIENCE

But how do we discover what the commands of divine law are? A Luther might have answered, "Read the Bible; it is the revealed word of God"; a medieval Scholastic might have answered, "Follow the traditions of the Church." But Locke wanted to put morality on a rational basis. Hence he maintained that the great principles of morality—those enunciated in divine law—are capable of demonstration.

> I am bold to think that morality is capable of demonstration, as well as mathematics: since the precise real essence of the things moral words stand for may be perfectly known, and so the congruity and incongruity of the things themselves be certainly discovered; in which consists perfect knowledge. Nor let any one object, that the names of substances are often to be made use of in morality, as well as those of modes, from which will arise obscurity. For, . . . when we say that man is subject to law, we mean nothing by man but a corporeal rational creature: what the real essence or other qualities of that creature are in this case is no way considered. And, therefore, whether a child or changeling be a man, in a physical sense, may amongst the naturalists be as disputable as it will, it concerns not at all the moral man, as I may call him, which is this immovable, unchangeable idea, a corporeal rational being. . . .

13 See pp. 266–74.

> The ideas that ethics are conversant about, being all real essences, and such as I imagine have a discoverable connexion and agreement one with another; so far as we can find their habitudes and relations, so far we shall be possessed of certain, real, and general truths.[i]

Examples of such "certain, real, and general truths," according to Locke, are "Where there is no property there is no injustice" and "No government allows absolute liberty." Unfortunately, these propositions, far from being rational truths, are only tautologies. Consider, for instance, what Locke himself said about his first proposition:

> "Where there is no property there is no injustice," is a proposition as certain as any demonstration in Euclid: for the idea of property being a right to anything, and the idea to which the name "injustice" is given being the invasion or violation of that right, it is evident that . . . I can as certainly know this proposition to be true, as that a triangle has three angles equal to two right ones.[j]

Obviously, if "property" is defined as "right" and "injustice" as "violation of right," "property" and "injustice" are mutually dependent: Where there is no property there can be no injustice. But such a truth throws no light on the problems, for instance, of public versus private ownership. Defining property as a right does not determine whether the owners of a public utility ought to be allowed to make as large a profit as they can. What it is important to know is what sorts of property are morally justified, and defining property as what is morally justified does not help at all.

The same is true with regard to the moral theorem "No government allows absolute liberty." Since "government" implies "law" and "law" implies "restriction on liberty," the theorem is necessarily true, because it is analytic. But this does not help to determine the restrictions on liberty that ought to be allowed. The fact is that according to Locke's own view his "eternal verities" are eternally true just because they are tautologies.

This is the old problem of universals. Locke ruled out a demonstrable science of physics because he believed that physics is concerned with the relations of coexistence and succession among ideas. Identical considerations apply in ethics. How can there be universal and necessary ethical truths unless there are real universals? If men know only particulars, what the Rationalists call a universal is merely the name of some "isolated" particular, it being quite immaterial whether the particular so isolated and so named is "fruit" or "iron" or "justice." It would seem, then, that all Locke's maxims are either tautologies (like those just discussed) or generalizations and summaries of past experience. The latter, of course, are identical with the law of opinion and correspond roughly to the empirical generalizations to which Locke believed the physical sciences to be limited.

AMBIGUITIES IN SOURCE OF MORAL LAW

This difficulty is a repetition, in the field of ethics, of the difficulty already noted in connection with Locke's account of substance.[14] Despite his empiricism, Locke was enough of a rationalist to believe in the essential rationality of the universe. It was therefore natural for him to hold that this rationality expresses itself (among other ways) in "eternal ethical verities," and to believe that man, as a part of this rational cosmos, is capable of understanding these principles and of acting on them. But in the world of fact with which the historical plain method was equipped to deal, there are no universal or necessary connections. The only way to get universality in such a world is by means of the decree of an omnipotent will. Hobbes recognized this; it was precisely for this reason that he introduced his absolute secular sovereign. Though it cannot be said that Locke was fully aware of the problem, it is suggestive that, side by side with passages in which he asserted the rationality of the moral law, there are passages in which he emphasized its dependence on a supreme will:

> He . . . that hath the idea of an intelligent, but frail and weak being, made by and depending on another, who is eternal, omnipotent, perfectly wise and good, will as certainly know that man is to honour, fear, and obey God, as that the sun shines when he sees it. . . . He will as certainly find that the inferior, finite, and dependent, is under no obligation to obey the supreme and infinite, as he is certain to find that three, four, and seven are less than fifteen.[k]

Another problem growing out of these ambiguities in Locke's account of the source of moral law is the question of the nature of a morally good motive. From what sort of motive ought men to obey the moral law? Locke's writings contain different answers, depending on which notion of moral law was uppermost in his mind as he wrote. When he was thinking of the moral law as an expression of divine will, he explained duty in terms of our status as the children of an omnipotent father and commander. When he was thinking of the moral law as a rational order in the universe, he explained duty in terms of our status as rational creatures. In both these cases, however much they otherwise differ, an intrinsic rightness attaches to the performance of acts commanded by the moral law, and it is significant that Locke often wrote as if doing one's duty (acting in conformity with the moral law) were good in itself. But, insofar as pleasure is the sole good, the motive for obeying the moral law is not a sense of duty, and obedience has no intrinsic worth. The motive is simply a calculation of long-range advantage.

In his conception of an eternal and unalterable moral law, Locke was looking back to the medieval tradition; in his conception of pleasure as the sole good, he was looking ahead to a secular and utilitarian ethics. The point at which these

14 See pp. 256–57.

two views came together in Locke's theory was his contention that divine law decrees what is actually productive of maximum pleasure. If all men were perfectly enlightened egoists, they would follow divine law simply because it contains better advice about how to maximize pleasure than is contained in the crude generalizations of the law of opinion. But alas, because of the "narrow scantling" of our human capacity, most of us choose an immediate, lesser good when it is in competition with the greater but more distant pleasure recommended by divine law. For this reason, God in His goodness has decreed *extra* sanctions (rewards and punishments in the afterlife), consideration of which may induce even the most shortsighted of us to follow God's law. Thus, whereas a really enlightened utilitarian would obey the moral law because of the long-range earthly pleasure of which it is known to be productive, less enlightened men obey it (and so get the same results) because of fear of hellfire and hope of heavenly bliss. Though this argument is not very edifying morally, it is logically satisfactory, providing (1) that one is a utilitarian and (2) that one accepts, as Locke did, the "evidences" of Christianity.

Political Theory

THE STATE OF NATURE

Although, as we have seen, Locke's ethical theory actually left the status of moral law in considerable doubt, his political theory rests on the assumption that the moral law is an "eternal verity" that guarantees to every man certain inalienable rights and imposes on every man certain duties. Because these rights and duties are imposed on us as men (that is, as creatures rational enough to recognize the eternal validity of the moral law), and not as citizens, Locke called the condition in which individuals are related by moral rather than political ties the "state of nature." Individuals in a state of nature may, if they choose to do so, agree to form themselves into a political state. If they do so, it is because they believe that advantages will accrue to them from taking this step.

This way of describing the origins of political societies suggests that there was a time when men actually lived in the condition Locke described, that is, with no political organization of any kind. Locke has consequently been criticized on the grounds that this is completely unhistorical: No such state of nature has ever existed. But, as a matter of fact, whether there ever was a time when men lived without political organization is irrelevant to Locke's main argument. His point was simply that the laws of nature are absolutely binding because of men's nature as men, and hence that they are without regard to temporal, or any other, conditions.

When Locke said that "in a state of nature men have such-and-such rights," he was not making a factual, historical statement that such-and-such liberties were actually appropriated by men at such-and-such times in the remote past. He was making a moral statement about what rights *ought* to be recognized at all times. "State of nature" is not antecedent to the political state; it is an ideal in terms of which all the various actual political states are to be evaluated. "State of nature" is what ought to be the case in all communities; "political state" is what actually is the case in some particular community at some particular time. Actual codes of legislation are to be evaluated by ascertaining the degree to which they implement men's natural (that is, moral) rights.

> To understand political power aright, and derive it from its original, we must consider what estate all men are naturally in, and that is, a state of perfect freedom to order their actions, and dispose of their possessions and persons as they think fit, within the bounds of the law of Nature, without asking leave or depending upon the will of any other man.
>
> . . . .
>
> But though this be a state of liberty, yet it is not a state of license; though man in that state have an uncontrollable liberty to dispose of his person or possessions, yet he has not liberty to destroy himself, or so much as any creature in his possession, but where some nobler use than its bare preservation calls for it. The state of Nature has a law of Nature to govern it, which obliges every one, and reason, which is that law, teaches all mankind who will but consult it, that being all equal and independent, no one ought to harm another in his life, health, liberty, or possessions; for men being all the workmanship of one omnipotent and infinitely wise Maker; all the servants of one sovereign Master, sent into the world by His order and about His business; they are His property, whose workmanship they are made to last during His, not one another's pleasure. And, being furnished with like faculties, sharing all in one community of Nature, there cannot be supposed any such subordination among us that may authorize us to destroy one another, as if we were made for one another's uses, as the inferior ranks of creatures are for ours. Every one as he is bound to preserve himself, and not to quit his station willfully, so by the like reason, when his own preservation comes not in competition, ought he as much as he can to preserve the rest of mankind, and not unless it be to do justice on an offender, take away or impair the life, or what tends to the preservation of the life, the liberty, health, limb, or goods of another.
>
> And that all men may be restrained from invading others' rights, and from doing hurt to one another, and the law of Nature be observed, which willeth the peace and preservation of all mankind, the execution of the law of Nature is in that state put into every man's hands, whereby every one has a right to punish the transgressors of that law to such a degree as may hinder its violation. . . .
>
> And thus, in the state of Nature, one man comes by a power over another, but yet no absolute or arbitrary power to use a criminal, when he has got him in his hands, according to the passionate heats or boundless extravagancy of his own will, but only to retribute to him so far as calm reason and conscience dictate, what is proportionate to his transgression, which is so

much as may serve for reparation and restraint. For these two are the only reasons why one man may lawfully do harm to another, which is that we call punishment. In transgressing the law of Nature, the offender declares himself to live by another rule than that of reason and common equity, which is that measure God has set to the actions of men for their mutual security, and so he becomes dangerous to mankind; the tie which is to secure them from injury and violence being slighted and broken by him, which being a trespass against the whole species, and the peace and safety of it, provided for by the law of Nature, every man . . . hath a right to punish the offender, and be executioner of the law of Nature.

. . . .

By the same reason may a man in the state of Nature punish the lesser breaches of that law, it will, perhaps, be demanded, with death? I answer: Each transgression may be punished to that degree, and with so much severity, as will suffice to make it an ill bargain to the offender, give him cause to repent, and terrify others from doing the like. Every offense that can be committed in the state of Nature, may, in the state of Nature, be also punished equally, and as far forth, as it may, in a commonwealth. For though it would be beside my present purpose to enter here into the particulars of the law of Nature, or its measures of punishment, yet it is certain there is such a law, and that too as intelligible and plain to a rational creature and a studier of that law as the positive laws of commonwealths, nay, possibly plainer; as much as reason is easier to be understood than the fancies and intricate contrivances of men, following contrary and hidden interests put into words; for truly so are a great part of the municipal laws of countries, which are only so far right as they are founded on the law of Nature, by which they are to be regulated and interpreted. . . .

'Tis often asked as a mighty objection, where are, or ever were, there any men in such a state of Nature? To which it may suffice as an answer at present, that since all princes and rulers of "independent" governments all through the world are in a state of Nature, 'tis plain the world never was, nor never will be, without numbers of men in that state. I have named all governors of "independent" communities, whether they are, or are not, in league with others; for 'tis not every compact that puts an end to the state of Nature between men, but only this one of agreeing together mutually to enter into one community, and make one body politic. . . .

To those that say there were never any men in the state of Nature, I . . . affirm that all men are naturally in that state, and remain so till, by their own consents, they make themselves members of some politic society . . . .[1]

In a word, the state of nature is not a condition in which some men actually find themselves; it is simply the inalienable rights and duties that belong to men as men. Our chief duty is easily stated: We must not interfere with other men's rights. Our rights Locke variously defined as "life, health, liberty, and possession," or, more simply, "life, liberty, and property." The underlying idea is that of equality. It is because all men are born equal[15] that it is wrong for one man to subjugate another, to destroy another (except as a just punishment), or to use another as an instrument.

This fundamental moral equality is quite compatible, Locke maintained, with social inequality (his was not an equalitarian state), with the obvious facts of physical and mental inequality, and (as we shall see) with economic inequality.

> Though I have said . . . "That all men by nature are equal," I cannot be supposed to understand all sorts of "equality." Age or virtue may give men a just precedency. Excellency of parts and merit may place others above the common level. Birth may subject some, and alliance or benefits others, to pay an observance to those to whom Nature, gratitude, or other respects, may have made it due; and yet all this consists with the equality which all men are in in respect of jurisdiction or dominion one over another, which was the equality I there spoke of as proper to the business in hand, being that equal right that every man hath to his natural freedom, without being subjected to the will or authority of any other man.[m]

POLITICAL EQUALITY

Thus, by liberty Locke meant *political* equality. And political equality does not mean that there ought to be no political subordination, no use of force at all. That would be equivalent to anarchy, the denial of political order. Rather, it means that the moral use of force depends on consent. In the *basic* decisions about the structure and organization of a society, every individual ought to count as one, that is, as the equal of every other man, regardless of how unequal men may be in other respects.

Perhaps the shortest way to state Locke's position is to say (1) that the people are, and remain, sovereign, and (2) that "the people" are a collection of autonomous and independent individuals. This formula, however, requires two modifications. In the first place, since (according to Locke) political power is limited by the laws of nature, the people are not sovereign in the full Hobbesian sense. In the second place, strictly speaking, it is not the whole people who are effectively sovereign, but a simple majority. Locke's position here is that, though no one can be compelled to join a community, citizens can be compelled *after* they join it. For when a man consents to join a community, he agrees to accept the decisions of the majority. Under these circumstances, Locke maintained, the use of force against "recalcitrant minorities" is morally justified, providing, of course, that no fundamental rights are violated.

> Men being, as has been said, by nature all free, equal, and independent, no one can be put out of this estate and subjected to the political power

15 Men are born equal, Locke held, in the sense that they are born *to* this full state of equality, not *in* it.

of another without his own consent, which is done by agreeing with other men, to join and unite into a community for their comfortable, safe, and peaceable living, one amongst another, in a secure enjoyment of their properties, and a greater security against any that are not of it. . . . When any number of men have so consented to make one community or government, they are thereby presently incorporated, and make one body politic, wherein the majority have a right to act and conclude the rest.

For, . . . it being one body, [it] must move one way . . . whither the greater force carries it, which is the consent of the majority; or else it is impossible it should act or continue one body, one community, which the consent of every individual that united into it agreed that it should. . . .

And thus every man, by consenting with others to make one body politic under one government, puts himself under an obligation to every one of that society to submit to the determination of the majority, and to be concluded by it; or else this original compact, whereby he with others incorporates into one society, would signify nothing, and be no compact if he be left free and under no other ties than he was in before in the state of Nature. . . .

For if the consent of the majority shall not in reason be received as the act of the whole, and conclude every individual, nothing but the consent of every individual can make anything to be the act of the whole, which, considering the infirmities of health and avocations of business, which . . . will necessarily keep many away from the public assembly; and the variety of opinions and contrariety of interests which unavoidably happen in all collections of men, 'tis next impossible ever to be had. . . .

Whosoever, therefore, out of a state of Nature unite into a community, must be understood to give up all the power necessary to the ends for which they unite into society to the majority of the community, unless they expressly agreed in any number greater than the majority.[n]

CONSENT

Though it cannot be said that Locke dealt adequately with the problems involved, he was one of the first political thinkers to emphasize the importance of consent. In his insistence on this fundamental right, he at once reflected the growing sense of individuality that was one of the marks of the new age and laid the basis for democratic theory and practice. Locke intended his doctrine of consent to provide a moral basis for the use of force; but there is no reason to suppose that a majority will be more wise, prudent, and restrained in using force than a single individual. If (as Locke rightly pointed out) it is reasonable to refuse to surrender oneself to the tender mercies of an absolute monarch, it is equally reasonable to be loath to surrender oneself to the tender mercies of an absolute majority. It is clear that Locke did not automatically secure a moral basis for the state by putting sovereignty into the hands of the majority of citizens. Later generations of democratic theorists have wrestled with this problem without complete success: Men are still faced with the paradox that they must sometimes be forced to be free.

PROPERTY

So far the rights to life and liberty, and what these rights entail, have been discussed. An account of the third basic right, property, remains to be given. Since God created the earth and endowed it with natural resources of all kinds for the benefit of man, "the earth and all that is therein . . . belong to mankind in common . . . and . . . nobody has originally a private domain, exclusive of the rest of mankind."

This doctrine was designed to counter royal claims to ownership, based on a theory of divine right. But it had the disadvantage of plunging Locke into state socialism. He extricated himself from this position by an ingenious argument derived from every man's right to his own body. If a man has a right to his body, he has a right, by extension, to his body's labor, and so to whatever natural objects he has "mixed his labour with."

> Though the earth and all inferior creatures be common to all men, yet every man has a "property" in his own "person." This nobody has any right to but himself. The "labour" of his body and the "work" of his hands, we may say, are properly his. Whatsoever, then, he removes out of the state that Nature hath provided and left it in, he hath mixed his labour with it, and joined to it something that is his own, and thereby makes it his property. It being by him removed from the common state Nature placed it in, it hath by this labour something annexed to it that excludes the common right of other men. For this "labour" being the unquestionable property of the labourer, no man but he can have a right to what that is once joined to, at least where there is enough, and as good left in common for others.
>
> He that is nourished by the acorns he picked up under an oak, or the apples he gathered from the trees in the wood, has certainly appropriated them to himself. Nobody can deny but the nourishment is his. I ask, then, when did they begin to be his? when he digested? or when he ate? or when he boiled? or when he brought them home? or when he picked them up? And 'tis plain, if the first gathering made them not his, nothing else could. That labour put a distinction between them and common. That added something to them more than Nature, the common mother of all, had done, and so they became his private right. . . .
>
> It will, perhaps, be objected to this, that if gathering the acorns or other fruits of the earth, etc., makes a right to them, then any one may engross as much as he will. To which I answer, Not so. The same law of Nature that does by this means give us property, does also bound that property too. "God has given us all things richly" is the voice of reason confirmed by inspiration. But how far has He given it us? To enjoy. As much as any one can make use of to any advantage of life before it spoils, so much he may by his labour fix a property in. Whatever is beyond this, is more than his share, and belongs to others. . . .
>
> I think it is plain that property in [the land] too is acquired as the former. As much land as a man tills, plants, improves, cultivates, and can use the product of, so much is his property. . . .

Nor was this appropriation of any parcel of land, by improving it, any prejudice to any other man, since there was still enough and as good left, and more than the yet unprovided could use. So that, in effect, there was never the less left for others because of his enclosure for himself. For he that leaves as much as another can make use of does as good as take nothing at all. Nobody could think himself injured by the drinking of another man, though he took a good draught, who had a whole river of the same water left him to quench his thirst. And the case of land and water, where there is enough of both, is perfectly the same.[o]

Locke gave an analogous account of the origin of the use of money. But since money does not "spoil," it is not immoral for men to accumulate more than they can use.

The greatest part of things really useful to the life of man . . . are generally things of short duration, such as—if they are not consumed by use—will decay and perish of themselves. Gold, silver, and diamonds are things that fancy or agreement have put the value on, more than real use and the necessary support of life. . . . He that gathered a hundred bushels of acorns or apples had thereby a property in them; they were his goods as soon as gathered. He was only to look that he used them before they spoiled, else he took more than his share, and robbed others. . . . If he gave away a part to anybody else, so that it perished not uselessly in his possession, these he also made use of. And if he also bartered away plums that would have rotted in a week, for nuts that would last good for his eating a whole year, he did no injury; he wasted not the common stock . . . . Again, if he would give his nuts for a piece of metal, pleased with its colour, or exchange his sheep for shells, or wool for a sparkling pebble or a diamond, and keep those by him all his life, he invaded not the right of others; he might heap up as much of these durable things as he pleased, the exceeding of the bounds of his just property not lying in the largeness of his possessions, but the perishing of anything uselessly in it.

And thus came in the use of money; some lasting thing that men might keep without spoiling, and that, by mutual consent, men would take in exchange for the truly useful but perishable supports of life.[p]

Although all this seemed to Locke an evident "law of reason," there are serious omissions in his defense of property. Though it may be allowed that every man has a right to the fruits of his own toil, Locke overlooked an important difference between money and the "acorns, apples, and plums" that money represents. Locke reasoned that since these fruits may be accumulated without prejudice to the rights of others (there being more than enough fruits to go around), there is no reason why gold and silver, which are merely valueless symbols, may not also be accumulated without prejudice to others, and indeed to the advantage of all. But is it true that "gold and silver may be hoarded up without injury to any one"? That depends on what is done with the accumulation.

Locke's rule was that "appropriation" must not "invade the rights of others." It is not self-evident that massive accumulation of capital in a few hands is harmless. Indeed, there may well be a contradiction between the political equality on which Locke insisted so eloquently and the economic inequality that his doctrine of property approves.

Locke's case rests on an alleged parallelism between agrarian and capitalistic societies—a parallelism that is plausible only so long as the power of capital is minimized. Though it is admittedly easier today to detect this weakness in Locke's argument than it would have been in Locke's own day, the Britain of 1688 was a long way from being a simple agrarian community, and the great Whig magnates, who were Locke's friends, were not in the least like the peasants whose simple transactions Locke described in these pages. One gets the impression, indeed, that Locke was more interested in finding a plausible defense of the status quo than in getting to the root of the matter.

UTILITY OF POLITICAL SOCIETIES

So much, then, for men's basic rights as Locke conceived of them—life, liberty, and property. The function of the state, as has been said, is to implement them—to insure that men actually have the rights that they ought to have. Men would not enter a political society unless they thought it would protect their lives, liberties, and properties. To justify its existence, and the various inconveniences it imposes on men (for example, taxes), the state must do a better job of preserving their rights than they could do for themselves.

> If man in the state of Nature be so free as has been said, if he be absolute lord of his own person and possessions, equal to the greatest and subject to nobody, why will he part with his freedom, this empire, and subject himself to the dominion and control of any other power? To which it is obvious to answer, that though in the state of Nature he hath such a right, yet the enjoyment of it is very uncertain and constantly exposed to the invasions of others. . . . This makes him willing to quit this condition which, however free, is full of fears and continual dangers; and it is not without reason that he seeks out and is willing to join in society with others who are already united, or have a mind to unite for the mutual preservation of their lives, liberties and estates, which I call by the general name—property.
>
> The great and chief end, therefore, of men uniting into commonwealths, and putting themselves under government, is the preservation of their property; to which in the state of Nature there are many things wanting.
>
> Firstly, there wants an established, settled, known law, received and allowed by common consent to be the standard of right and wrong, and the common measure to decide all controversies between them. For though the law of Nature be plain and intelligible to all rational creatures, yet men, being biased by their interest, as well as ignorant for want of study of it, are not apt to allow of it as a law binding to them in the application of it to their particular cases.

Secondly, in the state of Nature there wants a known and indifferent judge, with authority to determine all differences according to the established law. For every one in that state being both judge and executioner of the law of Nature, men being partial to themselves, passion and revenge is very apt to carry them too far, and with too much heat in their own cases, as well as negligence and unconcernedness, make them too remiss in other men's.

Thirdly, in the state of Nature there often wants power to back and support the sentence when right, and to give it due execution. They who by any injustice offended will seldom fail where they are able by force to make good their injustice. Such resistance many times makes the punishment dangerous, and frequently destructive to those who attempt it.

Thus mankind, notwithstanding all the privileges of the state of Nature, being but in an ill condition while they remain in it are quickly driven into society. . . .

But though men when they enter into society give up the equality, liberty, and executive power they had in the state of Nature into the hands of the society, to be so far disposed of by the legislative as the good of the society shall require, yet it being only with an intention in every one the better to preserve himself, his liberty and property (for no rational creature can be supposed to change his condition with an intention to be worse), the power of the society or legislative constituted by them can never be supposed to extend farther than the common good, but is obliged to secure every one's property by providing against those three defects above mentioned that made the state of Nature so unsafe and uneasy. And so, whoever has the legislative or supreme power of any commonwealth, is bound to govern by established standing laws, promulgated and known to the people, and not by extemporary decrees, by indifferent and upright judges, who are to decide controversies by those laws, and to employ the force of the community at home only in the execution of such laws, or abroad to prevent or redress foreign injuries and secure the community from inroads and invasion. And all this to be directed to no other end but the peace, safety, and public good of the people.[q]

THE POLITICS OF LOCKE AND HOBBES CONTRASTED

Locke's argument, like Hobbes's, has a utilitarian form: The justification for the inconveniences that the state entails lies in the fact that the state enables men to escape still greater inconveniences. But because Locke and Hobbes started from very different conceptions of human nature, this argument led them to very different conclusions. In Hobbes's view, man is so utterly the slave of passion and momentary self-interest that *anything* is better than life in a state of nature. In Locke's view, however, man is on the whole decent and reasonable; he is able to make a calm, long-range assessment of his interests and capable of acting in the light of this assessment. Since the Lockian man can get on better without the state than can the Hobbesian man, he is able to demand more of it before he consents to it. Because he does not have to make a forced sale, he can hold out for better terms.

This difference between the two thinkers' evaluations of human capacities reflects in part the difference between the courses of the two great revolutions that England experienced in the seventeenth century. Hobbes's opinions were formed in the years that led up to a bitter civil war. Locke, on the other hand, was only a child when Charles I was beheaded; but he was an active participant in the organization of the Whig Party and an interested onlooker at its parliamentary triumph. Granted, Hobbes would probably not have been convinced by the "Glorious Revolution"; he would doubtless have said that its glory lay in the fact that, whereas only a part of the nation had hated the Church of England in 1642, the whole nation feared the Church of Rome in 1688. The difference, he would have said, was not that men were more reasonable in 1688, but that they were more united in the object of their passion.

But for Locke the events of 1688 confirmed the more optimistic view of human nature and justified the theory of consent. Only a few years earlier, the English people had consented to James's rule because they believed that he would abide by his coronation oath to respect their age-old rights. Instead, he had tried to alter the form of government and had ruled by "arbitrary personal power." Accordingly, the contract lapsed; the people withdrew their consent and chose as king a man who acknowledged their inalienable rights. From Locke's point of view, the Glorious Revolution was no more a revolution than is the decision of the shareholders of a corporation to replace the management.

The Lockian state is, in fact, a joint-stock company whose members have entered into partnership for profit and have retained ultimate control of the enterprise. The management is but the agent of the owners; both its form and the conditions of its tenure are determined by them. If the owners choose to keep management in their own hands, the government is democratic; if they "put the power of making laws into the hands of a few select men, . . . then it is an oligarchy; if into the hands of one man, . . . then it is a monarchy." The owners have the further option to compound and mix these forms as they see fit.[r]

Locke himself preferred a mixed form, consisting of three distinct elements: (1) "a single hereditary person having the constant, supreme, executive power," (2) "an assembly of hereditary nobility," and (3) "an assembly of representatives chosen *pro tempore* by the people."[s] But he did not insist on this form. The main point, he believed, was that in all "well-framed governments" there should be a distribution of powers, with the legislative and the executive "in distinct hands."

The Lockian state, with its emphasis on the fundamental autonomy, independence, and equality of all citizens, is not very fashionable today. Many people, even those who sympathize with Locke's aim, would say that his concern for liberty led him to sacrifice the power that Bodin, Hobbes, and Machiavelli knew to be essential for efficient administration. Locke's reply to this criticism would of course be that these theorists overestimated the need for a supreme power because they underestimated man's abilities to govern and discipline himself.

RELIGION AND THE STATE

Locke's view of the way the state ought to handle the "religious problem" reflects this conviction. According to Bodin and Hobbes, religion is a dangerous passion, requiring strict control and constant vigilance on the part of the sovereign. According to Locke, these thinkers mistook an effect for a cause. A diversity of religious opinions endangers the public peace only if an attempt is made to suppress them. The cure for religious troubles is therefore not less, but more, toleration.

> You'll say, that assemblies and meetings endanger the public peace, and threaten the Commonwealth. . . . But if this be so, why is not the magistrate afraid of his own Church; and why does he not forbid their assemblies, as things dangerous to his government? . . .
>
> Let us therefore deal plainly. The magistrate is afraid of other Churches, but not of his own; because he is kind and favourable to the one, but severe and cruel to the other. . . . Let him turn the tables: or let those dissenters enjoy but the same privileges in civils as his other subjects, and he will quickly find that these religious meetings will be no longer dangerous. For if men enter into seditious conspiracies, 'tis not religion inspires them to it in their meetings, but their sufferings and oppressions that make them willing to ease themselves. Just and moderate governments are everywhere quiet, everywhere safe. But oppression raises ferments and makes men struggle to cast off an uneasy and tyrannical yoke. . . . Suppose this business of religion were let alone, and that there were some other distinction made between men and men, upon account of their different complexions, shapes, and features, so that those who have black hair (for example) or grey eyes, should not enjoy the same privileges as other citizens. . . . Can it be doubted but these persons, thus distinguished from others by the colour of their hair and eyes, and united together by one common persecution, would be as dangerous to the magistrate, as any others that had associated themselves merely upon the account of religion?[t]

Though Locke held that religion ought not to be oppressed, he did not maintain that every sort of regulation of religion is wrong. He distinguished, indeed, between (1) articles of faith and (2) practices and ceremonials. As regards the former, he held that

> . . . it is absurd that things should be enjoined by laws, which are not in men's power to perform. And to believe this or that to be true, does not depend on our will. . . . The business of laws is not to provide for the truth of opinions, but for the safety and security of the Commonwealth, and of every particular man's goods and person. And so it ought to be. For the truth certainly would do well enough, if she were once left to shift for herself. . . . The case of each man's salvation belongs only to himself. . . . Anyone may employ as many exhortations and arguments as he pleases, towards the

promotion of another man's salvation. But all force and compulsion are to be forbidden. . . . Every man, in that, has the supreme and absolute authority of judging for himself. And the reason is, because nobody else is concerned in it, nor can receive any prejudice from his conduct therein. . . . Men cannot be forced to be saved whether they will or no. And therefore, when all is done, they must be left to their own consciences.[u]

On the other hand, most sects enjoin, or at least encourage, certain overt practices and ceremonies. Here regulation is permissible, but only if the acts in question injure other men in their life or property. They are to be forbidden, in other words, not as religious rites, but as acts of such-and-such a kind. Thus

> . . . if any people congregated upon account of religion, should be desirous to sacrifice a calf, I deny that that ought to be prohibited by a law. *Meliboeus,* whose calf it is, may lawfully kill his calf at home, and burn any part of it that he thinks fit. For no injury is thereby done to anyone, no prejudice to another man's goods. And for the same reason he may kill his calf also in a religious meeting. Whether the doing so be well-pleasing to God or no, it is their part to consider that do it. The part of the magistrate is only to take care that the Commonwealth receive no prejudice, and that there be no injury done to any man, either in life or estate. . . . But if peradventure, such were the state of things, that the interest of the Commonwealth required all slaughter of beasts should be forborn for some while, in order to the increasing of the stock of cattle, that had been destroyed by some extraordinary murrain; who sees not that the magistrate, in such a case, may forbid all his subjects to kill any calves for any use whatsoever? Only 'tis to be observed that, in this case, the law is not made about a religious, but a political matter: nor is the sacrifice, but the slaughter of calves thereby prohibited. . . .
>
> Whatsoever is lawful in the Commonwealth cannot be prohibited by the magistrate in the Church. Whatsoever is permitted unto any of his subjects for their ordinary use, neither can nor ought to be forbidden by him to any sect of people for their religious uses. . . . But those things that are prejudicial to the commonweal of a people in their ordinary use, and are therefore forbidden by laws, those things ought not to be permitted to Churches in their sacred rites. . . .
>
> If each of them [state and Church] would contain itself within its own bounds, the one attending to the worldly welfare of the Commonwealth, the other to the salvation of souls, 'tis impossible any discord should ever have happened between them.

Locke's hands-off policy differs almost as much from the Thomistic position as it does from the Hobbesian position. Whereas Hobbes held that the state should be supreme over the Church, Thomas held that the Church should be supreme over the state. Locke agreed with Thomas that "there is nothing in this world that is of any consideration in comparison with eternity." But, because he adopted the characteristic Protestant position that salvation is a matter of each soul's direct and private relation with the Deity, he denied that the civil magistrate should be subordinate to any ecclesiastical authority whatever.

THE LAISSEZ-FAIRE STATE

What is true of religion is equally true, Locke believed, of the other departments of life. Although the government must have enough power to regulate abuses and to prohibit acts that conflict with the common good, government does not need great power, much less unlimited power. Men are essentially decent and self-respecting. Given the necessary opportunity, which a good education will provide, they will develop into mature and reasonable creatures, capable of assuming the responsibilities of citizenship.

Locke was thus aware of the important role of education in the democratic, laissez-faire state, and he was full of sound and interesting suggestions about educational reform to achieve this end. But the education of mature and responsible citizens is not as simple as Locke supposed. Locke was thinking primarily of formal education, but it is now believed that the whole social and physical environment is a part of the educational process—that proper diet, for example, is more important to overall development than proper training in "Scholastic" logic. This conception has led to a radical reassessment of Locke's idea of laissez faire, with a much greater emphasis on the need for positive action to help produce the kind of citizen that political democracy requires and moral decency demands.

Because the base of the electorate expanded far more rapidly in the nineteenth century than did the standard of living, the need for state assistance in the production of "maturity" became greater than ever before; and this occurred at precisely the time that the industrial revolution was changing the structure of society from rural to urban and introducing all sorts of additional complications, of which the problem of dietary deficiency is but one small example. Schooling, housing, sanitation, medical and old-age care, employment conditions, all were gradually brought into the sphere of political duties, and "the welfare state" was on its way, long before it appeared in headlines, brought on by the logic of Locke's own laissez-faire position.

Given the conditions of modern society (of which Locke did not dream), and in order to preserve the very rights he affirmed, citizens now authorize the state to perform activities that Locke thought could safely be left to individual initiative. These changes in emphasis have not occurred without subjecting the Lockian ideal to great strain. There would doubtless always be a certain tension in the Lockian state between the ideal of freedom and even the minimal requirements of organization, but this tension has been vastly increased in the last century. Indeed, the elaborate organization that now seems necessary to implement the Lockian system of rights may end by overwhelming the very rights it is designed to implement. Conflict over the antithetical claims of freedom of speech and security is merely one case in point. It is extremely difficult to draw the line between the laxity that might imperil this freedom and the rigorousness that would destroy what it seeks to preserve. Here, as in so many other departments of modern political life, one of the central problems for democratic societies is how to manage not to commit suicide while avoiding being murdered.

Locke and Ourselves

Nothing is easier than to point out inconsistencies in Locke's theory, such as the major conflict, running through his whole view, between his empirical method and his belief in all sorts of "rational" certainties. But Locke's successors, as we shall see, gained very little by being more consistent; they only ended in a blind alley that he had too much common sense to enter. And it was the same common sense, of course, that even more obviously helped him avoid the other extreme of early modern philosophy, that of rationalistic system-building.

Though Locke did not manage to combine the apparently contradictory claims of rationalism and empiricism into a sound theory of knowledge, he saw that both elements are necessary and he resisted the temptation to achieve an easy solution by ignoring either one or the other. In this respect—in his sense of the wholeness of philosophy—Locke was perhaps the most balanced modern thinker before Kant.

If consistency were the sole element in the philosophical ideal, it would be hard to understand the great influence of Locke's views in so many different fields. We have already examined his influence on the development of psychology; in the next chapters we will examine his influence on the development of epistemology. Even more important, perhaps, was his influence on democratic political theory. The spirit of the Declaration of Independence, of the Constitution, and of the Bill of Rights was thoroughly Lockian; indeed, the American political ideal today is still the Lockian state. But, extensive as Locke's influence has been, his appeal is less the appeal of theory than it is the appeal of a humane, generous, and honest mind. It is the appeal, too, of what may be called common sense—of a willingness to let things lie, instead of forcing issues or insisting on neat solutions.

The systematic type of mind is certainly valuable; consistency is obviously an important consideration in any kind of thinking. But systematic completeness can perhaps be too dearly purchased. Who can deny that the common-sense, Lockian type of mind is as valuable, in its own way, as the more systematic mind, or that it is as useful in the twentieth century as it was in the seventeenth?

CHAPTER 9

Berkeley

Life

George Berkeley (1685–1753) was born in Ireland of English parents and was educated at Trinity College, Dublin, where he remained for some years as a teacher. He took orders in the Church of England and eventually (in 1734) became a bishop. At one period in his life he interested himself greatly in the British colonies in the New World and sought to establish a university in Bermuda for the education of Americans. This project failed for want of government support, but not before Berkeley had spent some three years in Newport, Rhode Island.

Berkeley was a sincerely religious man, deeply impressed by the conflict between the scientific and the religious views of life that, so he thought, was revealed in the writings of Descartes, Locke, and other modern philosophers.

The root of the trouble, he held, was the belief that the object of scientific cognition is an independent and inert material substance: "All the monstrous systems of atheists" have relied on the alleged existence of material substance and the difficulty of understanding how it could be created out of nothing by God's fiat. The supposed independent existence of matter has made it easy for "impious and profane persons" to "deride immaterial substance," to suppose the soul divisible and corruptible like the body, to deny providence, and to attribute "the whole series of events either to blind chance or fatal necessity." Therefore, if the concept of matter can only be eliminated, "the atheist will want the colour of an empty name to support his impiety." [a] But how is it possible to deny the existence of matter without denying the validity of the whole scientific enterprise as well? This was the problem for which Berkeley believed he had found a solution. In 1710, at an age when a twentieth-century philosopher is just beginning to think about a likely topic for his projected Ph.D. dissertation, Berkeley published his *Principles of Human Knowledge,* which purported to vindicate the tenets of Christianity without undermining the sciences.

Arguments Against Material Substance

Berkeley thought he could show that nothing exists independently of minds and that the word "matter," when used (as most people use it) to designate such a supposedly independent existent, is merely a meaningless noise to which nothing in the real world corresponds.

PRIMARY AND SECONDARY QUALITIES

Berkeley had a number of arguments; a chief one may be called the "argument from primary and secondary qualities."

> They who assert that figure, motion, and the rest of the primary or original qualities do exist without the mind, in unthinking substances, do at the same time acknowledge that colours, sounds, heat, cold, and suchlike secondary qualities, do not; which they tell us are sensations, existing in the mind alone, that depend on and are occasioned by the different size, texture, and motion of the minute particles of matter. . . . Now, if it be certain that those *original* qualities are inseparably united with the other sensible qualities, and not, even in thought, capable of being abstracted from them, it plainly follows that *they* exist only in the mind. But I desire any one to reflect, and try whether he can, by any abstraction of thought, conceive the extension and motion of a body without all other sensible qualities. For my own part, I see evidently that it is not in my power to frame an idea of a body extended and moving, but I must withal give it some colour or other sensible quality, which is acknowledged to exist only in the mind. In short, extension, figure,

> and motion, abstracted from all other qualities, are inconceivable. Where therefore the other sensible qualities are, there must these be also, to wit, in the mind and nowhere else.[b]

This argument is extremely effective against Locke and Descartes, who held that color, sound, and odor are mind-dependent and yet denied that size and shape are. Strictly speaking, however, the argument shows only that primary and secondary qualities are "inseparably united." Hence those who did not agree with Locke and Descartes that the known facts about physiology "conclusively demonstrated" the mind-dependence of sense qualities would not be touched by this argument as it stands.

RELATIVITY-TO-OBSERVER

A second line of attack by Berkeley may be called the "relativity-to-observer argument":

> After the same manner as modern philosophers prove certain sensible qualities to have no existence in Matter, or without the mind, the same thing may be likewise proved of all other sensible qualities whatsoever. Thus, for instance, it is said that heat and cold are affections only of the mind, and not at all patterns of real beings, existing in the corporeal substances which excite them; for that the same body which appears cold to one hand seems warm to another. Now, why may we not as well argue that figure and extension are not patterns or resemblances of qualities existing in Matter; because to the same eye at different stations, or eyes of a different texture at the same station, they appear various, and cannot therefore be the images of anything settled and determinate without the mind?[c]

This argument shows that the colored surface I see and judge to be out there is not the surface you see and judge to be out there. But it does not prove that there is *no* colored surface out there. As Berkeley pointed out, the argument "does not so much prove that there is no extension or colour in an outward object, as that we do not know by sense which is the true extension or colour of the object." What is needed, therefore, is a further argument to show that the very idea of sensible qualities existing in outward objects is absurd. This Berkeley undertook to do in the following way:

PLEASURE-PAIN

> PHILONOUS.[1] Doth the *reality* of sensible things consist in being perceived? or, is it something distinct from their being perceived, and that bears no relation to the mind? . . .

1 [Philonous, whose name means "lover of mind" in Greek, represents Berkeley; Hylas, whose name is derived from the Greek word for "matter," is a Cartesian, or Lockian, dualist—AUTHOR.]

HYLAS. I mean a real absolute being, distinct from, and without any relation to, their being perceived.

PHILONOUS. Heat therefore, if it be allowed a real being, must exist without the mind?

HYLAS. It must.

PHILONOUS. Tell me, Hylas, is this real existence equally compatible to all degrees of heat, which we perceive . . . ?

HYLAS. Whatever degree of heat we perceive by sense, we may be sure the same exists in the object that occasions it.

PHILONOUS. What! the greatest as well as the least?

HYLAS. I tell you, the reason is plainly the same in respect of both. They are both perceived by sense; nay, the greater degree of heat is more sensibly perceived; and consequently, if there is any difference, we are more certain of its real existence than we can be of the reality of a lesser degree.

PHILONOUS. But is not the most vehement and intense degree of heat a very great pain?

HYLAS. No one can deny it.

PHILONOUS. And is any unperceiving thing capable of pain or pleasure?

HYLAS. No, certainly.

PHILONOUS. Is your material substance a senseless being, or a being endowed with sense and perception?

HYLAS. It is senseless without doubt.

PHILONOUS. It cannot therefore be the subject of pain?

HYLAS. By no means.

PHILONOUS. Nor consequently of the greatest heat perceived by sense, since you acknowledge this to be no small pain?

HYLAS. I grant it.

PHILONOUS. What shall we say then of your external object; is it a material Substance, or no?

HYLAS. It is a material substance with the sensible qualities inhering in it.

PHILONOUS. How then can a great heat exist in it, since you own it cannot in a material substance? . . . But, did you not say before that all degrees of heat were equally real; or, if there was any difference, that the greater were more undoubtedly real than the lesser? . . . How shall we be able to discern those degrees of heat which exist only in the mind from those which exist without it?[d]

This argument is very ingenious. It depends on but two suppositions, both of which Berkeley believed everyone would have to grant: (1) that pleasures and pains are mental states having no existence independent of minds, and (2) that what is true of any degree of a quality is true of all degrees. It is only necessary to point out that an intense heat *is* a pain in order to show that no degree of heat can have independent existence. The conclusion must be that qualities have no existence except as *sensible* qualities, that is, as qualities for a mind.

So far, however, the arguments apply only to qualities. They show that both the primary and the secondary qualities of things are relative to the perceiver, and that it is as meaningless to talk about unperceived qualities as it is to talk about unperceived pleasures and pains. But Descartes and the other defenders of material substance would hold that, whatever is proved true of *qualities,* matter itself necessarily exists. This being the case, whether or not it is perceived is quite irrelevant. Berkeley saw that Locke's historical plain method would demolish independent substance as completely as the arguments just cited had demolished independent qualities. In order to understand his reasoning here, let us examine his exposition of Locke's empirical criterion of meaning.

Critique of Abstract Ideas

Berkeley agreed with Locke that "it is evident to any one who takes a survey of the *objects of human knowledge,* that they are either *ideas* actually imprinted on the senses; or else such as are perceived by attending to the passions and operations of the mind; or lastly, *ideas* formed by help of memory and imagination—either compounding, dividing, or barely representing those originally perceived in the aforesaid ways."[e]

This provides a sure way of checking the aberrations of speculative philosophy. We have merely to look for the "original idea" that was the source of any speculative concept. If we can find it, well and good; if we cannot, we must abandon the concept as fictitious.

> No sooner do we depart from sense and instinct to follow . . . reason . . . ,
> but . . . we are insensibly drawn into uncouth paradoxes, difficulties, and
> inconsistencies, which multiply and grow upon us as we advance in specula-
> tion; till at length, having wandered through many intricate mazes, we find
> ourselves just where we were, or, which is worse, sit down in a forlorn
> Scepticism.[f]

The trouble, Berkeley believed, stems from a tendency to think in words instead of thinking about the things the words signify. "We need only draw the curtain of words, to behold the fairest tree of knowledge, whose fruit is excellent, and within the reach of our hand."[g] Berkeley therefore devoted the opening pages of the *Principles* to a study of the

> . . . nature and abuse of Language [which has] had a chief part in rendering
> speculation intricate and perplexed, and [has] occasioned innumerable errors
> and difficulties in almost all parts of knowledge. And that is the opinion that
> the mind hath a power of framing *abstract* ideas or notions of things. He
> who is not a perfect stranger to the writings and disputes of philosophers
> must needs acknowledge that no small part of them are spent about abstract
> ideas. These are in a more especial manner thought to be the object of those
> sciences which go by the name of logic and metaphysics, and of all that which

passes under the notion of the most abstracted and sublime learning. . . .

Whether others have this wonderful faculty of abstracting their ideas, they best can tell. For myself, I find indeed I have a faculty of imagining, or representing to myself, the ideas of those particular things I have perceived, and of variously compounding and dividing them. I can imagine a man with two heads; or the upper parts of a man joined to the body of a horse. I can consider the hand, the eye, the nose, each by itself abstracted or separated from the rest of the body. But then whatever hand or eye I imagine, it must have some particular shape and colour. Likewise the idea of man that I frame to myself must be either of a white, or a black, or a tawny, a straight, or a crooked, a tall, or a low, or a middle-sized man. I cannot by any effort of thought conceive the abstract idea of . . . *man*, or, if you please, humanity, or human nature.[h]

DIFFERENCE FROM LOCKE

In the main, of course, this was intended by Berkeley as a criticism of the speculations of the Continental Rationalists, but it was also directed against Locke, who, as Berkeley rightly saw, had formulated his historical plain method ambiguously and had not pressed it to its logical conclusion. Locke wrote as if he believed that what is before the mind when it thinks "triangle" is a generalized image—a triangle that is neither scalene nor equilateral. According to Berkeley, no such general image exists. What is before the mind is always some particular triangle, which stands for, or represents, every other particular triangle.

Thus, when Berkeley denied that men have the "faculty of abstracting their ideas," he was actually making two distinct assertions, though he did not distinguish them. He was asserting both a psychological thesis—that there are no generalized images, only specific ones—and an epistemological thesis—that there are no universals, only particulars. As regards the former, he and Locke differed. As regards the latter (which is, of course, the important one from the philosophical point of view), they were in agreement: when I think "man," for instance, what I am thinking about is nothing but particular human beings.

Since all ideas are concrete particulars, and since there are no real universals, it follows that a general name simply refers to (is the sign of) several particular ideas, all of which it indifferently represents, and some one of which is always actually present to the mind when it thinks about the meaning of this name. But if what is before the mind is always a particular, how can we ever know any general truths at all? If what one is thinking about is always some particular triangle (for example, a black equilateral triangle outlined in white), how can one be sure that the theorem about the interior angles equaling 180° is true of a white scalene triangle outlined in black? Berkeley's answer was that we can be sure that what is true of the one is true of the other because the particular properties that differ in the two triangles (white, black, and so on) do not enter into the proof.

MATTER AN ABSTRACT IDEA

The next step in Berkeley's attack on material substance was to show that this critique of abstract ideas applies to the notion of "matter." Just as the word "man" either names nothing at all or is simply a way of referring indifferently to John, to James, to Tom, to Dick, to Harry, so "matter" either names nothing at all or is merely a way of referring indifferently to a great many particular sense qualities.

Try, Berkeley urged, to find the "original" of the idea of matter. All one ever finds is particular apples, tables, men. Analyze any one of these. Is it possible to find any matter? No; one finds only such-and-such sensible qualities.

> As several of these are observed to accompany each other, they come to be marked by one name, and so to be reputed as one *thing*. Thus, for example, a certain colour, taste, smell, figure and consistence having been observed to go together, are accounted one distinct thing, signified by the name apple; other collections of ideas constitute a stone, a tree, a book, and the like sensible things.[i]

But in none of these is matter to be found. The conclusion that follows, which Locke ought to have drawn from his historical plain method, is that terms like "matter," "body," "material substance," should be dropped from the philosophical vocabulary. In the following passage Berkeley exposes the vacuity of these terms as they were employed in Cartesian dualism.

> HYLAS. . . . I find it necessary to suppose a *material substratum*, without which [the qualities] cannot be conceived to exist.
>
> PHILONOUS. *Material substratum* call you it? Pray, by which of your senses came you acquainted with that being?
>
> HYLAS. It is not itself sensible; its modes and qualities only being perceived by the senses. . . .
>
> PHILONOUS. It seems then you have only a relative *notion* of it, or that you conceive it not otherwise than by conceiving the relation it bears to sensible qualities?
>
> HYLAS. Right.
>
> PHILONOUS. Be pleased therefore to let me know wherein that relation consists.
>
> HYLAS. Is it not sufficiently expressed in the term *substratum*, or *substance?*
>
> PHILONOUS. If so, the word *substratum* should import that it is spread under the sensible qualities or accidents?
>
> HYLAS. True.
>
> PHILONOUS. And consequently under extension?
>
> HYLAS. I own it. . . .
>
> PHILONOUS. So that something distinct from, and exclusive of, extension is supposed to be the *substratum* of extension?
>
> HYLAS. Just so.

PHILONOUS. Answer me, Hylas. Can a thing be spread without extension? or is not the idea of extension necessarily included in *spreading?* . . .

HYLAS. Aye but, Philonous, you take me wrong. I do not mean that Matter is *spread* in a gross literal sense under extension. . . . You . . . take things in a strict literal sense. That is not fair, Philonous.

PHILONOUS. I am not for imposing any sense on your words: you are at liberty to explain them as you please. Only, I beseech you, make me understand something by them. You tell me Matter supports or stands under accidents. How! is it as your legs support your body?

HYLAS. No; that is the literal sense.

PHILONOUS. Pray let me know any sense, literal or not literal, that you understand it in. . . .

HYLAS. I declare I know not what to say. . . .

PHILONOUS. It seems then you have no idea at all, neither relative nor positive, of Matter; you know neither what it is in itself, nor what relation it bears to accidents?

HYLAS. I acknowledge it.

PHILONOUS. And yet you asserted that you could not conceive how qualities or accidents should really exist, without conceiving at the same time a material support of them?

HYLAS. I did.

PHILONOUS. That is to say, when you conceive the *real* existence of qualities, you do withal conceive Something which you cannot conceive.[j]

"ESSE EST PERCIPI"

Berkeley reinforced this line of reasoning by a somewhat different argument. What is meant, he asked,

> . . . by the term *exist* when applied to sensible things [?] The table I write on I say exists; that is, I see and feel it: and if I were out of my study I should say it existed; meaning thereby that if I was in my study I might perceive it, or that some other spirit actually does perceive it. . . . This is all that I can understand by these and the like expressions. For as to what is said of the *absolute* existence of unthinking things, without any relation to their being perceived, that is to me perfectly unintelligible. Their *esse* is *percipi;* nor is it possible they should have any existence out of the minds or thinking things which perceive them.[k]

In a word, what "nicer strain of abstraction" could there be than to separate the *being* of a sensible thing from its being perceived? Just as there is no universal "man" that is distinct from the particular Johns and Jameses, so there is no "being" that is distinct from being perceived. To be *means* to-be-perceived, that is, to be an object for some mind or other. Thus Berkeley was not content to say merely that since (as everyone agreed) the mind knows only its own ideas, it cannot *know* anything that is not an idea. He also maintained that there cannot *be* anything that is not for-a-mind. Try to think of anything that is not for-a-mind. It cannot be done, for whatever one thinks of is *eo ipso* for-a-mind. "All the Choir of Heaven and the furniture of earth," Berkeley urged in his florid eighteenth-century style, "in a word all those bodies which compose the mighty frame of the world, have no substance without a mind."

Berkeley's position is thus that "existence-independent-of-mind" is a contradiction in terms: It amounts to saying that we can conceive what is unconceived. To this Hylas replied that, though anything the mind can conceive is obviously conceivable, there may yet be something that is inconceivable. That is, unknown and unknowable objects may exist. Berkeley's answer was that Hylas could *talk*, if he chose, about a something entirely unknown, but "my inference shall be, that you mean nothing at all. . . . I leave it to you to consider how mere jargon should be treated."[1]

PUZZLE CONCERNING THE NATURE OF IDEAS

Hylas would have done better to ask what Berkeley meant by saying that all existence is "for" some mind or other. Even if it be agreed that the red that I see and the middle C that I hear are somehow relative to, and dependent on, myself as a perceiver, it does not necessarily follow that red and middle C are "ideas" in the sense of being mental images.

The trouble is that Berkeley had inherited the Cartesian and Lockian assumption that minds know bodies by means of ideas. He was quite critical about the "body" part of this assumption, for it offended his religious sensibilities. And when he saw that, in this view, bodies are unknowable, he was only too glad to drop them. But he was quite uncritical about the rest of the formula; it did not occur to him to ask himself whether the rest of the scheme might not be invalidated by the same line of argument. His position was that "of course" there are minds and "of course" each mind knows its own ideas. Hence, if there are no bodies for minds to know, reality naturally consists in minds and their ideas.

Dr. Samuel Johnson once undertook to refute Berkeley by kicking a stone. Although Berkeley had a perfectly good reply to this criticism as Johnson stated it, one can sympathize with the critic. What one kicks is not ideas, but stones. Why call the stone that I kick "my idea of a stone"? The truth is that "idea of" is as empty of meaning as "material substance"—a verbal complication that confuses, rather than assists, our efforts to think straight. Philonous is really not much better off than poor Hylas, who tried to defend his material substratum by arguing that if we admit properties, we must allow substances for them to inhere in. Similarly, Berkeley might say, "Nobody denies that there are minds, and what minds know is ideas." But, unfortunately, this is only a matter of definition. Of course minds know only ideas, if one defines the objects of knowledge as ideas! At times Berkeley seemed to see that calling the empirical data "ideas" was just a manner of speaking, and in more than one place he insisted that he had left the physical world just what it was before the theory was put forward.

Unfortunately, the term "idea" carried as many special connotations of its own as had the objectionable "material substance."[2] Berkeley pointed out a very important truth in insisting that a stone is just a set of coexisting data, not a material substratum with properties. But it was misleading to add that these data were private mental states.

The Physical World

In view of the ambiguities just noted, it is not surprising that many of Berkeley's contemporaries misunderstood the *esse est percipi* doctrine and assumed Berkeley to be holding that the world is a mere dream. But Berkeley had no trouble distinguishing between dream and reality. In a "real" stone, for instance, the visual ideas of such-and-such a colored shape coexist along with the ideas of resistance and pain, when these are accompanied by the muscular sensations called kicking. In an "imaginary" stone, the visual data are accompanied neither by tactile data nor by a sensation of pain.

Moreover, the various data (the color and the shape) making up the real stone are more vivid and more distinct than those making up the imaginary stone. Also, the data in the real stone are independent of one's will (for instance, if I look in the appropriate direction, I cannot but see the stone), whereas the data in the imaginary stone are dependent on one's will. "Dream" stones are to be distinguished from both imaginary stones and real stones, not on the basis of vividness or independence, but on the basis of confusedness and irregularity. Thus the distinctions on which Dr. Johnson rightly insisted can be accounted for in Berkeleian terms.

Nor was Berkeley's position, as he pointed out, in any way incompatible with the existence of scientific laws, as formulated in the "corpuscular" philosophy. He denied the existence, not of *bodies* (understood as stable collections of sensory data), but of *body* (the abstract idea). According to Berkeley, scientists may *talk* about the states of a material substance, but everything they say can be said far more simply and intelligibly by talking about the relations of certain ideas to certain other ideas.[3] A scientific law is thus a generalization about what ideas coexist with or follow other ideas in our experience. When we say that friction causes heat, we mean that certain ideas of rubbing are always accompanied by

---

2 "If it be demanded why I make use of the word *idea*, and do not rather in compliance with custom call them *things;* I answer, I do it for two reasons:—First, because the term *thing* . . . is generally supposed to denote somewhat existing without the mind: Secondly, because *thing* hath a more comprehensive signification than *idea*, including spirits, or thinking things, as well as ideas"—*Principles* (Fraser), Part I, §39. But, of course, the fact that "thing" is a bad term does not imply that "idea" is a good one.

3 "They who attempt to account for things do it, not by corporeal substance, but by figure, motion, and other qualities"—*Principles*, Part I, §50.

sensations of heat—in other words, that friction is the *sign* of heat. It is a mistake, therefore, to think that the natural sciences can ever be demonstrable; on the contrary, the function of physics is merely to describe with accuracy the observable relations between signs and things signified. Thus, a "law" like the inverse square law is nothing but a statement of the precise conditions under which some idea or set of ideas is experienced.

> The question whether the earth moves or no amounts in reality to no more than this, to wit, whether we have reason to conclude, from what has been observed by astronomers, that if we were placed in such and such circumstances . . . , we should perceive the [earth] move among the choir of the planets. . . . And this, by the established rules of nature, which we have no reason to mistrust, is reasonably collected from the phenomena.[m]

This is a much simpler interpretation of what science is about than the original scheme of bodies-in-motion-that-cause-sensations-in-minds. It is easy, however, to see why the latter seemed so natural, almost inevitable, to the first physicists and philosophers. Measurement was the indispensable preliminary for the new physics. Clearly, motion, size, and weight are more or less easily and directly measured. Hence these were the properties with which the new physics began. Because these properties thus seemed more important than others, it was assumed that they were also ontologically superior. Hence, again, when philosophers made a model of the universe that the new physics seemed to describe, they limited the real world to things that have these properties—in other words, they said that reality consists in bodies in motion. Since this scheme worked well, practical scientists did not worry about a little logical fuzziness.

But, as we have seen, this scheme caused great philosophical embarrassments, including such puzzles as the interaction of minds and bodies, and the peculiar status of phantasms in Hobbes's philosophy and of perception in Descartes' and Locke's. The advantage of Berkeley's analysis was that it showed that many (unfortunately, not all) of these puzzles are merely verbal. Instead, for instance, of talking about "reducing" everything to states of bodies in motion, Berkeley would have us talk about the relations that obtain among various experiences, which are all on the same ontological footing and which are organized on the basis of empirical relations of coexistence and succession, rather than on the basis of a metaphysical relation of material substance and properties.

God

Berkeley's proof of the existence of God is causal in form and proceeds by a process of elimination. What is the cause, he asked, of the order and regularity that men encounter in their experience? Various philosophers have suggested various possible causes. Berkeley eliminated each of these suggestions in turn, leaving God as the only possible cause.

First, there was the materialists' claim that regularities in the behavior of matter cause the order and regularity of our experience. Since Berkeley believed that he had shown that "matter" is an empty noise signifying nothing, he thought it sufficient to reply to the materialists, "I do by no means find fault with your reasoning, in that you collect *a* cause from the *phenomena:* but I deny that *the* cause . . . can properly be termed Matter."[n]

Second, there were ideas. Berkeley asserted that ideas are "visibly inactive"; being passive, they cannot be causes. Here Berkeley was simply following Locke and drawing the logical conclusion from his observations. What is observable is alteration, not the production of alteration. One experience (the perception of billiard ball B moving across the table) follows another (the perception of billiard ball A in contact with B), but we do not perceive in A any power or agency that causes B to move.[4]

Third, there was the self. According to Berkeley, the self is certainly active on occasion, and sometimes it is the cause of what it experiences—for example, in dream and in imagination. But it is equally evident that the self is by no means the cause of all that it experiences: "When in broad daylight I open my eyes, it is not in my power to choose whether I shall see or no . . . : so likewise as to the hearing and other senses; the ideas imprinted on them are not creatures of *my* will."[o]

The cause of our experience, with all its marvelous order and regularity, must be something like the self, but much greater. It must be active; specifically, it must be a mind—"How can that which is *inactive* be a *cause;* or that which is *un-thinking* be a *cause of thought?*" Hence, since the self does not produce the ideas, "there is some other Will or Spirit that produces them." And, since the orderliness of the ideas is very great, the will that produces them must be very powerful. Indeed, according to Berkeley, it must be infinite.

> If we attentively consider the constant regularity, order, and concatenation of natural things, the surprising magnificence, beauty and perfection of the larger, and the exquisite contrivance of the smaller parts of the creation, to-gether with the exact harmony and correspondence of the whole, but above all the never-enough-admired laws of pain and pleasure, and the instincts or natural inclinations, appetites, and passions of animals;—I say if we consider all these things, and at the same time attend to the meaning and import of the attributes One, Eternal, Infinitely Wise, Good, and Perfect, we shall clearly perceive that they belong to the aforesaid Spirit, "who works all in all" and "by whom all things consist."[p]

The attack on material substance thus served a double purpose for Berkeley: It removed the prop on which atheism rested, and it furnished "a direct and im-mediate demonstration of the being of God." Indeed, it demonstrated not only

4 See p. 250.

God's existence but also His goodness. If God sometimes chose to think "edible," and sometimes "poisonous," along with "red-sweet-spherical," our lives would be short. Life is viable only because we can safely take "red-sweet-spherical" as a sign of "edible"; and this is possible only because a beneficent God thinks them together regularly.

It will be seen that Berkeley abandoned the rationalistic attempt (which Locke had inconsistently retained) to prove the existence of God by an ontological type of argument. Berkeley saw that, given the premises of the historical plain method, no idea ever implies the existence of its object. He therefore tried to argue that observed facts can be explained only on the hypothesis of a divine cause. But, though Berkeley called his proof a "demonstration," it yields at best only a probable conclusion. It is impossible to say, for instance, that an infinite cause is *necessary* to produce the order in question. A very great cause might be sufficient to this purpose.

Spiritual Substance

At one point in the *Dialogues,* Hylas suggests to Philonous that the arguments the latter used so effectively against material substance might also be used against spiritual substance. If an apple is only a congeries of ideas, what about God and the self?

> HYLAS. Answer me, Philonous. Are all our ideas perfectly inert beings? Or have they any agency included in them?
> PHILONOUS. They are altogether passive and inert.
> HYLAS. And is not God an agent, a being purely active?
> PHILONOUS. I acknowledge it.
> HYLAS. No idea therefore can be like unto, or represent the nature of God?
> PHILONOUS. It cannot.
> HYLAS. Since therefore you have no *idea* of the mind of God, how can you conceive it possible that things should exist in His mind? Or, if you can conceive the mind of God, without having an idea of it, why may not I be allowed to conceive the existence of Matter, notwithstanding I have no idea of it? . . .
> You admit . . . that there is spiritual Substance, although you have no idea of it; while you deny there can be such a thing as material Substance, because you have no notion or idea of it. Is this fair dealing? To act consistently, you must either admit Matter or reject Spirit.q

And this line of reasoning applies even more obviously to the self:

> According to your own way of thinking, and in consequence of your own principles, it should follow that *you* are only a system of floating ideas, with-

out any substance to support them. Words are not to be used without a meaning. And, as there is no more meaning in *spiritual Substance* than in *material Substance*, the one is to be exploded as well as the other.[r]

The problem raised here by Hylas seems to have dawned on Berkeley only after the publication of the *Principles:* On Berkeley's own account of the nature of knowledge, men cannot know spirits or spiritual activity. For all that men ever know is ideas, and ideas are inert and passive. It was desperately necessary, Berkeley saw, to do something about this situation, and in subsequent editions of the *Principles* and in the *Dialogues* he tried to draw a distinction between ideas and "notions." Though it is true that we have no idea of God or of self, we do have a notion of them.

> I own I have properly no *idea*, either of God or any other spirit. . . . I do nevertheless know that I, who am a spirit or thinking substance, exist as certainly as I know my ideas exist. . . . I know this immediately or intuitively, though I do not perceive it as I perceive a triangle, a colour, or a sound.[s]

Though Hylas "owned himself satisfied on this point," he should have pressed Philonous more closely. Of course, Berkeley was conscious of his own existence as "something different" from his ideas—willings, doubtings, hopings, and hatings are experienced as "something different" from reds, sphericals, and sweets. But how does the difference between a "willing" and a "red" differ from the difference between a "red" and a "sweet"? That is the pertinent point. Neither "willing" nor "red," it would seem, is a self; each is but an element in experience, a part of the content of consciousness, distinguished qualitatively, of course, from other parts.

In a word, why distinguish between "ideas" and "notions"? Berkeley admitted that people use the two terms interchangeably, but he maintained that "it conduces to clearness and propriety to distinguish things very different by different names." It may be agreed that different things ought to be called by different names, but in this case, what are the distinguishing marks that justify different names? If "willing" and "red," as parts of the content of consciousness, are on the same footing, they should be called by the same name. If "red" is an idea, so is "willing." The problem of our knowledge of spiritual substance is not solved by drawing what amounts to a Scholastic distinction between "notion" and "idea."

The line of criticism Hylas might have developed here was later on carried much further by Hume.[5] For the present, let us continue to examine Berkeley's own argument. According to Berkeley, then, the self exists, and I know that it exists. Since I cannot have an idea of the self, it must be that I have a notion of it. What is more, I not only have a notion *that* I exist, but I also have a notion of myself as an indivisible and incorporeal, and so an immortal, soul. Of this, according to Berkeley, I am immediately and intuitively certain. From this certain self-

5 See pp. 304–11.

knowledge, Berkeley proceeded to a knowledge of God and of other selves. Though I have a direct intuition (that is, notion) only of my own existence, I know, from the causal argument already discussed, *that* God exists. I can come to understand His nature by reflecting on my own activities as a spirit and "heightening the powers and removing the defects" that I find in myself. As regards other finite spirits, my knowledge is similarly inferential. Berkeley saw that "we have neither an immediate evidence nor a demonstrative knowledge of the existence of other finite spirits," but he believed that we can infer their existence from the ideas they excite in us. Further, he held it possible to argue by analogy that these other spirits must be like the spirit that each of us experiences in himself.

Unfortunately (to mention but one of a number of difficulties with this reasoning), the inference to the existence of other selves seems to conflict with the inference to the existence of God. First Berkeley argued, in effect, that God must exist because nothing else could be the cause of the self's ideas. Then he turned around and maintained that, since some of the self's ideas are, after all, not caused by God (nor yet by the self), other spirits must exist to produce them.

Summary

It should be evident from Berkeley's discussion of our knowledge of spiritual substances that he was only a lukewarm empiricist. He was glad to use an empirical argument to destroy "material substance," and a very effective job he made of it. But he was totally unprepared for the way this instrument could be turned against those spiritual substances whose existence he wanted to validate.

Though the alternatives for Berkeley were either to throw out spiritual substance along with matter or to abandon the historical plain method, he never (at least officially) gave up either. He did what most people in similar circumstances do—first he tried to patch up the holes in his arguments; when that failed, he went quietly away and let the arguments stand. This was easy for Berkeley because, despite the verbal similarity to Locke, his mind was not critical in the Lockian sense. Locke *intended* to be rigorously critical. Berkeley did not. He never believed in the existence of matter, and he never stopped believing in the existence of spirits—in both cases, on grounds that had nothing to do with the historical plain method. He used the empirical method to disprove what he already disbelieved, and he abandoned it when it seemed to disprove what he wanted to believe.

This is shown conclusively by the final development of his thought. In his last work, *Siris* (1744), which was officially devoted to publicizing the medicinal virtues of tar water but ranged over the whole philosophical field as it did so, Berkeley continued to use his old terminology—but now with a new meaning. He still thought of the physical world as consisting of God's thoughts, but his interest was now in God the thinker rather than in the empirical relations discernible among the things God supposedly thought about. He now drew a distinction between the empirical data present to our minds (those "ideas" that he had formerly taken to be real) and reality, of which he now held ideas to be "appearances." Accordingly, sense perceptions were now compared very unfavorably with notions, which were virtually identified with Platonic forms. Thus Berkeley's final position was a Christian Neoplatonism in which the real world consisted in God's thoughts (Platonic archetypes), and the world of our "ideas," which the youthful Berkeley had taken to be real, was merely the wavering image of a truth that transcended it but of which we could catch faint reflections here below.

From his own point of view, then, Berkeley did not in the least belong in the succession from Locke to Hume. The reason for ignoring his later theories and insisting on his empiricism is that his later theories were neither original nor carefully worked out, whereas his earlier view was a significant stage in the dialectical development of the Lockian premises. In the history of philosophy, Berkeley is an empiricist in spite of himself.

CHAPTER 10

Hume

Life

David Hume's mind was as tough as Hobbes's. He had none of the piety of Locke and Berkeley, and none of the latter's mysticism.[1] This gave him the advantage (or disadvantage, depending on how one looks at it) of not feeling compelled to draw back from conclusions to which logic seemed to lead him. It must also be said that his logic was better than theirs; he saw more clearly than either Locke or Berkeley the implications of the premises they had accepted.

1 Boswell, Johnson's biographer, called on Hume a few weeks before Hume's death, when he was visibly failing. Under the circumstances, immortality seemed to Boswell an appropriate subject of conversation, and he questioned Hume closely about his beliefs. Was it not possible that there might be a future state? Yes, Hume replied; "It was [also] possible that a piece of

Hume was born in Edinburgh in 1711 into a family of country gentlemen of ancient lineage and modest circumstances. His father died when the children were young, but their mother saw to it that they were decently educated. When he was twenty-three he went to France, where by exercising the strictest economy he managed to subsist on the small allowance his family could afford to give him. He spent three years there writing the book with which he hoped to make his fortune. It was difficult to find a publisher, and when the *Treatise* appeared in 1738, to his bitter disappointment, "it fell" (as he related in his *Autobiography*) "dead-born from the press, without reaching such distinction as even to excite a murmur from the zealots." [2]

During the next ten years Hume acted variously as the paid companion of a mad marquis, who in intervals of sanity apparently admired the *Treatise*, as the private secretary of a general during an ill-conceived amphibious expedition against the coast of France, and as a member of the suite of the same general now turned British Ambassador to the courts of Vienna and Turin. He also published two volumes of *Essays* and drastically revised the unfortunate *Treatise*. The new version was published as *An Enquiry Concerning the Human Understanding* (in 1748) and *An Enquiry Concerning the Principles of Morals* (in 1751).

At about this time, he was appointed librarian of the Advocates' Library at Edinburgh, but the lawyers were scandalized by his selections for the library,[3] and he was soon obliged to resign. Meanwhile he had begun a *History of England* because, as he wrote to a friend, "there is no post of honor in the English Parnassus more vacant than that of history." He chose to begin with the Stuarts and once

---

coal put upon the fire would not burn." That men "should exist for ever" was "a most unreasonable fancy. . . . The trash of every age must [then] be preserved, and . . . new Universes must be created to contain such infinite numbers." When Boswell inquired whether Hume had ever "entertained any belief in Religion," Hume replied that, as a child, he had passed briefly through a period of piety, worrying greatly about his vices and especially about his pride. But what a childish folly this was, Hume continued. Why should a boy not be proud who knew that he excelled his fellow students? The trouble with Christianity was that it tried to extinguish, instead of moderating, the passions, and so ended in immorality. "He then said flatly that the Morality of every Religion was bad, and, I really thought, was not jocular when he said 'that when he heard a man was religious, he concluded he was a rascal, though he had known some instances of very good men being religious'"—quoted in *Private Papers of James Boswell*, edited by G. Scott and F. A. Pottle (W. E. Rudge, priv. printed, Mt. Vernon, N.Y., 1928–34), Vol. XII (1931), pp. 227–32.

2 Despite this appearance of *sang-froid*, Hume had toned the book down considerably in preparing it for publication, excising passages in which his sceptical conclusions were too plainly stated. In his own view, he wrote to a friend at the time, he had "castrated it by cutting off its nobler parts."

3 In 1754 Hume purchased, among other books, the *Contes* of La Fontaine and Bussy-Rabutin's *Histoire amoureuse des Gaules*. The curators objected that the books were "obscene," ordered them removed, and decreed that in the future the librarian must secure their approval before making any purchases. According to Hume, "if every book not superior in merit to *La Fontaine* be expelled from the Library, I shall engage to carry away all that remains in my pocket. I know not indeed if any will remain except our fifty pound Bible, which is too bulky for me to carry away. . . . *Bussi Rabutin* contains no bawdy at all, though if it did, I see not that it would be a whit the worse"—*Letters of David Hume*, edited by J. Y. T. Greig (Clarendon Press, Oxford, 1932), Vol. I, p. 212.

again he was assailed by "one cry of reproach, disapprobation and even detestation."[4] However, his books were now becoming well known on the Continent, especially in France. There came to be, indeed, almost a Humian cult, and when he finally returned to France in 1763, in the suite of the British Ambassador, he had an immense success—which he thoroughly enjoyed but which he did not allow to go to his head. After three years in France, he returned home to find that his fame had at last spread to Britain. His last years (he died in 1776) were spent in Edinburgh, where his even temper, his kindliness to young writers, and his agreeable company made him the center of Scottish literary society.

Theory of Knowledge

Like Locke and Berkeley, Hume was dissatisfied with the "abstruse speculations" that passed for philosophy among the learned. Such speculation, he thought, was inconclusive and did not touch the lives of the common men. It was useful only to those who had a theological ax to grind and who, "being unable to defend [their superstitious beliefs] on fair ground, raise these entangling brambles to cover and protect their weakness."

Like Locke and Berkeley, again, he believed that the

> . . . only method of freeing learning, at once, from these abstruse questions, is to enquire seriously into the nature of human understanding, and show, from an exact analysis of its powers and capacity, that it is by no means fitted for such remote and abstruse subjects. We must submit to this fatigue, in order to live at ease ever after: And must cultivate true metaphysics with some care in order to destroy the false and adulterate. . . . Accurate and just reasoning is the only catholic remedy, fitted for all persons and all dispositions; and is alone able to subvert that abstruse philosophy and metaphysical jargon, which, being mixed up with popular superstition, renders it in a manner impenetrable to careless reasoners, and gives it the air of science and wisdom. . . .
> It is remarkable concerning the operations of the mind, that, though most intimately present to us, yet, whenever they become the object of reflection, they seem involved in obscurity; nor can the eye readily find those lines and boundaries, which discriminate and distinguish them. The objects are too fine

---

4 Hume saw the struggle for the preservation of parliamentary rights as a product of religious bigotry. The parliamentarians were "dupes of their own zeal. . . . Equally full of fraud and of ardor, these pious patriots talked perpetually of seeking the Lord, yet still pursued their own purposes; and have left a memorable lesson to posterity, how delusive, how destructive that principle is, by which they were animated. . . . It is vain, therefore, to dignify this civil war, and the parliamentary authors of it, by supposing it to have had any other considerable foundation than theological zeal, that great and noted source of animosity among men." As for the Reformation itself, it had been a contest between "superstition" and "enthusiasm," and Hume made it clear that he had as little use for the one as for the other.

to remain long in the same aspect or situation; and must be apprehended in an instant, by a superior penetration, derived from nature, and improved by habit and reflexion. It becomes, therefore, no inconsiderable part of science barely to know the different operations of the mind, to separate them from each other, to class them under their proper heads, and to correct all that seeming disorder, in which they lie involved. . . . And if we can go no farther than this mental geography, or delineation of the distinct parts and powers of the mind, it is at least a satisfaction to go so far; and the more obvious this science may appear (and it is by no means obvious) the more contemptible still must the ignorance of it be esteemed, in all pretenders to learning and philosophy. . . .

Shall we esteem it worthy the labour of a philosopher to give us a true system of the planets, and adjust the position and order to those remote bodies; while we affect to overlook those, who, with so much success, delineate the parts of the mind, in which we are so intimately concerned?[a]

REFORMULATION OF LOCKE'S POSITION

Hume's first task was to reformulate Locke's theory of ideas. His version is a great improvement over Locke's. He abandoned Locke's distinction between ideas of sensation and ideas of reflection—which involved a metaphysics that ought to have been examined, not assumed uncritically at the outset. The basic distinction he introduced—a distinction between "impressions" and "ideas"— did not involve him (at least, not so obviously) in metaphysics. Further, it made possible a precise statement of Locke's historical plain method, that is, of an empirical criterion of meaning.

Every one will readily allow, that there is a considerable difference between the perceptions of the mind, when a man feels the pain of excessive heat, or the pleasure of moderate warmth, and when he afterwards recalls to his memory this sensation, or anticipates it by his imagination. These faculties may mimic or copy the perceptions of the senses; but they never can entirely reach the force and vivacity of the original sentiment. . . . The most lively thought is still inferior to the dullest sensation.

We may observe a like distinction to run through all the other perceptions of the mind. A man in a fit of anger, is actuated in a very different manner from one who only thinks of that emotion. If you tell me, that any person is in love, I easily understand your meaning, and form a just conception of his situation; but never can mistake that conception for the real disorders and agitations of the passion. When we reflect on our past sentiments and affections, our thought is a faithful mirror, and copies its objects truly; but the colours which it employs are faint and dull, in comparison of those in which our original perceptions were clothed. It requires no nice discernment or metaphysical head to mark the distinction between them.

Here therefore we may divide all the perceptions of the mind into two classes or species, which are distinguished by their different degrees of force and vivacity. The less forcible and lively are commonly denominated *Thoughts* or *Ideas*. The other species want a name in our language, and in most others; I suppose, because it was not requisite for any, but philosophical purposes, to rank them under a general term or appellation. Let us, therefore, use a little freedom, and call them *Impressions;* employing that word in a sense somewhat different from the usual. By the term *impression*, then, I mean all our more lively perceptions, when we hear, or see, or feel, or love, or hate, or desire, or will. And impressions are distinguished from ideas, which are the less lively perceptions, of which we are conscious, when we reflect on any of those sensations or movements above mentioned.

Nothing, at first view, may seem more unbounded than the thought of man, which not only escapes all human power and authority, but is not even restrained within the limits of nature and reality. To form monsters, and join incongruous shapes and appearances, costs the imagination no more trouble than to conceive the most natural and familiar objects. And while the body is confined to one planet, along which it creeps with pain and difficulty; the thought can in an instant transport us into the most distant regions of the universe; or even beyond the universe, into the unbounded chaos, where nature is supposed to lie in total confusion. What never was seen, or heard of, may yet be conceived; nor is any thing beyond the power of thought, except what implies an absolute contradiction.

But though our thought seems to possess this unbounded liberty, we shall find, upon a nearer examination, that it is really confined within very narrow limits, and that all this creative power of the mind amounts to no more than the faculty of compounding, transposing, augmenting, or diminishing the materials afforded us by the senses and experience. When we think of a golden mountain, we only join two consistent ideas, *gold*, and *mountain*, with which we were formerly acquainted. A virtuous horse we can conceive; because, from our own feeling, we can conceive virtue; and this we may unite to the figure and shape of a horse, which is an animal familiar to us. In short, all the materials of thinking are derived either from our outward or inward sentiment: the mixture and composition of these belongs alone to the mind and will. Or, to express myself in philosophical language, all our ideas or more feeble perceptions are copies of our impressions or more lively ones.

To prove this, the two following arguments will, I hope, be sufficient. First, when we analyze our thoughts or ideas, however compounded or sublime, we always find that they resolve themselves into such simple ideas as were copied from a precedent feeling or sentiment. . . . Those who would assert that this position is not universally true nor without exception, have only one, and that an easy method of refuting it; by producing that idea, which, in their opinion, is not derived from this source. It will then be incumbent on us, if we would maintain our doctrine, to produce the impression, or lively perception, which corresponds to it.

Secondly. If it happens, from a defect of the organ, that a man is not susceptible of any species of sensation, we always find that he is as little susceptible of the correspondent ideas. A blind man can form no notion of colours; a deaf man of sounds. . . .

Here, therefore, is a proposition, which not only seems, in itself, simple and intelligible; but, if a proper use were made of it, might render every dispute equally intelligible, and banish all that jargon, which has so long taken possession of metaphysical reasonings, and drawn disgrace upon them. All ideas, especially abstract ones, are naturally faint and obscure: the mind has but a slender hold of them: they are apt to be confounded with other resembling ideas; and when we have often employed any term, though without a distinct meaning, we are apt to imagine it has a determinate idea annexed to it. On the contrary, all impressions, that is, all sensations, either outward or inward, are strong and vivid; the limits between them are more exactly determined: nor is it easy to fall into any error or mistake with regard to them. When we entertain, therefore, any suspicion that a philosophical term is employed without any meaning or idea (as is but too frequent), we need but enquire, *from what impression is that supposed idea derived?* And if it be impossible to assign any, this will serve to confirm our suspicion. By bringing ideas into so clear a light we may reasonably hope to remove all dispute, which may arise, concerning their nature and reality.[b]

It will be seen that in distinguishing impressions from ideas, Hume allowed himself only an empirically observable difference—a difference in degree of "liveliness." That some of our experiences—whether of colors, like blue, or emotions, like love—are more "lively" than others is an empirical fact. The less lively ones Hume called "ideas"; the more lively ones he called "impressions." Though he actually believed in the existence of an external world,[5] he made no assumptions about where impressions come from, what causes them, or what makes them more vivid than ideas.[6] Yet despite all this care, one major assumption did slip in: Like Locke, Hume simply took for granted that every item in consciousness—every impression and every idea—is a distinct, separate, isolated unit.[7] This assumption—called "psychological atomism" because it parallels the atomistic view of physical reality—dominated psychology for more than a century. It led to the further assumption that the main business of psychology was to find the laws by which the supposedly separate "atoms" of experience become "associated."

5 See pp. 311–15.
6 "By the term of impression I would not be understood to express the manner, in which our lively impressions are produced in the soul, but merely the perceptions themselves"—*Treatise* (Selby-Bigge), I, i, 1, note.
7 "Simple perceptions or impressions and ideas are such as admit of no distinction nor separation. The complex are the contrary to these, and may be distinguished into parts. Tho' a particular colour, taste, and smell are qualities all united together in this apple, 'tis easy to perceive they are not the same, but are at least distinguishable from each other"—*Treatise*, I, i, 1.
   Some recent writers have denied that Hume really held this view. The point is discussed by H. H. Price in *Hume's Theory of the External World* (Clarendon Press, Oxford, 1940), pp. 73–74.

ASSOCIATION OF IDEAS

Since, according to Hume, every simple idea is an independent entity, it is theoretically possible that any one of our simple ideas might precede or follow any other simple idea, in any order whatever. But even the most superficial observation of the flow of ideas in our minds shows that this is not the case. On the contrary, when we engage in conversation or argument, even when we daydream, our ideas fall into regular patterns; the relations we observe among them are not merely random or chance. There must, then, be "some universal principles" at work among our ideas, "some bond of union among them, some associating quality, by which one idea naturally introduces another."[c] The three principles Hume believed to be involved are (1) resemblance, (2) contiguity, and (3) cause and effect.

> That these principles serve to connect ideas will not, I believe, be much doubted. A picture naturally leads our thoughts to the original:[8] the mention of one apartment in a building naturally introduces an enquiry or discourse concerning the others:[9] and if we think of a wound, we can scarcely forbear reflecting on the pain which follows it.[10] But that this enumeration is complete, and that there are no other principles of association except these, may be difficult to prove to the satisfaction of the reader, or even to a man's own satisfaction. All we can do, in such cases, is to run over several instances, and examine carefully the principle which binds the different thoughts to each other, never stopping till we render the principle as general as possible. The more instances we examine, and the more care we employ, the more assurance shall we acquire, that the enumeration, which we form from the whole, is complete and entire.
>
> These are therefore the principles of union or cohesion among our simple ideas. . . . Here is a kind of ATTRACTION, which in the mental world will be found to have as extraordinary effects as in the natural, and to shew itself in as many and as various forms. Its effects are every where conspicuous; but as to its causes, they are mostly unknown, and must be resolv'd into *original* qualities of human nature, which I pretend not to explain. . . .
>
> Amongst the effects of this union or association of ideas, there are none more remarkable than those complex ideas, which are the common subjects of our thoughts and reasoning, and generally arise from some principle of union among our simple ideas.[d]

Hume's position, then, is that complex ideas originate in our minds as a result of the operation of the three principles enumerated above. Consider those complex ideas that he classified as "abstract"—for instance, "triangle," "justice," "government," or "conquest." The principle of resemblance is responsible for the generation of all such ideas.

8 Resemblance.
9 Contiguity.
10 Cause and effect.

When we have found a resemblance among several objects, that often occur to us, we apply the same name to all of them, whatever differences we may observe in the degrees of their quantity and quality, and whatever other differences may appear among them. After we have acquired a custom of this kind, the hearing of that name revives the idea of one of these objects, and makes the imagination conceive it with all its particular circumstances and proportions.[11] But as the same word is suppos'd to have been frequently applied to other individuals, that are different in many respects from that idea, which is immediately present in the mind; the word not being able to revive the idea of all these individuals, only touches the soul, if I may be allow'd so to speak, and revives that custom, which we have acquir'd by surveying them. . . . The work raises up an individual idea, along with a certain custom. . . .

'Tis certain *that* we form the idea of individuals, whenever we use any general term; *that* we seldom or never can exhaust these individuals; and *that* those, which remain, are only represented by means of that habit, by which we recall them, whenever any present occasion requires it.[e]

THE EMPIRICAL CRITERION OF MEANING

This account of how abstract ideas are formed in the mind has brought Hume from psychology to epistemology and metaphysics; indeed, in the last paragraph of the long passage quoted earlier,[12] in which Hume formulated his version of the empirical criterion of meaning, he has already made this move. All simple ideas, he maintained, are memory copies of simple impressions; complex ideas are combinations of simple ones. Hence a term has meaning (that is, names an idea) only if there is an impression or combination of impressions of which it is a copy.

Nominalism was the inevitable result of (1) this criterion of meaning and (2) the psychological doctrine that impressions are "particular in their nature and at the same time finite in their number." On this basis there could obviously be no "real" universals, and Hume's argument for nominalism could, in effect, be a challenge: Show me a universal; I will believe it when you point it out to me. But you never show me more than (1) a term, (2) a number of particulars, or (3) a habit.

A philosophy that proposes to get on without universals is something of a novelty. There had been nominalists in the Middle Ages, but they had been able to rely on God's omnipotent will. Hobbes, too, had been a nominalist, but he had been less interested in epistemological questions than in political ones. Locke and Berkeley, who had been interested in epistemological questions, had

11 [When you say "dog," for instance, I always think of some particular dog—that is, I have an image of some dog of my acquaintance. Which of these I happen to imagine on any particular occasion can be accounted for by the principles of association. Today, for example, I may think of my neighbor's Sealyham, which kept me awake last night by its barking. This day last week I might have imaged the Irish Setter I had encountered a few hours earlier on a walk—AUTHOR.]

12 See p. 301.

inconsistently allowed themselves all sorts of universals, as well as spiritual activities and causes. Hume's theory is therefore of great importance. Because Hume was so thorough in developing the implications of his empirical and nominalistic starting point, one can almost say that if his conclusions are unacceptable, something must be wrong with this starting point and with the conception of the mind as a collection of simple impressions and ideas. Now, Hume's conclusions, as we shall see as we proceed, certainly differ widely from those of the traditional philosophy. Much that it had held to be true and important turned out, on Hume's premises, to be not merely false but nonsensical. But does this make Hume's conclusions unacceptable? The cleavage between the Humians and the anti-Humians (if a complex division of opinion may be thus oversimplified) is still one of the major issues in philosophy.

With this much as a preface, let us see how Hume applied his more rigorous version of the empirical criterion of meaning to the analysis of some of the great traditional concepts of philosophy. We shall start with substance. It will be seen that, unlike Berkeley, Hume did not attempt to exempt spiritual substance from the logic of the argument.

SUBSTANCE

> I wou'd fain ask those philosophers, who found so much of their reasonings on the distinction of substance and accident, and imagine we have clear ideas of each, whether the idea of *substance* be deriv'd from the impressions of sensation or reflexion? If it be convey'd to us by our senses, I ask, which of them; and after what manner? If it be perceiv'd by the eyes, it must be a colour; if by the ears, a sound; if by the palate, a taste; and so of the other senses. But I believe none will assert, that substance is either a colour, or a sound, or a taste. The idea of substance must therefore be deriv'd from an impression of reflexion, if it really exist. But the impressions of reflexion resolve themselves into our passions and emotions; none of which can possibly represent a substance. We have therefore no idea of substance, distinct from that of a collection of particular qualities, nor have we any other meaning when we either talk or reason concerning it.[f]

THE SELF

Next Hume applied his version of the empirical criterion of meaning to the supposed idea of self.

> There are some philosophers, who imagine we are every moment intimately conscious of what we call our SELF; that we feel its existence and its continuance in existence; and are certain, beyond the evidence of a demonstration, both of its perfect identity and simplicity. The strongest sensation, the most violent passion, say they, instead of distracting us from this view, only fix it the more intensely, and make us consider their influence on *self* either by their pain or pleasure. . . .

Unluckily all these positive assertions are contrary to that very experience, which is pleaded for them, nor have we any idea of *self*, after the manner it is here explain'd. For from what impression cou'd this idea be deriv'd? This question 'tis impossible to answer without a manifest contradiction and absurdity; and yet 'tis a question, which must necessarily be answer'd, if we wou'd have the idea of self pass for clear and intelligible. It must be some one impression, that gives rise to every real idea. But self or person is not any one impression, but that to which our several impressions and ideas are suppos'd to have a reference. If any impression gives rise to the idea of self, that impression must continue invariably the same, thro' the whole course of our lives; since self is suppos'd to exist after that manner. But there is no impression constant and invariable. Pain and pleasure, grief and joy, passions and sensations succeed each other, and never all exist at the same time. It cannot, therefore, be from any of these impressions, or from any other, that the idea of self is deriv'd; and consequently there is no such idea. . . .

For my part, when I enter most intimately into what I call *myself*, I always stumble on some particular perception or other, of heat or cold, light or shade, love or hatred, pain or pleasure. I never can catch *myself* at any time without a perception, and never can observe any thing but the perception. When my perceptions are remov'd for any time, as by sound sleep; so long am I insensible of *myself*, and may truly be said not to exist. And were all my perceptions remov'd by death, and cou'd I neither think, nor feel, nor see, nor love, nor hate after the dissolution of my body, I shou'd be entirely annihilated, nor do I conceive what is farther requisite to make me a perfect non-entity. If any one upon serious and unprejudic'd reflexion, thinks he has a different notion of *himself*, I must confess I can reason no longer with him. All I can allow him is, that he may be in the right as well as I, and that we are essentially different in this particular. He may, perhaps, perceive something simple and continu'd, which he calls *himself*; tho' I am certain there is no such principle in me.

But setting aside some metaphysicians of this kind, I may venture to affirm of the rest of mankind, that they are nothing but a bundle or collection of different perceptions, which succeed each other with an inconceivable rapidity, and are in a perpetual flux and movement. . . . The mind is a kind of theatre, where several perceptions successively make their appearance; pass, re-pass, glide away, and mingle in an infinite variety of postures and situations. There is properly no *simplicity* in it at one time, nor *identity* in different; whatever natural propension we may have to imagine that simplicity and identity. The comparison of the theatre must not mislead us. They are the successive perceptions only, that constitute the mind; nor have we the most distant notion of the place, where these scenes are represented, or of the materials, of which it is compos'd.[g]

IDENTITY

Questions about whether we have an idea of self are obviously tied up with questions about the concept of identity. I believe that the "I" who is now writing these words is the same I who, as a college student, heard lectures about Hume and was asked questions about his theories on a final examination in "History of Philosophy, 1b." What is meant by personal identity? Before we try to answer this question, we had better try to answer the simpler question (which is complicated enough) about the meaning of "identity" as applied to inanimate objects, to plants, and to animals.

A moment's consideration reveals that there is a paradox about identity. To say that two things are identical (for example, that the desk I see now is "identical with," or "the same as," the desk I saw last week) is to say that the two things (desk now, desk then) are the same and yet, because they are two, different. Identity is a relation involving at least a pair—but a pair are different, not identical.

> The view of any object is not sufficient to convey the idea of identity. For in that proposition, *an object is the same with itself*, if the idea express'd by the word, *object* were no ways distinguish'd from that meant by *itself*; we really shou'd mean nothing. . . . One single object conveys the idea of unity, not that of identity.
>
> On the other hand, a multiplicity of objects can never convey this idea, however resembling they may be suppos'd. The mind always pronounces the one not to be the other, and considers them as forming two, three, or any determinate number of objects, whose existences are entirely distinct and independent.[h]

The problem is to find a "medium" between unity and number (that is, between "same" and "different"), even though unity and number seem to be as mutually exclusive as existence and nonexistence.

> After one object is suppos'd to exist, we must either suppose another also to exist; in which case we have the idea of number [that is, difference]: Or we must suppose it not to exist; in which case the first object remains at unity [that is, we do not have a pair, so there is nothing for it to be identical with].
>
> To remove this difficulty, let us have recourse to the idea of time or duration. . . . Time . . . implies succession, and when we apply its idea to any unchangeable[13] object, 'tis only by a fiction of the imagination, by which the unchangeable object is suppos'd to participate of the changes of the co-existent objects. . . . This fiction of the imagination almost universally takes place; and 'tis by means of it, that a single object, plac'd before us, and survey'd for any time without our discovering in it any interruption or variation, is able to give us a notion of identity. . . . Here then is an idea, which is a medium betwixt unity and number.

13 [Hume meant "unchanging"—AUTHOR.]

Hume's analysis here is acute: First he points out that there is a logical paradox in judging that A is identical with B, since A, being A, is not B. Next he notes that, as a matter of psychological fact, people do make such judgments whenever they feel that there is only a temporal difference between A and B (A is earlier than B and differs from B only in being earlier). That is to say, in Hume's language, temporal difference provides the "medium" required between unity and number. Things that differ temporally, but *only* temporally, are felt to be different enough to be two, yet not too different to be called identical.

Hume's next question was whether there *are* any experiences that differ only temporally. At first sight this may seem a silly question; there are certainly a great many experiences that *seem* to differ only temporally. Thus, for instance, I say that the desk I am looking at now, at the end of one minute's observation, is "identical with" the desk I was looking at a minute ago, at the beginning of the period of observation. But are judgments of this kind warranted?

Now, there is no change, no succession, in the rectangular mahogany-colored datum in the center of my field of vision, but there is change and succession in the rest of the visual field and in the various somatic data—muscular relaxings and tensings, inhalings and exhalings of breath, and so forth—of which I am also aware. As long as I attend exclusively to the mahogany-colored datum, I get unchanging sameness (unity); as long as I attend to the somatic data, I get difference (number). In neither case do I get identity. If, however, I mix these two experiences together—if I transfer the succession that I experience in the somatic data to the continuing mahogany-colored datum; if I think of the mahogany-colored datum, which is really not a succession but a single unity, as if it were a succession, but a succession of "sames"—*then* I get the idea of identity.

In other words, when I say the present mahogany-colored datum is identical with the one a minute ago, I project into what is actually a continuous, unchanged datum (unity) a temporal difference obtained from my experience of a succession of somatic data (difference). Hence the supposedly "mere temporal difference" (datum then, datum now) is a fiction of my imagination. The mahogany-colored datum is not a succession; it is just "the same." The somatic data are a succession; they are "different." Because my mind "feigns" that the succession in the somatic data is in the mahogany-colored datum, I mistakenly conclude that I have experienced two temporally different but otherwise unchanged mahogany-colored data.

But, according to Hume, this is not yet the end of the muddle. Once we obtain the idea of identity through this kind of confusion, or mixture, of one datum's sameness with another datum's difference, we proceed to apply it, by a further exercise of imagination, to cases in which a datum is not even under continuous observation. Indeed, the usual situation in which we talk about identity is one in which we are not aware of the datum continuously. To say, for instance, that the mahogany-colored datum I see now is identical with the one I saw yesterday involves "feigning" or "imagining" (1) that the two data form the two ends, as it were, of a continuous experience and (2) that this unchanging, continuous experience is a succession.

Now, the first mahogany-colored datum differs, at least numerically, from the second. It is easy, having overlooked this difference, to overlook other differences and to "feign" that a second datum, which really only resembles the first, is identical with it. Thus, I saw "the desk" yesterday at noon; today I see it in late afternoon. Though the light is quite different at these hours, so that the mahogany-colored datum I now see only resembles the mahogany-colored datum I saw yesterday, I nevertheless identify them. The reason lies in still another natural tendency of the mind.

> Nothing is more apt to make us mistake one idea for another, than any relation betwixt them, which associates them together in the imagination, and makes it pass with facility from one to the other. Of all relations, that of resemblance is in this respect the most efficacious; and that because it not only causes an association of ideas, but also of dispositions, and makes us conceive the one idea by an act or operation of the mind, similar to that by which we conceive the other. . . . Whatever ideas place the mind in the same disposition or in similar ones, are very apt to be confounded.

This is just what happens in the case of the desk. My desk is so familiar, so much a part of my experience of this room, that instead of attending closely to the data before me, my mind takes them as the sign of the desk; at the same time, a familiar disposition is evoked in me—the disposition to sit down and get to work. Because the disposition evoked on separate occasions by different data is the same, and because the data are not examined on their own account but are taken as the sign of the desk, I assume that the data themselves are identical.

In this way, a "succession of different objects . . . connected together by a close relation" comes to be "confounded" with an unchanging object felt against a background of temporal change. If we were to attend closely to the former, we would see them for the different objects (or sense data) that they are, but we almost never give them the attention this would require.

> That action of the imagination, by which . . . we reflect on the succession of related objects, . . . facilitates the transition of the mind from one object to another, and renders its passage as smooth as if it contemplated one continu'd object. This resemblance is the cause of the confusion and mistake, and makes us substitute the notion of identity, instead of that of related objects. . . . Our propensity to this mistake is so great from the resemblance above-mention'd, that we fall into it before we are aware; and . . . boldly assert that these different related objects are in effect the same, however interrupted and variable. In order to justify to ourselves this absurdity, we often feign some new and unintelligible principle, that connects the objects together, and prevents their interruption or variation. Thus we feign the

continu'd existence of the perceptions of our senses, to remove the interruption; and run into the notion of a *soul,* and *self,* and *substance,* to disguise the variation. But we may farther observe, that where we do not give rise to such a fiction, our propension to confound identity with relation is so great, that we are apt to imagine something unknown and mysterious, connecting the parts, beside their relation; and this I take to be the case with regard to the identity we ascribe to plants and vegetables.[i]

All that is needed, Hume held, to confirm this account of the matter is careful attention to objects we commonly call identical. In every case, these objects prove to be "variable or interrupted" and to consist of a succession of related parts.

Hume gave a number of examples, or, as he called them, "experiments." These prepare the way for his attack on the idea of personal identity by analyzing other uses of the term "same"—uses that are simpler to deal with because the "self" is not involved.

Suppose any mass of matter, of which the parts are contiguous and connected, to be plac'd before us; 'tis plain we must attribute a perfect identity to this mass, provided all the parts continue uninterruptedly and invariably the same, whatever motion or change of place we may observe either in the whole or in any of the parts. But supposing some very *small* or *inconsiderable* part to be added to the mass, or subtracted from it; tho' this absolutely destroys the identity of the whole, strictly speaking; yet as we seldom think so accurately, we scruple not to pronounce a mass of matter the same, where we find so trivial an alteration. The passage of the thought from the object before the change to the object after it is so smooth and easy, that we scarce perceive the transition, and are apt to imagine, that 'tis nothing but a continu'd survey of the same object.

There is a very remarkable circumstance, that attends this experiment; which is, that tho' the change of any considerable part in a mass of matter destroys the identity of the whole, yet we must measure the greatness of the part, not absolutely, but by its *proportion* to the whole. The addition or diminution of a mountain wou'd not be sufficient to produce a diversity in a planet; tho' the change of a very few inches wou'd be able to destroy the identity of some bodies. 'Twill be impossible to account for this, but by reflecting that objects operate upon the mind, and break or interrupt the continuity of its actions not according to their real greatness, but according to their proportion to each other: And therefore, since this interruption makes an object cease to appear the same, it must be the uninterrupted progress of the thought, which constitutes the imperfect identity.

This may be confirm'd by another phaenomenon. A change in any considerable part of a body destroys its identity; but 'tis remarkable, that where the change is produc'd *gradually* and *insensibly* we are less apt to ascribe to it the same effect. The reason can plainly be no other, than that the mind, in following the successive changes of the body, feels an easy passage from the surveying its condition in one moment to the viewing of it in another and at no particular time perceives any interruption in its actions. From which continu'd perception, it ascribes a continu'd existence and identity to the object. . . .

There is . . . another artifice, by which we may induce the imagination to advance a step farther; and that is, by producing a reference of the parts to each other, and a combination to some *common end* or purpose. A ship, of which a considerable part has been chang'd by frequent reparations, is still consider'd as the same; nor does the difference of the materials hinder us from ascribing an identity to it. The common end, in which the parts conspire, is the same under all their variations, and affords an easy transition of the imagination from one situation of the body to another.

But this is still more remarkable, when we add a *sympathy* of parts to their *common end,* and suppose that they bear to each other, the reciprocal relation of cause and effect in all their actions and operations. This is the case with all animals and vegetables; where not only the several parts have a reference to some general purpose, but also a mutual dependance on, and connexion with each other. The effect of so strong a relation is, that tho' every one must allow, that in a very few years both vegetables and animals endure a *total* change, yet we still attribute identity to them, while their form, size, and substance are entirely alter'd. An oak, that grows from a small plant to a large tree, is still the same oak; tho' there be not one particle of matter, or figure of its parts the same. An infant becomes a man, and is sometimes fat, sometimes lean, without any change in his identity. . . .

We now proceed to explain the nature of *personal identity.* . . . Here 'tis evident, the same method of reasoning must be continu'd, which has so successfully explain'd the identity of plants, and animals, and ships, and houses, and of all the compounded and changeable productions either of art or nature. The identity, which we ascribe to the mind of man, is only a fictitious one, and of a like kind with that which we ascribe to vegetables and animal bodies. It cannot, therefore, have a different origin, but must proceed from a like operation of the imagination upon like objects.[j]

The idea of identity, therefore, does not refer to some particular impression of identity, as the idea of red refers to an impression of red. Identity is not a property of objects; it is a product of our minds. "Identity is nothing really belonging to these different perceptions, and uniting them together; but it is merely a quality, which we attribute to them because of the union of their ideas in the imagination, when we reflect upon them." Of course, there is *something* in the data that is the occasion of our uniting them. Data that are contiguous, data that resemble each other, data that are felt to be causally related, tend to be united (that is, associated). The imagination consequently passes easily from one such datum to its associated datum. Because it passes easily from one to the other, we tend to treat the two data as identical.

The whole of this doctrine leads us to a conclusion, which is of great importance in the present affair, *viz.* that all the nice and subtle questions concerning personal identity can never possibly be decided, and are to be regarded rather as grammatical than as philosophical difficulties. Identity depends on the relations of ideas; and these relations produce identity, by means of that easy transition they occasion. But as the relations, and the easiness of the transition may diminish by insensible degrees, we have no just standard, by which we can decide any dispute concerning the time, when they acquire or lose a title to the name of identity. All the disputes concerning the identity of connected objects are merely verbal, except so far as the relation of parts gives rise to some fiction or imaginary principle of union, as we have already observ'd.[k]

The External World

Hume did not deny, or even doubt, that there is a world outside man and his experience. He was merely concerned to show that neither he nor anyone else can produce any evidence to justify this belief: The arguments by which philosophers have sought to prove that an external world exists are all invalid. Hume's case against the philosophers consists merely in pressing home the consequences of the representative theory of perception. "The mind has never anything present to it but the perceptions, and cannot possibly reach any experience of their connexion with objects. The supposition of such a connexion . . . is, therefore, without any foundation in reasoning."[1]

Nothing more really needs to be said. But, because our belief in externality is so ingrained, Hume thought it desirable to examine this belief in detail, and especially to show why, though there is absolutely no evidence to support it, it is so persistent.

What is meant by an external world is "an existence distinct from the mind and perception." But there is, and can be, no *impression* of continued and distinct existence.

> That our senses offer not their impressions as the images of something *distinct*, or *independent*, and *external*, is evident; because they convey to us nothing but a single perception, and never give us the least intimation of any thing beyond. . . .
>
> It may perhaps be said, that . . . our own body evidently belongs to us; and as several impressions appear exterior to the body, we suppose them also exterior to ourselves. The paper, on which I write at present, is beyond my hand. The table is beyond the paper. The walls of the chamber beyond the table. And in casting my eye towards the window, I perceive a great extent of fields and buildings beyond my chamber. From all this it may be infer'd, that no other faculty is requir'd, beside the senses, to convince us of the external existence of body. But to prevent this inference, we need only weigh the three following considerations. *First,* That, properly speaking, 'tis not our body we perceive, when we regard our limbs and members, but certain impressions, which enter by the senses; so that the ascribing a real

and corporeal existence to these impressions, or to their objects, is an act of the mind as difficult to explain, as that which we examine at present. *Secondly,* Sounds, and tastes, and smells, tho' commonly regarded by the mind as continu'd independent qualities, appear not to have any existence in extension, and consequently cannot appear to the senses as situated externally to the body. . . . *Thirdly,* Even our sight informs us not of distance or outness (so to speak) immediately and without a certain reasoning and experience, as is acknowledg'd by the most rational philosophers.[m]

Hume supported this argument by additional considerations. It is clear that, "so far as the senses are the judges, all perceptions"—whether of pains and pleasures, of colors, tastes, and smells, or of figure, bulk, and motion—"are the same in the manner of their existence." But no one thinks that pleasures and pains have an independent and continued existence. Hence, if all our perceptions are "on the same footing," none of them has an independent and continued existence.

Consider, too, the following "experiments." I am now experiencing a mahogany-colored percept that I call my desk and that I believe to have a distinct existence independent of me and my perception. Now I press one eye with a finger; the desk becomes double. Do both these desks have independent existence? Obviously not. Well, then, which is independent and which dependent?

As we do not attribute a continu'd existence to both these perceptions, and as they are both of the same nature, we clearly perceive, and all our perceptions are dependent on our organs, and the disposition of our nerves and animal spirits. This opinion is confirm'd by the seeming encrease and diminution of objects, according to their distance; by the apparent alterations in their figure; by the changes in their colour and other qualities from our sickness and distempers; and by an infinite number of other experiments of the same kind; from all which we learn, that our sensible perceptions are not possest of any distinct or independent existence.[n]

BASIS FOR BELIEF IN EXTERNAL WORLD

In a word, the senses can "give us no notion of continued existence, because they cannot operate beyond the extent in which they really operate." Why then, Hume asked, does everyone, himself included, believe that an external world exists? The answer lies in the faculty of the imagination that we have already seen at work in the notion of identity. It works in much the same way to produce the notion of externality. Identity is, in fact, one of the properties that we attribute to so-called external objects. Thus, when I "feign" that today's percept of the desk is identical with yesterday's, I am assuming that the desk has had a continuous existence from yesterday to today. Since I assume continuity, though I know that I have not been continuously perceiving the desk, it follows that I also assume independence.

It remains to ask what characteristics of experience facilitate this easy passage of the imagination from one datum to another—a passage made so easily that we fail to observe that a passage is occurring. According to Hume, the characteristics in question are (1) constancy and (2) coherence.

(1) Whenever a series of regularly repeated percepts occurs, the mind has a tendency to pass from one percept to another without noticing the intervals between them. I observed a mahogany-colored percept yesterday; I observe one today. My mind proceeds to feign that the interval between yesterday's percept and today's is filled by unobserved mahogany-colored percepts exactly like those I actually observe. But since I know that I have not observed these data, I proceed, by a *further* fiction, to assume that these unobserved data exist independently of me: Having once started on this adventure of the imagination, my mind invents more and more elaborate fictions in an attempt to justify the first one.

(2) So far imagination has yielded only a continuous and independent *datum*, not a continuous and independent *object,* that is, a desk. This is where *coherence* comes in. When I look at what I call the top of the desk, I do not see the legs; when I look at the front, I do not see the back. What I always see is some particular datum. How do I come to put these together into the object that I call my desk? Hume's answer was that in my experience, these various data fall into certain patterns. If, after I see the datum I call "top of desk," I stoop over (which means experiencing a series of somatic data in legs and back), I then see the datum that I call "underside of desk." If I walk around the desk (which means experiencing further somatic data, plus various visual data of walls, floor, and so forth), I then see the datum that I call "back of desk." If I return, I see once again "front of desk," and so on. There is thus a kind of coherence, or pattern, among the data I experience. And this pattern facilitates the passage of the imagination in the same way that constant repetition of a datum does. In both cases, intervals occur between actual experiences; in both cases, the imagination bridges the intervals, or rather, *fills* the intervals with unobserved data. It supposes that "the irregular appearances [the differently shaped data of front and back, in this case] are joined by something of which we are insensible." [14]

TENSION BETWEEN REASON AND NATURE

If Hume's analysis is correct, there are no grounds for our belief in the existence of material objects and an external world. Or rather, the grounds are not logical; they are psychological. They lie in an empirically verifiable property of our imagination, namely, its tendency to bridge, or fill, any intervals between

---

14 This example of how the imagination constructs an object (for example, a desk) out of sense data by filling the intervals between them is, of course, greatly oversimplified. For an excellent expansion of Hume's abbreviated account, see Price, *Hume's Theory of the External World*, Chapter 3.

constant and coherent data. This is just a "natural propensity" of our minds, lacking a rationale of any kind. In strict logic, men ought, therefore, to abandon their belief in externality, continuity, and independence. But this natural propensity is stronger than logic and reasserts itself as often as we try to put our belief aside. The result is a tension between our natural, "instinctual" beliefs and reason.

There is a great difference betwixt such opinions as we form after a calm and profound reflection, and such as we embrace by a kind of instinct or natural impulse, on account of their suitableness and conformity to the mind. If these opinions become contrary, 'tis not difficult to foresee which of them will have the advantage. As long as our attention is bent upon the subject, the philosophical and study'd principle may prevail; but the moment we relax our thoughts, nature will display herself, and draw us back to our former opinion. . . .

But tho' our natural and obvious principles here prevail about our study'd reflections, 'tis certain there must be some struggle and opposition in the case; at least so long as these reflections retain any force or vivacity. In order to set ourselves at ease in this particular, we contrive a new hypothesis, which seems to comprehend both these principles of reason and imagination. This hypothesis is the philosophical one of the double existence of perceptions and objects; which pleases our reason, in allowing, that our dependent perceptions are interrupted and different; and at the same time is agreeable to the imagination, in attributing a continu'd existence to something else, which we call *objects*. This philosophical system, therefore, is the monstrous offspring of two principles, which are contrary to each other, which are both at once embrac'd by the mind, and which are unable mutually to destroy each other. The imagination tells us, that our resembling perceptions have a continu'd and uninterrupted existence, and are not annihilated by their absence. Reflection tells us, that even our resembling perceptions are interrupted in their existence, and different from each other. The contradiction betwixt these opinions we elude by a new fiction, which is conformable to the hypotheses both of reflection and fancy, by ascribing these contrary qualities to different existences; the *interruption* to perceptions, and the *continuance* to objects. Nature is obstinate, and will quit the field, however strongly attack'd by reason; and at the same time reason is so clear in the point, that there is no possibility of disguising her. Not being able to reconcile these two enemies, we endeavour to set outselves at ease as much as possible, by . . . feigning a double existence, where each may find something that has all the conditions it desires.

'Tis impossible upon any system to defend either our understanding or senses; and we but expose them farther when we endeavour to justify them in that manner. As the sceptical doubt arises naturally from a profound and intense reflection on those subjects, it always encreases, the farther we carry our reflections, whether in opposition or conformity to it. Carelessness and in-attention alone can afford us any remedy. For this reason I rely entirely upon them; and take it for granted, whatever may be the reader's opinion at this present moment, that an hour hence he will be persuaded there is both an external and internal world.°

Causality and Inductive Inference

The empirical sciences constantly argue from "some" to "all," or at least to "probably all." If every piece of ice we have heated has become liquid, we inductively infer that on all future occasions, pieces of ice will become liquid when they are heated. If we find that something that we thought was ice does not melt when heated, we are likely to say, "Well, what do you know! Though that looks like ice, it must be plastic or glass." That is, despite occasional mistaken predictions, we continue to believe in the uniformity of nature. This belief underlies all the empirical sciences, including physics. A physical law is the formulation of some uniformity, derived by an inference from "some" to "all." Galileo did not compute velocities for *all* bodies that roll down inclined planes; he could not have done so, for bodies have continued to roll until this day. He measured the velocity of some (relatively very few) bodies and concluded (that is, inferred) that what was true of those bodies is true of all bodies "under similar circumstances." What justifies this inference? What are the logical grounds for men's belief in the uniformity of nature?

NO NECESSARY CONNECTION

Before Hume, the usual answer to this question was in terms of "causal necessity": Everyone agreed that every event that occurs has some cause that necessarily produces it. The new scientific method rested on this belief, and the success of the method seemed to substantiate the belief. Accordingly, Hume set himself to examine the notion that a necessary connection can exist between two events, a connection such that if one of the events occurs, the other must inevitably also occur.

> There are no ideas, which occur in metaphysics, more obscure and uncertain, than those of *power, force, energy* or *necessary connexion,* of which it is every moment necessary for us to treat in all our disquisitions. We shall, therefore, endeavour, in this section, to fix, if possible, the precise meaning of these terms, and thereby remove some part of that obscurity, which is so much complained of in this species of philosophy.
>
> It seems a proposition, which will not admit of much dispute, that all our ideas are nothing but copies of our impressions, or, in other words, that it is impossible for us to *think* of any thing, which we have not antecedently *felt,* either by our external or internal senses.

To be fully acquainted, therefore, with the idea of power or necessary connexion, let us examine its impression; and in order to find the impression with greater certainty, let us search for it in all the sources, from which it may possibly be derived.

When we look about us towards external objects, and consider the operation of causes, we are never able, in a single instance, to discover any power or necessary connexion; any quality, which binds the effect to the cause, and renders the one an infallible consequence of the other. We only find, that the one does actually, in fact, follow the other. . . . There is not, in any single, particular instance of cause and effect, any thing which can suggest the idea of power or necessary connexion.

From the first appearance of an object, we never can conjecture what effect will result from it. But were the power or energy of any cause discoverable by the mind, we could foresee the effect, even without experience; and might, at first, pronounce with certainty concerning it, by mere dint of thought and reasoning.

In reality, there is no part of matter, that does ever, by its sensible qualities, discover any power or energy, or give us ground to imagine, that it could produce any thing, or be followed by any other object, which we could denominate its effect. Solidity, extension, motion; these qualities are all complete in themselves, and never point out any other event which may result from them. The scenes of the universe are continually shifting, and one object follows another in an uninterrupted succession; but the power or force, which actuates the whole machine, is entirely concealed from us, and never discovers itself in any of the sensible qualities of body. We know, that, in fact, heat is a constant attendant of flame; but what is the connexion between them, we have no room so much as to conjecture or imagine. It is impossible, therefore, that the idea of power can be derived from the contemplation of bodies, in single instances of their operation; because no bodies ever discover any power, which can be the original of this idea.

Since, therefore, external objects as they appear to the senses, give us no idea of power or necessary connexion, by their operation in particular instances, let us see, whether this idea be derived from reflection on the operations of our own minds, and be copied from any internal impression. It may be said, that we are every moment conscious of internal power; while we feel, that, by the simple command of our will, we can move the organs of our body, or direct the faculties of our mind. . . .

We shall proceed to examine this pretension; and first with regard to the influence of volition over the organs of the body. This influence, we may observe, is a fact, which, like all other natural events, can be known only by experience, and can never be foreseen from any apparent energy or power in the cause, which connects it with the effect, and renders the one an infallible consequence of the other. The motion of our body follows upon the command of our will. Of this we are every moment conscious. But the means, by which this is effected; the energy, by which the will performs so extraordinary an operation; of this we are so far from being immediately conscious, that it must for ever escape our most diligent enquiry.

For *first;* is there any principle in all nature more mysterious than the union of soul with body; by which a supposed spiritual substance acquires such an influence over a material one, that the most refined thought is able to actuate the grossest matter? . . .

Secondly, We are not able to move all the organs of the body with a like authority; though we cannot assign any reason besides experience, for so remarkable a difference between one and the other. Why has the will an influence over the tongue and fingers, not over the heart or liver? This question would never embarrass us, were we conscious of a power in the former case, not in the latter. We should then perceive, independent of experience, why the authority of will over the organs of the body is circumscribed within such particular limits. Being in that case fully acquainted with the power or force, by which it operates, we should also know, why its influence reaches precisely to such boundaries, and no farther. . . .

Thirdly, We learn from anatomy, that the immediate object of power in voluntary motion, is not the member itself which is moved, but certain muscles, and nerves, and animal spirits, and, perhaps, something still more minute and more unknown, through which the motion is successfully propagated, ere it reach the member itself whose motion is the immediate object of volition. Can there be a more certain proof, that the power, by which this whole operation is performed, so far from being directly and fully known by an inward sentiment or consciousness, is to the last degree mysterious and unintelligible? Here the mind wills a certain event: Immediately another event, unknown to ourselves, and totally different from the one intended, is produced: This event produces another, equally unknown: Till at last, through a long succession, the desired event is produced. . . . How indeed can we be conscious of a power to move our limbs, when we have no such power; but only that to move certain animal spirits, which, though they produce at last the motion of our limbs, yet operate in such a manner as is wholly beyond our comprehension?

We may, therefore, conclude . . . that our idea of power is not copied from any sentiment or consciousness of power within ourselves, when we give rise to animal motion, or apply our limbs, to their proper use and office. That their motion follows the command of the will is a matter of common experience, like other natural events: But the power or energy by which this is effected, like that in other natural events, is unknown and inconceivable.

Shall we then assert, that we are conscious of a power or energy in our own minds, when, by an act or command of our will, we raise up a new idea, fix the mind to the contemplation of it, turn it on all sides, and at last dismiss it for some other idea, when we think that we have surveyed it with sufficient accuracy? I believe the same arguments will prove, that even this command of the will gives us no real idea of force or energy.

First, It must be allowed, that, when we know a power, we know that very circumstance in the cause, by which it is enabled to produce the effect: For these are supposed to be synonimous. We must, therefore, know both the cause and effect, and the relation between them. But do we pretend to be acquainted with the nature of the human soul and the nature of an idea, or the aptitude of the one to produce the other? . . . We only feel the event, namely, the existence of an idea, consequent to a command of the will: But the manner, in which this operation is performed, the power by which it is produced, is entirely beyond our comprehension.

Secondly, The command of the mind over itself is limited, as well as its command over the body; and these limits are not known by reason, or any acquaintance with the nature of cause and effect, but only by experience and observation, as in all other natural events and in the operation of external objects. Our authority over our sentiments and passions is much weaker than that over our ideas; and even the latter authority is circumscribed within very narrow boundaries. Will any one pretend to assign the ultimate reason of these boundaries, or show why the power is deficient in one case, not in another.

Thirdly, This self-command is very different at different times. A man in health possesses more of it than one languishing with sickness. We are more master of our thoughts in the morning than in the evening: Fasting, than after a full meal. Can we give any reason for these variations, except experience? Where then is the power, of which we pretend to be conscious? . . .

But to hasten to a conclusion of this argument, which is already drawn out to too great a length: We have sought in vain for an idea of power or necessary connexion in all the sources from which we could suppose it to be derived. It appears that, in single instances of the operation of bodies, we never can, by our utmost scrutiny, discover any thing but one event following another, without being able to comprehend any force or power by which the cause operates, or any connexion between it and its supposed effect. The same difficulty occurs in contemplating the operations of mind on body—where we observe the motion of the latter to follow upon the volition of the former, but are not able to observe or conceive the tie which binds together the motion and volition, or the energy by which the mind produces this effect. The authority of the will over its own faculties and ideas is not a whit more comprehensible: So that, upon the whole, there appears not, throughout all nature, any one instance of connexion which is conceivable by us. All events seem entirely loose and separate. One event follows another; but we never can observe any tie between them. They seem *conjoined,* but never *connected.* And as we can have no idea of any thing which never appeared to our outward sense or inward sentiment, the necessary conclusion *seems* to be that we have no idea of connexion or power at all, and that these words are absolutely without any meaning, when employed either in philosophical reasonings or common life.[p]

Hume's conclusion, granting his premises, is inevitable. If every impression is a distinct item in our experience ("entirely loose and separate"), there can be no necessary connection between two ideas derived from two impressions, however closely juxtaposed ("conjoined") the original impressions may have been. That is all there is to it. The long analysis was necessary, not to prove Hume's case, but to convince his readers.

Hume realized, however, that the phrase "necessary connection" cannot be completely meaningless; if some idea, however vague and confused, were not named by these words, rationalist philosophers would willingly abandon the phrase. Accordingly, Hume set out to find the origin in experience of this confused idea. Now, many sequences occur in our experience that we do *not* think of as being necessary. For instance, immediately after writing the word "necessary" in the last sentence, I heard a car backfiring on the street outside. It did not occur to me that my writing "necessary" caused the car to backfire. But suppose that whenever I wrote "necessary," a car backfired in the street outside. After a time I would begin to listen for the backfire whenever I wrote the word. I have such a feeling of expectation whenever a sequence is frequently repeated, and this, according to Hume, is what I mistake for necessary connection.

Thus, the whole experiential origin of the supposedly profound idea that there is a necessary connection between cause and effect amounts to no more than (1) a repeated sequence of impressions and (2) the expectation that on its next occurrence, the first impression of the sequence will again be followed by the second. There is no *reason* in the nature of things why any event should not be followed by any other event whatever. It just happens that some events follow other events consistently and that, when they have done so often enough, we expect them to continue to do so. This is all there is to causality. Like our idea of identity, our idea of necessary connection is derived from something in us, not in the object; like the idea of identity, it is grounded in the human imagination, not in the rationality of the universe. There is no more a reason why the sun should rise tomorrow than there is a reason why writing "necessary" should cause cars to backfire. There is, of course, a reason why I *feel* differently about these two sequences, but this is merely a psychological fact about human nature.

> It appears, then, that this idea of a necessary connexion among events arises from a number of similar instances which occur of the constant conjunction of these events. . . . But there is nothing in a number of instances, different from every single instance, which is supposed to be exactly similar; except only, that after a repetition of similar instances, the mind is carried by habit, upon the appearance of one event, to expect its usual attendant, and to believe that it will exist. This connexion, therefore, which we *feel* in the mind, this customary transition of the imagination from one object to its usual attendant, is the sentiment or impression from which we form the idea of power or necessary connexion. Nothing farther is in the case. Contemplate the subject on all sides; you will never find any other origin of that idea. This is the sole difference between one instance, from which we can never receive the idea of connexion, and a number of similar instances, by which it is suggested. The first time a man saw the communication of motion by impulse, as by the shock of two billiard balls, he could not pronounce that the one event was *connected:* but only that it was *conjoined* with the other. After he has observed several instances of this nature, he then pronounces them to be *connected.* What alteration has happened to give rise to this new idea of *connexion?* Nothing but that he now *feels* these events to be *connected* in his imagination, and can readily foretell the existence of one from the

appearance of the other. When we say, therefore, that one object is connected with another, we mean only that they have acquired a connexion in our thought.q

SCIENCE LIMITED TO EMPIRICAL GENERALIZATION

It follows that the pretensions of the natural sciences to demonstrative certainty are utterly without basis.

> Past *Experience* . . . can be allowed to give *direct* and *certain* information of those precise objects only, and that precise period of time, which fell under its cognizance: but why this experience should be extended to future times, and to other objects, which for aught we know, may be only in appearance similar; this is the main question on which I would insist. The bread, which I formerly eat, nourished me; . . . but does it follow, that other bread must also nourish me at another time . . . ? The consequence seems nowise necessary. At least, it must be acknowledged that there is here a consequence drawn by the mind; that there is a certain step taken; a process of thought, and an inference, which wants to be explained. These two propositions are far from being the same, *I have found that such an object has always been attended with such an effect,* and *I foresee, that other objects, which are, in appearance, similar, will be attended with similar effects.* I shall allow, if you please, that the one proposition may justly be inferred from the other: I know, in fact, that it always is inferred. But if you insist that the inference is made by a chain of reasoning, I desire you to produce that reasoning. The connexion between these propositions is not intuitive. There is required a medium, which may enable the mind to draw such an inference, if indeed it be drawn by reasoning and argument. What that medium is, I must confess, passes my comprehension; and it is incumbent on those to produce it, who assert that it really exists, and is the origin of all our conclusions concerning matter of fact.
>
> This negative argument must certainly, in process of time, become altogether convincing, if many penetrating and able philosophers shall turn their enquiries this way and no one be ever able to discover any connecting proposition or intermediate step, which supports the understanding in this conclusion. But as the question is yet new, every reader may not trust so far to his own penetration, as to conclude, because an argument escapes his enquiry, that therefore it does not really exist. For this reason it may be requisite to venture upon a more difficult task; and enumerating all the branches of human knowledge, endeavour to show that none of them can afford such an argument.
>
> All reasonings may be divided into two kinds, namely, demonstrative reasoning, or that concerning relations of ideas, and . . . that concerning matter of fact and existence. That there are no demonstrative arguments in the case seems evident; since it implies no contradiction that the course of nature may change, and that an object, seemingly like those which we have experienced, may be attended with different or contrary effects. May I not clearly and distinctly conceive that a body, falling from the clouds,

and which, in all other respects, resembles snow, has yet the taste of salt or feeling of fire? Is there any more intelligible proposition than to affirm, that all the trees will flourish in December and January, and decay in May and June? Now whatever is intelligible, and can be distinctly conceived, implies no contradiction, and can never be proved false by any demonstrative argument or abstract reasoning *a priori.*

If we be, therefore, engaged by arguments to put trust in past experience, and make it the standard of our future judgment, these arguments must be probable only, or such as regard matter of fact and real existence, according to the division above mentioned. But that there is no argument of this kind, must appear, if our explication of that species of reasoning be admitted as solid and satisfactory. We have said that all arguments concerning existence are founded on the relation of cause and effect; that our knowledge of that relation is derived entirely from experience; and that all our experimental conclusions proceed upon the supposition that the future will be conformable to the past. To endeavour, therefore, the proof of this last supposition by probable arguments, or arguments regarding existence, must be evidently going in a circle, and taking that for granted, which is the very point in question.[r]

If Hume was correct, the sciences are limited to historical statements. They can only report past observations. They can say no more than that such-and-such an event x has been followed by such-and-such another event y. It is important to see that it is not merely a matter of not being certain that x will be followed by y in the future. It is much worse than this. No matter how often x has been followed by y in the past, we have no rational basis for thinking even that it will *probably* be followed by y in the future. Nothing is more probable than anything else. When every datum is "loose and separate," every occurrence is a brand-new event.[15] We start from scratch every moment. Inductive inference is not a way of reaching rationally justified conclusions; it is a leap in the dark.

Of course, we must make the leap. We cannot, practically, limit ourselves to historical statements. We have to act as if we knew past experience to be relevant to future situations. But, according to Hume, we must not fool ourselves about what we are doing. We must not mistake practical necessity for logical rationale. We jump because we have to jump. If we land on the other side, well and good. If we don't, we crash. But these leaps that we call inferences are justified, not by evidence, but by success.

The net result of Hume's analysis is this: All our knowledge of what, popularly speaking, is called "objects" (Berkeley's "Choir of Heaven and furniture of earth")

15 This can be illustrated from the "laws of probability." We think that the chances are 1/2 that a coin tossed into the air will fall heads. What are the chances that it will fall heads if tossed a second time? Still 1/2. Every toss is a separate occurrence to be calculated in isolation from other tosses. But, of course, in Hume's view there is not just an equal chance, each time, of heads and of tails; there is an equal chance of anything and everything. The penny might just as well stand on edge or burst out singing "The Star-Spangled Banner" as fall heads or tails. Hence the probability of its falling heads is not 1/2, but 1/infinity.

is merely knowledge of spatiotemporal relations among simple ideas or impressions (plus an act of the imagination). The same is true of our alleged knowledge of the self: It amounts to no more than a knowledge of the temporal relations among psychic states. This kind of knowledge Hume called "knowledge of matters of fact." We can only know that, as a matter of fact, such-and-such a datum is followed by such-and-such another datum, is above it, or is below it. We can never know that it *must* be so, for every fact could always be otherwise. Its "contrary . . . is still possible; because it can never imply a contradiction. . . . *That the sun will not rise tomorrow* is no less intelligible a proposition, and implies no more contradiction than the affirmation, *that it will rise.* We should in vain, therefore, attempt to demonstrate its falsehood." s

With knowledge of matters of fact Hume contrasted "knowledge of the relations of ideas."[16] Relations of ideas are knowable by logical reasoning, but they give us no information about what exists or about how the things that exist behave.

> Of [this] kind are the sciences of Geometry, Algebra, and Arithmetic; and in short, every affirmation which is either intuitively or demonstratively certain. *That the square of the hypotenuse is equal to the squares of the two sides,* is a proposition which expresses a relation between these figures. *That three times five is equal to the half of thirty,* expresses a relation between these numbers. Propositions of this kind are discoverable by the mere operation of thought, without dependence on what is anywhere existent in the universe. Though there never were a circle or triangle in nature, the truths demonstrated by Euclid would for ever retain their certainty and evidence.t

It will be seen that Hume agreed with the rationalists that there are absolutely certain, demonstrable truths. He differed with them—and this was an enormous difference—in holding that these truths are empty, devoid of information about matters of fact and existence.

Mathematics

Hume's account of demonstrable knowledge has brought us to mathematics. Unfortunately, his discussion at this point was complicated by the fact that, in the *Treatise* at any rate, he tried to distinguish between geometry on the one hand and arithmetic and algebra on the other. He thought that the latter two sciences concern proportion in number and that, since "we are possest of a precise standard, by which we can judge of the equality and proportion of

16 See p. 302.

numbers . . . ,we [can] determine their relations, without any possibility of error." This seemed to him to make arithmetic and algebra vastly superior to geometry. "When two numbers are so combin'd as that the one has always an unite answering to every unite of the other, we pronounce them equal; and 'tis for want of such a standard of equality in extension, that geometry can scarce be esteem'd a perfect and infallible science." [u]

What he had in mind is the following kind of difference. Suppose we are asked whether it is possible to draw two straight lines that have a common segment. At first the answer may seem obvious. When, for instance, we draw

"our ideas seem to give us a perfect assurance that no two straight lines can have a common segment." But if we consider the matter a little more closely, doubts creep in: "Where two [straight] lines incline upon each other with a sensible angle [as in the above figure], 'tis absurd to imagine them to have a common segment. But supposing these two lines to approach at the rate of an inch in twenty leagues, I perceive no absurdity in asserting, that upon their contact they become one." In a word, we know from experience that nature is "susceptible of prodigious minuteness"; and when the angle formed by *AB* and *CD* is very small, "we have no standard of a [straight] line so precise, as to assure us of the truth of this proposition." Hence, though "geometry . . . much excels . . . the loose judgments of the senses and imagination; yet [it] never attains a perfect precision and exactness." [v]

Suppose, on the other hand, that we have two piles of stones. Each of the stones in each pile is a separate entity, a unit. We can count, for each pile, "one," "two," "three," as we pick up each stone. If we end with the same number when we have finished picking up all the stones in both piles, we can be sure that the number of stones in the two piles was equal.

But these considerations do not support Hume's thesis. It may well be more difficult to measure angles accurately than it is to count stones correctly. If so, the application of geometry to concrete empirical situations (for example, surveying a field) is less certain than the application of arithmetic to concrete empirical situations (counting the stones in a pile). But Hume failed to distinguish pure mathematics from what he described in one place as "mixed" mathematics. The proposition, "*If* this is a triangle, its interior angles equal 180°," is just as true as the proposition, "*If* this pile contains five stones and that pile three stones, the two piles together contain eight stones." If it is harder to ascertain that this figure is a triangle than it is to ascertain that this pile contains five stones, it follows that there is a difference in certainty between mixed geometry and mixed arithmetic. But it does not follow that there is a difference in certainty between pure geometry and pure arithmetic.

In the *Enquiry* (where Hume seems to have held that geometry as well as arithmetic yields certain knowledge), he tried to distinguish between (1) knowledge of a relation between two distinct ideas (causality is such a relation), which can never be certain or demonstrative, and (2) knowledge that depends on the analysis of an individual idea. Anything found to be true about some such idea would continue to be true as long as the idea did not change: "It is from the idea of a triangle that we discover the relation of equality which its three angles bear to two right ones; and this relation is invariable as long as our idea remains the same."

But Hume forgot that, in his own view, what is before the mind is always either a simple idea (image) or a complex one. If it is complex, its parts are simple ideas, between which, according to his doctrine, no necessary relations hold. On the other hand, if it is a really simple idea with no parts, the question of necessary relations does not enter, since there are no relations at all. Actually, of course, the idea of a triangle is complex. It is possible to compute the angles of the particular triangle now before my mind and to ascertain that they equal 180°; it is also possible to compute the size of two right angles and to discover that they equal 180° (just as it is possible to count stones in piles). But this shows only that the angles of *this* triangle equal two right angles, and as soon as my view of the triangle is interrupted, I have to measure again, since, for all I know, it may have changed in the interval.

At this point perhaps someone will reply that the theorem under discussion is not about the particular image before my mind now; it is about the universal triangle. But, according to Hume, there is no more to the universal triangle than the term "triangle" plus various images of triangles. From his viewpoint, we can say, if we like, that the theorem is true of the term and of all the images that satisfy the term, but how do we know whether any particular image is the image of a triangle? We must measure, and quite apart from possible mistakes in measurement,[17] it is impossible to measure all the images that claim to be triangles. Thus the logical conclusion from Hume's premises is that certainty is limited to the term. Mathematical knowledge is "universal and exact" only because, as Hobbes maintained, it is about the agreement and disagreement of names. The certain and demonstrable knowledge that is to be contrasted with mere knowledge of "matters of fact" is not an analysis of a sensible idea (that is, an image) into its constituent parts, but an analysis of the definitions of terms. The contrast is between (1) knowledge of the spatiotemporal relations between sense data and (2) knowledge of the agreement and disagreement of names. The former is "instructive" (that is, informative) but always particular; the latter is universal but tells us nothing about matters of fact and existence.

---

17 That is, mistakes like those that might be made in surveying a field.

Unfortunately, Hume's account is marred by confusions—of which the following is an example.

> The great advantage of the mathematical sciences above the moral consists in this, that the ideas of the former, being sensible, are always clear and determinate, the smallest distinction between them is immediately perceptible, and the same terms are still expressive of the same ideas, without ambiguity or variation. An oval is never mistaken for a circle, nor an hyperbola for an ellipsis. The isosceles and scalenum are distinguished by boundaries more exact than vice and virtue, right and wrong. If any term be defined in geometry, the mind readily, of itself, substitutes, on all occasions, the definition for the term defined: Or even when no definition is employed, the object itself may be presented to the senses, and by that means be steadily and clearly apprehended.ʷ

It is evident that part of the time Hume was talking about sensible images and part of the time, about terms. Now, if what is being judged about is a sensible image, it is easy to distinguish a circle from *some* ellipses. But it is also possible to draw an ellipse whose foci are very close together and whose shape therefore is very nearly circular—so nearly circular that the distinction between the ellipse and a circle, far from being immediately perceptible, could not be detected by any but the most painstaking measurements. This, of course, was the doctrine of the *Treatise*. Nature is "susceptible of prodigious minuteness," and "where the differences are small . . . it is impossible to judge exactly." Hence it is only possible to be certain about the sensible image *now* before us; indeed, it may be impossible even to be certain about *it*.

But in the same passage Hume added that "if the term be defined . . . the mind substitutes the definition . . . for the term."[18] Under these circumstances, it is immaterial that some sensible figure cannot be determined to be a circle or an ellipse, for now the theorem is not about images at all, but about a definition. It thus becomes an empirical question in "mixed" mathematics whether such-and-such actual figures are instances of the definition. But now, having got clear, or so one might suppose, about the basis for mathematical certainty, Hume reverted to the imagistic view, unaware that he had done so: "Even when no definition is employed, the object itself may be steadily and clearly apprehended."

To summarize (and to oversimplify a complicated piece of Humian interpretation), it may be said that given his premises, Hume was correct in holding that if geometry is "instructive," it is not certain, and that if it is certain, it is "not instructive." Though he wavered between saying that it is instructive and saying that it is certain, he was quite clear that it could not be *both*. Hence he was fundamentally antagonistic to claims of rationalist philosophers that a priori insights into the nature of reality can be derived from mathematics.

18 He ought to have said "for the image."

'Tis usual with mathematicians, to pretend, that those ideas, which are their objects, are of so refin'd and spiritual a nature, that they . . . must be comprehended by a pure and intellectual view, of which the superior faculties of the soul are alone capable. The same notion runs thro' most parts of philosophy. . . . 'Tis easy to see, why philosophers are so fond of this notion of some spiritual and refin'd perceptions; since by that means they cover many of their absurdities, and may refuse to submit to the decisions of clear ideas, by appealing to such as are obscure and uncertain. But to destroy this artifice, we need but reflect on that principle so oft insisted on, *that all our ideas are copy'd from our impressions.* For from thence we may immediately conclude, that since all impressions are clear and precise, the ideas, which are copy'd from them, must be of the same nature, and can never, but from our fault, contain any thing so dark and intricate. An idea is by its very nature weaker and fainter than an impression; but being in every other respect the same, cannot imply any very great mystery. If its weakness render it obscure, 'tis our business to remedy that defect, as much as possible, by keeping the idea steady and precise; and till we have done so, 'tis in vain to pretend to reasoning and philosophy.[x]

God

Logically, there are two questions that any philosophy of religion must consider at the outset: Can the existence of God be proved? Can anything be known about His nature? If the answers to these questions are negative, the whole of the traditional theology—which has been concerned with such questions as the nature of man's duties to God—must be thrown out.

ONTOLOGICAL AND CAUSAL PROOFS

As regards the classic proofs of the existence of God, it is obvious that Hume would reject all versions of the ontological proof, for in his view all demonstrative knowledge is knowledge of the consequences of names. Again, for obvious reasons, he rejected all forms of the causal proof, whether the Cartesian or the Berkeleian. Such dicta as Descartes' "Every cause must have at least as much reality as its effect" were, for Hume, meaningless noises. Try to locate in experience any impressions that correspond to "must" and "reality" in this sentence. You will never find anything except regular sequences of data. But, more generally, if causality has turned out to be no more than the regular occurrence of phenomena plus subjective expectation on our part, it makes no sense to talk about a divine first cause. If belief in a real connection among these concrete data of experience is unjustified, metaphysicians are even less justified in affirming a "secret cause" outside, or beyond, the data. "Our ideas reach no farther than our experience. We have no experience of divine attributes and operations: I need not conclude my syllogism. You can draw the inference yourself."[y]

THE "ARGUMENT FROM DESIGN"

In addition to the traditional metaphysical proofs, there is, however, another, and a very old, argument for God's existence. Look around you, this argument runs. Observe the wonderful order and symmetry in every part of nature. Is it an accident that there is food for us to eat, air for us to breathe, water to drink and to wash in? Do not all these things bespeak a beneficent creator, looking out for man's interests? This "argument from design," as it is called, has always made a strong appeal to the feelings. It was used by Augustine; it colors Berkeley's version of the causal argument;[19] it was very popular among Hume's contemporaries; and it has survived to our own day, at least in popular writings.

Before attacking this argument, Hume stated it very fairly:

> Look around the world: contemplate the whole and every part of it: You will find it to be nothing but one great machine, subdivided into an infinite number of lesser machines. . . . All these various machines, and even their most minute parts, are adjusted to each other with an accuracy, which ravishes into admiration all men, who have ever contemplated them. The curious adapting of means to ends, throughout all nature, resembles exactly, though it much exceeds, the productions of human contrivance; of human design, thought, wisdom, and intelligence. Since therefore the effects resemble each other, we are led to infer, by all the rules of analogy, that the causes also resemble; and that the Author of nature is somewhat similar to the mind of man; though possessed of much larger faculties, proportioned to the grandeur of the work, which he has executed. . . . Whence arise the many conveniences and advantages which men and all animals possess? . . . Any one of them is a sufficient proof of design, and of a benevolent design, which gave rise to the order and arrangement of the universe.[z]

In both the *Enquiry* and the *Dialogues*, Hume subjected this line of reasoning to merciless criticism. Since his arguments are complex, it may be helpful to put down the four main points before considering them in detail: (1) If causality means regularity of sequence, it can, at best, refer only to *classes* of events; it is not possible, therefore, to talk about the cause of a singular event, as is the case when we talk about the cause of the universe as a whole. (2) The proof from design is admittedly an argument from analogy, and this type of argument is always very weak. If one argues from analogy at all, it is more plausible to conclude that the world is produced by some sort of vegetative process than that it proceeds in accordance with a rational plan. (3) Allowing that some parts of the universe (for example, animal organisms, including our bodies) have a means-end structure, it does not follow that this structure was designed. (4) Even allowing that it is legitimate to infer something like an intelligence as the author of nature, there is absolutely no evidence that this intelligence has moral characteristics.

19 See pp. 290–91.

THE ARGUMENT OF THE *ENQUIRY*

Let us now examine the argument of the *Enquiry*, which, it may be noted, Hume was careful to cast in the form of a conversation so that he could put the attack in the mouth of "a friend who loves sceptical paradoxes of which I can by no means approve."

When we infer any particular cause from an effect, we must proportion the one to the other, and can never be allowed to ascribe to the cause any qualities, but what are exactly sufficient to produce the effect. A body of ten ounces raised in any scale may serve as a proof, that the counterbalancing weight exceeds ten ounces; but can never afford a reason that it exceeds a hundred. If the cause, assigned for any effect, be not sufficient to produce it, we must either reject that cause, or add to it such qualities as will give it a just proportion to the effect. But if we ascribe to it further qualities, or affirm it capable of producing other effects, we can only indulge the license of conjecture, and arbitrarily suppose the existence of qualities and energies, without reason or authority.

The same rule holds, whether the cause assigned be brute unconscious matter, or a rational intelligent being. . . . No one, merely from the sight of one of Zeuxis's pictures, could know, that he was also a statuary or architect, and was an artist no less skillful in stone and marble than in colours. The talents and taste, displayed in the particular work before us; these we may safely conclude the workman to be possessed of. The cause must be proportioned to the effect; and if we exactly and precisely proportion it, we shall never find in it any qualities, that point farther, or afford an inference concerning any other design or performance. Such qualities must be somewhat beyond what is merely requisite for producing the effect, which we examine.

Allowing, therefore, the gods to be the authors of the existence or order of the universe; it follows, that they possess that precise degree of power, intelligence, and benevolence, which appears in their workmanship; but nothing farther can ever be proved, except we call in the assistance of exaggeration and flattery to supply the defects of argument and reasoning. So far as the traces of any attributes, at present, appear, so far may we conclude these attributes to exist. The supposition of farther attributes is mere hypothesis; much more the supposition, that, in distant regions of space or periods of time, there has been, or will be, a more magnificent display of these attributes, and a scheme of administration more suitable to such imaginary virtues. We can never be allowed to mount up from the universe, the effect, to Jupiter, the cause; and then descend downwards, to infer any new effect from that cause; as if the present effects alone were not entirely worthy of the glorious attributes, which we ascribe to that deity. The knowledge of the cause being derived solely from the effect, they must be exactly adjusted to each other; and the one can never refer to anything farther, or be the foundation of any new inference and conclusion.[a]

But, objected Hume in his temporary role as the defender of orthodoxy:

If you saw, for instance, a half-finished building, surrounded with heaps of brick and stone and mortar, and all the instruments of masonry; could you not *infer* from the effect, that it was a work of design and contrivance? And could you not return again, from this inferred cause, to infer new additions to the effect, and conclude, that the building would soon be finished, and receive all the further improvements, which art could bestow upon it? . . . Why then do you refuse to admit the same method of reasoning with regard to the order of nature? Consider the world and the present life only as an imperfect building, from which you can infer a superior intelligence; and arguing from that superior intelligence, which can leave nothing imperfect; why may you not infer a more finished scheme or plan, which will receive its completion in some distant point of space or time?

In reply, Hume's "friend" pointed out that the cases are not parallel. In the past we have seen carpenters completing unfinished buildings. Hence, when we now see an unfinished building, we are justified in inferring that in time it too will be finished. But suppose we had never before seen a finished building; the only building with which we are acquainted remains unfinished. We would certainly not be warranted in inferring that someday it will be finished. In a word, inductive inferences must be founded on experience.

In works of *human* art and contrivance, it is allowable to advance from the effect to the cause, and returning back from the cause, to form new inferences concerning the effect. . . . But what is the foundation of this method of reasoning? Plainly this; that man is a being, whom we know by experience, whose motives and designs we are acquainted with, and whose projects and inclinations have a certain connexion and coherence, according to the laws which nature has established for the government of such a creature. When, therefore, we find, that any work has proceeded from the skill and industry of man, as we are otherwise acquainted with the nature of the animal, we can draw a hundred inferences concerning what may be expected from him; and these inferences will all be founded in experience and observation. . . . We comprehend in [each] case a hundred other experiences and observations, concerning the *usual* figure and members of that species of animal, without which this method of argument must be considered as fallacious and sophistical.

The case is not the same with our reasonings from the works of nature. The Deity is known to us only by his productions, and is a single being in the universe, not comprehended under any species or genus, from whose experienced attributes or qualities, we can, by analogy, infer any attribute or quality in him. As the universe shews wisdom and goodness, we infer wisdom and goodness. As it shews a particular degree of these perfections, we infer a particular degree of them, precisely adapted to the effect which we examine. But farther attributes or farther degrees of the same attributes, we can never be authorized to infer or suppose, by any rules of just reasoning.

Up to this point, Hume allowed his reader to infer that God exists. He merely maintained that what can be inferred about His nature is severely limited. Now, at the end of the section, he introduced a further difficulty ("which I shall just propose to you without insisting on it, lest it lead into reasonings of too nice and delicate a nature") that challenges the validity of *any* inference from effect to cause in the present kind of case:

> I much doubt whether it be possible for a cause to be known only by its effect (as you have all along supposed) or to be of so singular and particular a nature as to have no parallel and no similarity with any other cause or object, that has ever fallen under our observation. It is only when two *species* of objects are found to be constantly conjoined, that we can infer the one from the other; and were an effect presented, which was entirely singular, and could not be comprehended under any known *species*, I do not see, that we could form any conjecture or inference at all concerning its cause. If experience and observation and analogy be, indeed, the only guides which we can reasonably follow in inferences of this nature; both the effect and cause must bear a similarity and resemblance to other effects and causes, which we know, and which we have found, in many instances, to be conjoined with each other. I leave it to your own reflection to pursue the consequences of this principle.

ARGUMENT OF THE *DIALOGUES*

In the *Dialogues,* Hume mustered additional arguments. He allowed that the argument from design has great appeal, but he urged that the basis for its persuasiveness lies, not in the evidence that can be marshaled for it, but in the "early education" of those whom the argument attracts. If men were to look at nature objectively, and without the predispositions inculcated by training in the traditional beliefs, who would find in it evidence of the God of Christian theology?

> But were this world ever so perfect a production, it must still remain uncertain, whether all the excellences of the work can justly be ascribed to the workman. If we survey a ship, what an exalted idea must we form of the ingenuity of the carpenter, who framed so complicated, useful, and beautiful a machine? And what surprise must we feel, when we find him a stupid mechanic, who imitated others, and copied an art, which, through a long succession of ages, after multiplied trials, mistakes, corrections, deliberations, and controversies, had been gradually improving? Many worlds might have been botched and bungled, throughout an eternity, ere this system was struck out: Much labor lost: Many fruitless trials made: And a slow, but continued improvement carried on during infinite ages in the art of world-making. In such subjects, who can determine, where the truth; nay, who can conjecture where the probability lies; amidst a great number of hypotheses which may be proposed, and a still greater number which may be imagined?

And what shadow of an argument, continued Philo,[20] can you produce, from your hypothesis, to prove the unity of the Deity? A great number of men join in building a house or ship, in rearing a city, in framing a common-wealth: Why may not several deities combine in contriving and framing a world? This is only so much greater similarity to human affairs. . . . You will find a numerous society of Deities as explicable as one universal Deity, who possesses, within himself, the powers and perfections of the whole society. All these systems, then, of scepticism, polytheism, and theism, you must allow, on your principles, to be on a like footing, and that no one of them has any advantages over the others.[b]

But why presuppose a conscious mind at all? If a dispassionate view of nature suggests any analogy at all, it is that of an organism rather than that of a machine. But organisms have an *internal* principle of life and of organization. Hence the fact that machines require a designer is irrelevant. If we are to conclude anything, it ought to be that the universe's origin is "to be ascribed to generation or vegetation [rather] than to reason or design."[c]

The world plainly resembles more an animal or a vegetable, than it does a watch or a knitting-loom. Its cause, therefore, it is more probable, resembles the cause of the former. The cause of the former is generation or vegetation. The cause, therefore, of the world, we may infer to be some thing similar or analogous to generation or vegetation.

But how is it conceivable, said Demea, that the world can arise from anything similar to vegetation or generation?

Very easily, replied Philo. In like manner as a tree sheds its seed into the neighbouring fields, and produces other trees; so the great vegetable the world, or this planetary system, produces within itself certain seeds, which, being scattered into the surrounding chaos, vegetate into new worlds. A comet, for instance, is the seed of a world; and after it has been fully ripened, by passing from sun to sun, and star to star, it is at last tossed into the unformed elements, which everywhere surround this universe, and im-mediately sprouts up into a new system. . . .

I understand you, says Demea: But what wild, arbitrary suppositions are these? What *data* have you for such extraordinary conclusions? And is the slight, imaginary resemblance of the world to a vegetable or an animal sufficient to establish the same inference with regard to both? Objects, which are in general so widely different; ought they to be a standard for each other?

Right, cries Philo: This is the topic on which I have all along insisted. I have still asserted, that we have no *data* to establish any system of cos-mogony. Our experience, so imperfect in itself, and so limited both in extent and duration, can afford us no probable conjecture concerning the whole of

20 [There are three characters in the *Dialogues,* each of whom represents a fairly well-defined attitude toward religion. *Philo* is a sceptic. *Demea* represents the opposite pole—extreme orthodoxy. *Cleanthes* is a more liberal theologian who emphasizes "reason" rather than dogma, and whose position is similar to Locke's—AUTHOR.]

things. But if we must needs fix on some hypothesis; by what rule, pray, ought we to determine our choice? Is there any other rule than the greater similarity of the objects compared? And does not a plant or an animal, which springs from vegetation or generation, bear a stronger resemblance to the world, than does any artificial machine, which arises from reason and design? . . .

In this little corner of the world alone, there are four principles, *reason, instinct, generation, vegetation*, which are similar to each other, and are the causes of similar effects. What a number of other principles may we naturally suppose in the immense extent and variety of the universe, could we travel from planet to planet and from system to system, in order to examine each part of this mighty fabric? Any one of these four principles above mentioned (and a hundred others which lie open to our conjecture) may afford us a theory, by which to judge of the origin of the world; and it is a palpable and egregious partiality, to confine our view entirely to that principle, by which our own minds operate. Were this principle more intelligent on that account, such a partiality might be somewhat excusable. But reason, in its internal fabric and structure, is really as little known to us as instinct or vegetation; and perhaps even that vague, undeterminate word, nature, to which the vulgar refer everything, is not at the bottom more inexplicable. The effects of these principles are all known to us from experience: But the principles themselves, and their manner of operation, are totally unknown: Nor is it less intelligible, or less conformable to experience to say, that the world arose by vegetation from a seed shed by another world, than to say that it arose from a divine reason or contrivance.[d]

Thus an impartial observer would be able to infer neither *one* cause nor an *intelligent* one. It is even more obvious, Hume held, that he could not infer a *beneficent* and *all-powerful* one. Look at the world with an unprejudiced eye— does it suggest an all-competent architect?

Did I show you a house or palace, where there was not one apartment convenient or agreeable; where the windows, doors, fires, passages, stairs, and the whole economy of the building were the source of noise, confusion, fatigue, darkness, and extremes of heat and cold; you would certainly blame the contrivance, without any farther examination. The architect would in vain display his subtilty, and prove to you, that if this door or that window were altered, greater ills would ensue. What he says, may be strictly true: The alteration of one particular, while the other parts of the building remain, may only augment the inconveniences. But still you would assert in general, that, if the architect had had skill and good intentions, he might have formed such a plan of the whole, and might have adjusted the parts in such a manner, as would have remedied all or most of these inconveniences. His ignorance, or even your own ignorance of such a plan, will never convince you of the impossibility of it. If you find many inconveniences and deformities in the building, you will always, without entering into any detail, condemn the architect.[e]

The same reasoning applies to the universe. The existence of evil, misery, and pain is incompatible with the God of Christian theology.

> But allowing you, what never will be believed; at least, what you never possibly can prove, that animal, or at least, human happiness, in this life, exceeds its misery; you have yet done nothing: For this is not, by any means, what we expect from infinite power, infinite wisdom, and infinite goodness. Why is there any misery at all in the world? Not by chance surely. From some cause then. Is it from the intention of the Deity? But he is perfectly benevolent. Is it contrary to his intention? But he is almighty. Nothing can shake the solidity of this reasoning, so short, so clear, so decisive. . . .
>
> But I will be contented to retire still from this intrenchment: For I deny that you can ever force me in it: I will allow, that pain or misery in man is *compatible* with infinite power and goodness in the Deity, even in your sense of these attributes: What are you advanced by all these concessions? A mere possible compatibility is not sufficient. You must *prove* these pure, unmixed, and uncontrollable attributes from the present mixed and confused phenomena, and from these alone. A hopeful undertaking! Were the phenomena ever so pure and unmixed, yet being finite, they would be insufficient for that purpose. How much more, where they are also so jarring and discordant!
>
> Here, Cleanthes, I find myself at ease in my argument. Here I triumph. . . .
>
> Look round this universe. What an immense profusion of beings, animated and organized, sensible and active! You admire this prodigious variety and fecundity. But inspect a little more narrowly these living existences, the only beings worth regarding. How hostile and destructive to each other! How insufficient all of them for their own happiness! How contemptible or odious to the spectator! The whole presents nothing but the idea of a blind nature, impregnated by a great vivifying principle, and pouring forth from her lap, without discernment or parental care, her maimed and abortive children.[f]

These arguments do more than merely elaborate the thesis of the *Enquiry* that it is illegitimate to impute more to the cause than the *minimum* required to produce a given effect. They make the further point that men's tendency to impute more to the cause results from a predisposition to accept the beliefs inculcated by "early education." Characteristically—as with his discussion of identity, substance, and other traditional concepts—Hume shows not merely that a widely held belief is mistaken, but he also shows why so mistaken a belief should be so widely held.

HUME'S CONCLUSION

Finally, what was Hume's own position? His last word on the subject, in fact his last word on any subject (for the following paragraph was added to the text of the as yet unpublished *Dialogues* just before his death), was that *order* is an empirical fact; that there is some slight evidence that it has a cause analogous to mind; but that there is no evidence at all for the God of religion.[21]

> If the whole of natural theology, as some people seem to maintain, resolves itself into one simple, though somewhat ambiguous, at least undefined proposition, *that the cause or causes of order in the universe probably bear some remote analogy to human intelligence:* If this proposition be not capable of extension, variation, or more particular explication: If it afford no inference that affects human life, or can be the source of any action or forbearance: And if the analogy, imperfect as it is, can be carried no farther than to the human intelligence; and cannot be transferred, with any appearance of probability, to the other qualities of the mind: If this really be the case, what can the most inquisitive, contemplative, and religious man do more than give a plain, philosophical assent to the proposition, as often as it occurs; and believe that the arguments, on which it is established, exceed the objections, which lie against it? Some astonishment indeed will naturally arise from the greatness of the object: Some melancholy from its obscurity: Some contempt of human reason, that it can give no solution more satisfactory with regard to so extraordinary and magnificent a question. But believe me, Cleanthes, the most natural sentiment, which a well-disposed mind will feel on this occasion, is a longing desire and expectation, that Heaven would be pleased to dissipate, at least alleviate, this profound ignorance, by affording some more particular revelation to mankind, and making discoveries of the nature, attributes, and operations of the divine object of our Faith. A person, seasoned with a just sense of the imperfections of natural reason, will fly to revealed truth with the greatest avidity: While the haughty dogmatist, persuaded that he can erect a complete system of theology by the mere help of philosophy, disdains any farther aid, and rejects this adventitious instructor. To be a philosophical sceptic is, in a man of letters, the first and most essential step towards being a sound, believing Christian.[g]

It is hard to see how this final sentence could be taken as anything but a characteristic piece of Humian irony. But it does not follow that Hume would have called himself an "atheist." In the first place, it is just as impossible, he held, to *rest* in religious scepticism as to rest in scepticism about the existence of an external world. Whatever one's theoretical doubts,

> ... the beauty and fitness of final causes strike us with such irresistible force that all objections appear (what I believe they really are) mere cavils and sophisms; nor can we then imagine how it was ever possible for us to repose any weight on them. ...

21 The question of what Hume's religious opinions really were has been much debated by commentators, and differences of opinion are facilitated (as Hume undoubtedly intended) by the dialogue form of exposition. Which character speaks for the author? Kemp Smith's study of the manuscript revisions of the *Dialogues* seems conclusive for the view that "Philo from start to finish represents Hume." For another point of view, however, see C. W. Hendel, *Studies in the Philosophy of David Hume* (Princeton University Press, 1925).

To whatever length any one may push his speculative principles of scepticism, he must act, . . . and live, and converse like other men. . . . It is impossible for him to persevere in total scepticism, or make it appear in his conduct for a few hours.[h]

One's reason may tell one that there is no more to the causal principle than a "lively anticipation." But, when the discussion ends, the sceptic leaves with the other guests via the stairs, not through the window. He may *know* that there is absolutely no evidence for the "law" of gravity, but he *acts* as if it were completely certain.

In the second place, according to Hume, "atheism" is largely a term of abuse, and disputes between atheists and believers are largely verbal. That this is so results from the fact that "suspension of judgment" (which is what the want of evidence calls for) is impossible.[22]

There is a species of controversy, which, from the very nature of language and of human ideas, is involved in perpetual ambiguity, and can never, by any precaution or any definitions, be able to reach a reasonable certainty or precision. These are the controversies concerning the degrees of any quality or circumstance. Men may argue to all eternity, whether Hannibal be a great, or a very great, or a superlatively great man, what degree of beauty Cleopatra possessed, what epithet of praise Livy or Thucydides is entitled to, without bringing the controversy to any determination. The disputants may here agree in their sense, and differ in the terms, or *vice versa;* yet never be able to define their terms, so as to enter into each other's meaning: Because the degrees of these qualities are not, like quantity or number, susceptible of any exact mensuration, which may be the standard in the controversy. That the dispute concerning theism is of this nature, and consequently is merely verbal, or perhaps, if possible, still more incurably ambiguous, will appear upon the slightest inquiry. I ask the theist, if he does not allow, that there is a great and immeasurable, because incomprehensible, difference between the *human* and the *divine* mind: The more pious he is, the more readily will he assent to the affirmative, and the more will he be disposed to magnify the difference: He will even assert, that the difference is of a nature which cannot be too much magnified. I next turn to the atheist, who, I assert, is only nominally so, and can never possibly be in earnest; and I ask him, whether, from the coherence and apparent sympathy in all the parts of this world, there be not a certain degree of analogy among all the operations of nature, in every situation and in every age; whether the rotting of a turnip, the generation of an animal, and the structure of human thought be not energies that probably bear some remote analogy to each other. It is impossible he can deny it: He will readily acknowledge it. Having obtained this concession, I push him still farther in his retreat; and I ask him, if it be not probable, that the principle which first arranged, and still maintains order

22 The following passage, too, was added in the final revision of the *Dialogues*, just before Hume's death.

in this universe, bears not also some remote inconceivable analogy to the other operations of nature, and among the rest to the economy of human mind and thought. However reluctant, he must give his assent. Where then, cry I to both these antagonists, is the subject of your dispute? The theist allows, that the original intelligence is very different from human reason: The atheist allows, that the original principle of order bears some remote analogy to it. Will you quarrel, Gentlemen, about the degrees, and enter into a controversy, which admits not of any precise meaning, nor consequently of any determination? . . .

It seems evident, that the dispute between the sceptics and dogmatists is entirely verbal. . . . No philosophical dogmatist denies, that there are difficulties both with regard to the senses and to all science: and that these difficulties are in a regular, logical method, absolutely insolvable. No sceptic denies, that we lie under an absolute necessity, notwithstanding these difficulties, of thinking, and believing, and reasoning with regard to all kind of subjects, and even of frequently assenting with confidence and security. The only difference, then, between these sects, if they merit that name, is that the sceptic, from habit, caprice, or inclination, insists most on the difficulties; the dogmatist, for like reasons, on the necessity.[i]

LIMITATIONS OF HUME'S VIEW

Hume realized, of course, that "believers" would not accept this version of the dispute. It is not just a matter, the religious man would say, of whether we use the term *God* or whether we "vary the expression" and use the term *mind*. The important thing is not the term used but what the term names. It is interesting, as a matter of fact, to see what Hume believed the religious man would miss from his account. "The doctrine of a future state is necessary . . . to morals," Cleanthes told Philo. "The proper office of religion is to regulate the heart of men, humanize their conduct, [and] infuse the spirit of temperance, order, and obedience." To this Philo replied in effect that religion ought to have no influence on conduct, and that whenever it does, its influence is evil. When religion departs from a philosophical contemplation of the possibility that something like a mind is at work in the universe—when it passes over into action—it descends at once into either superstition or enthusiasm, both of which history shows to have had a most deleterious effect on human life. To this argument, Philo thought that Cleanthes could make only the feeble reply that "religion however corrupted is still better than no religion at all."

It is characteristic of Hume's position that his Cleanthes and his Philo agreed that the only intelligible defense of the "religious hypothesis" is its utility, its possible impact on morals. They merely differed about whether this impact has been preponderately good or ill. Neither of Hume's characters saw that the "believer" might just possibly wish to take a different ground: that he might criticize Hume's conception not so much (as with Cleanthes) because it gives man nothing to fear as because it gives him nothing to worship. Indeed, such a critic might say that a religion limited, as Hume's is, to the contemplation of a possibility is no religion at all.

Moral Theory

ATTACK ON RATIONALISTIC ETHICS

During the Middle Ages the primary task of moral philosophy had been to systematize the various injunctions about conduct enunciated by Jesus and handed down by the Church fathers. If anyone were to ask, "Why should I be good?" that is, "Why should I do the acts prescribed?" it was enough to show that the acts *were* prescribed. The authority for conduct rested on the authority of the Church. When it came about that philosophers no longer accepted the authority of the Church, they merely looked for a new authority. This most of them found in reason. Descartes' proposals for an absolutely certain science of conduct and Locke's attempt to demonstrate the principles of ethics are examples of the tendency of thought that, according to Hume, "affirms that virtue is nothing but a conformity to reason; that there are eternal fitnesses and unfitnesses of things, which are the same to every rational being that considers them; that the immutable measures of right and wrong impose an obligation . . . on all human creatures; . . . that morality, like truth, is discern'd merely by ideas, and by their juxta-position and comparison."

Hume was, of course, entirely opposed to this way of thinking. Since the view that morality can be grounded in reason is still widely held, his arguments against it have more than a merely historical interest.

There are, in all, five arguments:

(1) "Reason judges either of *matter of fact* or of *relations.*" Consider, for instance, a moral judgment that condemns ingratitude by calling it a crime. "Where is that matter of fact which we here call *crime?*" The facts are good offices performed on the one side and a return of ill will or indifference on the other. "You cannot say that these, of themselves, always, and in all circumstances, are crimes. . . . Consequently, we may infer, that the crime of ingratitude is not any particular individual *fact;* but arises from a complication of circumstances," that is, from a relation. But this relation is not at all like the sort of relation that reason can demonstrate in mathematics.

(2) In mathematical (that is, demonstrative) thinking from "known and given relations," we infer "some unknown relation which is dependent on the former." In moral thinking, no new fact, no new relation, is inferred or discovered. Here thinking has the function of making us better acquainted with the facts. "But after every circumstance, after every relation is known, the understanding has no further room to operate, nor any object on which it could employ itself. The approbation or blame which then ensues [that is, the *moral* judgment] . . . is

not a speculative proposition or affirmation, but an active feeling or sentiment." Once the circumstances of the action are known (who was ungrateful to whom, under what circumstances, and so on), "nothing remains but to feel . . . some sentiment of blame or approbation; whence we pronounce the action criminal or virtuous."

(3) Moral goodness is comparable to natural beauty; and no one holds that the latter is a matter of judgment.

> Euclid has fully explained all the qualities of the circle; but has not in any proposition said a word of its beauty. The reason is evident. The beauty is not a quality of the circle. . . . It is only the effect which that figure produces upon the mind. . . . In vain would you look for [beauty] in the circle, or seek it, either by your senses or by mathematical reasoning, in all the properties of that figure. . . . Till . . . a spectator appear, there is nothing but a figure of such particular dimensions and proportions: from his sentiments alone arise its elegance and beauty. . . .
>
> (4) Inanimate objects may bear to each other all the same relations which we observe in moral agents; though the former can never be the object of love or hatred, nor are consequently susceptible of merit or iniquity. A young tree, which over-tops and destroys its parent, stands in all the same relations with Nero, when he murdered Agrippina; and if morality consisted merely in relations, would no doubt be equally criminal.
>
> (5) It appears evident that the ultimate ends of human actions can never, in any case, be accounted for by *reason,* but recommend themselves entirely to the sentiments and affections of mankind, without any dependance on the intellectual faculties. Ask a man *why he uses exercise;* he will answer, *because he desires to keep his health.* If you then enquire, *why he desires health,* he will readily reply, *because sickness is painful.* If you push your enquiries farther, and desire a reason *why he hates pain,* it is impossible that he can ever give any. This is an ultimate end, and is never referred to any other object.[j]

It is important to see that, in attacking rationalism in ethics, Hume was not denying that there is such a thing as moral judgment. That is, he was not saying that there is only "unthinking feeling," only an automatic emotive response to a situation. On the contrary, "*reason* and *sentiment* concur in almost all moral determinations and conclusions." Doubtless, every moral judgment depends ultimately on

> . . . some internal sense or feeling which nature has made universal in the whole species. For what else can have an influence on this nature? But in order to pave the way for such a sentiment, and give it proper discernment of its object, it is often necessary, we find, that much reasoning should precede, that nice distinctions be made, just conclusions drawn, distant comparisons formed, complicated relations examined, and general facts fixed and ascertained.[k]

In all these ways, then, reasoning enters into the moral conclusion, distinguishing it from any automatic emotive response to a situation. But the part reason plays is subordinate to sentiment and provides no basis for a demonstrative ethics. Hume summarized this in the aphorism, "Reason is, and ought only to be the slave of the passions, and can never pretend to any other office than to serve and obey them."[1]

EMPIRICAL AND NORMATIVE ETHICS CONTRASTED

Thus Hume's ethics was radically different from that of preceding philosophers. Where their approach was normative, his was empirical. For him, "being desired" or "being approved" was just another fact about a thing, like "being hot." According to him, neither can be deduced from the thing's nature. In both cases, the only possible basis for inference is experience. It simply turns out to be a fact that friction is associated with heat, that such-and-such objects are associated with desire or approval.

Accordingly, Hume did not ask, "What ought men do?" or "Why ought they do it?" He asked, "What do men mean by such terms as 'ought,' 'virtue,' 'moral'?" The "principles" for which he was searching were not metaphysical, religious, or moral ultimates; they were empirically verifiable relationships, such as the relationship between certain attitudes (for example, those called "approving" and "disapproving") and certain types of behavior. If it can be shown that all the activities that are approved fall into certain classes, moral approbation will have been explained in exactly the same way as heat is explained, by ascertaining the phenomena with which it is regularly conjoined. In a word, Hume ruled out a metaphysic of morals just as he ruled out a metaphysic of nature.

> In order to [discover the true origin of morals], . . . we shall endeavour to follow a very simple method: we shall analyse that complication of mental qualities, which form what, in common life, we call Personal Merit: we shall consider every attribute of the mind, which renders a man an object either of esteem and affection, or of hatred and contempt; every habit or sentiment or faculty, which, if ascribed to any person, implies either praise or blame, and may enter into any panegyric or satire of his character and manners. . . . The very nature of language guides us almost infallibly in forming a judgement of this nature; and as every tongue possesses one set of words which are taken in a good sense, and another in the opposite, the least acquaintance with the idiom suffices, without any reasoning, to direct us in collecting and arranging the estimable or blameable qualities of men. The only object of reasoning is to discover the circumstances on both sides, which are common to these qualities; to observe that particular in which the estimable qualities agree on the one hand, and the blameable on the other; and thence to reach the foundation of ethics, and find those universal principles, from which all censure or approbation is ultimately derived. As this is a question of fact, not of abstract science, we can only expect success, by following the experi-

mental method, and deducing general maxims from a comparison of particular instances. . . . Men are not cured of their passion for hypotheses and systems in natural philosophy, and will hearken to no arguments but those which are derived from experience. It is full time they should attempt a like reformation in all moral disquisitions; and reject every system of ethics, however subtle or ingenious, which is not founded on fact and observation.[m]

NATURE OF MORAL GOODNESS

According to Hume, an examination of the circumstances in which men use terms with moral connotations—terms such as "humane," "merciful," "beneficent," "just," "faithful," "truthful," "chaste"—shows that all the qualities constituting personal merit, the qualities described by these terms, are "either useful or agreeable to the person himself or to others." To prove this, Hume imagined a man being congratulated by his friends on the character of his prospective son-in-law:

> What so natural, for instance, as the following dialogue? You are very happy, we shall suppose one to say, addressing himself to another, that you have given your daughter to Cleanthes. He is a man of honour and humanity. Every one, who has any intercourse with him, is sure of *fair* and *kind* treatment.[23] I congratulate you too, says another, on the promising expectations of this son-in-law; whose assiduous application to the study of the laws, whose quick penetration and early knowledge both of men and business, prognosticate the greatest honours and advancement.[24] You surprise me, replies a third, when you talk of Cleanthes as a man of business and application. I met him lately in a circle of the gayest company, and he was the very life and soul of our conversation: so much wit with good manners; so much gallantry without affectation; so much ingenious knowledge so genteelly delivered, I have never before observed in any one.[25] You would admire him still more, says a fourth, if you knew him more familiarly. That cheerfulness, which you might remark in him, is not a sudden flash struck out by company: it runs through the whole tenor of his life, and preserves a perpetual serenity on his countenance, and tranquillity in his soul. He has met with severe trials, misfortunes as well as dangers; and by his greatness of mind, was still superior to all of them.[26,n]

It will be seen that Hume took no account of what he called the "monkish virtues"—celibacy, fasting, penance, mortification, self-denial, humility, silence, solitude. "They serve to no manner of purpose; neither advance a man's fortune in the world, nor render him a more valuable member of society; neither qualify

23 Qualities useful to others.
24 Qualities useful to the person himself.
25 Qualities immediately agreeable to others.
26 Qualities immediately agreeable to the person himself.

him for the entertainment of company, nor increase his power of self-enjoy-ment."° How, then, can they be virtues? Obviously they are not, if Hume's generalization about what actions men approve as virtues is correct. This gen-eralization was supposedly reached inductively from a study of how men actually evaluate conduct. But some men—many men, as a matter of fact—*do* approve humility, self-denial, penance. It would seem to follow that an adequate general-ization must take account of these facts, and that Hume's generalization is too narrow—not that the "monkish virtues" are not virtues. To this Hume could reply only that the upholders of the monkish virtues have been misled by "superstition and false religion" and that no one who "judged of things by rational unprejudiced reason" would ever conclude that such conduct was virtuous. But the upholders of the monkish virtues could just as well reply to Hume that only "atheists and epicureans," blinded by *their* false doctrines, would ever suppose that celibacy and penance were not virtues. The one line of argument proves as much as the other and convinces only those who are already persuaded.

This illustrates one of the difficulties with a purely empirical approach. If Hume had really considered all the varieties of ethical evaluations, it is hard to believe that the "principles" he claimed to find would have neatly emerged from the welter of details. What, for instance, do the value judgments made by a Socrates and by a Hitler have in common? We may suspect that Hume knew before he began what he was looking for, and that the induction in the *Enquiry* is no more than an ex post facto literary device.

This difficulty might, of course, be met by a more careful inductive procedure, as Bacon's hasty conclusions could be corrected by an improved methodology. A more fundamental question is whether even the most careful description of what people *think* is good throws any light on what is really good. Here is another parting of the ways in philosophy.

However this may be, Hume has now found—at least to his own satisfaction—the defining characteristic of everything that men call moral goodness, virtue, and merit (these are synonyms from Hume's point of view). To say that quality *x* is morally good is to say that *x* is useful or agreeable either to the man who has *x* or to other men. We have next to note the relation between moral goodness and goodness in general. "Whatever is valuable in any kind . . . classes itself under the division of useful or agreeable, the *utile* or the *dulce.*" Beauty is a case in point. Generally speaking, we find everything that is useful beautiful. "The conveniency of a house, the fertility of a field, the strength of a horse, the capacity, security, and swift-sailing of a vessel, form the principal beauty of these several objects. . . . Where any object, in all its parts, is fitted to attain any agreeable end, it naturally gives us pleasure, and is esteem'd beautiful." What is true of the beauty of natural objects is true of artistic beauty. "There is no rule in painting or statuary more indispensible than that of balancing the figures, and placing them with the greatest exactness on their proper centre of gravity. A figure, which is not justly balanced, is ugly; because it conveys the disagreeable ideas of fall, harm, and pain."ᴾ

But why, if the value of all values lies in their utility or pleasure, do men distinguish kinds of value? Why are some things called "good," some "beautiful," and some "morally good"? Hume's reply was that, although all values are pleasures, they are qualitatively distinguished by their different flavors.

> Under the term *pleasure*, we comprehend sensations, which are very different from each other. . . . A good composition of music and a bottle of good wine equally produce pleasure; and what is more, their goodness is determin'd merely by the pleasure. But shall we say upon that account, that the wine is harmonious, or the music of a good flavour? In like manner an inanimate object, and the character or sentiments of any person may, both of them, give satisfaction; but as the satisfaction is different, this keeps our sentiments concerning them from being confounded, and makes us ascribe virtue to the one, and not to the other. Nor is every sentiment of pleasure or pain, which arises from characters and actions, of that *peculiar* kind, which makes us praise or condemn. The good qualities of an enemy are hurtful to us; but may still command our esteem and respect. 'Tis only when a character is considered in general, without reference to our particular interest, that it causes such a feeling or sentiment, as denominates it morally good or evil. 'Tis true, those sentiments, from interest and morals, are apt to be confounded. . . . It seldom happens, that we do not think an enemy vicious, and can distinguish betwixt his opposition to our interest and real villainy or baseness. But this hinders not, but that the sentiments are, in themselves, distinct; and a man of temper and judgment may preserve himself from these illusions.q

DIFFERENTIAE OF MORAL GOODNESS

In a word, moral goodness (virtue) is distinguished from other kinds of goodness by two properties: (1) It is a pleasure resulting from a consideration of character or motive, and (2) it is a disinterested approbation.

Reference to character was Hume's way of interpreting the traditional Christian emphasis on inwardness. But, of course, if called on to defend this first differentia of moral goodness, he would not have appealed to the Christian tradition; he would merely have noted, as a matter of empirical fact, that when men pass moral judgment, they are judging about character.

> If any *action* be either virtuous or vicious, 'tis only as a sign of some quality or character. It must depend upon durable principles of the mind, which extend over the whole conduct, and enter into the personal character. . . .
> Actions are, indeed, better indications of a character than words, or even wishes and sentiments; but 'tis only so far as they are such indications, that they are attended with love or hatred, praise or blame.r

When people blame a man for not performing some action, it is because they take this as a sign of some deficiency in his character. "If we find, upon enquiry, that the virtuous motive was still powerful over his breast, tho' check'd in its operation by some circumstances unknown to us, we retract our blame, and have the same esteem for him, as if he had actually perform'd the action, which we require of him."ˢ

As regards the second supposed differentia of moral goodness, egoists like Hobbes have denied that disinterested approbation is possible.

> There is a principle, supposed to prevail among many, . . . that all *benevolence* is mere hypocrisy, friendship a cheat, public spirit a farce, fidelity a snare to procure trust and confidence; and that while all of us, at bottom, pursue only our private interest, we wear these fair disguises, in order to put others off their guard, and expose them the more to our wiles and machinations.ᵗ

Hume did not reply by denouncing egoism as "wrong" or "wicked," but by showing that it is not an adequate account of how men actually behave and of what moves them. His three arguments against egoism are devastating:

(1) The egoistic hypothesis seems to contradict obvious facts about conduct.

> The most obvious objection to the selfish hypothesis is, that, as it is contrary to common feeling and our most unprejudiced notions, there is required the highest stretch of philosophy to establish so extraordinary a paradox. To the most careless observer there appear to be such dispositions as benevolence and generosity; such affections as love, friendship, compassion, gratitude. . . . As this is the obvious appearance of things, it must be admitted, till some [other] hypothesis be . . . proved.ᵘ

No doubt it would be much more pleasant to have a neat, monistic explanation of behavior than to admit a plurality of irreducible motives. But "the love of simplicity . . . has been the source of much false reasoning in philosophy."

(2) To hold that our "real" motivation is always self-interest commits us to a most complicated psychological theory. It is as if, watching a wagon drawn by horses, we were to insist that "minute wheels and springs, like those of a watch give motion [to it]." Take the case of a man who grieves for the death of a friend. If the friend were rich and powerful, we might suppose hidden self-interest to be at work; but what if the friend were poor and without influence? It is not plausible to maintain that grief in such a case "arises from some metaphysical regards to a self-interest, which has no foundation in reality."

Or consider the motivation of animals, who "are found susceptible of kindness, both to their own species and to ours." Are we to say that our dog can make "refined deductions of self interest"? That our goat is a Machiavellian schemer plotting to curry our favor? Or are we to allow that disinterested benevolence moves them, while refusing to admit it in men?

(3) In any case, self-love cannot be men's *only* good, for its satisfaction depends wholly on the satisfaction of various particular desires.

> If I have no vanity, I take no delight in praise: if I be void of ambition, power gives me no enjoyment: if I be not angry, the punishment of an adversary is totally indifferent to me. In all these cases there is a passion which points immediately to the object, and constitutes it our good or happiness. . . . Were there no appetite of any kind antecedent to self-love, that propensity could scarcely ever exert itself; because we should, in that case, have felt few and slender pains or pleasures, and have little misery or happiness to avoid or to pursue.[v]

In other words, "self-love" is an abstraction invented by an overly rationalistic psychology. Attention to the empirical facts shows that it is an oversimplification to classify motives as simply egoistic or simply altruistic. There are, in the first place, certain "primary" appetites—such as the appetite of hunger and the appetite of thirst. The satisfaction of these appetites brings pleasure, and the thought of this pleasure can become the object of a "secondary" appetite. But unless there were a primary appetite for food, there could be no desire for the pleasure of eating. So, though I often eat for the sake of the pleasure it brings me, and though my motive is then self-love, this is possible only because there are other motives (for example, the satisfaction of hunger) that cannot properly be described as self-love. Further, it is not the case that a man's motive is sometimes purely self-love (pleasure-in-eating) and sometimes purely a specific satisfaction (cessation of hunger). Rather, both elements enter into a man's motivation whenever he eats.

> In all . . . cases there is a passion which points immediately to the object, and constitutes it our good or happiness [for example, the broiled steak, the compliment from a superior, the punishment of an adversary]; as there are other secondary passions which afterwards arise and pursue it as a part of our happiness, when once it is constituted such by our original affections.

And what is true of steaks is certainly true of friendship and benevolence.

> Where is the difficulty in conceiving, that . . . from the original frame of our temper, we may feel a desire of another's happiness or good, which, by means of that affection, becomes our own good, and is afterwards pursued, from the combined motives of benevolence and self-enjoyments? Who sees not that vengeance, from the force alone of passion, may be so eagerly pursued, as to make us knowingly neglect every consideration of ease, interest, or safety; and, like some vindictive animals, infuse our very souls into the wounds we give an enemy; and what a malignant philosophy must it be, that will not allow to humanity and friendship the same privileges which are indisputably granted to the darker passions of enmity and resentment.

Thus the trouble with the thesis that men are motivated entirely by self-love is not that it is immoral, but that it is poor psychology. Doubtless the force of benevolence varies from individual to individual. But "there is some benevolence however small, infused into every bosom. . . . Let these generous sentiments be supposed ever so weak . . . they must still direct the determinations of our minds, and, where everything else is equal, produce a cool preference of what is useful and serviceable to mankind."

Not only is it an empirical fact that all men experience (at least to some extent) the sentiment of benevolence. It is also an empirical fact that this sentiment underlies our moral judgments. That this is the case is shown by the way we use language. There are occasions on which we say, "He is a villain," not "He is offensive to me." There are occasions on which we say, "He is just," not "He has been generous to me." These linguistic differences correspond to differences in our attitudes toward the man whose conduct we are assessing. When we are concerned only with the effect of his conduct on ourselves, that is, when we are motivated by self-love, we do not use moral language; when we do use moral language, we are expressing concern for the effect of his conduct on the public generally, that is, we are animated by benevolence.

Thus the conclusion Hume reached by an analysis of moral language reinforces the conclusion he had reached by an examination of the role of reason in the moral judgment. In that case he realized that the ultimate basis of moral judgment could not be reason—it must be "some internal sense or feeling which nature has made universal in the whole species."[27] It is now clear what this feeling is. It is the sentiment of benevolence, which issues in judgments of disinterested approbation when we believe that the conduct we are appraising is useful to mankind generally.

IN WHAT SENSE MORAL JUDGMENTS ARE SUBJECTIVE

It follows that moral judgments are not independent of our feelings. In this sense, they are subjective; they are not judgments about a wholly external reality, and they cannot be demonstrated by a process of deductive reasoning like that employed in mathematics. But this does not mean that they are subjective in the sense that agreement about moral appraisals is impossible. Men do not judge exclusively about their own individual feelings, for, according to Hume, the feeling of benevolence, though it varies in strength from man to man, is universal. Hence disagreement over moral appraisals can be overcome.

Disagreement results, in the first place, from differences about whether the conduct being appraised is useful to mankind. This is an empirical question, and, as the relevant facts become known, men should be able to reach agreement. In the second place, disagreement over moral appraisals results from the fact that if the conduct being appraised touches a man closely, his feeling of self-love may bias his judgment. But since sentiments of benevolence really do operate, they enable men to get a perspective on things and so to counteract bias. My generous neighbor may excite more affection in me than the historical Marcus

27 See p. 338.

Brutus; but I can believe, through my reading of history, that had I known Marcus Brutus as well as I know my neighbor, I would have thought even more highly of his character than I do of my neighbor's. So I allow for this bias in my estimate of them and in the relative approval I give to their characters. Similarly, when I hear a singer whose appearance I dislike, I may be tempted to disapprove his voice; but I can correct for this by comparing his voice with that of some other singer about whose appearance I have no feeling one way or the other.

Further, because men live in a social world, it is advantageous for them to agree on common, or standard, evaluations, just as they agree on common, or standard, shapes and sizes and colors for objects. In my visual field, my desk varies in shape and size, depending on how far away from it I am. When I am sitting at it, it may occupy almost the whole of the field; when I am on the other side of the room, it occupies only a small portion of it. But because I "know" that its size remains constant, I learn to see it as the same size in both perspectives. In the same way, a standard evaluation of such-and-such a character may replace my personal estimate, even though, in a sense, the private feeling remains (as the desk continues to occupy different amounts of the visual field even after I learn to see it as constant in size).

Being thus acquainted with the nature of man, we expect not any impossibilities from him; but confine our view to that narrow circle, in which any person moves, in order to form a judgment of his moral character. When the natural tendency of his passions leads him to be serviceable and useful within his sphere, we approve of his character, and love his person, by a sympathy with the sentiments of those, who have a more particular connexion with him. We are quickly oblig'd to forget our own interest in our judgments of this kind, by reason of the perpetual contradictions, we meet with in society and conversation, from persons that are not plac'd in the same situation, and have not the same interest with ourselves. The only point of view, in which our sentiments concur with those of others, is, when we consider the tendency of any passion to the advantage or harm of those, who have any immediate connexion or intercourse with the person possess'd of it. And tho' this advantage or harm be often very remote from ourselves, yet sometimes 'tis very near us, and interests us strongly by sympathy. This concern we readily extend to other cases, that are resembling; and when these are very remote, our sympathy is proportionably weaker, and our praise or blame fainter and more doubtful. The case is here the same as in our judgments concerning external bodies. All objects seem to diminish by their distance: But tho' the appearance of objects to our senses be the original standard, by which we judge of them, yet we do not say, that they actually diminish by the distance; but correcting the appearance by reflexion, arrive at a more constant and establish'd judgment concerning them. In like manner, tho' sympathy be much fainter than our concern for ourselves, and a sympathy with persons remote from us much fainter than that with persons near and contiguous; yet we neglect all these differences in our calm judgments concerning the characters of men. Besides, that we ourselves often change our situation in this particular, we every day meet with persons, who are in a different situation from ourselves, and who cou'd never converse with us on any reasonable terms, were we to remain constantly in that situation and point of view, which is peculiar to us. The intercourse of sentiments, therefore, in society and conversation, makes us form some general inalterable standard, by which we may approve or disapprove of characters and manners. And tho' the *heart* does not always take part with those general notions, or regulate its love and hatred by them, yet are they sufficient for discourse, and serve all our purposes in company, in the pulpit, on the theatre, and in the schools.ᵂ

This is very ingenious; it almost certainly accounts, at least in part, for the way in which standard judgments about, say, historical figures arise. It also shows how a "corrected" moral judgment comes about; it shows, for instance, how a narrow sympathy, limited to a small circle of close acquaintances, may gradually be replaced by a wider benevolence, embracing persons remote from us. In this way Hume provides for moral criteria—not transcendental or logically necessary criteria, of course, but criteria that emerge in experience. He shows why men come to accept these criteria and how, in the course of time, they refine them. This may be enough "objectivity" for most people, but of course it will not satisfy those who believe in moral absolutes.

Philosophical Scepticism

DIFFICULTIES IN HUME'S POSITION

It remains to consider some difficulties in Hume's position. First, there is a problem with regard to his account of the self. According to his theory, I construct objects (for example, a desk) from discrete percepts by "feigning" data to fill the gaps between the percepts. But what is this self that constructs objects? Is *it* constructed? And if so, by whom? It would seem that the "I" who feigns the continuous mahogany-colored data and so constructs the desk cannot be "feigned" in the way that the desk is feigned. Surely, in order to feign the unity, identity, and continuity of the desk, the self must have a unity, identity, and continuity that are not feigned. This does not mean, of course, that the self is necessarily the metaphysically distinct and independently real substance of Cartesianism. It does mean, however, that it has more unity than Hume's theory can allow it. In a word, if the self were only a flickering succession of "loose and separate" ideas, as the theory asserts, it could never know even the fragmentary world the theory describes. Such a self would be too fragmentary even to know its own fragmentariness.

There is also a puzzle about Hume's attack on the causal principle: It is almost too successful. Constant succession, he maintained, causes "a lively anticipation" that is mistaken for "necessary connection." But is there a necessary connection between constant successions and lively anticipations, or is there only a lively anticipation? The argument that purports to prove that inductive inference cannot be rationally justified rests—covertly, to be sure—on inductive inferences about human nature and the workings of the mind. Hume's critique of science cannot apply to the science of psychology, though there are no logical grounds for exempting this science from the general critique.

Hume was aware of these paradoxes and seems to have been of two minds about his own philosophy. At times he was almost bewildered by the position in which he found himself and was at a loss as to how to proceed. His recognition of "the wretched condition, weakness and disorder of the faculties" filled him with "melancholy" and "desponding reflections." He was "affrighted and confounded with that forlorn solitude" in which he was placed by his philosophy.

> Where am I, or what? From what causes do I derive my existence, and to what condition shall I return? Whose favour shall I court, and whose anger must I dread? What beings surround me? and on whom have I any influence, or who have any influence on me? I am confounded with all these questions, and begin to fancy myself in the most deplorable condition imaginable, inviron'd with the deepest darkness, and utterly depriv'd of the use of every member and faculty.
>
> Most fortunately it happens, that since reason is incapable of dispelling these clouds, nature herself suffices to that purpose, and cures me of this philosophical melancholy and delirium. . . . I dine, I play a game of backgammon, I converse, and am merry with my friends; and when after three or four hours' amusement, I wou'd return to these speculations, they appear so cold, and strain'd and ridiculous, that I cannot find in my heart to enter into them any farther. . . .
>
> I am ready to throw all my books and papers into the fire, and resolve never more to renounce the pleasures of life for the sake of reasoning and philosophy. . . . [Nevertheless] I cannot forbear having a curiosity to be acquainted with the principles of moral good and evil, the nature and foundation of government, and the cause of those several passions and inclinations, which actuate and govern me. I am uneasy to think I approve of one object, and disapprove of another; call one thing beautiful, and another deform'd; decide concerning truth and falsehood, reason and folly, without knowing upon what principles I proceed.[x]

It is not surprising to find Hume writing in this vein. After all, he lived in the "Age of Reason." There ought to be, there must be, rational principles in the universe, principles that provide a basis for intelligent choice and enlightened conduct. But when Hume searched in experience (and where else can one search?) for these principles, he failed to find them. So far from finding objective, rational principles, he found only the imagination—a private, subjective principle that feigns to be objective and rational but is really "inconstant and fallacious." No wonder Hume protested his despair. Yet somehow the passage does not ring true. One who could write so smoothly of "melancholy and despondency" could hardly feel as disturbed as Hume professed to be. Hume was not really as gloomy as he sounded.

ALTERNATIVES TO HUME'S DILEMMA

The fact is that when one gets oneself in the kind of jam into which Hume was led by following out the Lockian premises, there are really only three possibilities. First, one can conclude that something is wrong with the premises from which one started and begin to work out a rational philosophy on a different basis. Second, one can take refuge in some sort of extrarational authority ("to be a philosophical sceptic is . . . the first . . . step towards being a sound, believing Christian"). Third, one can boldly face life in a world without certainty and make the best of it.

Here, once again, is a fundamental parting of the ways, where choices are probably determined by basic temperamental differences. The first of these choices was adopted by Kant when (as he said) Hume roused him from his "dogmatic slumbers" by demonstrating that the old version of rationalism was no longer viable. Philosophers as different as Hegel and Whitehead continued this effort to rehabilitate rationalism, but in the nineteenth century, and in our own time, the second and third choices have been increasingly adopted. The second has taken many (and in certain respects antithetical) forms—a revival of Catholicism, romanticism, political totalitarianisms of the right and the left. The third—abandonment of the quest for certainty, acceptance of provisional solutions as long as they work, and readiness to discard them when changing conditions make them no longer appropriate—has been the solution favored by pragmatists and radical empiricists. The interplay among these responses to Hume's attack on rationalism, and the manifold variations and permutations that they have undergone, make the study of recent cultural history a fascinating but complex undertaking.

HUME'S "MITIGATED" SCEPTICISM

There is, however, no doubt about where Hume's own sympathies would lie—with pragmatism and radical empiricism. But though Hume's temper was radically empirical, he did not work out a pragmatic theory of experience. Indeed, his theory of experience was completely atomistic, as has been shown. Moreover, Hume shared the belief of his contemporaries and his predecessors that knowledge is something that happens to men, not something that men make happen by what they do. The discovery that knowledge occurs as a result of men's interaction with their environment was not made until much later. Hume's contribution—and it was an important one—was rather the discovery that criticism does not destroy belief nor render men impotent. Men go on living as if inductive inference were rationally justified, as if there were an external world, and so on. "Total scepticism," in a word, is impossible. "Nature, by an absolute and uncontrollable necessity has determined us to judge as well as to breathe and feel." "Nature will always maintain her rights, and prevail in the end over any abstract reasoning whatsoever."[y]

What is called instinct is observed in animals, that is, attitudes and behavior patterns "in which they improve little or nothing by the longest practice and experience"—the digging instinct in the dog, the nesting instinct in the bird, the anti-dog instinct in the cat, and so on. Now, there are instincts in men too; and of these the most important is what Hume called the instinct for "experimental reasoning." This is something that, as a matter of fact, men share with the animals. It involves "a prepossession to repose faith in the senses" and in the existence of an external world. On it

> . . . the whole conduct of life depends. . . . [It] is nothing but a species of instinct or mechanical power,[28] that acts in us unknown to ourselves; and in its chief operations, is not directed by any such relations or comparisons of ideas, as are the proper objects of our intellectual faculties. Though the instinct be different, yet still it is an instinct, which teaches a man to avoid the fire; as much as that, which teaches a bird, with such exactness, the art of incubation, and the whole economy and order of its nursery.[z]

If, then, no amount of philosophical reasoning can destroy these instinctive ways of behaving, does it follow that there is no difference at all between the philosophical sceptic and the unthinking man to whom doubt has never occurred? On the contrary. Though the former's "common conduct will [not] be found different from those who have never formed any opinions in the case," once he has "accustomed himself to sceptical considerations or the uncertainty and narrow limits of reason, he will not entirely forget them when he turns his reflections on other subjects."[a]

He will know that absolute rational certainty is unattainable except in pure mathematics. He will not be deceived, as the vulgar are, by the pretensions of metaphysicians and theologians to a knowledge that he knows to be impossible. He will "run over libraries, [and taking] in . . . hand any volume; of divinity or school metaphysics [he will] ask, *Does it contain any abstract reasoning concerning quantity or number?* No. *Does it contain any experimental reasoning concerning matter of fact and existence?* No. Commit it then to the flames: for it can contain nothing but sophistry and illusion."[b]

The philosophical sceptic, in a word, reserves his scepticism for abstract reason, having made his peace with concrete experience. He has come to see that action, not certainty—experience, not logic—is the criterion a man ought to accept. It is true that "if we reason *a priori*, anything may appear able to

---

28 [By "mechanical," Hume presumably meant merely that it is not a deliberate and rational process—AUTHOR.]

produce anything. The falling of a pebble may, for aught we know, extinguish the sun; or the wish of a man control the planets in their orbits."[c] They *may* do so, but in point of fact they do not; at least, they have not done so yet. Experience shows great regularity in the behavior of nature; on this basis, men can form generalizations, make plans, live successfully. What more does a *reasonable* man want?

> Man is a reasonable being; and as such, receives from science his proper food and nourishment: But so narrow are the bounds of human understanding, that little satisfaction can be hoped for in this particular, either from the extent of security or his acquisitions. Man is a sociable, no less than a reasonable being: But neither can he always enjoy company agreeable and amusing, or preserve the proper relish for them. Man is also an active being; and from that disposition, as well as from the various necessities of human life, must submit to business and occupation: But the mind requires some relaxation, and cannot always support its bent to care and industry. It seems, then, that nature has pointed out a mixed kind of life as most suitable to the human race, and secretly admonished them to allow none of these biases to *draw* too much, so as to incapacitate them for other occupations and entertainments. Indulge your passion for science, says she, but let your science be human, and such as may have a direct reference to action and society. Abstruse thought and profound researches I prohibit, and will severely punish, by the pensive melancholy which they introduce, by the endless uncertainty in which they involve you, and by the cold reception which your pretended discoveries shall meet with, when communicated. Be a philosopher; but, amidst all your philosophy, be still a man.[d]

Scepticism, in a word, is not a resting-place; it is a propaedeutic. It has a cathartic function: It purges the mind of delusions of grandeur; it brings men down from the clouds and sets them firmly on their feet; it reorients the intellectual enterprise, turns it away from the vain pursuit of certainty and toward "action, employment and occupations of daily life." Far from inhibiting action, it frees men from the metaphysical mazes in which they have been wandering and enables them to contemplate without distress "the whimsical condition of mankind, who must act and reason and believe; though they are not able, by their most diligent enquiry, to satisfy themselves concerning the foundation of these operations, or to remove the objections, which may be raised against them."[e]

Not everyone, certainly, will be satisfied with this "mitigated" scepticism of Hume's. The urge to understand, the faith that things are meaningful, is one of man's deepest passions. In Hume's view, this urge cannot be satisfied, for the universe is not the sort of thing of which an account can be given. But if mitigated scepticism is not the noblest of philosophical ideals, it is certainly not the meanest. Indeed, in a time like ours, when so many seem to have surrendered to fanaticism and dedicated themselves to bigotry and violence, it surely has much to recommend it.

Notes

Chapter 1 / Renaissance

a   *The Inferno*, translated by J. Ciardi (New American Library, New York, 1954), Canto XXVI, ll. 106–12.

b   Quoted in J. A. Williamson, *The Voyages of the Cabots and the Discovery of North America* (Argonaut Press, London, 1929), p. 26.

c   Quoted in P. Smith, *The Age of the Reformation* (Holt, New York, 1920), p. 729.

d   Quoted in A. B. Kerr, *Jacques Coeur* (Scribner's, New York, 1927), p. 83.

e   *De Monarchia*, translated by P. H. Wicksteed (Dent, London, 1929), I, 5.

f   *Ibid.*, III, 16.

g   Marsiglio, *Defensor Pacis*, I, iv, quoted in F. W. Coker, *Readings in Political Philosophy* (Macmillan, New York, 1938), p. 247.

h   Marsiglio, *Defensor Minor*, i, 2 and 4, quoted in G. H. Sabine, *A History of Political Theory* (Holt, New York, 1937), p. 295.

i   *Six Books Concerning the State*, translated by W. T. Jones, in *Masters of Political Thought* (Houghton Mifflin, Boston, 1947), p. 62, n. 1.

j   *Ibid.*, p. 57.

k   *Ibid.*, pp. 81–83.

l   *Ibid.*, p. 60, n. 1.

m   *Discourses on the First Ten Books of Titus Livius,* translated by C. E. Detmold, in *The Writings of Niccolo Machiavelli* (Houghton Mifflin, Boston, 1891), Vol. II, Bk. II, Ch. 22, p. 286.

n   *Ibid.*, Bk. I, Ch. 37, p. 174; Bk. II, Introduction, p. 225.

o   *Ibid.*, Bk. II, Ch. 2, pp. 232–33.

p   *Ibid.*, Bk. I, Ch. 55, pp. 209–11.

q   *The Prince,* translated by Luigi Ricci, revised by E. R. P. Vincent (Modern Library, New York, 1940), Chs. 5 and 8, pp. 18–19 and 35.

r   *Ibid.*, Chs. 17–18, pp. 61 and 63–65.

s   *Discourses,* translated by Detmold, *op. cit.,* Vol. II, Bk. I, Ch. 11, p. 127; Bk. I, Ch. 12, pp. 129–30; Bk. I, Ch. 14, pp. 134–35.

t   *Ibid.*, Bk. I, Ch. 52, p. 203.

u   *Ibid.*, Bk. II, Ch. 29, p. 309.

v   Petrarch, *The Ascent of Mont Ventoux,* translated by H. Nachod, in *The Renaissance Philosophy of Man,* edited by E. Cassirer, P. O. Kristeller, and F. H. Randall, Jr. (University of Chicago Press, 1948), pp. 36–37, 41, and 43–46.

w   Petrarch, *On His Own Ignorance,* translated by H. Nachod, in *The Renaissance Philosophy of Man,* edited by Cassirer, Kristeller, and Randall, *op. cit.,* p. 108.

x   *Ibid.*, pp. 57–59.

y   *Ibid.*, pp. 62 and 75.

z   Pico della Mirandola, *Oration on the Dignity of Man,* translated by E. L. Forbes, in *The Renaissance Philosophy of Man,* edited by Cassirer, Kristeller, and Randall, *op. cit.,* pp. 223–25, 227, and 229.

a   Baldesar Castiglione, *Book of the Courtier,* translated by L. E. Opdycke (Scribner's, New York, 1903), p. 9.

b   See, for instance, J. Burckhardt, *The Civilization of the Renaissance in Italy,* translated by S. G. C. Middlemore (Allen and Unwin, London, 1928), pp. 190–91.

c   *Book of the Courtier,* translated by Opdycke, *op. cit.,* p. 26.

d   *Ibid.*, p. 59.

e   *Ibid.*, pp. 62 and 64.

f   *Ibid.*, pp. 250–51.

g   *Ibid.*, pp. 294–95.

h   *Ibid.*, p. 305.

i   *Ibid.*, p. 286.

Chapter 2   /   Reformation

a   J. Gerson, *On the Way to Unite and Reform the Church in a General Council,* quoted in C. Beard, *The Reformation of the Sixteenth Century* (Williams and Norgate, London, 1903), p. 12.

b   Quoted in J. Burckhardt, *The Civilization of the Renaissance in Italy,* translated by S. G. C. Middlemore (Allen and Unwin, London, 1928), p. 464.

c   *A Treatise on Christian Liberty,* translated by W. A. Lambert, in *Works of Martin Luther* (A. J. Holman, Philadelphia, 1915), Vol. II, pp. 312–15 and 318.

d   *Ibid.*, pp. 320 and 323; and *An Open Letter to the Christian Nobility,* translated by C. M. Jacobs, in *Works of Martin Luther, op. cit.,* Vol. II, pp. 66–68.

e   *An Argument in Defense of All the Articles of Dr. Martin Luther Wrongly Condemned in the Roman Bull,* translated by C. M. Jacobs, in *Works of Martin Luther, op. cit.,* Vol. III, pp. 108–11.

f   *Tischreden* (Weimar), I, 1009; II, 2654a.

g   *A Treatise on Good Works*, translated by W. A. Lambert, in *Works of Martin Luther, op. cit.*, Vol. I, p. 191; and *A Treatise on Christian Liberty*, translated by Lambert, *op. cit.*, Vol. II, pp. 335–36.

h   *Secular Authority: To What Extent It Should Be Obeyed*, translated by J. J. Schindel, in *Works of Martin Luther, op. cit.*, Vol. III, p. 236.

i   *A Treatise on Good Works*, translated by Lambert, *op. cit.*, Vol. I, pp. 263–64.

j   *Ibid.*, pp. 262–63.

k   Quoted in A. C. McGiffert, *Martin Luther: The Man and His Work* (Century Co., New York, 1911), p. 350.

l   *Secular Authority: To What Extent It Should Be Obeyed*, translated by Schindel, *op. cit.*, Vol. III, pp. 251 and 253–54.

m   Quoted in McGiffert, *Martin Luther: The Man and His Work, op. cit.*, p. 308.

n   Quoted in J. Köstlin, *The Theology of Luther*, translated by C. E. Hay (United Lutheran, Philadelphia, 1897), Vol. II, p. 261.

o   Quoted in Beard, *The Reformation of the Sixteenth Century, op. cit.*, p. 163.

Chapter 3   /   Science and Scientific Method

a   *The Literary Works of Leonardo da Vinci*, edited by J. P. and I. A. Richter (Oxford, London, 1939), Vol. II, p. 85.

b   *Ibid.*, pp. 239–41.

c   William Gilbert, *On the Loadstone and Magnetic Bodies*, translated by P. F. Mottelay (Wiley, New York, 1893), Bk. I, Ch. I.

d   *Ibid.*, Bk. V, Ch. I.

e   Quoted in R. W. Church, *Bacon* (Harper, New York, 1902), p. 67.

f   *Great Instauration*, Proeminum and Plan of Work, in *The Works of Francis Bacon*, edited by J. Spedding, R. L. Ellis, and D. D. Heath (Longman & Co., London, 1857–74), Vol. IV (1868), pp. 7 and 26–27.

g   *Novum Organum*, in *Works*, edited by Spedding, Ellis, and Heath, *op. cit.*, Vol. IV (1868), Part I, Sec. 25.

h   *Ibid.*, Part I, Secs. 14 and 24.

i   *Ibid.*, Part I, Secs. 41 ff.

j   *Ibid.*, Part I, Secs. 18 and 36.

k   See *ibid.*, Preface.

l   *Great Instauration*, Plan of Work, *op. cit.*, Vol. IV (1868), p. 26.

m   This and the following passages are from *Novum Organum, op. cit.*, Vol. IV (1868), Part II, Secs. 11 ff.

n   *Great Instauration*, Preface, *op. cit.*, Vol. IV (1868), p. 19.

o   Quoted in E. A. Burtt, *The Metaphysical Foundations of Modern Physical Science* (Kegan Paul, London, 1925), p. 38; and W. C. D. and M. D. Whetham, *Cambridge Readings in the Literature of Science* (Cambridge University Press, 1928), p. 13.

p   Quoted in W. C. Rufus, D. J. Struik, and E. H. Johnson, *Johann Kepler* (Williams and Wilkins, Baltimore, 1931), p. 14.

q   *Ibid.*, pp. 26–27.

r   F. W. Westaway, *The Endless Quest* (Blackie, London, 1934), p. 146.

s   *The Sidereal Messenger*, translated by E. S. Carlos, in Whetham and Whetham, *Cambridge Readings in the Literature of Science, op. cit.*, pp. 17, 26–28, and 30.

t   Quoted in W. T. Sedgwick and H. W. Tyler, *A Short History of Science* (Macmillan, New York, 1917), p. 222.

u   *Ibid.*, pp. 222–23.

v   Galileo Galilei, *Dialogues Concerning Two New Sciences*, translated by H. Crew and A. de Salvio (Northwestern University Press, 1950), pp. 1–6.

w *Ibid.*, pp. 153–54.
x *Ibid.*, p. 162.
y *Ibid.*, pp. 166–67.
z *Ibid.*, pp. 174–76.
a *Ibid.*, pp. 170–72.
b *Ibid.*, pp. 178–79.
c *Il Saggiatore*, quoted in Burtt, *The Metaphysical Foundations of Modern Physical Science, op. cit.*, p. 75.

Chapter 4 / Hobbes

a Quoted in L. Stephen, *Hobbes* (Macmillan, London, 1904), pp. 17–18.
b *Elements of Philosophy*, in *The English Works of Thomas Hobbes*, edited by Sir W. Molesworth (J. Bohn, London, 1839–45), Vol. I (1839), Ch. 1, Secs. 8–9.
c *Ibid.*, Ch. 26, Sec. 1.
d *Ibid.*, Ch. 26, Sec. 2.
e *Ibid.*, Ch. 9, Secs. 1 and 3; Ch. 10, Sec. 5.
f *Ibid.*, Ch. 11, Secs. 1–2 and 7.
g *Ibid.*, Ch. 15, Secs. 2–3.
h *Ibid.*, Ch. 25, Sec. 1.
i *Leviathan*, in *Works*, edited by Molesworth, *op. cit.*, Vol. III (1839), Part II, Ch. 31.
j *Human Nature*, in *Works*, edited by Molesworth, *op. cit.*, Vol. IV (1840), Ch. 2, Sec. 10.
k *Leviathan, op. cit.*, Vol. III (1839), Part I, Ch. 2.
l *Ibid.*, Part I, Ch. 3.
m *Ibid.*, Part I, Ch. 1.
n *Human Nature, op. cit.*, Vol. IV (1840), Ch. 4, Secs. 9–10.
o *Elements, op. cit.*, Vol. I (1839), Ch. 2, Secs. 4 and 9; Ch. 3, Secs. 7–8.
p *Leviathan, op. cit.*, Vol. III (1839), Part I, Ch. 5.
q *Ibid.*, Part I, Ch. 7.
r *Elements, op. cit.*, Vol. I (1839), Ch. 25, Sec. 1.
s *Ibid.*, Ch. 27, Sec. 4.
t *Leviathan, op. cit.*, Vol. III (1839), Part I, Ch. 6.
u *Ibid.*, Part I, Chs. 11 and 13.
v *Ibid.*, Part I, Ch. 12.
w *Ibid.*, Part II, Ch. 18.
x *Ibid.*, Part I, Ch. 6.
y *Ibid.*, Introduction.
z *Ibid.*, Part I, Chs. 14–15.
a *Ibid.*, Part II, Ch. 17.

Chapter 5 / Descartes

a *Discourse on Method*, translated by E. S. Haldane and G. R. T. Ross, in *The Philosophical Works of Descartes* (Cambridge University Press, 1931), Vol. I, pp. 83–87.
b *Rules for the Direction of the Mind*, translated by Haldane and Ross, in *Works, op. cit.*, Vol. I, pp. 5, 7–9, 14–17, and 22.
c *Discourse on Method*, translated by Haldane and Ross, *op. cit.*, Vol. I, p. 87.
d *Ibid.*, pp. 81–82.
e *Ibid.*, p. 85.
f *Ibid.*, pp. 92–94.

g "Mathematics and the Laws of Nature," one of a series of radio talks sponsored by U. S. Rubber Company and published by them, 1947.

h G. H. Hardy, *A Mathematician's Apology* (Cambridge University Press, 1940), pp. 63–64.

i *Discourse on Method,* translated by Haldane and Ross, *op. cit.,* Vol. I, p. 89.

j *Meditations on First Philosophy,* translated by Haldane and Ross, in *Works, op. cit.,* Vol. I, pp. 145–48.

k *Ibid.,* pp. 149–50.

l *Ibid.,* pp. 162–67.

m *Third Set of Objections with Author's Reply,* translated by Haldane and Ross, in *Works, op. cit.,* Vol. II, pp. 66–67 and 69.

n *Second Set of Objections,* translated by Haldane and Ross, in *Works, op. cit.,* Vol. II, pp. 25–26.

o *Meditations,* translated by Haldane and Ross, *op. cit.,* Vol. I, pp. 185 and 190–91.

p *Principles of Philosophy,* translated by Haldane and Ross, in *Works, op. cit.,* Vol. I, pp. 239–40.

q *Considerations upon the Reputation, Loyalty, Manners, and Religion of Thomas Hobbes Written by Himself,* in *The English Works of Thomas Hobbes,* edited by Sir W. Molesworth (J. Bohn, London, 1839–45), Vol. IV (1840), p. 247; and *Leviathan,* in *Works,* edited by Molesworth, *op. cit.,* Vol. III (1839), Part III, Ch. 34.

r *Principles of Philosophy,* translated by Haldane and Ross, *op. cit.,* Vol. I, pp. 255–56, 259–60, 262, and 264–67.

s *Ibid.,* p. 269.

t *Ibid.,* pp. 223 and 232.

u *Ibid.,* pp. 234–36.

v *Meditations,* translated by Haldane and Ross, *op. cit.,* Vol. I, pp. 159–60.

w *Ibid.,* pp. 160–61.

x *Ibid.,* pp. 194, 187, and 193.

y *Ibid.,* pp. 196–98.

z *Principles of Philosophy,* translated by Haldane and Ross, *op. cit.,* Vol. I, p. 223.

a *The Passions of the Soul,* translated by Haldane and Ross, in *Works, op. cit.,* Vol. I, p. 382.

b *Meditations,* translated by Haldane and Ross, *op. cit.,* Vol. I, pp. 192 and 196; and *The Passions of the Soul,* translated by Haldane and Ross, *op. cit.,* Vol. I, pp. 345–46.

Chapter 6 / Spinoza

a *Ethics,* translated by R. H. M. Elwes (Bell, London, 1919), Part I, pp. 39–42.

b *Ibid.,* Part I, Prop. viii, note ii; Props. xi and xiv.

c *Ibid.,* Part I, Prop. xv, note; Prop. xvii, Coroll., note.

d *Ibid.,* Part II, Prop. vii, Coroll., note.

e *Ibid.,* Part I, Prop. xv, note.

f *Ibid.,* Part II, Lemmas i and iii and Coroll.; Ax. ii and Def.

g *Ibid.,* Part IV, Preface.

h *Ibid.,* Part IV, Prop. xxviii.

i *Ibid.,* Part V, Preface.

j *Ibid.,* Part V, Props. ii, iii, and iv, Coroll.; Prop. vi and note.

k *Ibid.,* Part V, Prop. xlii.

Chapter 7 / Leibniz

a *Letter to M. Bayle,* translated by P. P. Wiener, in *Leibniz: Selections* (Scribner's, New York, 1951), pp. 182–84.

b *Letter to De Volder,* translated by Wiener, in *Leibniz, op. cit.,* pp. 157–58; and *Specimen Dynamicum,* translated by Wiener, in *Leibniz, op. cit.,* pp. 119–21.

c *Specimen Dynamicum*, translated by Wiener, *op. cit.*, p. 130.
d *The Principles of Nature and of Grace, Based on Reason*, translated by Wiener, in *Leibniz, op. cit.*, §§1–2, pp. 522–23; and *Monadology*, translated by Wiener, in *Leibniz, op. cit.*, §§7–16, pp. 533–36; §§66–67 and 69–70, p. 547.
e *The Principles of Nature and of Grace*, translated by Wiener, *op. cit.*, §§3–4, pp. 523–24; and *Monadology*, translated by Wiener, *op. cit.*, §§49–52, pp. 542–43; §62, p. 546.
f *Monadology*, translated by Wiener, *op. cit.*, §§44–45 and 53–59, pp. 541–45.
g *Ibid.*, §17, p. 536.
h *Ibid.*, §58, p. 544.

Chapter 8 / Locke

a Quoted in H. R. Fox Bourne, *The Life of John Locke* (Harper, New York, 1876), Vol. I, pp. 43 and 48.
b *Ibid.*, Vol. II, p. 557.
c *An Essay Concerning Human Understanding*, edited by A. C. Fraser (Clarendon Press, Oxford, 1894), "Epistle to the Reader," p. 9.
d From a paper (written in 1669) on "The Art of Medicine" (quoted in Fox Bourne, *The Life of John Locke, op. cit.*, Vol. I, p. 224).
e *Essay*, edited by Fraser, *op. cit.*, IV, xix, 14.
f *Ibid.*, IV, vii, 11.
g *Ibid.*, I, iii, 24–25.
h See *ibid.*, IV, ii, 1; vii, 19.
i *Ibid.*, II, i, 2–5.
j *Ibid.*, II, ii, 1–2.
k *Ibid.*, II, iv, 1 and 4.
l *Ibid.*, II, v, 1.
m *Ibid.*, II, xii, 1.
n *Ibid.*, II, xiii, 4.
o *Ibid.*, II, xvii, 8.
p *Ibid.*, II, xvii, 7.
q *Ibid.*, II, xxiii, 1–5.
r *Ibid.*, II, xxi, 4.
s *Ibid.*, II, xxi, 1.
t W. James, *The Principles of Psychology* (Holt, New York, 1890), Vol. I, p. 224.
u *Essay*, edited by Fraser, *op. cit.*, IV, i, 1–2.
v *Ibid.*, IV, ix, 3.
w *Ibid.*, IV, x, 3–6.
x *Ibid.*, IV, xi, 1–2 and 8–9.
y See *ibid.*, III, iii, 15; II, xxxi, 6.
z *Ibid.*, IV, i, 4.
a *Ibid.*, III, iii, 7–8.
b *Ibid.*, II, xx, 2.
c *Ibid.*, II, xxi, 35.
d *Ibid.*, II, xxi, 44–45 and 60–61.
e *Ibid.*, II, xxviii, 5–7.
f *Ibid.*, II, xxviii, 10–11.
g *Ibid.*, II, xxviii, 12.
h *Ibid.*, II, xxviii, 8.
i *Ibid.*, III, xi, 16; IV, xii, 8.
j *Ibid.*, IV, iii, 18.
k *Ibid.*, IV, xiii, 4.

l   *Of Civil Government* (Dent, London, 1924), Secs. 4–15.
m   *Ibid.*, Sec. 54.
n   *Ibid.*, Secs. 95–99.
o   *Ibid.*, Secs. 26–27 and 30–32.
p   *Ibid.*, Secs. 46–47
q   *Ibid.*, Secs. 123–27 and 131.
r   *Ibid.*, Sec. 132.
s   *Ibid.*, Sec. 213.
t   *Letter on Toleration*, in *The Works of John Locke* (A. Bettesworth, London, 1727), Vol. II, p. 252.
u   *Ibid.*, pp. 248, 252, and 254.

Chapter 9 / Berkeley

a   *A Treatise Concerning the Principles of Human Knowledge,* edited by A. C. Fraser, in *The Works of George Berkeley* (Clarendon Press, Oxford, 1901), Vol. I, Part I, §93.
b   *Ibid.*, Part I, §10.
c   *Ibid.*, Part I, §14.
d   *Three Dialogues between Hylas and Philonous*, edited by Fraser, in *Works, op. cit.*, Vol. I, pp. 384–86.
e   *Principles*, edited by Fraser, *op. cit.*, Vol. I, Part I, §1.
f   *Ibid.*, Introduction, §1.
g   *Ibid.*, Introduction, §24.
h   *Ibid.*, Introduction, §§6 and 10.
i   *Ibid.*, Part I, §1.
j   *Three Dialogues*, edited by Fraser, *op. cit.*, Vol. I, pp. 408–10.
k   *Principles*, edited by Fraser, *op. cit.*, Vol. I, Part I, §3.
l   *Three Dialogues*, edited by Fraser, *op. cit.*, Vol. I, pp. 437–38.
m   *Principles*, edited by Fraser, *op. cit.*, Vol. I, Part I, §58.
n   *Three Dialogues*, edited by Fraser, *op. cit.*, Vol. I, p. 430.
o   *Principles*, edited by Fraser, *op. cit.*, Vol. I, Part I, §29.
p   *Ibid.*, Part I, §146.
q   *Three Dialogues*, edited by Fraser, *op. cit.*, Vol. I, pp. 447 and 449.
r   *Ibid.*, p. 450.
s   *Ibid.*, pp. 447–48.

Chapter 10 / Hume

a   *An Enquiry Concerning the Human Understanding*, edited by L. A. Selby-Bigge (Clarendon Press, Oxford, 1894), §I.
b   *Ibid.*, §II.
c   *A Treatise of Human Nature*, edited by L. A. Selby-Bigge (Clarendon Press, Oxford, 1896), I, i, 4.
d   *Enquiry*, edited by Selby-Bigge, *op. cit.*, §III; and *Treatise*, edited by Selby-Bigge, *op. cit.*, I, i, 4.
e   *Treatise*, edited by Selby-Bigge, *op. cit.*, I, i, 7.
f   *Ibid.*, I, i, 6.
g   *Ibid.*, I, iv, 6.
h   *Ibid.*, I, iv, 2.
i   *Ibid.*, I, iv, 6.
j   *Ibid.*

k *Ibid.*

l *Enquiry*, edited by Selby-Bigge, *op. cit.*, §XII, Pt. I.

m *Treatise*, edited by Selby-Bigge, *op. cit.*, I, iv, 2.

n *Ibid.*

o *Ibid.*

p *Enquiry*, edited by Selby-Bigge, *op. cit.*, §VII, Pts. I and II.

q *Ibid.*, §VII, Pt. II.

r *Ibid.*, §IV, Pt. II.

s *Ibid.*, §IV, Pt. I.

t *Ibid.*

u *Treatise*, edited by Selby-Bigge, *op. cit.*, I, iii, 1.

v *Ibid.*, I, ii, 4; iii, 1.

w *Enquiry*, edited by Selby-Bigge, *op. cit.*, §VII, Pt. I.

x *Treatise*, edited by Selby-Bigge, *op. cit.*, I, iii, 1.

y *Dialogues Concerning Natural Religion*, edited by N. Kemp Smith (Nelson, Edinburgh, 1947), Pt. II.

z *Ibid.*, Pts. II and VIII.

a This and the following passages are from *Enquiry*, edited by Selby-Bigge, *op. cit.*, §XI.

b *Dialogues*, edited by Kemp Smith, *op. cit.*, Pts. V and VI.

c *Ibid.*, Pt. VII.

d *Ibid.*

e *Ibid.*, Pt. XI.

f *Ibid.*, Pts. X and XI.

g *Ibid.*, Pt. XII.

h *Ibid.*, Pts. X and I.

i *Ibid.*, Pt. XII.

j *An Enquiry Concerning the Principles of Morals*, edited by L. A. Selby-Bigge (Clarendon Press, Oxford, 1894), Appendix I.

k *Ibid.*, §I.

l *Treatise*, edited by Selby-Bigge, *op. cit.*, III, ii, 3.

m *Enquiry Concerning Morals*, edited by Selby-Bigge, *op. cit.*, §I.

n *Ibid.*, §IX, Pt. I.

o *Ibid.*

p *Treatise*, edited by Selby-Bigge, *op. cit.*, III, iii, 1; and *Enquiry Concerning Morals*, edited by Selby-Bigge, *op. cit.*, §VI, Pt. II.

q *Treatise*, edited by Selby-Bigge, *op. cit.*, III, i, 2.

r *Ibid.*, III, iii, 1.

s *Ibid.*, III, ii, 1.

t *Enquiry Concerning Morals*, edited by Selby-Bigge, *op. cit.*, Appendix II.

u *Ibid.*

v *Ibid.*

w *Treatise*, edited by Selby-Bigge, *op. cit.*, III, iii, 3.

x *Ibid.*, I, iv, 7.

y *Ibid.*, I, iv, 1; and *Enquiry*, edited by Selby-Bigge, *op. cit.*, §V, Pt. I.

z *Enquiry*, edited by Selby-Bigge, *op. cit.*, §IX.

a *Dialogues*, edited by Kemp Smith, *op. cit.*, Pt. I.

b *Enquiry*, edited by Selby-Bigge, *op. cit.*, §XII, Pt. III.

c *Ibid.*

d *Ibid.*, §I.

e *Ibid.*, §XII, Pt. II.

Suggestions for Further Reading

The best course to pursue is to turn directly to the various great texts from which the selections in this volume have been drawn. Thus, instead of being content with the extracts given here, read the whole of Descartes' *Meditations,* of Hume's *Enquiry,* and so on. Information concerning translations and editions will be found in the bibliographical notes section.

Beyond the masters themselves, here is a short list of books about them and their times that should help to make their theories more intelligible.

HOBBES

T. E. Jessop: *Thomas Hobbes* (London, 1960). This short essay maintains that "if Hobbes was an atheist, he was in *Leviathan* a perfectly hypocritical one."

J. Laird: *Hobbes* (London, 1934). A well-balanced study containing a useful account of Hobbes's influence.

R. Peters: *Hobbes* (New York, 1956). A judicious discussion of most of the central problems raised by Hobbes's theories.

Also useful:

L. Stephen: *Hobbes* (London, 1904).
A. E. Taylor: *Hobbes* (London, 1908).
H. Warrender: *The Political Philosophy of Hobbes* (Oxford, 1957).

DESCARTES

W. Doney (editor): *Descartes: A Collection of Essays* (New York, 1967). Contains sixteen studies, some unpublished elsewhere, on various aspects of Descartes' thought.
A. B. Gibson: *The Philosophy of Descartes* (New York, 1932). Considers Descartes' thought from the point of view of his own interests rather than from the point of view of the development of his ideas by others.
N. Kemp Smith: *Studies in Cartesian Philosophy* (London, 1902). Especially good on the Occasionalists and other thinkers whom Descartes influenced.
A. Sesonski and N. Fleming (editors): *Meta-Meditations: Studies in Descartes* (Belmont, Calif., 1965). A collection of journal articles by contemporary philosophers.

Also useful:

A. G. A. Balz: *Descartes and the Modern Mind* (New Haven, 1952).
E. S. Haldane: *Descartes: His Life and Times* (New York, 1905).
S. V. Keeling: *Descartes* (London, 1934).

SPINOZA

S. Hampshire: *Spinoza* (London, 1956). An acute and sympathetic study by a writer who does not share Spinoza's devotion to metaphysics.
H. H. Joachim: *A Study of the Ethics of Spinoza* (Oxford, 1901). Excellent, though perhaps difficult for the beginning student.
H. A. Wolfson: *The Philosophy of Spinoza* (Cambridge, Mass., 1934). Emphasizes the Hebraic and Arabic background of Spinoza's thought and holds him to have been "the last of the Mediaevals and the first of the moderns."

Also useful:

R. McKeon: *The Philosophy of Spinoza* (Boston, 1928).
L. Roth: *Spinoza* (Boston, 1929).

LEIBNIZ

H. W. Carr: *Leibniz* (Boston, 1929). Regards Leibniz as "the first philosopher of the modern period to indicate the true nature of idealism."
B. Russell: *A Critical Exposition of the Philosophy of Leibniz* (London, 1937). Holds that the theory of monads is "a rigid deduction from a small number of premises," some of which are unfortunately mutually inconsistent.

Also useful:

H. W. B. Joseph: *Lectures on the Philosophy of Leibniz* (Oxford, 1949).

LOCKE

M. Cranston: *Locke* (London, 1961). A short but interesting account of Locke's life, emphasizing his lack of candor and his occasional "neurotic" secrecy.

J. Gibson: *Locke's Theory of Knowledge* (New York, 1917). Holds that the "sensationalistic atomism" of the *Essay* has been overemphasized.

J. W. Yolton: *John Locke and the Way of Ideas* (London, 1956). Examines the reactions of Locke's contemporaries to the *Essay* and concludes that it "had a disturbing effect on the traditional moral and religious beliefs of his day."

Also useful:

S. Alexander: *Locke* (New York, 1908).

A. C. Fraser: *Locke* (New York, 1901).

S. P. Lamprecht: *The Moral and Political Philosophy of John Locke* (New York, 1918).

BERKELEY

G. D. Hicks: *Berkeley* (London, 1932). A well-rounded study.

G. A. Johnson: *The Development of Berkeley's Philosophy* (New York, 1923). Undertakes "a careful study of his works in their chronological sequence and by detailed reference to his relations with his predecessors and contemporaries."

J. Wild: *George Berkeley* (New York, 1936). Holds that the late, Neoplatonic phase of Berkeley's thought has been neglected and that there is a continuous development of these ideas from his earliest works.

HUME

N. Kemp Smith: *The Philosophy of David Hume* (London, 1941). Undertakes to show that Hume's "philosophy originates in his preoccupation with moral questions."

E. C. Mossner: *The Life of David Hume* (Austin, Tex., 1954). A full-length study, with interesting material quoted from letters.

J. A. Passmore: *Hume's Intentions* (Cambridge, 1952). Holds that Hume's "great achievement lies in his contribution to a conception of science in which speculation, not security, is the key-note" and in which "reason appears in its true colours, as a form of human enterprise."

H. H. Price: *Hume's Theory of the External World* (Oxford, 1940). A very acute and useful analysis of one of the central problems raised by Hume.

A. Sesonski and N. Fleming (editors): *Human Understanding: Studies in the Philosophy of Hume* (Belmont, Calif., 1965). A collection of articles by contemporary philosophers.

Also useful:

B. M. Laing: *David Hume* (London, 1932).

J. Laird: *Hume's Philosophy of Human Nature* (London, 1932).

J. B. Stewart: *The Moral and Political Philosophy of David Hume* (New York, 1963).

GENERAL

C. L. Becker: *The Heavenly City of the Eighteenth Century Philosophers* (New Haven, 1932). Maintains with wit and learning that "the *philosophes* demolished the Heavenly City of St. Augustine only to rebuild it with more up-to-date materials."

J. Burckhardt: *The Civilization of the Renaissance in Italy.* This classic study is available in many editions, some well illustrated.

E. A. Burtt: *The Metaphysical Foundations of Modern Physical Theory* (New York, 1925). Discusses the metaphysical assumptions underlying the work of the early modern scientists and shows how these assumptions influenced the thinking of philosophers.

H. Butterfield: *The Origins of Modern Science* (London, 1949). Stresses the "moments that seem pivotal, those cases in which men not only solved a problem but had to alter their mentality in the process."

E. Cassirer: *The Philosophy of the Enlightenment,* translated by F. C. A. Koelln and J. P. Pettegrove (Princeton, N. J., 1951). Holds that the course of thought in the eighteenth century led "from mere geometry to a dynamic philosophy of nature, from mechanism to organism, from the principle of identity to that of infinity, from continuity to harmony."

G. N. Clark: *The Seventeenth Century* (Oxford, 1950). "The purpose of this book is to examine some of the more important activities of the seventeenth century, distinguishing their mutual relations and their places in the great transition."

A. Cobban: *In Search of Humanity: The Role of the Enlightenment in Modern History* (London, 1960). Holds that modern society has forgotten what was fundamental in the eighteenth-century world view—the belief in the capacity of reason to discover absolute political and ethical norms.

W. K. Ferguson: *The Renaissance in Historical Thought* (Boston, 1948). A history, not of the Renaissance itself, but of five centuries of changing interpretations of the Renaissance.

R. H. Tawney: *Religion and the Rise of Capitalism* (New York, 1926). Examines the relations between economic conditions and religious doctrine.

H. O. Taylor: *Thought and Expression in the Sixteenth Century* (New York, 1920). A thorough and valuable treatise.

B. Willey: *The Eighteenth Century Background* (London, 1940). Illustrates the importance in the eighteenth century of the idea of "nature" in religion, ethics, philosophy, and politics.

————: *The Seventeenth Century Background* (New York, 1958). Discusses the impact on "traditional beliefs, and especially theological and poetical beliefs, of the scientific world view with its new conceptions of truth and explanation."

Glossary

Short, dictionary-type definitions of philosophical terms are likely to be misleading, for philosophers use terms in many different ways and with little regard to common usage (on which, of course, dictionary definitions are based). Accordingly, many of the definitions given in this Glossary are accompanied by references to places in the text where the terms in question appear in a concrete context. For terms not defined in the Glossary, consult the Index; for fuller treatment of them and of other philosophical terms, see *The Encyclopedia of Philosophy*, edited by P. Edwards (Free Press, New York, 1967). Also available are the *Dictionary of Philosophy*, edited by D. D. Runes (Philosophical Library, New York, 1942), and *Dictionary of Philosophy and Psychology*, edited by J. M. Baldwin (Macmillan, New York, 1925). The *Encyclopaedia Britannica* (eleventh edition) contains excellent articles on many philosophical terms, including some of those in this Glossary.

Abstraction: The power of separating, in thought, one part of a complex from the other parts and attending to it separately. Thus, to consider the color of an apple in isolation from the apple's other qualities would be to abstract this quality for attention.

A priori: What is known independently of sense perception and for this reason held to be indubitable. The doctrine of innate ideas (see definition) was an attempt to account for the alleged existence of a priori knowledge.

Attribute: See **Substance**.

Axiom: A proposition held to be self-evidently true and so neither requiring nor indeed capable of proof. Hence a first principle from which all proofs start. Those who deny the self-evident truth of axioms hold them to be simply postulates from which such-and-such theorems can be deduced. Thus, according to this view, the axioms of one deductive system may be deduced from another set of postulates in some other deductive system. See, for instance, Spinoza's use of axioms in his *Ethics* (pp. 194–95).

Conceptualism: The view that universals are neither independently existing entities nor mere names, but are concepts formed in the mind. See **Nominalism, Realism,** and **Universal**.

Contingent: That which may be and also may not be. Hence an event whose occurrence is not necessarily determined (see **Determinism**) by other events.

Cosmology: The study of the universal world process. Distinguished from ontology (see definition) chiefly by the fact that, whereas the latter asks what reality *is*, cosmology asks how reality unfolds and develops in successive stages.

Deduction: A type of inference (see definition) that yields necessary conclusions. In deduction, one or more propositions (called "premises") being assumed, another proposition (the conclusion) is seen to be entailed or implied. It is usually held that in deduction the movement of thought is from premises of greater generality to a conclusion of lesser generality (from the premises "All men are mortal" and "All Greeks are men," we deduce that "All Greeks are mortal"), but the chief mark of deduction is the necessity with which the conclusion follows from the premises.

Determinism: The theory that denies contingency (see **Contingent**) and claims that everything that happens happens necessarily and in accordance with some regular pattern or law. There are three main types, or versions, of determinism: (1) a *scientific determinism* (in which all events are determined by antecedent events in time), (2) a *logical determinism* (as with Spinoza [see pp. 203–05]), and (3) a *teleological determinism* (in which all events are held to be determined in accordance with God's plan).

Discursive: The characteristic of the human intelligence that limits it, in the main, to a step-by-step reasoning—from premises to conclusion, from this conclusion to another, and so on. Hence to be contrasted with the all-inclusive vision of the mystic, with the possible operation of a suprahuman intellect, and with the way in which, according to some writers, axioms (see **Axiom**) and other self-evident principles are comprehended by the mind. See Descartes' account of the distinction between "intuition" and "deduction" (p. 157).

Dualism: Any view that holds two ultimate and irreducible principles to be necessary to explain the world. Descartes' two-substance theory (thinking substance, or mind, and extended substance, or body) is an example of dualism (see pp. 176–77).

Empiricism: The view that holds sense perception to be the sole source of human knowledge. Locke's "historical plain method" is an example of empiricism (see pp. 245–46).

Epistemology: From the Greek terms *episteme* (knowledge) and *logos* (theory, account). Hence the study of the origins, nature, and limitations of knowledge.

Essence: The that-about-a-thing-that-makes-it-what-it-is, in contrast to those properties that the thing may happen to possess but need not possess in order to be itself. Thus it is held (1) that we have to distinguish between those properties of Socrates that are "accidental" and so nonessential (for example, dying by hemlock) and those properties that are essential (for example, those traits of character and personality that made him the man he was). Further, it is held (2) that we have to distinguish between essence and existence (see definition): It is possible (according to this view) to define Socrates' essence exhaustively; yet when we have done so, the question still remains whether any such being exists. Holders of this view would maintain that there is only one object in which essence and existence are inseparable; this object is God. (For Spinoza's discussion of this point, see pp. 198–99.)

Eudaemonism: From the Greek term *eudaimonia*, usually translated as "happiness." Hence the view that the end of life consists in happiness, conceived of as an all-round, balanced, long-range type of well-being, in distinction from pleasure. Contrasted with hedonism (see definition).

Existence: Actuality or factuality. Contrasted with essence (see definition).

Experiment: A situation arranged to test an hypothesis. Contrasted with "mere" observation.

Free will: The doctrine of contingency (see **Contingent**) applied specifically to human behavior; the denial that men's acts are completely determined (see **Determinism**). The question of free will is important because many philosophers hold that "ought" implies "can"—that moral judgments of approbation and disapprobation are meaningless unless the acts judged about are free, that is, under the control of the agent, who, had he so chosen, might have done otherwise. The main problems connected with free will are (1) what meaning, if any, can be attached to the notion of a free choice and (2) how the possibility of being otherwise is compatible with either (a) belief in an omnipotent and omniscient Deity or (b) the doctrine of universal causal determinism. See Index.

Hedonism: The view that pleasure is man's good. Contrasted with eudaemonism (see definition). *Ethical hedonism* holds either (1) that a man's own pleasure is the sole end worth aiming at or (2) that other people's pleasure is to be taken into account. *Psychological hedonism* holds that, whatever men ought to aim at, they do in fact aim at pleasure. (For an attack on psychological hedonism, see pp. 343–45.)

Humanism: A variously used term. Employed (1) to describe the type of view that distinguishes man from the animals on the ground that man has certain moral obligations. Also used (2) to contrast a secular type of ethics with a religious ethics. Thus Plato's and Aristotle's ethics could be called "humanistic," in contrast with the ethics of Augustine, on the ground that they hold man himself, rather than God, to be the supreme value. Also used (3) to designate a particular historical movement, beginning in the fourteenth century, that emphasized the study of classical literature and the revival of classical ideals (see pp. 33–43).

Idealism: In general, any view that holds reality to be mental or "spiritual," or mind-dependent. *Subjective idealism* emphasizes the ultimate reality of the knowing subject and may either admit the existence of a plurality of such subjects (as with Berkeley [see pp. 292–93]) or deny the existence of all save one (in which case the view is called solipsism [see definition]). *Objective idealism* denies that the distinction between subject and object, between knower and known, is ultimate and maintains that all finite knowers and their thoughts are included in an Absolute Thought.

Induction: A type of inference (see definition) in which (in contrast to deduction [see definition]) the movement of thought is from lesser to greater generality. Thus induction begins, not from premises, but from observed particulars (for example, the observation that A, B, and C all have the property *x*) and seeks to establish some generalization about them (for example, that all members of the class *y*, of which A, B, and C are members, have the property *x*). The main problem connected with induction is the difficulty of determining the conditions under which we are warranted in moving from an observed "Some so-and-so's have such-and-such" to the unobserved "All so-and-so's probably have such-and-such." (For Hume's criticisms of induction, see pp. 315–22.)

Inference: The movement of thought by which we reach a conclusion from premises. Thus we speak of inductive and of deductive inference.

Innate ideas: According to the doctrine of innate ideas, we must distinguish between (1) ideas that we acquire in the course of our experience and (2) ideas that we possess antecedently to all experience. Holders of this view—among them, Descartes (see pp. 182–83) and Leibniz (see pp. 244–45)—would allow that some experience may be the occasion of our becoming consciously aware of an innate idea, but they would argue that the idea itself (for example, the idea of absolute equality) can never be found in experience. (For Locke's attack on the doctrine of innate ideas, see pp. 242–43.)

Intuition: Direct and immediate knowledge. To be contrasted with discursive (see definition) knowledge.

Judgment: The movement of thought by which, for example, we assert (or deny) some predicate of a subject, or, more generally, by which we connect two terms by some relation. Thus, when we say "This rose is red" or "New York is east of Chicago," we judge. Following Kant, most philosophers distinguish between (1) *analytical judgments,* in which the predicate concept is contained in the subject concept, and (2) *synthetical judgments,* in which the predicate concept is not so contained; and also between (3) *a priori judgments,* which are universal and necessary, and (4) *a posteriori judgments,* which are not universal and necessary.

Law of nature: See **Natural law.**

Materialism: The doctrine that reality is matter. Whereas idealism (see definition) holds that matter is "really" the thought of some mind or other, materialism holds that minds and all other apparently nonmaterial things (for example, gods) are reducible to the complex motions of material particles. Hobbes's theory (see pp. 122–27) is an example of materialism.

Metaphysics: The study of the ultimate nature of reality, or, as some philosophers would say, the study of "being as such." To be contrasted, therefore, with physics, which studies the "being" of physical nature; with astronomy, which studies the "being" of the solar system; with biology, which studies the "being" of animate nature; and so on. By "being as such," these philosophers mean, not the special characteristics of special kinds of things (for example, living things), but the most general and pervasive characteristics of all things. What Hobbes called "first philosophy"—the theorems that he held to be true of all bodies everywhere—is the materialistic equivalent of metaphysics (see pp. 122–23). (For Hume's criticism of metaphysics, see pp. 303–11.)

Monism: The view that everything is reducible to one kind of thing, or that one principle of explanation is sufficient to explain everything. No Christian philosopher could be a monist, for the Christian must insist on an ultimate and irreducible distinction between God the Creator and the universe He created.

Mysticism: The view that reality is ineffable and transcendent, that it is known, therefore, by some special, nonrational means; that knowledge of it is incommunicable in any precise conceptual scheme; and that it is communicable, if at all, only in poetic imagery and metaphor.

Naturalism: Another variously used term. (1) In one meaning, naturalism is a view that excludes any reference to supernatural principles and holds the world to be explicable in terms of scientifically verifiable concepts. In this meaning, naturalism is roughly equivalent to secularism and, like humanism (see definition), can be contrasted with a religiously oriented theory like Neoplatonism. (2) In another meaning, the emphasis is on the unity of behavior; any difference in kind between men and animals is denied, and human conduct and human institutions are held to be simply more complex instances of behavior patterns occurring among lower organisms. In this sense, naturalism is to be contrasted with humanism.

Natural law: This term may designate (1) a pattern of regularity that holds in physical nature. Thus people talk about the "law" of gravity and hold it to be a law of nature (or a natural law) that bodies attract each other directly with their masses and inversely with the square of their distance. Those who affirm the existence of natural laws in this sense hold that these laws are necessary and universal (not merely empirical generalizations concerning observable sequences) and that they are discoverable by reason. Or the term may designate (2) a moral imperative—not a description of what actually happens in the physical world, but a description of what *ought* to happen in men's relations to one another. In this sense, too, these laws would be regarded by those who affirm their existence as being of universal application and discoverable by reason. (For Locke's view of natural law, see pp. 261–66.)

Nominalism: The view that only particulars are real and that universals (see **Universal**) are but observable likenesses among the particulars of sense experience. For an example of nominalism, see p. 303.

Objective: To say that anything is "objective" is to say that it is real, that it has a public nature independent of us and of our judgments about it. Thus the question of whether or not values are objective turns on whether or not values are more than private preferences. If they are private preferences, our value judgments are subjective, and there is no more disputing about them than there is about judgments of taste: My good is what *I* prefer; yours is what *you* prefer. On the other hand, if values are objective, it follows that when we differ about them, at least one of us is mistaken.

Ontology: From the Greek terms *ontos* (being) and *logos* (theory, account). About equivalent in meaning to metaphysics (see definition). When we inquire about the "ontological status" of something, say, perception, we ask whether the objects of perception are real or illusory, and, if real, what sort of reality they possess (for example, whether they are mind-dependent or whether they exist independently of minds), and so on.

Pantheism: From the Greek terms *pan* (all) and *theos* (god). Hence the view that all things share in the divine nature, or that all things are parts of god. Pantheism represented a danger that Christian thinkers, who were committed to a transcendent God, had at all costs to avoid.

Phenomenalism: A type of view that, like idealism (see definition), holds that what we know is mind-dependent, but that, unlike idealism, holds that reality itself is not mind-dependent. Usually, phenomenalism does not attempt to inquire into the possible underlying causes of events, but limits itself to generalizing about empirically observable sequences.

Primary qualities: Those qualities thought to belong to bodies. To be distinguished from secondary qualities, which are held to be products of the interaction between our sense organs and the primary qualities of bodies. The distinction was introduced, in connection with the development of modern science (see pp. 115–17), to account for the status of colors, sounds, and tastes. It was held that these were less real than such properties as motion and weight, which were capable of analysis in the new mechanics.

Rationalism: (1) As contrasted with empiricism (see definition), rationalism means reliance on reason (that is, on deduction, on the criterion of logical consistency). (2) As contrasted with authoritarianism or mysticism (see definition), rationalism means reliance on our human powers.

Realism: (1) As contrasted with nominalism (see definition), realism holds that universals are real, and more real than the particulars of sense experience. (In this sense Descartes was a realist and Hobbes was a nominalist.) (2) As contrasted with idealism (see definition), realism holds that the objects of our knowledge are not mind-dependent but are independently existing entities. (In this sense, Descartes and Hobbes were both realists, whereas Berkeley was an idealist.) (3) As contrasted with idealism in still another sense, realism is the point of view that interests itself in men and institutions as they are, rather than as they ought to be. (In this sense, Machiavelli and Hobbes were both realists.) In this sense, also, realism is almost equivalent to naturalism (see definition).

Relativism: The view that maintains our judgments to be relative to (that is, conditioned upon) certain factors such as cultural milieu or individual bias. Hence the view that we do not possess any absolute, objective (see definition) truth. The relativist need not hold that all judgments are relative; it is possible, for instance, to hold that the physical sciences yield absolute truth while maintaining that in other fields (for example, ethics and religion) there is no absolute truth.

Scepticism: The position that denies the possibility of knowledge. Here, as with relativism (see definition), it is possible either to have a total scepticism or to limit one's scepticism to certain fields. Thus it is possible (as with Plato) to be sceptical of sense perception while holding that we can reach the truth by means of reason, or (as with St. Bernard) to be sceptical of reason while holding that we can reach the truth in a mystical experience (see **Mysticism**).

Solipsism: From the Latin *solus* (alone) and *ipse* (self). Hence the view that everything other than oneself is a state of oneself.

Subjectivism: See **Objective, Relativism,** and **Scepticism.**

Substance: Another variously used term. (1) In one meaning, substance is simply that which is real. Thus Aristotle called those amalgams of matter and form that he took reality to consist of "substances." (2) In another meaning, substance is about equivalent to essence (see definition). Also, (3) substance is contrasted with attribute (or property, or quality) as that which *has* the attributes. Thus substance is the underlying (and unknown) ground in which properties are thought to inhere; it is that about which we are judging when we assert properties of a subject, for example, when we say "The rose is red." Hence (4) substance is that which, unlike an attribute or property, exists in its own right and depends on nothing else. (For an attack on the doctrine of substance, see p. 304.) See Index.

Teleology: From the Greek terms *telos* (end, goal) and *logos* (theory, account). Hence the view that affirms the reality of purpose and holds the universe either to be consciously designed by God or to be the working out of partly conscious, partly unconscious purposes that are immanent in the developing organisms. (For an attempt to reconcile teleology and mechanism, see pp. 230–33. For an attack on the concept of divine teleology, see pp. 326–27.)

Universal: A universal is that which is predicable of many. Thus "man" is a universal because it is predicable of Washington, Jefferson, Hamilton, and all other individual men. The main problem about universals concerns their ontological status (see **Ontology**). Are they (1) separate entities distinct from the individuals of which they are predicable, (2) real but not separable, or (3) not real at all, but merely the names of likenesses shared by certain particulars? See **Nominalism, Realism,** and Index.

Index

This is primarily an index of proper names. Thus titles and principal topics of discussion are indexed under the authors. Topics that recur in the work of several philosophers are also indexed as main entries. Page numbers in *italics* refer to quotations; those in **boldface** refer to major discussions.

God *(continued)*
213, *213,* 214, 216, *217,* 218; Thomas Aquinas on, 20, 33, 167, 199, 200, 259; as transcendent Other, 200, 200 n. *See also* Religion; Theology.
God, proof of existence of: Anselm's, 167; Berkeley's, 290–92, *291;* Descartes', *165–67,* 165–71, *167–68, 168,* 173, 173 n., 183 n., 201, 326; Hume's rejection of, 326–37, *328, 329, 330, 330–31, 331–32, 332, 333, 334;* Leibniz's, 229–30, *229–30;* Spinoza's, 196–99, *197–98*
Great Schism, in Catholic Church, 45, 49
Greig, J. Y. T., 297 n.
Grisar, H., 58 n.
Guicciardini, Francesco, *50,* 50 n.
Guilds, medieval. *See* Medieval guilds.

Hardy, G. H., *161*
Hegel, Georg Wilhelm Friedrich, 349
Hendel, C. W., 334 n.
History of the Reformation, A (Lindsay), 48 n.
Hobbes, Thomas, 3, **118–53,** 119 n., 219, 239; on association of ideas, *131,* 131–32; and Berkeley, 290; on body (matter), *122–23,* 122–27, *124–26;* on causality, *124–25;* on cogitating motions, 128–30; and Descartes, 159–61, 167–68, *167–68,* 176, 188; *Elements of Law* by, 121 n.; *Elements of Philosophy* by, *121,* 121 n., *122–23, 124–26, 126–27, 133;* on "first philosophy," *122–23,* 122–24, 126, 134; on God, *121, 150, 167–68,* 168; *Human Nature* by, 121 n.; and Hume, 296, 303, 343; on identity, 124, *125–26;* on laws of nature, 145–48, *146–47;* and Leibniz, 219, 233; *Leviathan* by, 120, 121 n., *130–31, 131, 134, 137–38, 140–42, 142–43, 145, 146–47, 149–50;* life of, 118–20; and Locke, 265, 274–75, 276, 277; on man, 128–44, *130–31, 131, 133, 134, 137–38, 140–42, 142–43,* 274; on mathematics, 119, *119,* 133–37, 159–62; as monist, 117; on motion, 122, 126–27, *126–27;* on nominalism, 136, 196, 303; and phantasms, doctrine of, 128–29, 131, 133, 138, 139, 290; on philosophy, 120–21, *121;* on physics and psychology, relation between, 140–42, *140–42;* place of, in history of philosophy, 153; and Plato, 136; political theory of, 151, 152, 274–75; on psychology and physics, relation between, 140–42, *140–42;* on reality, 122, 123; on religion, *142–43,* 142–44, 276; on science, 127, 133–37, 153, 176, 179; on sensation, 129, 130–31, *130–31;* on sovereignty, 148–51,

149–50, 265; and Spinoza, 193, 196, 214; on the state, 144–52, *145, 146–47, 149–50,* 274, 275, 277; on substance, *175;* and Thomas Aquinas, 120, 122, 147; on thought, distinguished from sensation, 132–33, *133;* on voluntary motions, *137–38,* 137–39
Humanism: and empiricism, 68–69; ideal of, 39–41, 43; in the Renaissance, 33–43
Humanists, Christian, 50–53
Hume, David, 3, **296–351,** 297 n., 298 n.; on association of ideas, *302,* 302–03, *303;* on atheism, 335, *335–36; Autobiography* by, 297; and Berkeley, 293, 295, 296, 298, 303, 304; on causality and inductive inference, *315–18,* 315–22, *319–20, 320–21,* 347–48; and Descartes, 326, 337; *Dialogues Concerning Natural Religion* by, 327, *327,* 330, *330–31,* 331 n., *331–32, 332, 333, 334, 334* n., *334–35,* 335 n., *335–36;* difficulties in position of, 347–49, *348;* on egoism, *343,* 343–45, *344; An Enquiry Concerning the Human Understanding* by, 297, 298–99, *299–301,* 302, *303, 304, 304–05, 306, 308, 308–09, 309–10, 310–11, 315–18, 319–20, 320–21,* 322, 324, 325, 327, 328, *328,* 329, 330, 333; *An Enquiry Concerning the Principles of Morals* by, 297, 338, *339–40, 340,* 341, *343, 344,* 350, *351; Essays* by, 297; on ethics, 337–47, *338, 339–40, 340;* on the external world, *311–12,* 311–15, *312, 314–15;* on God, 326–37, *327, 328, 329, 330, 330–31, 331–32, 332, 333, 334, 334–35,* 335–36; *History of England* by, 297; and Hobbes, 296, 303, 343; on identity, 305–11, *306, 308, 308–09, 309–10, 310–11,* 312; on impressions, *300–01,* 301, 303, 304, *304,* 311, *311–12;* on inductive inference and causality, *315–18,* 315–22, *319–20, 320–21,* 347–48; on knowledge, theory of, *298–99,* 298–311, *299–301,* 302, *303,* 304, *304–05, 306, 308, 308–09, 309–10, 310–11;* on "knowledge of matters of fact," 322; on "knowledge of relations of ideas," 322; life of, 296–98, 297 n.; and Locke, 296, 298, *299–301, 299–301,* 303, 337; on mathematics, 322, 322–26, *325, 326;* on meaning, empirical criterion of, *303,* 303–04; on nature and reason, tension between, 313 15, *314–15;* nominalism of, 303–04; on pleasure, *342;* on probability, 321 n.; on reason and nature, tension between, 313–15, *314–15;* on religion, 296–97 n.; and scepticism, 334, *334–35,* 335, *335–36, 347–51, 348, 350,* 351; on science,

Universals: Aristotle on, 183; Francis Bacon on, 86–87; Berkeley on, 285; Descartes on, 161, 169, 183; Hume on, 303; Leibniz on, 244–45; Locke on, 244–45, 264; and mathematics, 161; Plato on, 183

Valla, Lorenzo, 37
Vittorino da Feltre, 40

Weyl, Hermann, *160–61*
Whitehead, Alfred North, 349

N 0
O 1
P 2
Q 3
R 4
S 5
T 6